THE IDB

A History of Canada's Industrial Development Bank

E. RITCHIE CLARK

Published for the
Federal Business Development Bank by
UNIVERSITY OF TORONTO PRESS
Toronto Buffalo London

© Federal Business Development Bank 1985
Printed in Canada

ISBN 0-8020-3404-7

Canadian Cataloguing in Publication Data

Clark, E. Ritchie
The IDB: a history of Canada's Industrial Development Bank
Bibliography: p.
Includes index.
ISBN 0-8020-3404-7.
1. Federal Business Development Bank (Canada) – History. I. Federal Business
Development Bank (Canada). II. Title.
HG2710.0841532 1985   332.3'7'0971   c85-098378-9

To the men and women who

worked in the IDB

and made it successful

Contents

Photographs

Tables and charts

CHARTS

Preface

In the summer of 1978, I was invited by Guy Lavigueur, president of the Federal Business Development Bank (FBDB), and Eric Scott, vice-president, to write a history of the predecessor institution, the Industrial Development Bank (IDB). I was somewhat dismayed at the prospect, having had no previous experience of writing on this scale, but I was also happy to accept their invitation because I felt that the IDB had such achievements to its credit that they deserved to be recorded in a permanent form.

It could hardly be expected that I would view the IDB without some prejudice in its favour, since I served in it for twenty-eight years, and in various positions from credit officer to chief general manager. Nevertheless, I have tried to present its history honestly and truthfully and without personal bias. So far as possible, the history is based on documentary support, and not on opinion or the unreliable impressions of hazy recollection.

It has been impractical to include in the narrative everything that happened in the Bank. In deciding what to include and what to leave out, I have tried to bear in mind the different concerns of the various groups that might have an interest in its history. IDB borrowers, chartered banks and other Canadian financial institutions, development banks in other countries, teachers and students, politicians and civil servants, employees of the Federal Business Development Bank, former employees of the IDB, and finally the ordinary Canadian who was the ultimate owner of the IDB will, I hope, find their differing interests in the Bank's history reflected in the telling of it.

The narrative starts with an introductory chapter that gives a general outline of the character of the Bank, the economic conditions in which it operated, and an overall view of its accomplishments. The history itself is then divided into five parts. Each covers a period of years during which the Bank was, by reason of some event marking the beginning or end of the period, a somewhat different creature than it had been before. It is hoped that this will help the reader follow what is really a very complex story. Also, following the narrative through from one period to another in this way emphasizes the way in which the Bank steadily evolved through facing a wide variety of practical problems as they presented themselves from day to day and honestly seeking realistic solutions to them.

The first part of the book deals with the beginnings of the IDB and ends with the passage by Parliament of the act incorporating the Bank in 1944. The second part deals with the Bank's early years, and the development of its organization, policies, and procedures in the eleven years up to and including fiscal 1955. The third part starts with fiscal 1956, when a broadened field was opened up to the Bank by an amendment to the IDB Act making more types of business eligible for assistance. This part ends in fiscal 1961, when the act was amended again to make virtually every type of business eligible. The fourth part starts in fiscal 1962, when these amendments became effective, and deals with the operations of the Bank in the still broader field that the amendments opened up. This part runs to fiscal 1967. The last part covers the IDB's final years and starts in fiscal 1968, when a major reorganization of the Bank on more pronouncedly regional lines was completed. The story ends with the conversion of the Bank into the FBDB at the end of fiscal 1975.

Since pictures sometimes speak better than words, this book includes photographs of the places of business or the activities of some of the IDB's customers. Although such a relatively small number of cases could hardly be fully representative of the 48,000 businesses the Bank helped, they have been selected to give as clear a picture of the Bank's work as such a small sample could do. Many of the businesses shown, building on initial loans from the IDB of relatively small amounts such as $12,000, $15,000, or $25,000, grew to become very large corporations of national or international importance, with sales revenues of many millions of dollars.

I have not tried to assess the relative merit or worth of the contributions to the Bank's work made by the various individuals involved in it. Names are simply mentioned as these come up naturally in the telling. The Bank owed a great deal to those who occupied influential positions in it from time to time, particularly to those who led it in its early years and laid down the principles on which it was to operate. At the same time, there was such a strong feeling of participation on the part of its whole staff that one would not be far wrong in attributing to each one a measure of the credit for the Bank's success. In any event, I think it would be difficult, if not actually improper, for someone who, like myself, worked in the Bank for twenty-eight years to do more. At the same time, I hope that there does emerge from the book a sense of the dedication and enthusiasm with which the Bank's staff were thoroughly imbued, and of the honesty and sincerity with which they sought to perform the difficult role given to the Bank.

Although this is the first full study of the IDB to be published, a review of the Bank's history was written in the mid-1970s. In 1973, W.E. Scott, who had just retired as inspector general of banks (i.e. of the chartered banks), was asked by the IDB to gather together its historical material and prepare a monograph or long memorandum on the Bank's history. Mr Scott was well qualified for this since, as an officer of the Bank of Canada, he had been closely associated with Graham Towers, then governor of the Bank of Canada, in bringing the IDB into being and had drafted the original IDB bill. Mr Scott completed his monograph in 1976. His research into the Bank's early days has been most useful in writing this book, and he has been kindness itself in providing further information and comment.

In addition to using the material on the Bank's beginnings gathered by Mr Scott, I have gone through scores of IDB files and have perused thousands of letters, memoranda, and reports. I have also examined 25 boxes of Bank of Canada files relating to the IDB that are now in the custody of the FBDB, as well as 30 boxes of files in the archives of the Bank of Canada itself. I have consulted such relevant information as there is in the National Library, Ottawa, with the patient assistance of Heather Cameron of the library staff. In the Public Archives of Canada, Ottawa, Glen Wright of the Archives' staff dug out for me whatever government material was available there; I am greatly indebted to him. For parliamentary and journalistic material, I have used not only the National Library but also the McLennan Library of McGill University, Montreal; the John Robarts Library and the library of the Faculty of Management of the University of Toronto; the Metro Central Reference Library, Toronto; the library of Maclean Hunter Ltd, Toronto; and the library of the Royal Bank of Canada, Montreal. I am most grateful to all these libraries for making it easy for me to use their facilities.

For general political background, I have drawn on articles in the annual publication *The Britannica Book of the Year*, published by Encyclopaedia Britannica Inc. with the University of Chicago, and the *Canadian Annual Review*, published by the University of Toronto Press, and its successor, the *Canadian Annual Review of Politics and Public Affairs*, also published by the University of Toronto Press, but with the support of York University. For economic background, I have used the same publications and *Annual Reports*, *Statistical Summary*, and *Monthly Review* of the Bank of Canada, and the usual publications of Statistics Canada.

I have had assistance of one kind or another from many people. I owe a large debt of gratitude to Guy Lavigueur and Eric Scott for placing the IDB records held by the FBDB freely at my disposal. I am similarly grateful to John Roberts, former secretary of the Bank of Canada, and his successor, Tim Noël, to C.R. Tousaw, of the secretary's department, and to Jane Witty, archivist, for arranging for me the same freedom of research of papers dealing with the IDB that are in the archives of the Bank of Canada. G. Murphy, in charge of the Bank of Canada file repository, was most helpful. N.C. Tompkins, who was one of the first regional supervisors of the IDB and who died just as the writing of this history was completed, lent me material from his own files and was generous of his time in discussing the Bank's past with me or in writing to me about it.

W.C. Stuart, another long-time senior officer of the Bank, has assisted greatly by drawing on his unrivalled recollections, particularly in connection with the Trans-Canada Pipe Lines episode in 1955. For this I have also consulted J.E. Coyne, who was governor of the Bank of Canada and president of the IDB at that time; R.B. McKibbin, who was then a deputy governor of the Bank of Canada and headed the team for negotiating with Trans-Canada Pipe Lines Limited; and the Hon. Jack Davis, MLA, who was then director of economic research in the Economics Branch of the federal Department of Trade and Commerce and acted as a special assistant to the minister in energy matters. All of them were most helpful.

I am very grateful to J.R. Belcher of the Air Transport Association and G. Phillips of the Air Transport Committee of the Canadian Transport Commission for assistance in determining the number of commercial air services in operation in Canada; to Tom Trbovick of the Ottawa office of the Progressive Conservative party for permission to consult the party's archives; to Rolland P. Poirier, chairman of the Farm Credit Corporation, for sending me a great deal of information about the corporation; to Henry R. Juelich for supplying data on the operations of the Adjustment Assistance Board; to John Thompson, president of RoyNat Inc., for supplying a record of that company's prime interest rates and giving permission for their publication; to Stokes Tolbert, director of the Industrial Development and Finance Department of the World Bank, Washington, DC, for lending me some publications of the World Bank; to William Diamond and David L. Gordon, formerly directors of the

Development Finance Companies Department of the World Bank, for help in looking into the origin of the term *Industrial Development Bank*; to Seaton Findlay of Crawley Films Limited for supplying information about the Bank's films; to R.B. Bryce for guiding me to source material on the Canadian government's planning for the post-war period; to W.A. Kennett, for help regarding thoughts in governmental circles behind the conversion of the IDB into the FBDB; to Louis Rasminsky, formerly governor of the Bank of Canada and president of the IDB, and J.R. Beattie, formerly deputy governor of the Bank of Canada, for very helpful suggestions. Mr Beattie and Guy Bourbonnière, formerly vice-president, administration, for the FBDB, read an early draft of the complete book and suggested numerous textual improvements.

I received help from so many within the FBDB, as well as from former colleagues in the IDB, that it would be impossible for me to name them all. To them I extend my sincere thanks for the cheerful and generous way in which they spoke or wrote to me about their recollections or obtained information for me. I was happy to have these opportunities to renew cherished friendships. However, I am particularly indebted to E.A. Bell, Marie-Marthe Bergeron, G.A. Elliott, W.F. Farquharson, K.K. Hay-Roe, B.K. Heron, J.R. Millard, K.A. Powers, H.J. Russell, H.M. Scott, J.W. Sivers, H.R. Stoker, and R.H. Wheeler, who were colleagues in the IDB and are now retired, and to Margaret Byrne, H.P. Carmichael, R.F. Harriman, Y. Milette, M. Naggar, J.E. Nordin, J.O. Skerry, and D.R. Urquhart, formerly associates in the IDB and now employed in the FBDB.

Mr R.I.K. Davidson, editor (social sciences), for the University of Toronto Press has been most helpful in offering welcome encouragement, giving valuable advice, and making suggestions for improvements and enlargements of the text, particularly in those parts dealing with the background of the IDB.

Although all this assistance is gratefully acknowledged, it must be understood that the author is responsible for the contents of the book and for any opinions expressed in it.

For research in the Bank's records, I depended heavily on the constant, almost daily, assistance of Helen Shantz, manager, records, for the FBDB, and her staff.

I am also deeply grateful to D.R. Johnson of the FBDB, who was given the responsibility of steering the book through publication and did this with great competence and cheerfulness.

Some of the photographs in the book were supplied by the following individuals and companies, to all of whom I am most grateful: Bank of Canada (G.F. Towers, J.E. Coyne, L. Rasminsky, G.K. Bouey); Maxwell

Ward, president of Wardair International Ltd (the photo of a commercial air service); Les Industries Provinciales Ltée of St-Damien, Comté Bellechasse, Québec (the photo of a plastic-injection moulding machine); Corlab Ltd, Montreal (H.M. Scott); the *Gazette*, Montreal (J.C. Ingram, H.R. Stoker); La Société des Enfants Infirmes du Québec (L. Viau); Mrs F.M. Aykroyd (F.M. Aykroyd); Mrs C.E. De Athe (C.E. De Athe); Mr Tom Muskett (D.T. Muskett); Mrs N.C. Tompkins (N.C. Tompkins); E.C. Scott (the second training seminar); C.B. Ready (the fourth training seminar); and W.C. Stuart and I.D. MacLaren, who, like the writer, supplied photos of themselves.

Many others have assisted in the arduous task of locating photographs, but I am particularly grateful to K.E. Neilson, Jean Constable, Helen Shantz, Carolyn McCourt, Margo Chadwick, R.P. Dohan, R. Dupuis, C.B. Ready, and T.H. Measham of the FBDB; Dennis Ryan of MacLaren Advertising Ltd, Montreal; Agnes McFarlane, librarian of the *Gazette*, Montreal; and Marion Duncan, librarian of the *Financial Post*, Toronto.

Most of the photographs of IDB officers and activities reproduced here were accumulated by the Bank over the years. Efforts have been made to trace and credit as many of the photographers as possible. To those who could not be identified I extend my apologies; and to all of the photographers, my sincere thanks for the contribution their pictures have made to the history. I am also grateful to Mr Aldo Dolcetti for the cartoon from *Rapport*, which he drew when he was a legal officer in the Bank's Toronto office.

Most of the typing was done by a number of secretaries on the staff of the FBDB as an addition to their regular work. I am grateful to all of them, but particularly to Carolyn McCourt, who typed most of the early drafts, to Maureen Morganstein, and to Assunta Pannunzio and Micheline Thibault, who typed the final corrections and alterations. Most of the last drafts were typed by Nan Pope, who, in addition to being an excellent typist, assisted with a deep understanding of, and feeling for, style.

Finally, I must acknowledge my profound debt to my wife, Eileen, who has not only endured my complete preoccupation with this work for three years but also contributed enormously to its final form through reading and criticizing innumerable drafts, holding me firmly to the right line whenever my loyalty to grammatical principles faltered, and through valiant assistance during the arduous chore of proof-reading.

E.R.C.

Montreal

February 1982

Abbreviations and explanations

AAB Adjustment Assistance Board
CGMO Chief General Manager's Office
FBDB Federal Business Development Bank (successor to the IDB)
GMO General Manager's Office
IDB Industrial Development Bank
IRD Industrial Research Division (of the IDB)
SBLA Small Business Loans Act

Abbreviations and short titles used in the notes are given in the introduction to that section.

When the word 'Bank' appears with a capital letter, it refers to the IDB.

When a year is referred to, whether in the text, tables, charts, or appendices, it means the fiscal year of the Industrial Development Bank, that is, from 1 October to 30 September, unless otherwise stated.

The word 'Brief' in the sources of tables refers to the brief submitted by the IDB in 1962 to the Royal Commission on Banking and Finance (the Porter Commission).

Wherever there is reference to Canada's gross national product, the figures are expressed in constant (1971) dollars.

THE IDB

A History of Canada's Industrial Development Bank

Introduction

Canada's Industrial Development Bank was established in 1944 as a federal crown corporation, partly to assist Canadian businesses to adjust to peace-time conditions after the Second World War, and partly to provide a much-needed source of term financing for small and medium-sized businesses. In many ways, it was an unusual institution. Although it was a crown corporation, it was not owned directly by the government. It was, instead, a subsidiary of another crown corporation, the Bank of Canada, and, indeed, the only subsidiary that bank ever had. It reported directly to Parliament, but it did not receive any money or financial support from Parliament. It reported through the minister of finance, but since his contacts with the IDB's president were usually in connection with the latter's very important role of governor of the Bank of Canada, their normal consultations rarely touched on the affairs of the IDB; the minister had no contact whatever with the general manager of the Bank who directed its operations. Although the IDB was, then, a government bank, it operated entirely free from any political or governmental interference, and with virtually no contact with government departments or departmental officials, apart from the presence on its board of directors and/or executive committee of two (for a short time, three) deputy ministers. Even the bill by which the Bank was established was not the product of a government department, but was drafted within the Bank of Canada.

The IDB was called a bank, but it was not like the commercial banks that Canadians were used to: it did not take deposits or do many other things usually associated in the public mind with banks. In spite of any inferences that might be drawn from the IDB's name, its incorporating statute bestowed on it no responsibility or authority to initiate or promote developmental projects. It was intended simply that it should give financial assistance to as many as possible of those eligible businesses that might apply for it. Even then the Bank was only to provide assistance if it was of the opinion that the funds would not otherwise be available on reasonable terms and conditions. The IDB was not expected to operate with a view to profit, but neither was it expected to lose money. It was supposed to function beyond the limits of the ordinary business judgment of commercial lenders, but it was expected to do so in a businesslike way.

It is perhaps hardly to be wondered at that the IDB's operations were occasionally puzzling to politicians and general public alike, and that sometimes those working in it felt that the only people who really understood the Bank were themselves.

The IDB was one of a number of steps taken by the federal government in 1944, a year before the European war ended, to assist in bringing the Canadian economy and society back to a peace-time basis at the war's end. These steps included social measures such as family allowances and war veterans' gratuities and benefits and three acts to provide direct support to the economy – the Export Credit Act, to provide insurance for exports; the National Housing Act, to support residential construction; and the Industrial Development Bank Act. Each of these last three measures, in addition to playing a temporary role during the period of post-war adjustment, met also fundamental, long-term needs in the economy, and the three crown corporations that resulted became a permanent part of the business scene.

Although the post-war years were anticipated with some apprehension by business and federal government, the transition from war to peace was accomplished much more quickly and successfully than had been anticipated. The war had greatly accelerated Canada's industrialization, and the country 'emerged from the war in a strong economic position'. Within two years, i.e. by 1947, economic activity was at a peace-time peak; the amount spent on construction that year was the largest ever spent in one year up to that time; non-governmental expenditures on plant, equipment, and housing were more than 50 per cent higher than the previous year; and employment reached such a high level that the number of those who were unemployed fell during the year to only 1.4 per cent of the labour force.[1]

In fact, during the IDB's 31 years, from 1945 to 1975 inclusive, the Canadian economy was generally in a state of growth. The population nearly doubled, increasing from 12 million to 23 million people, and the gross national product (expressed in constant 1971 dollars) increased in most years by 4–9 per cent per annum. Over the entire period, the GNP multiplied four times.[2] On the whole, then, the IDB operated at a time of economic expansion. This favoured the work of the Bank, both in terms of the demand for loans and in the chances of its being able to dispose, successfully and without loss, of buildings or equipment held as security for any loans so unsatisfactory as to require liquidation.

Against this background of general expansion, however, the economy faced some quite serious problems. First, there were intervals when the rate of growth fell away significantly. In 1954, the gross national product actually dropped slightly below that of the preceding year. In the years 1957–61 inclusive, the rate of growth averaged only 2.8 per cent per annum, and rates similarly low occurred in 1967 (3.3 per cent) and 1970 (2.5 per cent). The rate of growth fell drastically from 7.2 per cent in 1973 to 0.6 per cent in 1975.[3]

Second, unemployment sometimes reached fairly high levels, even when the GNP seemed to be increasing satisfactorily. In 1958–61, unemployment ran around 7.0 per cent of the labour force, well above the levels of preceding years. During the 1960s, it dropped gradually to 3.6 per cent in 1966, but from then on it climbed until it reached 6.9 per cent in 1975, on its way to much higher levels in succeeding years.[4]

Third, a major concern throughout the period 1945–75 was the threat of inflation. The last surge of the post-war rise in prices occurred in 1948, when price controls were removed and the consumer price index climbed by 14.4 per cent. From then on, until 1971, prices rose much more slowly, even though steadily. For the 23 years from 1949 to 1971 inclusive, the consumer price index increased annually by only 2.6 per cent on the average; the largest individual yearly increases in those years were 10.5 per cent in 1951 (the Korean War had started in mid-1950) and 4.6 per cent in 1969. After 1971 prices rose rapidly, the increase in 1974 being 10.9 per cent and in 1975 10.8 per cent; by the latter year, the index was more than three times what it had been in 1946, following the end of the Second World War.[5]

Although general growth in the economy and the accompanying problems formed the background of the IDB's operations, it is probable that, until the Bank reached its greatest size in its last few years, it was not really big enough to be affected sensitively, in the volume of loans it made, by these broad variations in business conditions. The management of the Bank had, of course, to take account of such obvious things as marked business recessions, fluctuations in interest rates, current lending policies of other sources of financing, shortages of industrial raw materials, availability of building supplies, and conditions in particular industries within which loans were applied for. It is noteworthy that during the years 1945–55 and 1963–8, when there was substantial growth in the economy, the volume of loans made by the Bank each year remained relatively stable. However, in 1956 and 1962, changes in the definition of businesses eligible for IDB loans stimulated a marked surge in loan approvals that lasted, in each case, for about one year and seemed to move the Bank's operations to a new plateau.

These considerations suggest that, while the Bank's loan activity was undoubtedly affected by the economic environment, it was probably influenced to an even greater extent by other circumstances. These would include the periodical enlargements of the definition of eligible businesses, as just mentioned; the opening up, by these changes (as by the founding of the Bank), of a great and unsatisfied need on the part of businesses of all kinds for the sort of financing provided by the IDB; and factors within the IDB such as branch openings, publicity, and the evolution of policies and attitudes determining the Bank's responsiveness to loan applications.

Fourth, and finally, in the last 10 years of the Bank's operations, interest rates on the money markets, which had been relatively stable from 1948 to 1965, with a general tendency to rise gradually, became very volatile. They rose and fell in rapid and drastic jumps, trending all the time to ever higher levels. Between 1948 and 1965, the average yield for 10 industrial bonds generally ranged between $3\frac{1}{2}$ per cent and $5\frac{1}{2}$ per cent. By 1975, it was $11\frac{1}{2}$ per cent.[6]

One aspect of economic developments that did concern the IDB was the recurrence of periods of credit stringency arising from efforts of the Bank of Canada to combat tendencies toward inflation, from pressure on the country's productive capacity, and from occasional shortages of liquidity on the part of the chartered banks. From 1945 to 1975 there were at least eight such occasions. Some lasted less than a year, while in other cases several years elapsed before the management of the IDB considered the policies based on them to have become unnecessary.

On such occasions, and particularly those that reflected action by the Bank of Canada, the IDB would, in fairness to other lenders, follow policies intended to steer it away from making loans that would otherwise have been made by another lender, and more particularly by a chartered bank. Nevertheless, although the Bank tried to be entirely scrupulous in this policy, it may not have affected its lending volume to any great extent. Invariably, the Bank of Canada, when involved with the chartered banks in considering such situations, urged them not to allow times of credit stringency to interfere with their lending to small businesses. Admonitions to this effect appear repeatedly in Bank of Canada annual reports from 1948 on.[7] This was, of course, the area in which the IDB was most interested and where it made most of its loans.

When the IDB was first proposed in 1944, many said it was unnecessary. They claimed that existing financial institutions and the kinds of financing available could take care of the requirements of any credit-worthy business; the IDB would help only bankrupts and 'lame duck' businesses. In spite of these gloomy forecasts, the IDB, in its 31 years, authorized some 65,000 loans totalling $3 billion for 48,000 businesses that were considered by the Bank (as required by the IDB act) to be unable to obtain the financing elsewhere on reasonable terms and conditions. These businesses were far from being bankrupts or lame ducks, for well over 90 per cent of them were successful in establishing themselves and retiring their IDB loans. It was estimated that they employed close to 900,000 people.

The Bank assisted just about every kind of business and program imaginable, from setting up a new pipe mill or refinery to helping a young lawyer acquire his own law library. It was active in every part of Canada, and in some remote areas such as the Yukon was a major factor in economic growth. The IDB was probably the most important source of financial support for commercial air services apart from the mainline operations, for motels and other kinds of tourist services, and for many kinds of manufacturing such as small and medium-sized lumber operations and the production of hosiery. Most of the Bank's borrowers were small; the (mean) average loan was $47,000, and 48 per cent of the loans authorized were for $25,000 or less.

The Bank was successful in conducting its affairs in a businesslike way, both from its own standpoint and from that of its clients. It financed the cost of its operations entirely out of its own earnings. From these it paid for salaries, rent, advertising, and all other operating and capital expenses; it paid interest, on the funds it borrowed to finance its lending, at a rate above that payable on federal government bonds; it covered any losses on loans that had to be written off; and it set aside reserves to take care of estimated future write-offs. At the end of its last fiscal year, on 30 September 1975, these reserves equalled 2½ times the losses foreseen on loans then outstanding. It also paid, from earnings, the expenses of the non-revenue-producing programs it set up to help the operators of small businesses to improve their management skills. After covering all expenses and provision for reserves, it was able to show a profit every year. By 30 September 1975 these profits, which were accumulated in a reserve fund, amounted to a total of $37 million.

In addition to extending a substantial amount of assistance itself directly to businesses, the Bank also helped, by its example and satisfactory experience, to establish term mortgage financing in Canada as a normal source of funds for small and medium-sized businesses. When the Bank was founded in 1944 there was little financing of this sort being done. By the time the IDB was converted into the FBDB in 1975, the chartered banks, with the help of an amendment to the Bank Act, were operating vigorously in the term loan field; some finance companies had special divisions to handle this kind of financing; institutions specializing in it had appeared; and just about every province had its own 'development financing' organization.

The IDB was one of the first and one of the largest development banks in the world and had an international reputation as one of the most successful. Many similar institutions in other countries sent their officers to Canada's Industrial Development Bank for training.

In the eyes of those who worked in the IDB and of many thousands of businessmen and women whom it helped, it fully realized the expectation expressed by Dr W.C. Clark, the deputy minister of finance when the Bank was founded, in his testimony before the House of Commons Committee on Banking and Commerce in 1944: 'I think you will be proud of the results of the working of this bank.'

PART I

The beginnings of the Bank 1943–4

CHAPTER ONE

Background

Financing problems of small and medium-sized businesses and the role of development banks

Lord Macmillan, chairman of the committee that studied Britain's financial systems in 1929–31, could hardly have anticipated that, long after his report had become just another piece of economic history, it would have brought him immortality of a sort as the discoverer of an area of financial need that came to be known as the Macmillan gap.[1] This gap in the financial structures of Britain was described in the report as lying in the 'difficulty ... experienced by the smaller and medium-sized businesses in raising the capital which they may from time to time require, even when the security offered is perfectly sound.'[2] By 'capital' was meant funds provided either by a permanent investment made in a business or by long- or medium-term loans repayable over a period of years, and it was financial assistance of this sort that small and medium-sized businesses were considered to lack.

Although specialized institutions to fill this 'gap' were established in a number of countries, including the United States and the United Kingdom, prior to the Second World War,[3] the total amount of credit provided by them was relatively small. Few realized the importance of Lord Macmillan's discovery. In 1938, the Assembly of the League of Nations asked the Economic and Financial Organization of the Council of the League 'to study methods of providing medium-term credit to industry.'[4] The Financial Committee of the Organization reported in 1939.[5] After describing the difficulties faced by medium- and small-sized businesses in seeking medium- or long-term accommodation, and referring to a 'presumption that some credit institutions should exist for the provision of medium-term credit to small- and medium-sized industry,'[6] it came to the conclusion that there was no great unsatisfied demand for such accommodation:

Perhaps the most striking feature ... of the machinery for the provision of medium-term credit in various countries is the fact that the total amount of credit extended by the institutions established for the purpose has been very limited. This is not to say that the question of medium-term credit is unimportant. But the small volume of credit extended does strongly suggest that there is no great unsatisfied legitimate demand at the present time. As business revival becomes more general, the demand will doubtless grow, and there are good reasons for believing that in most countries the supply will keep pace. Where gaps exist in the financial machinery, they are narrow and are gradually being closed.[7]

Of course, the committee was not concerned only with the needs of small business. Indeed, it seemed to regard the matter of extending medium-term credits to small industries with a good deal of wariness: 'The risks of lending are especially heavy in small industries, where future success is more than usually difficult to evaluate, and where the continuity of efficient management cannot readily be assured in the event of personnel changes.'[8]

Subsequent developments in Canada and elsewhere would suggest modifications to both these conclusions − that there was no great unsatisfied legitimate demand for medium-term credit, particularly on the part of small businesses, and that extending such credit would be highly risky. The last forty years have seen the emergence into the financial world of new, specialized institutions, the 'development banks' − financial 'institutions, public or private, which have as one of their principal functions the making of medium- or long-term investments in industrial projects.'[9] The investment might be by way of a loan or by equity, and it would often be the case that the financing provided by a development bank would not otherwise have been forthcoming. The World Bank has sponsored approximately 110 such banks in developing countries and regions. Counting others set up by governments in developed countries, and private institutions, there are likely well over 200 development banks in operation.

Many differences in purpose, outlook, and method of operation distinguish development banks from one another.[10] Some assist only industrial businesses, while others also lend to agriculture. Some lend only to manufacturers; others lend to service industries as well. Some, particularly in developing countries, may actively identify and promote industries for development; others may merely hold themselves ready to consider requests for financial assistance. Some may concentrate on large-scale industry; some cater specifically to small and medium-sized business in the belief that these have particular difficulty in raising long- or medium-term funds through conventional sources. In countries where a development bank has been set up with this latter orientation, it may have been believed that, while short-term credit would usually be available, generally speaking, to all businesses of any size through the ordinary banking system, longer-term funds would be less easily found by small enterprises than by large corporations.

The need of a small or medium-sized business for long-term financing may arise from a number of causes. One business may want to expand or replace its plant to meet an increased demand on its products or to permit the manufacture of a new product. Another may be establishing a new enterprise and have insufficient equity funds invested in it by its owners to take care of all its needs; it has not enough money to provide working capital, cover initial operating losses, and take care of the other costs that can confront a new business and at the same time provide for the cost of its buildings and machinery. Another company may have found itself under pressure from rapidly growing sales demands and have involved itself in a program of capital expenditures that, having depleted its working capital, have left it with insufficient funds to finance day-to-day operations.

Some businesses, even small or medium-sized ones, may be earning such large profits that they can divert relatively large sums into a plant program and away from the financing of ordinary operations. Even if they have not enough cash available for the purpose, they may be able to finance their program with short-term credits and retire these rapidly from profits. But many perfectly healthy businesses may not be in this position and may have to find large amounts of some kind of permanent or long-term capital.

Funds of this sort were and are found relatively easily by large, creditworthy corporations by means of stock or debenture issues on the public money markets or through an investment dealer. These corporations will probably be well-known to prospective purchasers of their shares or bonds, their financial record can easily be presented and analysed, and the costs of the financing can be comfortably borne by such a corporation, having regard for its size and the magnitude of the financing involved. These recourses are not, however, so readily open to smaller businesses. For relatively small sums such as $15–25,000 – or even several hundred thousand dollars – stock or public debenture financing would be almost unthinkable. Proposals of these magnitudes would really be of no interest to investment dealers, and, in any event, the cost of trying to raise money in this way, if it were possible, would be greatly disproportionate to the amount involved and much too great for a small or medium-sized business.

Proposal for a special institution in Canada

In Canada, there is no record of there having been any discussion, prior to 1943, of difficulties encountered by small and medium-sized businesses in raising long- or medium-term capital. Even Lord Macmillan, whose report in 1930 identified this as an unfilled need in Great Britain, made no mention of it in 1933 in the report of the Canada Royal Commission on Banking and Currency over which he also presided as chairman.[11] When, however, during the Second World War, the Canadian government and its advisers considered what would need to be done at the end of the war to convert the economy back to a peacetime basis, one of the problems to which they turned their minds was that of the Macmillan gap.

Planning for the end of the war started within a few months of the war's beginning. In December 1939, the cabinet set up a committee to study the ultimate reintegration into the civilian world of members of the armed forces. This remained the principal goal of all post-war planning, but very soon, as various committees and study groups were set up through 1940–2, broader concerns were examined.[12] As J.L. Granatstein says in *Canada's War: Politics of the Mackenzie King Government, 1939–45*, 'Everyone in government, in the civil service, and in industry seemed afraid that the dislocations that would accompany the reconversion would be marked with massive unemployment and popular unrest.'[13]

The annual report of the Bank of Canada for 1943 (issued in February 1944) outlined the basic facts that lay behind these apprehensions. It estimated that about 1,900,000 persons were then 'engaged in the armed forces, in supplying the weapons of war, or in producing the food required for special wartime exports,' out of a total of 5,100,000 gainfully employed. The report estimated that at least 1,500,000 more persons would be available for civilian jobs after the war than the 3,200,000 so employed then, an anticipated increase of nearly 50 per cent! A working force of this size would be able to produce a much greater volume of civilian goods and services than Canada had ever known. It was believed that 'a vastly increased volume of consumption and capital development will be necessary if this output is going to be fully absorbed and high employment maintained.'[14]

Of the various study groups set up by the government, one of the most important was the group known as the Economic Advisory Committee, comprising a number of senior civil servants, including Dr W.C. Clark, deputy minister of finance, and Graham Towers, governor of the Bank of Canada. In January 1943 this committee was asked to organize the study of post-war problems by government departments and agencies.[15] Prominent among the problems studied were those arising from the financing of the conversion of industrial plants, and particularly of small and medium-sized ones, from wartime to peacetime production. In September 1943 the committee decided to determine how far these financial needs might be met by existing private and public financial agencies, what changes were necessary to stimulate the operations of private lending institutions to meet these needs, and what public financial institutions might be advisable to fill in any gap that existed.[16] Such a study would normally have been made within the Department of Finance, but, since Dr Clark was preoccupied with many other matters at the time, he asked Mr Towers to study the question within the Bank of Canada. This led ultimately to the conclusion that a special institution should be established, the principal role of which would be the making of industrial term loans, particularly to small or medium-sized businesses.

There were several reasons for this conclusion. First, it was expected that many small industries, which had financed the plant expansions required by the war effort without much difficulty on the strength of government orders, subcontracts, or advance payments on contracts, might face real problems in financing conversion to peacetime operations. With limited resources of their own, they would be seriously disadvantaged as compared with large corporations able to confront the problems of reconstruction with technical staffs and considerable financial resources.[17] The proposed agency would be able, where necessary, to redress this balance on behalf of the smaller enterprises.

Second, it was thought that many returning soldiers would want to set up new businesses or re-establish old ones in which they had been involved previously, and in either case they might encounter difficulty in obtaining from normal commercial sources the term financing that might be required.

Third, it was considered that Canada had its own Macmillan gap. For the chartered banks, the traditional role was the provision of short-term credits, not long- or medium-term loans. At that time, they had no power, under the Bank Act, to make loans against mortgage security, and they showed little interest in entering the field of term lending. They normally limited their lending to credits of no more than one year's duration. It was expected by a bank that a business loan or credit, primarily to finance day-to-day operations, would 'revolve' on a yearly basis. Ideally, the outstanding balance of such a credit would be cleaned up every now and then, and at least once a year. For longer-term capital needs, a business would be expected to look elsewhere. For a small or medium-sized Canadian business, there were few if any places to turn to. Even insurance companies and trust or mortgage companies, which made mortgage loans for housing, made few or no mortgage loans to small industries. In the absence of institutional sources to which such a business might turn, an owner had probably to canvass private sources of money. If financing were found in this way, the owner might well have to pay a high price for it, either in the rate of interest that might be charged for a loan or in the surrendering of a substantial portion of the equity in the business, and perhaps even its control.[18]

Other means of meeting the need were examined. In an unpublished monograph on the history of the IDB, W.E. Scott, who worked on the plans for the IDB with Graham Towers, has written:

One alternative to be considered was to provide a system of Government guarantees to the chartered banks for term loans to industry along the lines of the Home Improvement Loan program which had been operative since 1936. Such a policy would have the advantage of making the maximum use of the existing banking system and would avoid creating a facility which might appear to be competing with the present banks. However, a policy of guaranteeing lenders against losses seemed to be suited to situations where there would be a large number of quite small loans of a fairly uniform character. Under these conditions the guarantor could stipulate general rules and regulations but would not normally have to concern itself with individual loan applications and a common pool guarantee with a fixed percentage of loss to be covered by the guarantor would be operative. It did not seem at all likely that applications for industrial term loans would have these characteristics. Another question to be considered was how quickly the chartered banks would respond to the availability of a Government guarantee in this kind of lending. If for any reason — such as the percentage of guarantee being deemed inadequate in particular cases — the banks were unwilling to make loans, the Government would not be able to take any initiative. In view of the expected seriousness of post-war economic problems it was thought desirable to be able to act quickly and effectively. So it was felt that it would be unwise to place complete reliance on a system of guarantees in the case of industrial term loans.[19]

The results of the study made by the Bank of Canada were accepted by the government, which then asked the Bank of Canada to develop the project and take on the new agency as a subsidiary once it was established.

For the government, planning for the post-war years had taken on fresh urgency, for in 1943 it was defeated in several by-elections. Acting on the practical principle that 'people will vote for the party most likely to do what is needed to provide maximum employment and a measure of social insurance in the future,' the government developed a broad legislative program to re-establish the returning soldiers, expand public and private enterprise to provide employment, and provide some social security.[20] On 4 January 1944, the Hon. J.L. Ilsley, minister of finance, wrote to the Rt Hon. W.L.M. King, prime minister: 'As you know, I am also recommending that legislation be introduced at this session to provide for the setting up of an Industrial Credit Bank as a subsidiary of the Bank of Canada. This would be for the primary purpose of assisting industry in its reconversion program and providing capital, fixed as well as working, for the needs of small and medium-sized businesses particularly.'[21]

The government's program, announced at the opening of Parliament on 27 January 1944 as intended to establish 'a national minimum of social security and human welfare,'[22] included the Export Credit Corporation, authorized to insure exports to the extent of $100 million; the National Housing Act, expected to stimulate $1 billion in new construction; support for agricultural and fish prices at an estimated cost of $225 million; government guarantees for bank loans for farm improvements; family allowances estimated at $200 million per annum; war veterans' gratuities and benefits amounting to more than $1 billion; and, finally, the Industrial Development Bank,[23] with financing up to $100 million.

CHAPTER TWO

Legislation

Introduction of the IDB bill

A bill to set up the Industrial Development Bank was introduced in the House of Commons on 28 February 1944.[1] Second reading was debated 2–14 March and then referred to the Standing Committee on Banking and Commerce. The committee considered the bill in detail on 23 and 29 March and 2–10 August. On 11 August the bill was given third reading and, after passing the Senate the same day, received royal assent on 14 August.

Although the bill was criticized in Parliament, no objections were entered by other financial institutions. In fact, on 11 March 1944, the *Financial Post* said: 'In financial circles interviewed by the Financial Post, the Industrial Development Bank itself, as proposed, was seen as probably filling a gap in the Canadian credit organization whereby credit would be made available to enterprises which, while desirable, have not sufficient standing to obtain credit in the ordinary way, from established credit agencies, such as the chartered banks or by means of an issue of securities through an investment dealer.'

Later, in 1945, the journal of the Canadian Bankers' Association, the *Canadian Banker*, made the following editorial comment regarding the IDB: 'Brought into being at the 1944 session of parliament, the Bank has been organized in the interests of manufacturers with borrowing requirements of longer term than usual commercial banking and not within the field covered by the underwriting investment houses. There may be many cases, creditworthy though they are, that fall outside the orbits of both of these lending agencies and it is for them that the Industrial Development Bank has been designed ... Earnest wishes are extended for the success of the Industrial Development Bank.'[2]

The terms of the act of incorporation are important for understanding the history of the Bank since they established the framework within which it was to operate. The debates and discussions are also important because the two 'sponsors' of the bill, Mr Towers and Dr Clark, in their answers to certain criticisms of the bill, enunciated principles that were to be of enormous importance in the Bank's operation. Before we review the debates that took place, it might be said that almost none of the fears expressed then as to the Bank's prospects were confirmed by its experiences, apart from suggestions that the financial resources it was to have were too small and that its scope might have been made broad enough to include all types of business.

Name of the IDB

The first thing mentioned in the bill (section 3) was the name of the new institution, and this provoked about as much debate as any other part of the proposal. Those drafting the legislation used the name Industrial Credit Bank in their first drafts of legislation and in their early discussions. The name finally used was introduced in the fourth or fifth draft (there were eight or nine before the bill took final form). The change was made because it was thought that the word 'credit' suggested the kind of short-term accommodation usually supplied by chartered banks. Accordingly, 'development' was substituted. The name 'development bank' has come to describe a group of specialized, term-financing institutions that have appeared around the world.[3] In many cases the name of the Canadian bank has been fully imitated, and there are now Industrial Development Banks in Kenya, Turkey, India, Pakistan, Ivory Coast, Jordan, Israel, and elsewhere, and regional development banks in Asia, Africa, the Caribbean, and South America.

During the parliamentary discussion, there was objection to the use of the word 'Bank' in the name of the new institution. It was claimed that, with the exception of the Bank of Canada, the word was reserved for chartered banks by the Bank Act and that the new institution, which did not come under the Bank Act, would have a quite different character. It was even suggested that the record of the Canadian chartered 'banks' had come to be synonymous with 'safety,' a word not expected to be appropriate for the IDB.[4] In the end, the name remained as proposed in the bill.

During his testimony before the standing committee, Mr Towers expressed the opinion that it did not matter whether the word 'bank' appeared in the corporate name or not.[5] This was not the view later held by the staff of the IDB. It attached a great deal of importance to the word and felt that it was a constant reminder to everyone – those applying for assistance, other institutions, politicians, government officials, and, indeed, the IDB staff itself – that this was a business institution run on business-like principles. Being called a bank probably also helped to establish cordial and co-operative relations between officers of the IDB and those of the chartered banks, particularly at the branch level. It created a certain fraternal feeling between them.

To be a subsidiary of the Bank of Canada

The new bank was to be a wholly owned subsidiary of the Bank of Canada, which was to hold the shares for the full amount of authorized capital of $25 million (section 12). The initial issue of shares was to be for $10 million, after which the Bank of Canada was to subscribe in such amounts and at such times as the board might determine. This latter provision was to enable the board to maintain whatever relationship it considered appropriate between the amounts made available to the new bank in the form of equity and the amounts that it might borrow.

For funds beyond share subscriptions, the Bank was empowered to sell bonds and debentures (section 13). During the hearings of the standing committee, it seemed to be expected that these securities would be sold to the Bank of Canada,[6] the governing act of which was amended to permit this. However, there was no restriction in the IDB Act itself as to possible purchasers of the Bank's debentures, and Mr Towers expressed the view that the debentures might be bought by another financial institution or by the general public.[7] Whatever market was envisaged for the debentures, it appears to have been recognized by those drafting the bill that the notes and debentures of the Bank would not come within the definition of 'trustee' securities and so would not be eligible for life insurance company investment unless (a) they were government guaranteed, (b) they were specifically secured by the pledge of real estate and equipment, (c) they were specifically secured by securities that were 'trustee' securities, or (d) the Bank had regularly paid dividends in full for five years. It was decided not to attempt to meet any of these conditions in the legislation. In practice, the IDB never sold its debentures to anyone other than the Bank of Canada.

The only limitation put on the Bank's power to raise money was that the aggregate of its total direct and contingent liabilities should not exceed three times the aggregate amount of the paid-up capital and the Reserve Fund, i.e. accumulated profits (section 14). This meant that the act placed a limit of $100 million or slightly more on the size of the Bank.

The Industrial Development Bank was to have the same board of directors as the Bank of Canada, and the governor of the Bank of Canada was to be president of the IDB (section 6). The act did not designate him as chief executive officer of the IDB. This was in contrast with the Bank of Canada Act which did designate the governor as chief executive officer, adding 'and shall on behalf of the Board have the direction and control of the business of the Bank' with reservations as imposed by the act or the by-laws.[8] In a memorandum written in 1953, D.G. Marble, secretary of the Bank of Canada and of the IDB and later general manager of the IDB, explained the reasons for the difference between the two acts. Pointing out that section 10 of the IDB act provided that the board of directors might delegate its authority to the president or any officer, agent, or employee of the Bank, he said, 'Section 10 was worded quite deliberately because it was not intended that the President would be active in the day-to-day conduct of the affairs of the Bank, and it was intended that the General Manager, who is not mentioned in the Act in any place, would do so.' This view was confirmed by Mr Towers in a memorandum written a few weeks later.

The connection with the Bank of Canada was opposed by some members of Parliament in the House and on the banking committee. It was objected that there would be a conflict of interest if the Bank of Canada were to regulate the country's economy and at the same time be involved in lending to businesses. Dr Clark, however, argued that the link between the two banks would be beneficial to the central bank. It would have 'more intimate contact ... with the conditions and the problems of small and medium-sized industries.' Further, 'the operations of the Industrial Development Bank will naturally have to dovetail into the country's monetary policy,' and a corporate link between the two banks would make this easier.[9]

Apprehensions of political pressure

Probably more important to the government than these considerations were its trust in the ability of the Bank of Canada, and particularly Graham Towers, to get the Bank set up soundly and its view that a link with the central bank would protect the new bank against political pressures. Some MPs thought the possible exposure of the IDB to these pressures (which many seemed to think were inevitable) was an argument against a connection with the Bank of Canada. They believed the new bank would bring the central bank into political involvements from which it should be aloof. They did not believe the Industrial Development Bank would be able to withstand political pressure. As one member put it, 'You will find you will be very much a branch of the government. You have got 245 constituencies in the Dominion of Canada and you will probably get ... pressure of geographical availability for industries, pressure of raw materials ... pressure from the maritimes, pressure from western Canada ... You will be under pressure because you are a public institution for the assistance over a long period of certain industries, the giving of capital assistance from this government bank.'[10]

Even observers outside Parliament saw political pressure as the great hazard facing the new bank. In its issue of 29 April 1944, the *Financial Post* listed the following as among the questions that Canadians were asking: 'How will the IDB stand up to pressure from politicians who want friends backed: who want special help for their constituencies?' 'How will the IDB deal with sectional demands for industrialization? ... Will such loans be made to promote a sectional interest or because the individual borrower has a sound proposition?'

Events proved such concerns to be unwarranted. Throughout its life, the Industrial Development Bank reached decisions on all loan applications strictly on the basis of business considerations.

Some members thought the new bank might better be a private institution, set up, perhaps, by the chartered banks and other private financial institutions. However, Dr Clark pointed out that what the bank was to do had not been done in the past by private enterprise and would not likely be done in the future. The type of loan expected of the new bank would not attract private interests because the chances of profit were small and the risks of loss high.[11]

Possibility of losses

This last comment prompted the further criticism that it would be unsound for the central bank to be associated with an institution that had large losses such as critics of the proposed new bank assumed it would have. However, both Mr Towers and Dr Clark, while conceding the possibility of losses on individual loans, believed that overall the new bank would earn a modest profit. As Dr Clark said, 'It seems to me appropriate that the type of institution you set up to perform this function should be essentially a non-profit-making institution which goes out to render a service that is needed rather than to make profits primarily ... If we get a reasonably efficient management, what I would expect is that there would be a modest or relatively moderate profit rather than large profits.'[12]

The view that the Bank would inevitably operate at a loss was frequently expressed in the debates: 'Will the banks use this industrial bank as a safeguard for their bad loans; that is, industries that are about to go bankrupt?' 'We are going to have the taxpayer entering into the business of making commercial loans that are ... non-economic and terribly risky, when none of the companies, whose business is that of lending money, will touch it.' 'We are going into the bad loan business.' 'I would suggest that the name of this bank be changed to lame ducks incorporated.' 'Sure losers incorporated would be another good name for it.' 'It is paternalism for shifty borrowers who cannot get it through the regular sources.'[13]

These views were a challenge, of course, to the basic idea that there was a 'gap' in Canada's financial structure, and on this all Mr Towers and Dr Clark could do was to keep reiterating their opinion that there was such a gap and that because of it some sound, creditworthy businesses could not borrow the money they needed. As Mr Towers said: 'I think I would like to point out that loans made by the Industrial Development Bank would not be "cats and dogs" which were avoided by other lenders because they bear a terrifically high loss ratio. They would be loans which, because they were for periods of several years and in rather small amounts, were not suited to other financial institutions.'[14]

Regarding loan losses, he went on to say: 'The fact that such advances were of the type I have described would probably lead to the Industrial Development Bank incurring somewhat larger proportional losses than do the makers of ordinary short-term loans ... It is hardly necessary for me to add, of course, that any institution in the banking business must or should make losses because a bank which never makes a loss is no good to man or beast. No losses mean that a bank is operating so extraordinarily conservatively that it is not performing its function in the community.'

He estimated that the IDB might write off loans to the extent of $1\frac{1}{2}$ per cent of loans per annum, approximately double the rate experienced by the chartered banks. Although this was just a guess on his part, it was extraordinarily close to the proportion of disbursed loan proceeds that the IDB actually wrote off.

To supplement other financial institutions

According to the act, the Bank was not to displace other lending organizations but rather 'to supplement' their activities; this was said in the preamble to the act. It was provided in section 15 that financing was to be extended only 'if, in the opinion of the Board, credit or other financial resources would not otherwise be available on reasonable terms and conditions.' This provision was one of the main foundation stones of the Bank – it was to supplement, not compete with other financial institutions. Throughout its life the Bank had to concern itself with the possibility that any loan it was asked for might be available somewhere else. The problem of determining beyond doubt whether the funds applied for were available elsewhere was never completely solved to the satisfaction of the Bank's critics, and other financial institutions were often sceptical as to the respect paid by the Bank to this particular requirement.

It is curious to note in retrospect, however, that neither the chartered banks nor any other financial institutions entered any objections to the creation of the Bank when the bill was under consideration. In fact, on behalf of investment dealers, it was stated flatly by H.R. Jackman, MP for Rosedale, during the sittings of the standing committee, that 'there is no antipathy on the part of the investment banker or investment dealer community against a bill like this if it is otherwise sound.' He added, 'The more industry there is, the more banking there is to do and the more refunding there is as loans mature. Furthermore, if it were possible for the industrial bank to get going and to nurse young businesses in their early days, businesses which were unsuitable for public financing because of the high degree of risk attached to them or because of their smallness, the Industrial Development Bank might well prove a fruitful source of business for investment dealers, because in the more profitable stages of the business, with an assured credit rating, their securities could be sold to the public.' This was one prediction that proved to be correct. However, Mr Jackman said, in another part of the debate, 'I think this bank should never be set up. I think there is no need for it whatsoever.'[5]

Some MPs expressed great puzzlement as to how the new bank could satisfy this condition about the availability of funds elsewhere in the case of every application and were concerned about the legal difficulties that would arise if procedures in this regard fell short of perfection. Their concern arose partly from the simple wording of the condition as it appeared in the version of the bill as first presented to Parliament. This empowered the IDB to provide financing 'which would not otherwise be available on reasonable terms and conditions,' which seemed to imply that the Bank must be satisfied on this point beyond all possible challenge. However, the government, during the hearings of the standing committee, altered the clause, and in the end it read, 'if in the opinion of the Board [of Directors], credit or other financial resources would not otherwise be available on reasonable terms and conditions.' Basing this restriction on an opinion, and not on an absolute statement as in the original version, certainly made it much less difficult for the Bank to comply with the law in this matter.[16]

During the committee hearings, Mr Towers commented on the suggestion made by several members that the Bank would have to require an applicant to canvass every potential lender:

Obviously it would not be practicable for the management to go to any such lengths ... My opinion is that the Bank would have to operate along the following lines: if an applicant wanted a loan of a type in which a commercial bank might reasonably be interested the Industrial Development Bank would see that he discussed the matter with at least one representative bank normally doing this kind of business; if the credit requested was one which might be expected to be available by the issue of securities I think the development bank would want to know that he had talked to someone in that business to see if arrangements could be made; and similarly if it was the type of business which might well be done by an insurance company or a mortgage or trust company he should have some contacts of that kind before coming to us. The wording of Section 15, so far as I understand it, was intended to confirm the thought expressed in the preamble of the Bill that the Industrial Development Bank was to supplement existing lenders rather than displace them. For practical reasons I do not see how an absolute guarantee can be given that every potential lender in the country will be approached, in fact I am not sure that this would be entirely desirable. Perhaps the public interest would be better served by leaving lenders some incentive to look for business themselves.[17]

In actual practice, the Bank's procedures went beyond these ideas, as will be explained later, but Mr Tower's comments very well express the general attitude that guided the Bank in this matter throughout its life.

Powers to provide financial assistance to businesses

The act gave the Bank power (section 15) to extend financing by lending or guaranteeing loans, by entering into underwriting agreements, or by purchasing shares, bonds, or debentures of a corporation 'with a view to resale thereof.' The last phrase was intended to make clear that the Bank was not to become a permanent partner in a business. The interpretation of this phrase raised problems for the Bank, however, and may well have inhibited to some degree efforts made from time to time to develop a major activity in providing assistance through the purchase of shares. The Bank ultimately learned to live with the phrase by not interpreting it too closely, but for a long time the Bank's staff felt concerned that, if it acquired shares in a company, it might end up holding them for too long a period to satisfy the condition laid down in the act.

In any event, throughout the life of the Bank, loans repayable over a period of years were by far the main medium used for assisting businesses. During the debates in Parliament, several members suggested that guarantees would be a much better vehicle for the new bank to use in extending assistance. One member suggested a system of government guarantees of loans from conventional lenders as a means of avoiding the setting up by the new bank of a branch structure, which he saw as a duplication of existing banking services. Another suggested it as a means of avoiding the 'overhead and cost' of the new bank. It was also thought that such an arrangement would make the maximum use of the existing banking system.[18]

During the debate, however, it was pointed out in reply by J.L. Ilsley that a policy of guaranteeing lenders against losses seemed to be suited to situations where there would be a large number of quite small loans of a fairly uniform character. Under these conditions the guarantor could stipulate general rules and regulations but would not normally have to concern itself with individual loan applications, and a common pool guarantee with a fixed percentage of loss to be covered by the guarantor could be operative. The system of Home Improvement Loans was cited as an example of this. It did not seem at all likely that applications for industrial term loans would have these characteristics, and so one could not base a system of aid on guarantees exclusively. In his remarks before the standing committee, Mr Towers did seem to envisage some activity on the part of the IDB in guaranteeing loans made by others. 'Under the bill, the Industrial Development Bank direct loans would be confined to those cases where, for one reason or another, private lenders were not interested in making the loan even with a substantial guarantee from the Industrial Development Bank.' The comment was made in response to a suggestion that the Bank should have power only to guarantee, but Mr Towers pointed out that 'the effect of this [i.e. limiting the Bank to guarantees] would be that other institutions would have really a veto over any credit activities of the Industrial Development Bank.'[19]

Once it was operating, the IDB rarely had a guarantee proposed or sought either by an applicant or by his chartered bank. Also, it hardly ever encountered a case where a loan would not accomplish what was needed better than a guarantee. It found that guaranteeing a chartered bank loan did not put the IDB close enough to a borrower's operations or problems to give the Bank a satisfactory ongoing intimacy with them. Also, it found that it had little control or influence over the security since this was held, in the first instance, by the chartered bank concerned. Since the IDB had to charge a fee for its guarantee, expressed as a percentage of the outstanding balance owed to the chartered bank or other lending institution, it usually meant that a guarantee would be more expensive for the 'borrower' than a loan from the IDB. As a result, the number of cases in which the bank was involved in a guarantee was relatively small.

Particular consideration for small businesses

In the preamble of the act it was stated that the IDB was to provide capital assistance to industry 'with particular consideration to the financing problems of small enterprises.' Although it was repeatedly emphasized during the parliamentary debate that the Bank was to serve small and medium-sized businesses, this is the only reference to this in the act.

During debate there was much discussion of possible ways of ensuring that the Bank concentrated on this field. Most members, even those who criticized the bill, expressed sympathy for those owning small or medium-sized businesses, and many thought there should be legislative limits on the size of loan that the Bank could make. However, Mr Towers and Dr Clark steadfastly maintained their view on this, as on some other matters, that the Bank should not be hobbled by specific restrictions and stipulations in the act. The government did insert in the bill a complicated set of clauses (subsection 15[3]) designed to put a brake on any tendency on the part of the Bank to swing toward large loans. These clauses set a limit of $15 million on the aggregate of all loans, guarantees, etc, on which more than $200,000 was owing. This limit was increased by later amendments as the bank grew and actually became effective in the last year or two of the Bank's existence, when it had to refrain for several months from making loans for more than $200,000 each in order to comply with this restriction.[20]

Mr Towers's view was that the availability of financing to larger businesses from conventional sources would automatically ensure that the new bank's loans would be made mainly to small and medium-sized businesses.[21] The experience of the Bank confirmed this view completely. In the life of the Bank, 92 per cent of its loans were for $100,000 or less, and 48 per cent were for $25,000 or less.

Restricted eligibility of borrowers

Section 15(1) of the act restricted the Bank to assisting 'industrial enterprises,' which were defined as businesses 'in which the manufacture, processing or refrigeration of goods, wares and merchandise or the building, alteration or repair of ships or vessels or the generating or distributing of electricity is carried on.' This seems a curious mélange of businesses, but in practice the Bank's activity was for many years mostly in the fields of manufacturing or processing, although there was a fairly important demand in the field of refrigeration.

Some members of Parliament thought the scope of the bill was too narrow, one going so far as to describe the limited field set out in it as 'class legislation.'[22] Broader coverage of types of business to include trades, services, and construction, as well as transportation and communications, had been considered by those who prepared the legislation, but Mr Towers was quite definitely against it. In a letter to Dr Clark in 1943 he said: 'The credit requirements of merchandising and other establishments ... are relatively much smaller than in the case of industrial enterprises and, in addition, are largely of a short-term character which can be met by credits from trade and ordinary bank channels. I believe that the Industrial Development Bank should not attempt to cover a wider field than is necessary in the national interest. The problem of obtaining adequate staff is a major argument against following any other course for the time being.'

The considerations weighed by those drafting the bill for and against broadening the Bank's scope illustrate the problems faced by those setting up a new institution to operate in an unknown field doing things not done before. First, it was argued against broadening the scope that the trade and services groups, being typically small and difficult to deal with, should be excluded on grounds of expediency. It was considered doubtful whether very many of those that could not get credit elsewhere would be in a condition to get an advance from the new bank, and the investigation of many applicants that would almost certainly be unacceptable as credit risks would thus be avoided. Ironically, this was simply a narrow form of the basic argument voiced in the debate in Parliament against the creation of the bank at all – that a small business that could not get money from conventional sources would not be creditworthy.

Second, it was argued that for trading companies credit was easily available from suppliers of merchandise. This overlooked, of course, the high cost of such credit and the possibility that dependence on it might hamper a business in efforts to obtain additional assistance from other sources, such as the chartered banks. In fact, both of these considerations were, later on, reasons for the IDB's making some loans to retailers and wholesalers, and, indeed, to manufacturers as well, particularly those operating in rented premises.

Mr Towers, however, was opposed to broadening the scope of the

Bank's operations in the initial legislation,[23] and it was not done for many years. Quite apart from the considerations mentioned above, he was influenced by what he felt to be very practical factors. In considering reasons for starting the Bank, he gave high priority to anticipated post-war conditions; in the retail and wholesale fields, he thought there would be such an upsurge in civilian demand for goods that traders' inventories would turn over rapidly so that financing them would not be a problem or require special assistance. He also believed that from the standpoints of staffing the new Bank and gaining experience in a new field, it would be well that it should start small.

During the hearings of the standing committee, J.L. Ilsley also opposed broadening the scope of the new bank, but he argued on a somewhat different line. He claimed that to enlarge its field would make it a very different institution from what was intended; it would have 'a very large number of branches,' probably would have 'serious personnel problems,' and would be dealing with 'a large number of persons.' He proved to be correct in this, following the enlargement of the Bank's field to include any kind of business in 1961. In its last year of operation, 1975, it had eighty branches, was dealing with 27,000 accounts, and had become a very different institution from what was originally anticipated. Mr Ilsley also commented that, if the scope of the Bank were enlarged, 'we would be running into the danger of some of the inefficiencies that arise from public ownership and operation.' In any event, he said, no complaints had been received from the businesses not included in the act.[24]

Criteria for loans

The act laid down no rules as to the circumstances in which the Bank might extend financial assistance, Mr Towers and Dr Clark insisting that this should be left to the judgment of those managing it.[25] The Bank itself never set up any rigid rules of this character either. The act did, however, contain some general provisions that were important in the Bank's operations. In the preamble it was stated that the Bank was to be concerned with 'the availability of credit to industrial enterprises which may reasonably be expected to prove successful if a high level of national income and employment is maintained.' This fixed the role of the Bank: it was to help businesses that it believed would succeed. It was not specifically required by the act to seek to increase employment, protect jobs, prolong the life of faltering businesses, divert industry from one area to another, or ease regional disparities – all tempting goals for a government-related institution. While many of its loans did one or more of these things (to the great satisfaction of the Bank), the critical test for a loan was to be whether the borrowing business would be successful.

During the hearings of the Standing Committee on Banking and Commerce, Mr Towers stated very concisely how the IDB throughout its life would see its role on the basis of its act of incorporation: 'The objective is to ensure that any sound new development, that is, a new enterprise, and the expansion or modernization of existing enterprises, shall not be handicapped by lack of ability on the part of the enterprisers to obtain credit within amounts to which they might reasonably be entitled.'[26]

The cautious prudence of the requirement in the preamble that any business assisted should have reasonable prospects of success was modified by the provision that the Bank need only weigh up the chances of an applicant's success on the assumption that general economic conditions would remain at a high level.

By sections 16–23 of the act, the Bank was given power to take and realize upon pretty well any type of security – pledges of stock or bonds, warehouse receipts or bills of lading, inventories, mortgages or hypothecs of real or personal, movable, or immovable property. In practice, most loans were made against mortgages or hypothecs charging fixed assets, although, as will be explained later, the security for a loan would often comprise several items.

Although the Bank was given extensive powers to take security, the act laid down no requirements as to what security the Bank should take, or as to whether it took any at all, and there were no requirements as to how much the owners of a borrowing business should have invested in it. In the standing committee there was criticism on both these counts. Regarding security, Mr Towers replied: 'It is impossible to ensure prudent management by setting up legislative provisions covering such matters ... The management of this Bank would, I think, have every incentive to be prudent, although I hope they would not be timorous. I do not think that laying down specific collateral requirements would be of any help. If the requirements were not stringent, there might be a tendency to bring the standard of security down to the minimum prescribed. If, on the other hand, the requirements were too stringent, the deserving borrowers would not get assistance.'[27]

During the hearings of the standing committee, one member suggested that the act should require that the principals of any borrowing business have a certain investment in the business.[28] As a result, the government inserted into the bill a requirement (subsection 15[1]) that 'the amount of capital invested in or to be invested in' the borrowing business must, in the opinion of the board, be 'such as to afford the Bank reasonable protection.'[29] This is the only reference in the act to the basis on which loans might be made. It certainly left the Bank's management great leeway as to what investment it might require an applicant to have or to make in a project and, indirectly, as to what security might be required, or even what balance sheet position on the part of an applicant might be accepted.

The act did not limit the Bank as to the kinds of loans it made, but, in practice, they were invariably made for a period of years, with retirement usually effected by periodic instalments of principal plus interest.

One feature of the bill (section 7) was that the executive committee, consisting of the president (i.e. the governor of the Bank of Canada), the deputy governor, and two directors, was to have the full powers of the board of directors. For the first sixteen years or so of the Bank's existence, the committee operated pretty freely on this basis. This had some advantages, since the committee met much more frequently than the full board and so was able to provide quicker action and decisions than dependence on the authority of the full board would have entailed. In its last fourteen years or so, however, perhaps because by that time the Bank was quite large and complex, the executive committee, on its own initiative, refrained sometimes from exercising final authority in dealing with large loan proposals and would tend to refer such cases to the full board for final disposal, if time permitted.

Other terms of the bill

There were a number of other relatively minor provisions in the act. The board was empowered to delegate to the president or any other officer authority to act in all matters that were not, by the act or the by-laws of the Bank, reserved to be done by the board or the executive committee (section 10). For approving loans, however, no delegation of authority took place for some years, and only slowly was it extended to embrace, finally, most of the loan authorizations made. By the end of the Bank's existence, 99 per cent of loans were being approved by authority delegated by the board to lower levels within the Bank.

The bill provided that the Bank would have the same auditors as the Bank of Canada (section 27). This meant that it had two auditors at one time, usually one English-speaking and one French-speaking. They served for overlapping terms of two years each and worked jointly on the audit.

The Bank was required to set up a reserve fund (section 26) to which it was to transfer any profits after providing for bad and doubtful loans, depreciation, and so on. If the reserve fund ever exceeded the paid-up capital, however, the excess could be applied in payment of a dividend not exceeding 4 per cent of its paid-up capital. It is clear from the proceedings of the House of Commons banking committee that the new bank was not expected to operate at a loss. Mr Towers said: 'It is obvious the intention is that the bank should try to avoid making a net loss on its operations.'[30] At the same time, it was not expected to earn large profits. On this, Dr Clark said, 'The chances of profit in the operation of an institution like this are, I think, very modest, and the risks are probably considerable ... The profit possibilities in relation to the risks are not, I think, such as to attract private capital to this kind of business. Therefore, it seems to me appropriate that the type of institution you set up to perform this function should be essentially a non-profit making institution which goes out to render a service that is needed rather than to make profits primarily ... what I would expect is that there would be a modest or relatively moderate profit rather than large profits.'[31]

Section 34 provided for the act's coming into force on two separate dates. All but section 15 was proclaimed in effect on 30 September 1944, and section 15 (frequently referred to above and including the power to make loans and extend credit) was proclaimed as of 1 November 1944. This delay in proclaiming section 15 was intended to give the Bank one month in which to recruit staff and prepare operations.

PART II

The early years
1945–55

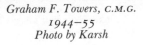

Graham F. Towers, C.M.G.
1944–55
Photo by Karsh

J.E. Coyne
1955–61
Photo by Karsh

L. Rasminsky, C.C., C.B.E.
1961–73
Photo by Paul Horsdal

G.K. Bouey
1973–5
Photo by Studio von Dulong

S.R. Noble, O.B.E.
Joined Bank 1944;
general manager 1944–53;
vice-president 1953–4; retired 1954
Photo by Karsh

D.G. Marble, C.B.E.
Secretary 1944–53;
general manager 1953–62;
special consultant 1962; died 1962
Photo by Karsh

A.N.H. James
Joined Bank 1944;
executive assistant 1944–53; assistant
general manager 1953–62; general
manager 1962–9; retired 1969
Photo by Arnott Rogers Batten Ltd

E.R. Clark
Joined Bank 1947; supervisor,
Winnipeg, 1957–9; supervisor,
Montreal, 1959–62; assistant general
manager, GMO, 1962–6;
deputy general manager 1966–9;
general manager 1969–73;
chief general manager 1973–5
Photo by Arnott Rogers Batten Ltd

*The Bank of Canada building, Victoria Square, Montreal (top),
completed in 1950. The IDB's General Manager's Office and all lending
operations based in Montreal were for many years housed on
the sixth floor. In 1974 two more floors were added; by then GMO alone
occupied all but the seventh floor and the first two floors,
as well as space in nearby buildings.
Photo by Fraser Films Limited, Montreal*

*The first general manager, S.R. Noble, in his office (centre).
The desk shown was used by all succeeding general managers
and later by the chief general manager of the Bank.
Photo by Fraser Films Limited, Montreal*

H.M. Scott
Joined Bank 1944;
directed legal work of bank;
chief, Legal Department, 1956–66;
general solicitor 1966–72;
retired 1972
Photo by Arnott Rogers
Batten Ltd

N.C. Tompkins
Joined Bank 1945;
supervisor, Vancouver, 1945–56;
assistant general manager,
British Columbia, 1956–61;
retired 1961

L. Viau
Joined Bank 1945;
deputy secretary 1948–59;
assistant supervisor,
Montreal, 1959–66;
assistant general manager,
Quebec Region,
1966–72;
retired 1972
Photo by Wm Notman
& Son, Montreal

D.T. Muskett
Joined Bank 1946;
supervisor, Winnipeg,
1946–57; resigned
1957

J.C. Ingram
Joined Bank 1945;
supervisor, Toronto, 1945–56;
resigned but rejoined bank as
supervisor, Winnipeg, 1962–3;
supervisor, Prairie Region,
1963–6; assistant general
manager, Prairie Region,
1966–73; retired 1973

W.C. Stuart
Joined Bank 1946;
supervisor, GMO, 1955–6;
supervisor, Toronto, 1956–62;
supervisor, Central Region, 1962–6;
ass't gen mgr, Ontario Region,
1966–73; general manager,
Ontario Region, 1973–4;
retired 1974
Photo by Ashley & Crippen, Toronto

*The company that built this factory (top), located in a small Quebec town,
received a series of a dozen or more IDB loans, starting with
one for $15,000. It is now one of Canada's major producers
of plastic articles, and employs 450 people.
Photo by Les Photographes Kedl (1976) Ltée, Quebec*

*With this aircraft (centre), financed with a small IDB loan, and himself
as the lone employee, the owner began in 1953 to build an air service
in the Arctic. With further loans the company grew; today it is an
international business with two thousand employees and annual revenues
in the hundreds of millions of dollars.
Photo by the Boeing Company*

Cultivator parts are shot-blasted to increase surface hardness (top left). This manufacturer of agricultural implements was established in Manitoba with the assistance of an IDB loan.

In a West Coast lumber mill (top right), one of many lumber companies financed by the Bank, a log is positioned for sawing. Photo by B.C. Jennings, Vancouver

This large industrial concern (centre) with substantial foreign sales in heating equipment, here in the process of being assembled, was started in a basement by several veterans of the Second World War. A small IDB loan helped to finance the company's first building.

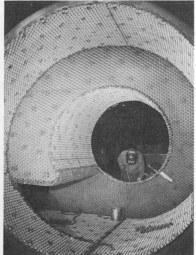

Starting with an IDB loan of $12,000 in 1952, this manufacturer of small electrical appliances (top left) grew until, with sales of millions of dollars per annum, it was able to finance further expansion through commercial sources of financing.
Photo by Dwight E. Dolan, Montreal

When this sheet-metal manufacturer (top right) received its first very small loan in 1948, it had annual sales of $100,000. By the sixties, after several more loans, it had annual sales of many millions of dollars. The picture shows a spiral dust-collector being welded.
Photo by David Bier Studios, Montreal

When the IDB made its first small loan to this manufacturer of aluminum products (centre), the business employed twenty people. With the help of additional loans it grew to be one of the largest companies in its field, with seven hundred employees. Here, aluminum ingots are prepared for processing.
Photo by Graetz Bros Ltd, Montreal

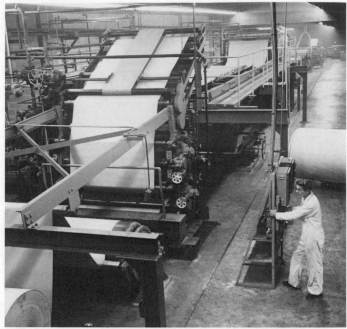

*A continuous web of paperboard is prepared for the production of cartons
and boxes (top). Starting as a very small business with an IDB loan
of a few thousand dollars, this company grew, with the help of additional
loans, to be a major manufacturer of paper boxes.
Photo by B.C. Jennings, Vancouver*

*This meat-packing business (centre) in the Atlantic Provinces started
with a very small IDB loan. Additional loans over the years helped it
to expand and upgrade plant facilities and to become
a major business in its area.*

CHAPTER THREE

Early organization

Operational headquarters in Montreal

With this chapter, we open our consideration of the IDB's first phase following the passage in Parliament of its act of incorporation. The IDB Act fixed the site of its head office as Ottawa,[1] where the head office of the Bank of Canada was located. Once the act was proclaimed, however, in the fall of 1944, the new bank established its operational headquarters at Montreal. This was probably regarded at the time as merely a practical decision. There developed a tradition in the IDB that it arose from the fact that S.R. Noble, the first general manager of the Bank, had a home there and had no intention of living anywhere else. In any event, the decision proved to be one of those small acorns from which great oaks grow, for it had important effects on the way in which the Bank's management functioned.

There were practical advantages in having the operational head-quarters of the Bank located in a major business and financial centre. Since many of the head offices of other financial institutions were also in Montreal, placing the operational headquarters there would permit the management of the IDB to maintain an acquaintance and liaison with these institutions. Perhaps, too, a location in a commercial centre would suggest to clients of the Bank and applicants for loans, as well as to the Bank's own staff, that the Bank was intended to operate free of any political or governmental involvements, and on strictly business-like principles. The separation probably helped to ease those pressures from the political world to which, as we have seen, many MPs expected the new bank to be subject. The operational headquarters in Montreal was free to concentrate on the business affairs of the Bank, while the head office, comprising the governor and certain other officers of the Bank of Canada in Ottawa, could act as a buffer against political pressures. This was a role, on the part of the Bank of Canada, to which the operating personnel of the IDB attached great importance.

It was unusual that the president and head office of a corporation should be physically separated by 125 miles from the general manager and his central operational staff. It meant that, in effect, the Bank had two 'head offices' which divided between them the functions that normally would belong to a corporation's central management. The secretary of the Bank of Canada was also the secretary of the IDB, and he and his staff were located in Ottawa. The two banks had the same board of directors and executive committee, with the later exception that, for the IDB, the deputy minister of trade and commerce was added to each body. The board and executive committee usually met in Ottawa.

At the first meeting of the board of directors in 1944, the general manager was authorized 'for and on behalf of the Bank to act in the conduct of the business of the Bank in all matters which are not by the Act to incorporate the Bank or by the by-laws specifically reserved to be done by the Board or by the Executive Committee,' phraseology partially drawn from the section of the Bank of Canada Act describing the responsibilities of the governor.[2] In practice, the general manager was responsible for the operating of the Bank, under the oversight of the president, executive committee, and board.

At first, all decisions to approve a credit had to be made by the committee or board. If a branch office of the Bank came to a favourable conclusion on an application, it recommended the proposal to the general manager; if he concurred, he in turn recommended it to head office for a final decision. If he did not concur in the recommendation, he would advise the branch it was declined, but it was several years before he was given authority to approve a loan himself.

Principles of general policy were the responsibility of the board of directors and/or executive committee. As questions on policy matters arose in the field, they were directed to the general manager, who, if unable to deal with them on the basis of principles previously laid down, would refer them to the president, who would, when necessary, refer them in turn to the board or committee.

While the General Manager's Office (GMO) handled all bookkeeping having to do with the Bank's loans, the general ledger and all operating expense accounts were maintained in Ottawa. The work of an internal audit was performed by the internal auditor of the Bank of Canada, who reported directly to the president of the IDB. Staff records for such matters as payroll, medical claims, pensions, and group insurance benefits were all administered by the head office in Ottawa. In some cases, such as pensions and group insurance, this was inevitable because they were basically the Bank of Canada plans of which employees of the IDB were made members. From the standpoint of the General Manager's Office, of course, it was very convenient that these routine administrative details should be attended to elsewhere. The IDB was charged an annual fee by the Bank of Canada for these services, but it would likely have been more expensive for the IDB, particularly when it was small, to set up new departments to do this work. Further, it would not then have had the advantage of the central bank's expertise in these administrative matters.

Relations between the president and the general manager

The separation of the offices naturally affected contacts between the president and the general manager. They could always communicate with each other by letter, memorandum, or telephone, but the separation must have had an influence in this regard just the same. Because the president was also governor of the Bank of Canada, a very time-consuming and taxing responsibility, he was undoubtedly limited in the amount of time he could devote to the affairs of the IDB. Much of the contact with the general manager on the president's behalf was done by the deputy governor or the secretary. Mr Towers had a considerable input into the policies of the Bank in its early years, but even in his day a good deal of the communication with the General Manager's Office in Montreal was handled by Mr Marble, the secretary.

The general manager invariably attended meetings of the board of directors, but the distance between Montreal and Ottawa made it impractical for him to attend always the weekly meetings of the executive committee. In fact, there would be long periods when he would only rarely do so. For many years, this gave rise to the curious situation of credit proposals recommended by the general manager as chief operational officer sometimes being disposed of without his being present if they were being finally dealt with by the executive committee. This placed on the secretary the responsibility to prepare and submit credit material to the executive committee.

In the later years of the Bank, when the volume of business was enormously increased, some of these earlier practices were altered, and responsibility for preparing material on credits for submission to the board or executive committee was assumed by the General Manager's Office. The general manager then invariably, as previously, attended meetings of the board of directors, but, in addition, either he or another senior officer from his office would attend meetings of the executive committee when IDB credit proposals were to be dealt with.

Staff members of the IDB always took great pride in the connection with the Bank of Canada and, in particular, in the fact that the governor, naturally an eminent and distinguished Canadian, was their president. He was regarded with respect and affection and, to some extent, awe by the employees of the IDB. At the same time, in their daily work, they looked for direction to the general manager, and it must have strengthened his position as chief operational officer of the Bank that he was located in his own separate office in Montreal.

It is obvious from all the above that the overall management of the Bank's affairs depended very much on a harmonious relationship between the president and the general manager, and between the general manager and other members of the staff in head office. Rarely was this harmony disturbed. The responsibilities of the general manager were not precisely defined, except regarding any authority he might be given to approve loans. Judgment and custom determined just what the limits to his authority in other areas were. The general manager knew he always had available to himself, in the president, the counsel and advice of an extremely able and sincere person who was as deeply interested in the success of the IDB as anyone, but who was able to take a somewhat more objective view of problems than those immersed in them daily might be able to do.

Freedom of Bank from political or departmental involvement

As a consequence of the separation of offices, head office in Ottawa tended to handle any contacts with the government or with politicians. Any correspondence with politicians was usually dealt with by the secretary or the president, whose prestige was valuable in this. Apart from questions about the Bank's use of lawyers, which will be referred to later, inquiries from politicians usually had to do with information about a prospective applicant or the Bank's operations generally, or about the progress being made with a particular application or a loan proposal that had been declined. For a long time, inquiries of the last two sorts would be turned aside unless they were accompanied by specific authorization from the applicant or borrower to answer such inquiries. In the later years of the Bank, however, the view was taken that an inquiry about an application by a member of Parliament implied that consent to release basic information had been given by the applicant, and information on the progress being made with an application or on the reasons why one was turned down would then be released. If an MP complained of a negative decision on an application, he might be told that the applicant could always ask for further consideration, especially if he had more information to supply.

Of course, nothing is all good nor all bad, and the effective insulation of the Bank's operations from political influences meant that members of the government and MPs did not have many occasions to hear about the Bank from those fully engaged in its work. As a result, when, in the later years of the Bank, fundamental questions were being raised in government circles about the Bank and its future, there was no background of acquaintance or familiarity between, on the one hand, ministers, members of Parliament, or civil servants and, on the other hand, the operational personnel of the Bank, even those of senior rank. Whether this unfamiliarity was good or bad is a legitimate question, but one thing it accomplished was to establish a clear tradition on the operational side of the Bank of aloofness from matters political. Among the staff of the Bank, no tradition was stronger than this one.

So jealous was the Bank of its independence and of the free exercise of its honest judgment on loan applications that it even came to regard with wariness any involvement, not only with politicians, but with federal government departments as well. The Hon. Walter Gordon, when minister of finance, was heard to remark that the IDB was 'as independent as a hog on ice.' Just what the metaphor meant to Mr Gordon is not known, but those in the IDB regarded it as a compliment.

In 1951, the federal Department of Fisheries wanted the Bank to join with it in a special study of the fishing industry to 'assess the feasibility of the development and expansion of processing facilities.' In his reply to this request, the general manager of the Bank, Mr Noble, said, 'Our function is primarily a financial one and must so remain. It is our function to consider enquiries strictly from a business point of view although of course we have to give some weight to the general factors involved in the industry as a whole.'

Proposals by government departments that the IDB administer their programs of financial assistance, or should assist with them, were turned aside. The people in the Bank did not see themselves in this role at all. They saw the Bank as established to do only certain things set out clearly in its act of incorporation and believed they would best perform these tasks if they did not become involved with other programs or with government departments.

Early offices and officers

The first office of the Bank, housing the general manager and his staff, was at 201 Notre Dame Street West, Montreal. In 1947, it moved to the Aldred Building on Place d'Armes. In 1950, it moved to the new Bank of Canada building on Victoria Square where it remained. At first the Montreal office was the only office the Bank had. All the first loan proposals received were dealt with there, and those investigating them would travel out from Montreal. However, in 1945 regional offices were opened in Toronto and Vancouver, and in 1946 a regional office was opened in Winnipeg. For ten years, these remained the only offices of the Bank. The Montreal office served eastern Ontario as far as Ottawa and Kingston, all of Quebec, and the Atlantic provinces. The Toronto office served southern Ontario and northern Ontario as far west as Sault Ste Marie (a limit that was later moved to Port Arthur). The Winnipeg office looked after Saskatchewan, Manitoba, and northwestern Ontario, and the Vancouver branch served British Columbia, Alberta, and the two territories.

The regional offices in Toronto, Vancouver, and Winnipeg were each under a supervisor who reported to the general manager in Montreal. A curious feature of the Bank's initial organization (and one that persisted for fifteen years to 1959), was that the office in Montreal in which the general manager and his supporting administrative staff were located also functioned as a 'branch' office under the general manager himself, dealing with loan applications from the public. The Bank was operating in an entirely new field in which the real demand had yet to be determined and the best way of operating established, and it was sensible that those responsible for its direction should be directly involved in its operations so that they could have a personal understanding of the nature of the problems with which the Bank was going to have to deal.

In November 1956, the Chambre de Commerce de Montréal wrote to the president of the Bank, J.E. Coyne, forwarding a recommendation that the General Manager's Office should transfer responsibility for the Bank's work in Quebec to a separate regional office such as served other parts of the country. Mr Coyne thought that such an arrangement would involve duplication of offices 'in view of the fact that the General Manager's Office for the entire nation is located in Montreal and for purposes of simplicity in organization incorporates within it the regional office for the province in which it is situated.' Later, in the late 1960s, regional offices, which had been exercising the function of direct lending to the public as well as that of supervising the operation of other branches, were separated from the first of these functions and their responsibilities confined to that of supervision. By this, the overall operations of the Bank benefitted greatly, and the same result might have come from setting up earlier a GMO with only a supervisory role.

As early as 1947, consideration was given to establishing an office in the Atlantic provinces – understandably, given that that entire area was being served by someone travelling from Montreal. The problem was believed to be solved in 1952, at least for a period of years, by appointing as supervisor, Atlantic provinces, Mr Frank Aykroyd, who, though stationed in Montreal, was to look after the Atlantic provinces. Not until 1956, with the opening of the Halifax branch, was there an office in the Atlantic provinces.

The serving of enormous areas by the Montreal, Winnipeg, and Vancouver offices was accomplished by what were called 'swings,' in which one or two officers would travel for a period of days through the distant territories served by these offices. While this seemed to serve the purposes of the Bank in its early years, it had serious disadvantages. It did not overcome the appearance of remoteness of the Bank from the small businesses it was supposed to serve. It meant that one or two officers were for long periods of time absent from their offices and unavailable for anything else; when they returned to their base office, they would have so many memoranda and reports to write that they were virtually out of action for a further period. Also, it presented practical obstacles of distance to many small business proprietors who might want to approach the Bank for assistance.

The history of the IDB was really one of people. The Bank showed an extraordinary ability to weld its employees into a loyal and dedicated team, highly competent and, indeed, outstanding in the Bank's field of term lending to small and medium-sized businesses. When a new employee joined the Bank in its formative years he was usually given two things, a slide-rule and a brief-case. The slide-rule was to enable him to make rapid calculations during his discussions with loan applicants as well as during the analysis of information supporting the applications (before the days of pocket computers), and the brief-case was so that he could take work home! So interesting was the work of the Bank and so successful was it in motivating its employees that overtime work, which might well have seemed onerous in other employment, became commonplace within the IDB. The Bank dealt with its employees on a humane, individual basis, and, even when it became quite large in its later years, it endeavoured strenuously to maintain this tradition.

In any event, few organizations, either public or private, can have had a staff as loyal and dedicated as that of the IDB. In fact, a sense of 'loyalty' seemed to embrace even those, who, for one reason or another, left the Bank for other employment. The training and experience they received in the IDB was unique in Canada and made them very attractive to other employers. Among former employees of the IDB would be found a president of a chartered bank, the general manager of another chartered bank, vice-presidents of a nation-wide trust company, the vice-president of a steel company, the treasurer of a provincial hydro corporation, senior officers of almost every provincial government lending corporation, the president and senior staff of a large private corporation operating in the industrial mortgage field, and senior officers of other large private corporations. Even these regarded themselves as 'old boys' of the IDB.

It was a characteristic of the IDB that its employees felt a deep involvement in the Bank, and all considered themselves to be direct participants in its evolution. Those who formed the early management group, however, were particularly important in establishing and developing the basic practices and procedures by which the Bank operated.

Before the IDB bill was passed by Parliament, Mr Towers discussed with W.E. Scott, his principal assistant in the Bank of Canada in planning the IDB, where they might find a suitable person to be general manager of the new bank. Mr Scott was then responsible for liaison between the central bank and the commercial chartered banks. Early in 1944 he called on the senior officers of the Royal Bank of Canada. In reporting back to Mr Towers, he mentioned that he had run into S.R. Noble, an assistant general manager of the Royal Bank who had been loaned to the government during the war as sugar administrator for the Wartime Prices and Trade Board, and vice-president of the Commodity Prices Stabilization Corporation Ltd. Mr Scott said that Mr Noble seemed to be winding down his government work in Ottawa, but was not yet back into full work at the Royal Bank. Mr Towers immediately exclaimed, 'That's the man we want.' Before his appointment to the Bank of Canada, Mr Towers had been an assistant general manager at the Royal, and he and Mr Noble had a high regard for each other. Mr Towers then spoke to S.G. Dobson, vice-president and general manager of the Royal Bank, who consented to Mr Noble's being approached. The latter accepted appointment as general manager of the IDB.

On the day the IDB bill passed Parliament, Mr Noble approached A.N.H. James, one of his senior assistants, to be his assistant in the new bank, and in October Mr James was appointed to this position with the title of executive assistant. He had been with Barclay's Bank for many years and, prior to the war, with Barclay's (Canada) Ltd, by whom he had been loaned to the government for the duration of the war. A couple of weeks later they were joined by H.M. Scott, a young lawyer from Winnipeg, who had had several years' experience in the mortgage field and who took charge of the Bank's legal department.

Other early officers were J.C. Ingram, who had been in the special accounts section of the Canadian Bank of Commerce and was put in charge of the Toronto office of the IDB as supervisor; D.R. Muskett, an officer of a trust company in Toronto, who opened the Bank's office in Winnipeg as supervisor; N.C. Tompkins, who had been inspector for the Royal Bank for eastern Canada and had been on loan to the Wartime Prices and Trade Board, who was appointed supervisor of the IDB's office in Vancouver; Lucien Viau, who was then a branch manager with the Banque provinciale in Montreal and who became the Bank's principal French-speaking officer; and W.F. Farquharson, who became the principal investigating officer at the Toronto office. The first engineering officer of the Bank was Eric Adams, who joined the staff in December 1944, but he left the service of the Bank a few years later. Important contributions to the Bank's early development were made also by Donald Gordon, deputy governor of the Bank of Canada and a director of the IDB, and D.G. Marble, secretary of the Bank of Canada and the first secretary of the IDB. The group of early officers mentioned includes three – Messrs Noble, Marble, and James – of the four general managers who successively directed the operations of the Bank. The fourth general manager (the author) joined the Bank in 1947 from the Bank of Nova Scotia.

The early management group represented a great deal of practical banking experience. Of the persons mentioned, eight had worked for chartered banks. In addition to those whose banking background has been mentioned, Mr Gordon, deputy governor, had been secretary of the Bank of Canada and prior to that manager of the Toronto branch of the Bank of Nova Scotia; Mr Marble, prior to his joining the Bank of Canada, had been personnel supervisor for the Royal Bank of Canada. In the early years of the Bank, all these men contributed constantly and intimately to establishing policies and procedures for the new Bank.

Because of the arrangements by which some of the administrative functions normally associated with a head office were attended by Bank of Canada personnel in Ottawa, most of the people taken on the staff of the

IDB, apart from those involved in loan accounting and other administrative duties, were directly employed in handling credit applications and inquiries. These personnel were divided into five categories: credit officers, engineers, lawyers, insurance officers, and secretaries. Initially, many of the credit officers were drawn from one or other of the chartered banks, since the IDB was starting from scratch and could not take time to train new credit officers in the matter of lending. Recruiting among the banks required the exercise of a good deal of tact and discretion. The banks themselves faced staffing problems in the post-war period, and, since the IDB needed a harmonious relationship with the banks, it could not simply plunge into the market and induce bank employees to switch over to it. Any intention to approach the employee of a bank about transferring to the IDB would usually be cleared first with the appropriate senior officer of the chartered bank concerned. For the same reason, the IDB tended to spread its recruiting around among the chartered banks so that it did not lean too heavily on any one of them. As a result, all the major banks were represented among the early senior officers and credit officers of the IDB.

The recruiting of lawyers, engineers, and other specialists did not present the same problems although, like the credit officers obtained from the banks, almost all those taken on initially had had practical business experience in their special fields before joining the Bank. It was perhaps for this reason that for many years the Bank did not require formal programs for training new employees. A new credit officer or engineer would be attached to someone else for a few weeks or months as an understudy and then function on his own.[3]

Secretaries and clerical staff also played important parts in helping to set the new bank up and get it operating, and these positions comprised, in the early years, the Bank's female staff. Among the secretaries, however, there were very able women who, in another day, would have qualified for senior posts. These women, many of whom stayed with the IDB or its successor, the FBDB, to retirement, or who still work for the FBDB, contributed directly and materially to the Bank's success by their loyalty, intelligence, and diligence. Later the Bank deliberately set itself to broaden its employment of women. Some of the early female employees were then appointed to responsible administrative posts, and women appeared in the ranks of credit officers, lawyers, and other important positions.

The employment on staff of engineers, lawyers, and insurance specialists was an innovation in Canadian banking. Engineers were for many years stationed at each branch and involved in dealing with the technical aspects of credit applications. Lawyers were also attached to the branch offices, with occasional exceptions, and supervised the preparation by outside lawyers of the security documents for approved loans. Insurance officers checked on compliance with loan conditions involving insurance.

Industrial Research Division

The IDB also very early set another precedent for Canadian banking institutions by using technical research studies to assist in dealing with applications. In 1945, it arranged with the Bank of Canada that the latter's research department would do such studies for the IDB when requested. These would cover the general situation in the industry with which an application was concerned, markets available, competition to be faced, imports and exports, raw material supplies, types of machinery available, price trends of materials and finished products, and so on. For these studies, information would be obtained, confidentially, from government departments, trade associations, large department stores, and any other suitable source.

Soon the research department of the Bank of Canada set aside for this a separate section known within the IDB as the industrial research division (IRD). It was located in Ottawa at head office, but shortly after it was set up arrangements were made for members of the staffs of the IDB's branch offices to make, on the division's behalf, such local inquiries in a branch's area as a particular study might require.

When the research work started, great importance was attached to the preparation of full-length studies on particular industries to be used by credit officers and engineers as reference material if an application in one of these industries was received. These covered every aspect of an industry, even to the point of including photographs and descriptions of machinery used in the industry. In spite of the enormous amount of work devoted to these special 'industry studies' and their very high quality, they were found to have limited practical value. By the time a study was completed any statistics or data in it might be out of date, and it was often found that, in spite of the depth of investigation represented by the study, it was not always relevant to the minutiae of the issues on which a loan to some small business would ultimately be decided. For the most part, therefore, studies and reports by IRD were done in response to specific requests for information on individual applications.

In 1968, IRD became a part of the IDB itself under Lorne Barclay, and it concentrated almost entirely on specific research for individual applications. In the later years of the Bank, as applications came increasingly from retail, wholesale, and service industries which did not lend themselves to this type of research, IRD was involved in a diminishing proportion of the Bank's total loans. None the less, it produced annually 300 to 400 reports that were most valuable for the applications concerned.

In 1946, it was proposed by Eric Adams, the senior engineer on the Bank's staff, that the functions of engineering supervision and industrial research be combined at the General Manager's Office in Montreal into one investigation and research department, with the engineers in the regional offices being field members of this department. This might have avoided certain administrative and personnel problems that later appeared in both these functions, but the suggestion was not adopted.

Organization

In 1946, a practice was established which, although not a formal part of the Bank's organization, was one of the most important parts of it. This was the holding every year or so of a supervisors' conference at the General Manager's Office in Montreal attended by all the regional supervisors, the general manager and other senior officers from his office, and the president, the deputy governor, and the secretary from Ottawa. These meetings usually lasted two days and covered all aspects of policy and procedures, upon many of which decisions would be reached following a free discussion. This established early the custom of contributions from all parts of the Bank to decisions on these matters.

For its first eleven years, the Bank functioned with few changes in the simple organization with which it started. Operations were directed from Montreal by a general manager and an assistant general manager (this title replaced executive assistant in 1953). The only other persons with appointed titles at GMO were two deputy secretaries, C.I. Stuart and L. Viau, the former concerning himself mainly with administration, the latter occupied principally on the credit side. There were specific departments at GMO for legal, insurance, loan accounting, and credit work, but, though the first three at least operated from the beginning under well-recognized leaders, they had no official titles. Credit work at GMO was carried on at first under the direct supervision of the general manager and his executive assistant (later, assistant general manager). In April 1955, the position of supervisor of the General Manager's Office was created, but the appointee, W.C. Stuart, was made supervisor of the Toronto office eleven months later, and the position lapsed.

Each of the three field offices was under the direction of a supervisor, and all four offices had a staff of credit officers to process loan applications. Montreal, Toronto, and Vancouver also had legal, insurance, and engineering officers. The Winnipeg office was not large enough to support a staff of specialists in these areas. For legal and insurance work, it depended on GMO in Montreal, but for the investigations then done at other offices by one of the Bank's engineers, it anticipated what was to be a common practice fifteen years later by usually using its credit officers for this work.

CHAPTER FOUR

Procedures

Role of the IDB

Although the act creating the IDB did not limit it to providing any particular type of financing, it was expected that its principal role would be the financing of building and equipment programs. Most of its loans were indeed of this character, but even in its early years it moved fairly quickly from this position. It provided financing to businesses so that they could put back into their working capital money tied up in a building or equipment program, perhaps completed or partially completed, for which term financing had not been arranged. The Bank saw itself, in these cases, as doing after the event what it might have done before had the applicant business planned its financial affairs better. Whatever purpose was served by the Bank's loans, they were invariably made on a medium- or long-term basis, with repayment generally by regular instalments of principal (usually monthly or quarterly) plus interest, on the basis of a formal written loan contract between the Bank and the borrower.

During the parliamentary debate in 1944, critics of the proposal to create the Industrial Development Bank claimed that most businesses that needed assistance should be able to get it from a chartered bank. If they could not, it must mean that they were not creditworthy because the chartered banks were experts in lending; to hold a contrary view was to reject the opinion of experts.[1] This argument overlooked the fact that the type of lending normally provided by the chartered banks and that to be supplied by the IDB were entirely different. The chartered banks were accustomed to providing short-term credit accommodation to cover a borrower's daily working capital needs. There would not usually be any formal written agreement as to when the bank loan would be paid off, other than that the loan might be made by means of a demand or short-term note or notes. The bank would generally expect that the loan would be reduced to zero some time during the ensuing year, but otherwise it might fluctuate up and down as the needs of the borrower changed.[2]

Since the IDB was entering a more or less new field of lending, it had to develop its own methods of operating and of examining credit proposals. The chartered banks, when considering a credit proposal or administering a loan, would give particular attention to those elements in a borrower's balance sheet that formed part of its working capital position – inventories, accounts receivable and the ageing of these, and accounts payable and their ageing. The lender would be concerned constantly, perhaps even daily, as to the way in which the borrower's current assets were turning over and the success with which it was able to keep its current liabilities in line. The chartered bank would be alert to danger signals among these balance sheet items that might require a quick reaction on its part to protect its loan.

The IDB, however, while concerned with the working capital position of a borrower as being critical to the latter's success, was also very concerned about the borrower's longer-term prospects. Since any loan that the Bank might make would be tied up for a long period of time – perhaps ten or fifteen years – it had a much keener interest in assessing the longer view of the business than might its short-term lending counterpart. As a result, while deeply interested in a borrower's current position, it was interested also in other parts of the borrower's balance sheet, including the fixed assets that would constitute the main security for a loan, and in analysing in some detail the market, operating costs, efficiency, cost controls, and elements of the borrower's long-term prospects. All this required a careful study of the applicant's plans – their soundness and adequacy, established costs, and technical aspects of the proposal – as well as an analysis in depth of the applicant's financial position and a consideration of the quality and continuity of management in the applicant business.

Processing of loan applications

For the first few weeks after the Bank started operations, applications were handled as best they might be without a formal procedure. In November 1944, Mr Towers wrote: 'Industrial Development Bank is now rejoicing in a staff of four, and is swamped with applications, many of which look perfectly reasonable. I hope that the pace slackens. If it does not, I am afraid we shall get a bad reputation for delay in doing business.' However, regular procedures were soon established, and although they were modified several times in later years to expedite the processing of applications, particularly for small amounts, the concepts embodied in them formed the basis of the Bank's procedures to the end.

They included two important elements – a detailed study of financial aspects of a proposal and of an applicant's previous record if it was not a new business, and an inspection visit to the applicant's place of business to study its operations and discuss the proposal 'on the spot.' When businessmen or businesswomen wanted to inquire about the possibility of getting a loan, they would either write to or call at an office of the Bank, probably giving some information about their business. They would be referred to a credit officer who would explain to the inquirers (who were usually as curious about the Bank as the Bank was about them) what the Bank's role was, the information that would be needed to support an application, the usual terms of a loan, the way in which the security of the loan would be taken, and the manner of disbursement. The credit officer would question the inquirers in detail about their business – its history, structure, products, past financial record, the purpose of the loan, and so on. Discussions of this sort would usually take about $1\frac{1}{2}$ hours. During the discussion the credit officer would try to form an opinion as to whether the proposition seemed to be one that the Bank could reasonably take under consideration. He would have to concern himself, of course, with whether or not the business was eligible under the act and whether the funds required could be obtained elsewhere and discuss these things with the applicant. If he thought that the proposed application was premature or unsatisfactory in some way, he would explain this to the applicant and perhaps indicate where the proposal should be strengthened before it could be considered. If the application seemed appropriate for consideration, he would then brief the applicant on the information that should be supplied to support it and give out a printed application form to be submitted.

Following such an interview (called inside the Bank an 'enquiry'), the credit officer wrote, for the Bank's files, a full memorandum on the discussion. He did the same for any subsequent interviews so that the files had a full record of all talks with an applicant. In the early years of the Bank, a copy of each of these memoranda was sent to GMO. This was considered necessary so that troublesome questions of policy could, if not raised at the branch level, be anticipated by the General Manager's Office which, if it thought necessary, might intervene regarding such questions.

When all the information required was received along with the signed application form, the credit officer would write a letter to the manager of the applicant's chartered bank branch describing the proposal that had been submitted, inviting the manager to express his opinion of it, and asking for a confidential report on the applicant business. The authority for his doing this was provided on the application form signed by the applicant. He would also analyse the information received with the application and very likely have another interview with the applicant to clear up further questions that had arisen.

The procedure for analysis was basically the same whether the application was for $5,000 or $5 million. Balance sheet figures for the business for as many years as were available would be set down on large ruled sheets in parallel columns year by year, and details of the operating statements would be set down in the same way. All items of cost for each year would be expressed as a percentage of the value of sales for that year. All these figures and percentages would then be compared from year to year, and any marked changes or variations would be questioned.

For many applicants, dealing with the Bank was an education in itself. The comparisons made between the yearly figures, the relating of cost items to sales figures, and the insights these exercises provided were a great novelty to many. Some applicants were not in the habit of preparing proper statements or even keeping proper books. How to prepare an operating forecast had, in some cases, to be patiently explained in detail. For many the idea of a formal costing system had never even been entertained. For example, one applicant was found to have been in the habit of preparing his operating statement by working back from an assumed net profit! The profit he was sure he knew, for he had complete confidence in his 'costing' by which he put down a figure for labour, material, and overhead costs for each batch of production as it went through his factory. When he came to add up his accounts at the end of the year, the one figure he felt unsure of was the final total cost of materials because, apart from his assumptions regarding each batch of production, he did not know how to handle the basic elements of this cost – purchases of raw materials, work-in-progress, and finished goods. As a result, the figure he put into his operating statement for material was whatever was necessary to produce the net profit he 'knew' he had earned! This business ultimately went under.

When the credit officer had studied the financial statements and other information submitted by an applicant, the credit officer would refer the application to one of the branch's engineers (unless, like Winnipeg, it did not have one). The engineer would visit the applicant's place of business and discuss all aspects of the application – the working capital position of the business, production flow, plant layout, any production problems, the type of equipment used, raw material used, costing method, markets, prospects for the future, plans for new buildings or the purchase of new machinery, and so on – and form an opinion of the probable value of the fixed assets forming the Bank's security in the event the loan had to be liquidated. A field investigation of this sort would usually take about a day. When the engineer returned to the office, he would write a report on his findings on all aspects of the application; the report might run anywhere from ten to thirty pages in length. This employment of full-time engineers was unusual among Canadian financial institutions. It meant that in the file of every application there was a clear account of the applicant's operations, needs, and problems written from a technical standpoint but with a view to helping those dealing with the application to reach a conclusion on it. Although, as will be seen later, the role of engineers changed as the Bank gained experience and the nature of applications altered, in the formative years of the Bank their contribution in developing experience and judgment within the Bank was invaluable.

The discussions that an applicant would have with the Bank's engineer were also of real value to the former. In many cases it was the first opportunity the proprietor or manager had had to talk about the business with a technical and practical person. Such questions as production flow, types of machinery, plant layout, building costs, and manufacturing costs were areas in which the Bank's engineers provided loan applicants with important assistance.

Many an applicant discovered, to his or her astonishment, that the product that was regarded as the applicant's leader and staple was losing money on every sale, and the business benefitted from the advice of the Bank's investigating engineer in correcting the situation. W.F. Farquharson, senior engineer at the Toronto regional office, has recalled investigating an applicant who was very pleased with himself because he had just purchased a costing 'system' from a friend. The latter operated a quite different business, and it took some argument to show that the system was not suited to the applicant's operation.

Once the engineer's report was completed and any further information from the applicant that it might have suggested had been obtained, the credit officer, the engineer, and the branch supervisor (or a senior officer of the Bank in the case of the Montreal office) would discuss the application. If their decision was negative, the applicant would be informed of this by letter, although the full reasons for the decision might not be given in the letter. For these, the applicant would preferably be invited to come to the Bank's office for a further discussion. It was felt that the reasons why an application was turned down could be explained much more satisfactorily verbally than by letter. Even so, explanations to an applicant of a negative decision were treated, in these early years, with some delicacy. As one general manager of the early years expressed it, 'Reasons given for a refusal should be as few as possible, and stay off controversial ground such as management.'

If the decision was favourable, a discussion with the applicant would take place as to the possible terms of a loan if one were approved by the Bank. Credit officers were expected to avoid giving the impression that the local office had reached a decision in favour of the application and was recommending it to the general manager. This was to avoid the awkward situation that was thought to arise if the final decision at GMO or the board was negative, in which event the Bank might appear to be divided in its reaction to the application. It was considered most important that whatever decision was reached should be regarded and spoken of as the Bank's decision.

One time an application from a business in Kitchener was, after analysis, favourably regarded by the branch office of the IDB and recommended to GMO. There it was turned down, and this decision was given to the company. At the discussion at which this decision was communicated, the auditor for the company, a very eminent member of his profession, took violent exception to the negative decision on the grounds that the credit officer, had, in the course of the initial interview, encouraged the applicant to expect approval of his proposal. When pressed, he attributed this favourable impression to the fact that the credit officer had smiled a lot and been very friendly! However, in spite of the fact that the credit officer and the branch supervisor had, indeed, supported the proposal and recommended it to the general manager, this was not disclosed to the applicant, who went away very disgruntled.

Although the procedures outlined above were the basis for dealing with credit applications throughout the Bank, there were some differences between offices in the way they were applied. These differences partly reflected the personality of the local supervisor, who often had his own ideas about how the procedures should be employed. Regional offices had from the beginning a great deal of freedom in how they functioned. There was no system of inspection by which offices were visited to ensure their adherence to laid-down procedures, and senior officers from Montreal would, in these early years, rarely visit the field offices. This left a great deal of room for imagination and initiative on the part of regional supervisors.

When an application was recommended to the general manager, it was accompanied by a letter of some length called a 'submission,' analysing all aspects of the proposal and the financial and operating position of the applicant and accompanied by large columned sheets on which the financial record of the business was set out in great detail year by year. This arduous process was followed with every application, no matter how small. Later, when the Bank was much larger and had more experience, these procedures were modified for small applications in the interests of saving time, but as a training for the credit officers of the Bank they could hardly have been surpassed.

If the application was approved by head office or by the general manager (until 1947 all proposals had to be submitted to head office in Ottawa for authorization via GMO in Montreal), a letter was written to the applicant setting out the terms for the proposed loan and giving a period of time – from two to three weeks – within which the terms were to be accepted in writing. If they were accepted, the legal department of the Bank then instructed an outside firm of solicitors to search land titles, to prepare lists of equipment to be charged, and to prepare the security for the loan. Each loan was different from every other, so that the security documents required separate preparation in each case. The outside lawyers would then submit the security documents to the Bank's legal department for a final check, following which the documents would be executed by the borrower and any registrations required made, and the loan would then be ready for disbursement. For a building or equipment program of some sort, disbursement took place gradually as the program was carried out. The borrower would submit to the Bank invoices or vouchers indicating either that he was being billed for the expense of the program or had already paid for it, and disbursement would take place in response to the submission of these vouchers.

The above recital will undoubtedly have created the impression that obtaining a loan from the IDB was not a quick process. During the period 1945–55, five or six weeks might elapse from the time the Bank received the information supporting an application till a decision on the application was reached; large applications could very well take longer than this. The preparation of the security might well take ten weeks or more, following which disbursement of the loan would itself be extended over a period of time as the program being financed was carried out. That the Bank was slow was a criticism heard frequently. The operating personnel felt that, to a large extent, the critics did not appreciate the problems frequently encountered in obtaining from unsophisticated businessmen the information needed to appraise a proposal and prepare the security documents. Nevertheless, the Bank was very much aware of the desirability of speeding up its processes as much as possible.

It sought to do this first by transferring from the board of directors to the general manager some of the power to authorize loans. In 1947, the general manager was given authority to deal with applications of up to $25,000. At the same time, the board was prepared to see the power to authorize loans of up to $5,000 or $10,000 delegated to the field supervisors. However, since this latter category embraced a small proportion of loans and in any event was going to require the submission by the supervisors to the General Manager's Office of exactly the same amount of information as they were required to submit for loans that were to be approved by the general manager or head office, the delegation of authority offered the supervisors was declined.

Security for loans and other conditions

The loans of the IDB constituted, in effect, miniature mortgage bonds. They provided for the small and medium-sized business the same kind of financing arrangement that was available to large corporations when they would sell bonds on the public market. Each loan was based on a contract designed for that particular loan. The main security for a loan was usually a charge on the fixed assets of the borrower, that is, land, buildings, and equipment. If the borrower occupied a building as a tenant, the main security would consist of a charge on his equipment, although this presented the Bank with certain problems because the landlord might well have some claim against the equipment in the event that rent was not paid. The Bank sought sometimes to protect itself against this situation by taking a mortgage on the building lease.

The Bank would also, of course, take an assignment of fire or other suitable insurance on the fixed assets. This was most important to the Bank, and the specialists in its insurance department would review the borrower's coverage to be sure it was adequate and in good shape. Even in the most unlikely cases, the Bank followed its set procedures and insisted on good fire insurance coverage. R. McMurray has recalled that, when he was insurance officer at the Vancouver office, the Bank insisted on the assignment of fire insurance on an outdoor 'bed' for making pre-stressed concrete beams. The borrower was mystified as to why such a contraption required fire insurance, and even Mr McMurray felt a little embarrassed about it. As it happened, however, the bed was sheltered in winter by plywood sheets and warmed by a blower; the plywood caught fire, the stressing cables buckled, and there was an insurance claim of $19,000.

If a loan went into liquidation, the insurance department was responsible for keeping the assets forming the Bank's security covered. This was not always easy. One borrower had had so many fires that when the Bank took possession of his plant no insurance agent could be persuaded to insure it, even after the Bank became its owner. Once they heard the address, they listened no more!

An even more unhappy (from the Bank's standpoint) experience in which insurance was not collected involved a vessel that the Bank had seized that had a completely inoperable power plant. The vessel had to be towed up the Bay of Fundy to the drydock at Saint John for repairs, and en route it encountered a severe storm. It started to roll to such an extent that it threatened to sink. It was, of course, adequately insured, so that had misfortune overtaken it, the Bank might have seen in this the hand of a beneficent providence. The tug-captain, however, responded to the threat to the vessel's safety so valiantly that with ropes and cables he saved the vessel. The Bank did not collect insurance, it had to spend great sums subsequently to fix up the vessel and to sell it – and it had to pay the captain a large reward for saving the vessel!

An interesting by-product of the Bank's security was that, because of the IDB's charges on the fixed assets and the assignment of fire and other insurance, and because of the need for the legal and insurance departments of the Bank to satisfy themselves as to the Bank's position in both these matters, a borrower would usually end up with insurance and titles to real estate, and perhaps also to equipment, that was in a better state than before the loan was made.

As part of its security, the Bank might ask for a personal guarantee of some amount, particularly in the case of a private company dependent on one or two principals for its successful operation. The idea was to tie in the interests of these people and put them behind the responsibility of the company to pay back the IDB loan. This was not fully successful: if the business were sold (which the Bank could not normally prevent if its loan was in good standing) the Bank could scarcely, as a rule, insist on retaining the guarantee of the previous owner. It might then find itself unable to obtain a substitute for the guarantee. In addition, personal guarantees were not easy to enforce. If a business were unsuccessful, the principal would quite likely have been left with few resources by the failure of the business. Sometimes when the Bank had to liquidate its security, it was obliged by practical considerations to reach a compromise with the guarantor by which it would accept monthly or annual payments for a period of time and for a lesser amount than the original guarantee.

The security for a loan might also include the assignment of life insurance on some key individuals – owners or employees. This was difficult to keep in force if the business were sold or the employee left the business, or if the Bank had to realize on its tangible security following the failure of a borrowing business. While the assignment of life insurance was for some time a fairly common feature of the Bank's loans, it was rarely of consequence in protecting the Bank's position. In only a handful of cases during the history of the Bank was the assignment of life insurance a factor in protecting the Bank from a loss. However, the assignment of the life insurance often proved to be a very good thing for the borrower. If the borrowing company found itself in difficulties because of the death of some key individual upon whom it had been required by the Bank to obtain life insurance, the Bank might, even though the policy was assigned, release the proceeds to the company if the Bank was satisfied with its position on other scores. Often this would provide a company in this difficult situation with a very welcome windfall.

W.F. Farquharson was once required to visit a borrowing business that was in great trouble. It depended on the technical knowledge and skills of one shareholder who was the only one really active in it. Mr Farquharson explained to the other shareholders that they too would have to pitch in and take some of the load off their key associate as otherwise it would kill him. The shareholders retired to discuss this suggestion, but they had obviously learned the value of insurance protection, for they returned to inform Mr Farquharson that there was no need to be worried about the possibility that overwork might kill their colleague, because they had his life insured!

Often the means by which the Bank would take a charge on a borrower's equipment was a chattel mortgage; for many years, this was not popular with some of its borrowers because such a step was traditionally regarded in trade circles as a sign that a business was in difficulties. Chattel mortgages were regularly reported by the credit-reporting agencies, and some borrowers feared that this might alarm trade creditors or other lenders. Ultimately, the Bank was able to persuade borrowers that giving a chattel mortgage to the IDB was likely to be regarded as a favourable sign. If the IDB were willing to lend to a business, it must be satisfied that the business had good prospects.

In addition to the various security requirements, a loan contract also established other understandings between the borrower and the Bank. A borrower would be required to supply annual audited statements and very often quarterly or even monthly interim statements. These latter could be prepared by the borrower and so did not have the standing of the annual audited statement, but they were regarded as useful because they provided a frequent point of contact between the borrower and the Bank by which the latter could keep in touch with the borrower's affairs and try to steer the borrowing business away from trouble. The statements were often also a valuable disciplinary exercise for any borrower who had not previously been in the practice of preparing such statements.

There would usually be a limitation put on how much a borrower could spend on fixed assets in any one fiscal year without first getting the consent of the Bank. In the case of an incorporated company there would usually also be a limitation on dividends or the redemption of stock, both of which would require the consent of the Bank, and in the case of a smaller private company there would very likely be a limitation on the amount that the proprietor could withdraw from the business in any one year without first getting the Bank's consent. These conditions were intended to protect the company's working capital and ensure that, before it launched itself on some program or expenditure that might drain away its working capital and compromise its future earnings, it would review the whole project with the Bank as an agency interested in the company but able to take a more objective view of its plans.

Loans were usually repayable over a number of years, with ten years being about the maximum term in the early years of the Bank. From 1944 to 1955, the average term was approximately six years. Repayment was usually by semi-annual, quarterly, or monthly instalments of principal plus interest. The term of years was usually based on the borrower's anticipated earning power. A term too short would mean that the company would undoubtedly be operating under difficulties as it sought to meet its payments, and if the term were too long it would mean the company was paying interest on borrowed money when it did not need to do so. Occasionally repayment was by equal amortized instalments including both principal and interest or by seasonal instalments.

The administration of a loan once disbursed would normally rest with the credit officer who originally processed the application. As financial statements came in from the borrower at least annually, but sometimes also quarterly or semi-annually, these would be transcribed to large columned sheets so that figures for a large number of periods could be easily compared. If any questions arose from examining the figures, they would be taken up with the borrower. If they seemed serious, an engineer might be asked to visit the borrower's plant. A visit to each borrower once a year in any event was the target of each office, although this was not always possible.

In the early years, the analyses of the borrower's financial statements, even the interim and unaudited ones, were sent by the field offices to the General Manager's Office in Montreal. In fact, copies of most correspondence and memoranda were also sent to GMO, so that the latter was very close to the operations of the Bank in all its parts. However, although the volume of new loans handled by the Bank remained relatively constant during the first eleven years, with little growth from year to year, the steady increase in the number of loans under administration, and the growing complexity of policy problems faced by the Bank, soon made it imperative that the flow of paper within the Bank be diminished.

Problems of time taken to process applications and delegation of power to approve loans

The painstaking analyses and studies of credit applications described above remained the classic concept within the Bank as to the best way of dealing with a proposal, but modifications of the procedures were soon made. As mentioned previously, in 1947 the general manager was given authority to approve loans of up to $25,000, but the authority was given in a curious way. The IDB Act required of the board or committee that, when it approved a loan, it must be of the 'opinion' that credit 'would not otherwise be available on reasonable terms and conditions' and that the 'amount of capital invested or to be invested ... by persons other than the Bank ... is such as to afford the Bank reasonable protection.'[3] To cover these two legal requirements, the resolution of the board delegating authority to the general manager expressed a blanket 'opinion' on the part of the board to the above effects about any loan of up to $25,000 that might be approved by the general manager, if 1 / the applicant's chartered bank had not been willing to make the loan after discussing the proposal with the applicant, and 2 / the capital in the borrowing business (including surplus and loans by shareholders that were frozen or were subrogated to the Bank) was at least equal to the loan to be made by the Bank. While the general manager did subsequently approve loans of up to $25,000, these requirements set by the board as required for its blanket 'opinion' were not actually communicated to the field offices of the Bank. All applications were, by normal procedures, discussed with an applicant's bankers, but this was not the only consideration given by the credit officers to the availability of financing elsewhere, even for loans of under $25,000. Also, it was not a fixed requirement that the investment in the borrowing business must be at least equal to the IDB's loan. The Bank got the reputation of making such a stipulation, but in fact loans were made, even in those early years, that exceeded the investment in a borrowing business. The credit officers were expected to be more careful on the first score and more flexible on the second than the directions issued by the board in connection with the delegation of authority.

In 1948, an attempt to reduce work by using preprinted forms was made with the introduction of a printed form, no. 73, to record the terms of a credit as recommended within the Bank and approved. This was a historic form within the Bank and was used virtually unchanged for nearly twenty-five years. This was a small gesture, however, and by 1952 the amount of paperwork required to process a credit application – the interview memoranda, investigation report, and submission letter – was causing concern. In that year, the general manager, Mr Noble, wrote to one of the field offices: 'Practically all the engineering reports which we received from your office could be improved by condensing them ... They are quite complete but I am sure the same information could have been given in about half the space.' Complaints of this sort did not have much effect, and in 1954 an attempt was made to control the size of reports and submission letters by prescribing the headings to be used in them. On this, Mr Towers said, with some exasperation: 'While I agree with the desirability of trying to achieve greater uniformity in the points and their sequences, I fear that unless we press the point this is not going to lead to greater brevity ... In the sample, the Engineer's report is 15 pages and the Supervisor's is 7 pages. But we certainly would not want the simpler accounts to run to this length simply because the Engineer or Supervisor felt that he should say a fair amount under each of the headings suggested.'

In April 1954, the board was prepared to give the general manager lending authority for amounts of up to $100,000 and to give authority up to $25,000 to the supervisors. The Bank's outside counsel, however, advised it that the IDB Act did not give the board power to delegate in the curious way that had been used. The action taken in 1947 was rescinded, and, pending an amendment to the act, other means of reducing the flow of paper were tried. Credit proposals of up to $25,000 were to be submitted by branches to the general manager on a one-page foolscap memorandum that came to be known as a 'Summary.' A submission letter was no longer required for these small loans, but a brief supplementary letter could be used to cover any special points. The so-called summary was similar to the document that Mr Marble (now general manager) had prepared for submitting credits to the board when he was secretary at head office. For credits of over $25,000, branches were still to use a submission letter when sending them to the general manager, but of these credits those of between $25,000 and $100,000 were to be sent on also to the board by the general manager by means of a one-page summary prepared at his office, and without the branch's submission letter. In this way, the paperwork at least conformed to the delegation of authorizing limits that had been intended. Only credits of over $100,000 were now to reach the board by means of a full submission letter.

The introduction of the summary one-page memorandum for submitting some credit proposals presented problems of its own. The rule that it must use only one page was rigidly enforced, but sometimes to compress the analysis of a proposal into this space seemed to take about as much of a credit officer's time as preparing a full submission letter. Short words would be sought to replace long words; letters, words, and lines would be carefully counted so that the best deletions could be made in an over-long summary to squeeze it into one page. Small-print typewriters were resorted to, and finally one supervisor was constrained to urge that larger foolscap paper should be permitted! The problems of reducing paperwork and streamlining procedures were far from solution when fiscal 1955 ended.

CHAPTER FIVE

Policies

Problems of eligibility

As a new organization operating in a new field, the Bank had to establish in its early years principles to govern its operations. These reflected generally the practical application of the terms of the IDB Act. It is important to note that, in spite of the Bank's name, it was not given the responsibility or power to seek out or promote developmental projects. Rather, the Bank responded to approaches made to it by business people or entrepreneurs for assistance in financing plans or projects that they themselves had planned or developed.

For every loan application, the Bank had first to reach a decision on the 'eligibility' of the business concerned as an 'industrial enterprise' as defined by the act. There the definition was 'a business in which the manufacture, processing or refrigeration of goods, wares and merchandise or the building, alteration or repair of ships or vessels or the generating or distributing of electricity is carried on.' This was not, in the act of 1944, a matter of 'opinion' on the part of the board of directors, unlike the matter of the availability of funds elsewhere.[1] This meant that the personnel of the Bank had to be very careful about the 'eligibility' of an applicant. Presumably, any loan made to an 'ineligible' business would be an illegal act. Accordingly, the Bank very early adopted the practice of referring the more difficult eligibility questions to its legal advisers. As Mr Towers explained in a letter to the general manager, 'Opinions had to err on the side of ruling many operations ineligible for fear of making loans which might later be declared ultra vires.'

In 1949, the act was amended to make eligibility a matter of 'opinion' on the part of the board of directors,[2] which eased the situation somewhat, but referring borderline cases still required a good deal of time, and principles for determining eligibility had to be established and carefully followed. Again, in Mr Towers's words:

The chief point of difficulty concerns the meaning of the word processing. It would generally be agreed that this excludes primary operations such as financing, fishing, logging, mining, quarrying, and generally the first action of extracting materials from their natural environment.

Undoubtedly in many cases the line between extracting and processing is very thin ... The [Executive] Committee felt that practical considerations should govern, and that regard must be had to the purpose of the operation and its relative importance in the total enterprise, in order to decide whether the activity carried on in a particular business constitutes an industrial enterprise ... The Act contemplates that the Bank is to provide capital for industrial enterprises, not for industrial activities which are purely incidental to other aspects of a non-industrial business and are not carried on in a business way for their own sake.

Understandably, applicants were puzzled by concerns of this sort and, regardless of explanations of the legal problems, tended to see in the whole thing a reflection of the stuffiness and conservatism that they instinctively associated with bankers.

By far the greatest number of applicants were from the field of manufacturing, so that in most cases 'eligibility' was determined by deciding whether or not an applicant was actually a manufacturer or a processor. One principle followed was that, to qualify, a process must result in some fundamental change in the material used. For example, a company engaged merely in the assembling of parts manufactured for it by others might not be regarded as a manufacturer. A decision to this effect in such a case was often a baffling surprise to the owner of the business. Logging was not considered eligible, whereas lumber mills were. The view was taken that a tree, when cut down and lying on the ground, was not really changed from its original state when it stood as a growing tree, whereas sawing the same log into lumber was a manufacturing process. Fine distinctions were made between two businesses employing very similar processes but marketing the end product in different ways and on different scales. A business that cooked and packaged food for sale in retail stores was considered a manufacturer or processor, but one that cooked food to be eaten only at tables on the premises was a restaurant and, being therefore regarded as engaged in a service industry, was not eligible. The dehydrating and desalting of crude oil were considered an eligible process, but the re-refining of used oil was regarded as doubtful. The breaking up and sweetening of imported blocks of shredded coconut was considered ineligible because there was not 'a sufficient change in the nature and characteristics of the subject matter to change its identity which is the criterion we have gone by in other cases.' A dairy engaged in the homogenization and pasteurization of fluid milk was not considered eligible as a processor, but it was considered eligible if the manufacture of some dairy product such as butter or cheese was also carried on and formed a substantial proportion of the dairy's turnover.

One ingenious applicant who wanted to set up an insurance business to offer a package deal combining life, sickness, and accident insurance argued that working out such a policy plan could reasonably be considered as 'processing' a tangible object culminating in the 'manufacture' of a specific policy to perform a specific function, i.e. to protect the insured from certain hazards just as an overcoat protects a person from the cold! The argument was carefully considered by the Bank, but not accepted.

The staff of the Bank became so accustomed to taking a serious view of the question of eligibility that applicants engaged in some other form of business such as assembling, warehousing, or one of the service industries were looked at almost askance, as if they were engaged in improper activities because they were not engaged in the eligible fields of manufacturing or processing!

An applicant once approached one of the officers of the Bank and gave as his business that of steel warehousing. Of course, this was not eligible. The legal adviser who accompanied the applicant then questioned him closely to see if there was not something in the operation of the warehouse that might enable the business to be classified as a manufacturer. Could the man not cut the steel or trim it or do something of that nature to it? In each case, the answer was in the negative, until finally in desperation the lawyer suggested to his client that he might at least paint the steel, in which event he might be considered eligible. Even at this, however, the applicant shook his head sadly.

Great difficulty arose in ruling on what the Bank called 'mixed' businesses, i.e. those in which both eligible and ineligible activities were carried on. A business that assembled parts manufactured by others, as well as parts made by the business itself, might or might not qualify to apply to the Bank. One had to decide whether the manufacture of parts by the applicant business was sufficiently important in its overall operation to make the business as a whole eligible. Various means were used to assist in such a decision, such as the distribution of plant floor area between the eligible and ineligible activities, the distribution of fixed asset investment, the relative dollar value of the manufactured parts and those obtained from others, and so on. No method was wholly satisfactory, and it was almost impossible to maintain consistency between cases.

A troublesome case of a mixed business was a printing shop. It had been decided very early that, as a matter of policy, the Bank would not make loans to newspapers, it being considered that their role of commenting freely and vigorously on public affairs and government policy made it inappropriate that a crown corporation such as the IDB should be financially involved with them. They might have strong political affiliations, and they might want to take a position for or against some governmental activity in which the IDB, as a crown corporation, might be directly or indirectly involved. This was one Bank policy with which the politicians seemed to agree. When, in 1961, the scope of the Bank was greatly enlarged, the Hon. Donald Fleming, the minister of finance, was most insistent that broadening the scope of the Bank must not alter its policy of not lending to daily newspapers.

Many companies publishing newspapers, however, also operated job printing businesses, and it hardly seemed reasonable that if an eligible part of the business needed some assistance, perhaps for building or equipment additions, it should be left without financial support because of its being associated with a daily newspaper. Establishing a principle that would easily and equitably solve this problem was very difficult. Even if such a business were ruled eligible, the Bank had the further problem of ensuring that any loan it might make was directed both in its amount and in its use toward the eligible activity within the business. Under these circumstances it is scarcely to be wondered at if, to some critics, the Bank seemed bound up in red tape and pedantry.

Another eligibility problem arose with respect to the sale of alcoholic beverages. Although it may seem strange today, in the early years there was a good deal of opposition on the part of the management of the Bank, and particularly of Graham Towers, to involving the Bank's 'public' money in businesses associated with alcoholic beverages and, in particular, their manufacture. Mr Towers felt it would be highly improper for 'public' money to be used in this way. None the less, he allowed himself to be persuaded in 1947 to make a loan to a new brewery. Perhaps he got a certain amount of satisfaction from the fact that the brewery was a complete failure, a situation from which the Bank was saved only by reason of the plant's being purchased by another brewery. In 1950, it was decided that the Bank would not, as a matter of policy, make loans to a brewery or distillery. This new policy was tested in 1953 when a Nova Scotia company producing 'apple wine' and cider applied for a loan. The combination of agricultural produce and a less-than-favoured province pointed the way to an answer, and the view therefore was taken that 'since this could not be considered as a brewery or distillery and because of its importance even as a relatively small consumer of apple products in the Annapolis Valley, it would be reasonable for us to consider the business as eligible.' Some alarm arose when it was learned that, in spite of their humble origins, the cider and 'apple wine' were sold exclusively to provincial liquor commissions which might, it was feared, place the lowly 'apple wine' in an undesirable light. However, the ruling held firm and the business was still considered eligible.

It may seem ironic that when, in 1961, restaurants and hotels were made eligible, the Bank was very quickly forced to a position where, in many cases, an application was declined unless the applicant had a liquor licence!

A situation that gave rise to a lot of difficulty was that of a manufacturer who operated a business in a building that, for tax or some other corporate reasons, was the property of another company owned by the same principal. The manufacturing business might require an enlargement of the building, but the IDB could not lend to the property-owning company because it was not engaged in manufacturing. Various devices were invented to try and get around this problem, but none of them was wholly satisfactory.

Difficulties arose also with respect to refrigeration. A business that stored goods in cold storage for its own use was not considered to be 'a business in which the ... refrigeration of goods, etc. is carried on,'[3] but one that stored goods for others in a refrigerated building was eligible. Refrigeration for the storage of fur coats was not considered eligible. Inevitably, an undertaker did actually claim to qualify for assistance under this part of the act, but he was not accepted.

Availability of funds elsewhere

The question of the availability of funds elsewhere, which later became a difficult matter, was usually dealt with in the early years with less difficulty than that of eligibility, although those MPs who took part in the debate on the act would have been surprised at this. When the Bank first started operations there were few other financial institutions to which a business seeking a small amount of term assistance might turn. On the application form submitted to the IDB by anyone seeking assistance the applicant had to make a declaration that he had been unable to obtain the money required elsewhere. For amounts of upwards of $75–100,000 or so, the applicant might be directed to contact one of the insurance companies as an alternative source; for larger amounts he or she might be asked to approach a broker who might be willing to entertain proposals of that size. However, whether the applicant would actually be asked to make these further efforts to obtain financing would depend on the nature of the program for which financing was sought and on the applicant's financial position. If the former were a mixed collection of purposes with a varied bundle of security offered, and the financial position were not too strong or healthy, it would not be considered necessary to send the applicant off on a further search for funds because even the few lenders that might have been interested at that time in this sort of financing would probably not look at a mixed-up kind of program supported by a mixed bag of security.

Practically all of the IDB's borrowers were also, of course, customers of a chartered bank. When the IDB received an application, the credit officer wrote to the branch manager of the bank with which the applicant dealt, explaining the program applied for and asking the manager for any opinion he might have about it and for a general report on the applicant. Authority to approach the branch manager in this way was given to the IDB by the applicant on the application form. The reply from the chartered bank was, of course, confidential.

The intention to follow this procedure in dealing with the chartered banks was explained by Mr Towers to representatives of the chartered banks in October 1944. The banks, uncertain how the IDB would fit in with their own operations, planned to have any branch manager receiving such a request from the IDB submit his intended reply to his head office before dispatching it. This cumbersome procedure delayed IDB applications and was soon abandoned by most chartered banks, and their branch managers would reply direct to the IDB. One chartered bank, however, maintained the procedure, at least partially, throughout the life of the IDB. Although the chartered bank probably intended thereby to ensure that it did not miss any chances to make a loan that might otherwise go to the IDB, the procedure had no effect on the number of clients of the particular bank that borrowed from the IDB. Each bank shared, through its customers, in IDB loans in just about the same proportions as each shared in the total amount of business loans made by the banks themselves.

Within the IDB the letter to the branch manager of a chartered bank was regarded as notice to that bank that a loan was under consideration by the

IDB and provided the chartered bank with an opportunity to make the loan itself if it wished to do so. Sometimes this opportunity would be taken, but many times, particularly in the early days of the IDB, any latent willingness on the part of an applicant's chartered bank to undertake the financing sought seemed more likely to be aroused when the IDB had completed its investigation and actually offered the applicant a loan.

Policies on prepayment of loans and various fees

Very early the IDB had to consider the prospect that its loans might be paid ahead of time, either in part or in full. The development of its policy in this matter illustrates the manner in which it gradually felt its way by experience into a posture proper for a crown corporation intended to serve the needs of small and medium-sized businesses, yet having due consideration for the normal practices of other lenders. Since it was not to compete with others, it could not ignore their practices completely in determining its own operational policies. However, its special responsibility toward the needs of small businesses might require it to modify somewhat, in its practices, those followed by commercial lenders. The IDB had also to remember that, while it was not expected to earn big profits, it was expected to conduct its affairs in such a manner as to pay its own way. It also had to work out its policy lines so as to treat its borrowers uniformly; being a crown corporation, it felt it would be exposed to awkward pressures and arguments if it followed varying practices based only on negotiations with its borrowers in individual cases.

Commercial lenders making term mortgage loans to businesses usually set up conditions to govern prepayments. Some would bar them altogether, at least for the early years of their loans. When a prepayment was permitted, the indemnity to be paid would generally be a matter of negotiation. For the IDB, considering that it was entering a field that many thought was extremely risky, the prospect of a prepayment on a loan was, for the first few years, accepted with satisfaction. This was particularly so if the prepayment came from the borrower's earnings. For a while the Bank accepted all prepayments without requiring any notice or the payment of an indemnity. It was soon apparent, however, that some prepayments were coming, not from earnings, but from borrowings from someone else, and the Bank felt it should take a different view of these. In such cases, it saw itself as having, in the first instance, taken a risk no other lender was prepared to take when the IDB made its loan. If, after the loan was made and the borrower's program was completed, the borrower was able to demonstrate the soundness of his program and the success of his business to the point that some lender who had originally been unwilling to assist him was now prepared to do so by providing money to prepay the IDB's loan, then the Bank felt that it should receive compensation for the expense and trouble of having analysed the proposal and authorized, and perhaps administered, a loan.

Accordingly, in May 1947, the Bank, while continuing to accept without notice or indemnity any prepayment that came from a borrower's earnings, established a policy of requiring an indemnity equal to six months' interest on any prepayment from some other source on all loans over $25,000. In November 1948 the rule was applied to all loans regardless of amount.

Experience soon showed that it was not always easy to tell whether or not a prepayment had come from earnings. The Bank found itself faced with arguments from ingenious accountants and borrowers to prove it had, whereas the Bank sometimes felt it had equally good grounds for suspecting the opposite. As a result, in September 1949 it was decided that, while all loan contracts would still permit prepayment without notice, any prepayment, regardless of its source, would require the payment of an indemnity of six months' interest; as a matter of practice, the Bank would still continue to accept prepayments from a borrower's earnings without an indemnity, but by leaving reference to this practice out of the loan contract the Bank would be in a position to form its own opinion, without challenge, as to whether the prepayment did actually come from earnings.

Even this modification did not lift these matters out of the area of argument, and in December 1953 the practice of accepting prepayments from earnings without an indemnity was terminated. From then on, while a prepayment could still be made at any time without notice (which the Bank regarded as a significant concession in itself), all prepayments required the payment of an indemnity.

In September 1955, the policy was modified further to exempt from an indemnity prepayments from the proceeds of fire loss or life insurance claims, and in addition supervisors were given authority to waive the indemnity on prepayments on a loan in any year up to the amount of the regular principal instalments due in that year.

Another practice that the Bank adopted early as a matter of policy was the levying of a 'commitment fee.' This was a fee payable by a business that had accepted the terms of a loan as authorized but later changed its mind and withdrew its acceptance. The fee was first introduced in 1946, and in 1951 it was set in a form that lasted until 1957. It amounted to 1 per cent per annum on the amount of the authorized loan for the period from the date of advice of the authorization to the applicant to the date of cancellation of the credit. The purpose of the fee was partly to compensate the Bank for the time and effort that it had expended on the loan. It was also, however, intended to protect the Bank against what it saw as unreasonable use (or misuse) of its operations by applicants and perhaps by other lenders who might be more willing to extend assistance to a particular business after the IDB had gone to the expense of thoroughly analysing a proposal and come to a favourable conclusion on it. The IDB felt that it should have some protection against this sort of thing, and compensation if it happened.

As an alternative, the Bank considered the possibility of charging a fee for investigating a proposal. This would have been levied on all applications at the time of their submission and collected as part of the requirements of the Bank to investigate the application. Paradoxically, it might well have been easier to collect and to explain than the commitment fee itself proved sometimes to be. The Bank adhered, however, to the commitment fee in place of an investigation fee. The letter of offer that was sent to an applicant when a loan was authorized left two or three weeks for a reply, and during this interval the applicant could, of course, explore other avenues of possible assistance, knowing that it had the assurance of financing from the IDB. Sometimes the period for acceptance would be extended, even though the IDB suspected that the applicant was actually using the letter of offer as a basis on which to approach other lenders. The fee did not become applicable during the interval allowed for acceptance, but once the terms of the Bank's offer of a credit were accepted in writing the Bank regarded itself as entitled to compensation in the form of a commitment fee in the event that the authorized loan was not taken up.

Guarantees

Another area in which the Bank had to establish policies was that of guaranteeing loans by others. Although, as will be recalled, Mr Towers and Dr Clark had rejected this as the sole method of operation, it was expected at first that, in working closely with chartered bank branches to solve the financial problems of applicants, the Bank would extend a good number of guarantees. Neither the chartered banks nor the clients, however, showed much interest in guarantees, and since such arrangements left the Bank with poor control of a situation in case of trouble and involved many administrative and supervisory difficulties, relatively few guarantee arrangements were entered into. For such as were made, it was decided to levy a charge of 2 per cent on the amount of the guarantee. There was some concern over the rate of interest that might be charged by a chartered bank on a loan supported by an IDB guarantee lest the total cost of the interest and the guarantee fee should exceed what would have been the IDB's rate of interest had it made a loan itself. Not enough cases occurred, however, to bring this issue to a matter of policy.

More difficult policy questions arose from a guarantee of a different character, one extended by a provincial government to the IDB as part of the latter's security for a loan by the Bank. Mr Towers said in a letter to the general manager, in 1952, 'There are many objections to such guarantees. If we have occasion to alter the terms of our arrangements with borrowers, the guarantors in the form of provincial governments have to be consulted and their agreement obtained; they may or may not support us in pressing a certain course of action on borrowers, and the handling of the accounts may be complicated in various other ways. Moreover, collecting under such guarantees in case of need has its delays and difficulties. We should, therefore, avoid these provincial guarantees if it is at all possible to do so.'

This, then, was the Bank's policy, but it was modified by the qualification that it should not be carried to the point of refusal, if, 'a) the enterprise appears to be soundly conceived and has a reasonable chance of success, b) the caliber of the management is good, and c) there appears to be no reasonable prospect of other lenders undertaking the business with the provincial guarantee. It is assumed, of course, that even if conditions a) and b) are fulfilled, the risk for the Bank is more than we would feel justified in accepting without a guarantee.' On this basis, a few loans were approved in the early years on the basis of provincial guarantees, but the Bank's policy became established as opposed to it.

Acquisition of shares

The IDB Act gave the Bank power to acquire shares in a business 'with a view to resale.'[4] The exact meaning of this phrase was a source of uncertainty to the Bank in contemplating the purchase of equities. Legal advice in 1946 was to the effect that in acquiring shares the Bank need have only a general intention to resell them and 'need not have a specific resale in contemplation, nor need it have a certain prospect' that the shares could be resold. In any event, there was little interest on the part of applicants in seeing the Bank acquire shares in their companies.

The Bank was occasionally interested in such a possibility if it thought that a loan was so risky as to require extra compensation such as sharing in the profits or growth of the borrowing business, and acquiring shares was one way of doing this. Other more direct ways of benefitting from a borrower's success were difficult to administer. Sometimes a loan agreement might require additional repayments on the principal of a loan if a borrower's profits exceeded some agreed-upon level in the future. If profits were of this magnitude, however, such success on the part of a borrower implied that the concerns as to risk that had prompted the Bank to make such a condition were set at rest and it no longer needed its loan paid off quickly. Under these circumstances, the requirement for an accelerated repayment amounted to giving the borrower a chance to make a prepayment without an indemnity. If, however, the Bank's concerns about a borrower's chances of success proved correct and earnings fell below expectations, there was no basis for an accelerated repayment, dearly as the Bank would have liked to receive one.

On one early loan the Bank sought extra compensation for unusual risk and a shortage of equity on the part of the borrower by asking for special bonus payments out of earnings if earnings exceeded a certain level. These payments were not to be applied on the principal of the loan but to be regarded as a bonus additional to the payment of interest. The borrower would have preferred that the extra risk be reflected in a higher rate of interest, since this expense would have been recognized as a cost in calculating income tax and there was a possibility that the bonus payment would not be so regarded. Mr Towers was unwilling, however, to see the Bank in the position of setting an interest rate at the high level this would have required. The bonus payment was, of course, easily avoided by the borrower by preparing his financial statements so as to keep his earnings below the critical level so that, although the business may have done extremely well, no extra benefit accrued to the Bank from the bonus clause.

Participating in equity as a means of extra compensation for very risky loans was free of these particular problems, but it raised others. Circumstances that might warrant sharing in profits (or equity) would be those in which the capital invested in a business was 'thin' or a loan by the Bank depended heavily for protection on the success of the business rather than on whatever value there might be in the fixed assets pledged as security. It was believed that if the Bank wanted extra compensation in such cases (and there were relatively few in which it did) the proper procedure for the Bank would be to lend part of the money needed and put part in shares. The value of these would grow with the earning of profits, and the Bank would hope to reap (some time) an extra reward for its original risks by selling these shares (or 'reselling' them as the act put it) at their increased value. Between 1944 and 1955, there were only nineteen cases in which the acquisition of an equity interest in a business by the Bank was approved,[5] and in each case this was accompanied by a loan.

Some applicants objected very strongly to the Bank's acquiring shares in their business. If the owner believed the business would succeed, such a proposal seemed an outrageous device for taking away the fruits of hard work and business acumen and singularly inappropriate in a crown corporation that, as many saw it, was supposed to help people and not make money. The view that the Bank needed extra compensation of this sort for a particularly risky loan depended partly on its opinion as to the security value of the pledged fixed assets. This opinion might put such values far below those established in the minds of the applicants and make any suggestion that a share of equity form part of the price for a loan appear scandalous to them.

The prospect of extending financial assistance by means of stock purchase had always a glamorous attraction for the Bank's officers, but in the initial years such purchases were invariably made as a means of enhancing the compensation for a particularly risky loan.

Criteria for lending

Although it may seem paradoxical, the one subject on which the Bank remained almost entirely free of rigid rules or regulations was that of lending. That this was so was probably one of its greatest strengths. The reader will recall that, during the parliamentary debate on the IDB Act, Graham Towers and W.C. Clark resisted any suggestion that the act should include guidelines or regulations on the Bank's lending operations.[6] This attitude was continued within the Bank itself.

Apart from the requirement that the Bank should satisfy itself that the financing requested by a business would not be available elsewhere on reasonable terms and conditions, the only stipulations in the act regarding the Bank's work were that it give particular attention to the needs of small and medium-sized businesses and that the investment in a business to which assistance was extended should be such as to afford the Bank reasonable protection. Regarding the first stipulation, the Bank followed the principle suggested by Mr Towers during the hearings of the House of Commons committee that the generally easier availability of credit to large corporations could be depended on to ensure that most of the Bank's activity would be in assisting small and medium-sized businesses, subject to an opinion by the Bank's directors that the assistance sought would not otherwise be available on reasonable terms and conditions. The second stipulation was expressed in such broad terms as to leave the Bank virtually free to make any loan in which it saw reasonable chances of repayment. The Bank set up no regulations about the amount of investment that might be expected in a borrowing business.[7]

What investment might be needed would depend on the requirements of each individual case. This particular aspect would be discussed with an applicant in terms of the business's needs. If it was a new business, it was pointed out to the applicant that the business would need money from some source such as equity investment by the proprietors to cover other essential needs. These included pre-operation expenses, initial operating losses which would be inevitable and extend over a period of time, working capital needs of the business to provide for the financing of operations, and a contribution to the cost of the fixed assets, since the Bank would expect normally to lend something less than the cost of these so that it would have a reasonable amount of security protection.[8] A discussion along these lines with an applicant, however, was not based on any rule or regulation as to what should be invested but was simply in the interests of ensuring that, from the Bank's and from the applicant's standpoint, the program and the loan, if the latter were approved, would both appear to be reasonable business propositions.

The Bank was at first more cautious in its attitude to the investment in a business than it later became and acquired a reputation of being unwilling to make a loan for an amount greater than was the equity in the borrowing business. Nevertheless, it made many loans even in those early years that exceeded the borrower's equity. In any event, the Bank had no rules or regulations on the matter beyond general injunctions to its officers not to be overly concerned with security, but to be more concerned with management and prospects and not to shrink from risk if a venture seemed worthwhile.

There were no rules about the earnings record of an applicant, about what working capital the business should have before a loan could be approved, or indeed about any aspect of an applicant's financial position. There were no rules about the structure of a borrowing business, and the Bank extended financing to incorporated companies, to partnerships, to individuals in business for themselves – in short, to any form of business. There were no rules as to the relationship between the amount of a loan and the cost of the fixed assets pledged to the Bank to support it, or even their 'security' value, i.e. what they might be expected to fetch if the Bank had to seize and sell them in order to retire its loan. Some loans might appear quite conservative relative to the value of the fixed assets, while others might be very close to, equal to, or even greater than the asset valuation. It was expected, however, that normally a loan would be covered by the estimated liquidation value of the security.

Throughout the life of the Bank, as it sought to increase its responsiveness to applications, instructions issued to its branches progressively diminished the emphasis to be placed on security as a factor in reaching a decision on a loan application. In practice, nevertheless, security was always a very important, and often a vital, consideration, even though the weight given it depended on the judgment of the Bank's officers as to the prospects of the business, the quality of its management, and so on.

The one major principle that the Bank's officers were expected to follow was that the applicant's working capital, investment, plant, market, costing system, and profit margin must be adequate for success; the loan proposal must be a reasonable business proposition, from the standpoint of the Bank and that of the applicant, and there must be reasonable prospects that the loan could be repaid. The Bank believed that it owed an obligation in this regard to the applicant and to itself. The attitude taken was well-expressed in an advertisement by the government of Manitoba in 1945 that recommended the IDB's services: 'If you intend to make an application remember that the Industrial Development Bank is *not* giving money away. You will have to satisfy them that you know what you are talking about – that your business is a good investment and that you know how to run it.'[9] The IDB was sometimes criticized for not taking enough risk in its loans, a conclusion based presumably on the amount of money it reported as having written off. Critics seemed to forget, however, that whenever the Bank had a loss that it could afford to absorb some small businessman or businesswoman had undoubtedly lost everything he or she had in their business. The Bank did not shrink from risks when these appeared reasonable, but it did not seek to enhance its own image as a risk-taker by drawing borrowers into hazardous ventures in which they seemed likely to lose everything.

From a policy standpoint, the IDB saw its role as defined in its act of incorporation. It took particular satisfaction in any loans that seemed likely to contribute significantly to the economic growth of a community or region, that had a good chance of displacing imports in favour of domestically made products, that launched a new industry, or that were expected to contribute to the general economic good of the country in some other way. The employees of the Bank saw themselves as doing something of social value in helping small businesses establish themselves soundly. They derived enormous satisfaction from setting up a small industry in a small village in Quebec or from helping a small lumber operator in British Columbia make a niche for himself among the giant mills and perhaps become a mini-giant. They did not, however, assume social responsibilities not assigned to the IDB in its act of incorporation. The Bank did not make a loan merely to maintain employment in a business or to fend off bankruptcy for a business that had no grounds for looking forward to reasonable success in the future. It did not make loans to support the development of one region of the country in preference to another. It gave a particularly warm welcome to proposals from the less well-developed regions and might seek eagerly for a way to make a proposition from these regions viable, but it did just as much for a borderline proposal from any region.

This attitude often puzzled critics of the Bank, who were much more accustomed to government programs directed exclusively toward under-developed regions. The view in the IDB, however, was that a small business struggling to establish itself without adequate financing represented 'underdevelopment,' whether it was located in the Atlantic provinces or in the suburbs of Toronto; if it could not get assistance from someone else, it was entitled to ask for the Bank's help.

This was not always understood by observers outside the Bank. One time a professor at McGill University in Montreal telephoned the writer, then general manager of the IDB, and invited him to give a talk on the Bank to a group of government officials from underdeveloped countries to whom the university, under the sponsorship of the Canadian Depart-ment of External Affairs, was giving a course on various aspects of Canadian society. The writer expressed great willingness to oblige and asked what he should say about the Bank. The professor suggested that he explain the way in which the IDB made a cost-benefit analysis of its loans. On being asked what this meant, he said that the Bank must have a means of deciding whether a loan had been successful. The writer replied that the Bank used a very simple test for this – if a loan was paid off by the borrowing business, it was a success. This the professor received with scornful scepticism and asked how, in that event, the Bank decided between making a loan in Gaspé and making one in Montreal. The reply was that this was a decision the Bank did not make; any reasonable proposition from either place would get a loan. Whether the professor believed that this was really the Bank's method of cost-benefit analysis is not known, but he apparently did not want to expose his visitors from the underdeveloped countries to such crudities, for he carried the matter no further!

Apart from such effects as may have flowed from the actual physical location of its branches in certain places, the IDB did not, in its lending policy, favour one area over another or one industry over another. It made no attempt normally to decide what industries should, from some abstract or social standpoint, be encouraged and what industries should be discouraged. It assessed all applications as to their being reasonable business propositions on their own individual merits.

As the Bank extended its network of branches and moved with increasing confidence into the providing of credit to small and medium-sized businesses, it became, in fact, a major factor in the economic growth of some of the less well-developed sections of the country. These matters will be discussed later, but an outstanding example of this was that in the Yukon the IDB had, by 1975, authorized 295 loans, i.e. one loan for every seventy people. It is no wonder that the commissioner for the Yukon, James Smith, said, at a public dinner in Whitehorse in 1973 to mark a visit by the board of the Bank of Canada and the IDB, 'The Yukon would not be where it is today without the Industrial Development Bank.'

Publicity

During the Bank's first decade, the criticism was frequently made that its services were not widely known and that it was not doing enough to correct this situation. The appropriate policy on publicity and advertising was a matter on which the management of the Bank was uncertain during its early years. It has to be remembered that the Bank was expected to supplement other lenders and not compete with or supplant them. Accordingly, it had to be very careful about thrusting itself forward aggressively in advertising. Certainly, the validity of this apprehension was confirmed in later years when other lenders followed the Bank's advertising with a suspicious and sceptical eye. Further, the management of the Bank was fearful in the early years of overloading its staff, which might be unable to cope with an upsurge in business such as an advertising campaign might produce.

It was expected at first that the branch managers of the chartered banks would be an avenue of publicity, because it was thought that much of the Bank's business would be in the form of joint loans with a chartered bank or, sometimes, of guarantees of chartered bank loans. It was also thought that chartered bank branch managers might even help businessmen prepare their applications to the IDB. None of these things happened, and as early as 1946 the Bank was casting around for ways of making its services better known. Nothing emerged from this except an information brochure that was supplied to chartered bank branches and various business associations, occasional speeches by the Bank's officers to business and service organizations, and a few articles on the Bank in newspapers and magazines. In addition, whenever an officer from the General Manager's Office in Montreal planned to visit the Atlantic provinces, where there was not, until 1956, a regional office, an announcement of the visit would be placed in the newspaper of a town to be visited with an invitation to all those interested in applying for a loan to call on the Bank's representative. However, these advertisements appeared only at lengthy intervals and assumed, perhaps without great justification, that the financial needs of local business people would come to a head coincidentally with a visit of this kind. The advertisements were very modest and quiet in appearance and tone.

In 1946, the suggestion was made within the Bank that the Bank's brochure should be mailed directly to established businesses across the country accompanied by a 'carefully considered' letter, written in terms 'to safeguard it from outward appearances of competition with regular lending institutions.' Mr Towers apparently lacked confidence in such a 'safeguard' and turned the idea down. In 1948, a proposal was made to the Bank for the production of a short publicity film. Although Mr Noble thought the suggested script to be a 'snappy little number,' the idea was apparently dropped.

In 1949, Don Muskett, the supervisor at Winnipeg, suggested that members of the staff of the IDB regional offices should make trips through their regions visiting chambers of commerce, bank managers, managers of local industries, and provincial authorities to explain the Bank's role. He suggested also that the Bank would get valuable publicity and perform useful work by holding seminars or courses on 'Better Management' in various towns in conjunction with chartered banks, chambers of commerce, provincial bureaux, and so on. Both these ideas were followed in later years, but the Bank was not ready for them in 1949. The general manager's comment was:

I am not particularly in favour of looking for publicity in the way of addressing public gatherings, etc. ... We are subjected to a constant barrage of representations from ... well-meaning but misguided people who seem to think that we were organized to take abnormal risks. It is true, of course, that a general explanation of our functions and limitations might do something to counteract this, but it could also have the opposite effect ... Most of the small manufacturers display lamentable weakness in the way of general business administration, particularly bookkeeping, cost accounting, budgetting, etc. I certainly think that where we can help to correct these difficulties we should do so and, unquestionably, we are doing a great deal through our engineering staff, all of whom have a considerable understanding of these matters, but it is another thing to conduct a general public campaign along this line. It seems to me that about all we can afford to do at present is to give what help is possible in individual circumstances.

By 1954 (when the Bank was ten years old), the problem of reaching out to the small businessman to inform him of the IDB's services was becoming acute, but the hesitancy with which the Bank moved into advertising is illustrated by the following extracts from a memo written that year by the president, Graham Towers:

When I was in Toronto the other day, the Supervisor said that on various occasions he had been struck by the lack of knowledge in Ontario of the existence and facilities of IDB. While the banks and their branches and a fair number of other people are, of course, aware of our presence and purpose, I dare say he is right because in this province in particular we are a relatively small frog in a large puddle. In the past, we have been content that this should be the case. Should we now give consideration to some form of advertising? I don't like the idea or expense of putting anything in the daily newspapers, but we might well be able to think up some other form of reminder of our existence. If we do anything at all, perhaps it would be difficult to confine it to Ontario – but Ontario is the place where our business is remarkably small in relation to our activities elsewhere.

To this, Mr Towers added in a pencilled marginal note: 'We might manage to confine it to Ontario.' In spite of this cautious feeling, in the very next year the IDB put its first advertisement in twenty-one business journals and financial newspapers. The idea of advertising in daily newspapers was turned down as too expensive. The Bank expected to operate with a narrow margin of profit, and it was felt that large expenditures on advertising which could not be depended on to yield commensurate benefits should be avoided. Mr Marble set out the views of management in a letter to one of the supervisors: 'Press advertising is a matter which has been considered by the Board of Directors and as you can appreciate, there is a mixture of feelings, one view being that we should make our existence known to those who might have need of our facilities and the other that an attempt to advertise our wares is always subject to the criticism of competition. It was in an attempt to steer a middle course that our advertising in the business journals has been so severely plain and limited as to media. The question did come up of insertions in general newspapers and was ruled out, largely on the matter of cost.'

The extracts below from an editorial in the Toronto *Globe and Mail* of 2

January 1951 provide some background to the diffidence and circumspection with which the Bank approached publicity. It had just issued its 1950 annual report, a modest booklet containing its balance sheet, operating statement, tables of loans by size, province, and industry, and about six pages of comment. Copies of the annual reports were often given out to people seeking assistance in order to explain the Bank's role. Accordingly, to improve the public understanding of what the IDB did, the Bank had inserted in its 1950 report eight black-and-white photographs of businesses to which the Bank had made loans. The *Globe and Mail's* comments were, in part:

It is a very nice piece of typography, with eight full pages of illustrations, decorated with original art work on the cover and some inside pages [a small patch of colour bearing the Bank's logo on the cover and on the title-page] *and printed on expensive paper in two colours* [black for the type-face, and reddish-brown for headings].

A single letter to the Minister and single mimeographed sheets of summarized statistics ... would have served the purpose equally well – at a very small fraction of the price for the de luxe work of printing art ...

In 1939 the Government's total expenses for such printing and stationery amounted to only $2.5 million. Last year it was reported at the hugely swollen aggregate of close to $13 million. For the current year it will skyrocket far above that figure if all such relatively small subdepartments and agencies as the IDB (assets just over $31 million) continue to waste both materials and labour on merely routine reports.

Considering that the report cost only $2,500, of which the photographs accounted for approximately $500, these comments might appear rather strong. Nevertheless, such views sufficed to cause the Bank to draw back quickly from even this small step toward greater publicity. Not until 1961 was it again so bold as to embellish its annual report with pictures of its borrowers' businesses.[10]

From 1945 to 1947 the only expenditures on publicity were for printing the annual report. This was a very modest brochure and cost approximately $2,000 a year. For the fiscal years 1948–54 inclusive, total publicity expenditures, apart from the annual report, were $10,700, representing an average of only $1,500 per annum. In 1955, however, when the series of advertisements appeared in twenty-one business journals and papers, expenditures for this program alone were $10,000; the printing of the annual report was $2,500, bringing total expenditures on publicity that year to $12,500. This was a relatively modest sum, but it was by far the largest amount spent in any year up to that time.

CHAPTER SIX

Finances

Rates of interest on loans

A matter of early importance to the Bank was the income it received through the rate of interest charged on its loans. The question of what rate of interest to charge was under consideration even before the Bank was in operation. The chartered banks were reported as lending at rates around 3 per cent for 'medium-term' loans, and, lacking any other yardstick, it was natural that the IDB should set its rate at a point bearing a reasonable relation to that of the chartered banks. Of course, medium-term loans of the banks at that time had little in common with IDB loans: they were not usually supported by specific mortgage security or by a formal, detailed written contract, and the term of repayment might be based on only an understanding, and a verbal one at that. However, using this bench-mark, the IDB in 1945 set its rate at 5 per cent, 'with few, if any, exceptions.'

This immediately established two principles. First, the IDB's rate was to be slightly above the 'market' rate (whatever market might be chosen for comparison). It was felt that if the rates of the other lenders were 'reasonable' (that is, presumably, in line with what general market conditions might lead one to expect) the Bank 'should not compete by offering lower rates; and it might even be argued that it should name slightly higher rates in order to avoid any element of competition.' Second, all borrowers, with only occasional exceptions, were to pay the same rate. In a 1945 article about the IDB in the *Canadian Banker*, S.R. Noble explained the Bank's initial interest rate policy: 'At present, a standard interest rate of five per cent is charged to all applicants, regardless of size, term of loan or security. Good arguments can be made for both a flat rate and differential rates of interest but, in the interests of simplicity and in fairness to all concerned, it seemed better to begin operating under a flat-rate policy. This has obvious disadvantages for the Bank itself, since the costs of investigating and supervision are often much higher proportionately on small than on larger loans. The decision emphasized our hope to help small business. In instances where a lower rate than 5% is justified it might be considered evidence that the necessary facilities are available elsewhere.'[1]

The costs of investigation, supervision, and so on for small loans were considered to be at least as high as for large loans and proportionately higher when these costs were expressed as a percentage of the loan. There was at first an inclination to think that this should be taken into account in setting the rates of interest for loans and that the large loans should be conceded the relative cost advantages of their size. This would mean setting their interest rates at a lower level than those of the smaller loans. However, it was established very early that there would be 'few, if any, exceptions' to the standard rate.

By 1947, the rate charged by the chartered banks on good commercial loans was up to $4\frac{1}{2}$ per cent,[2] but the IDB held its rate at 5 per cent, believing that the spread between the two rates was still adequate. Indeed, the management of the Bank was inclined to the view that for larger loans, i.e. over $100,000, a better comparison of rates might be with those of the security markets rather than with those of the chartered banks, and since the former were somewhat lower than the latter, the IDB was ready to consider a lower rate than 5 per cent in exceptional cases for larger loans.

By 1949, the president was concerned as to whether a 5 per cent loan rate would be high enough to cover operating expenses and losses and yield a suitable return on the Bank's equity capital (for which 3 per cent was suggested). Mr Towers was most anxious that the IDB should 'stand on its own feet.' This meant that for the next few years head office leaned toward an upward movement in the IDB lending rate, while GMO, more directly concerned with the problems of nursing this new Bank into an active and lively role, leaned toward holding the rate down. Even those who held the latter view, however, believed that the IDB would have to raise its rate. Mr Noble wrote that he 'would be the last to advocate no change [i.e. no increase in the IDB rate] if a change in general conditions should make our rates competitive with other financial institutions. If we got to the stage where this was the case we would in a few years be doing all the business of the character we were set up to finance, because no intelligent borrower can believe that, at the same rate, he is not in better hands with us than with any private lender!'

By February 1951, pressure from rising costs and slowly increasing rates on the markets brought an increase in the IDB's rate to 5½ per cent, with the expectation that 6 per cent might be charged for increases in existing loans where there had been extra work in trouble and supervision or for 'cases when the size and character of the borrower and his prospects would make it reasonable for us to claim some reward for our advice and financial support.' By 'size' was presumably meant the larger borrowers, and by 'character' those businesses big enough and strong enough to pay for the extra benefits of advice and guidance that usually accompanied an IDB loan.

One might see in this last thought the foreshadowing of a third principle in the establishment of interest rates which represented a departure from the principle of 'the same rate for all loans' and was not fully effective until much later in the Bank's history, namely, setting for large loans a higher schedule of interest rates than for small loans. Since the costs of making and managing a small loan were likely to be much the same as the costs of a large loan, the latter represented potentially a much larger margin of profit for the Bank. At first the Bank responded as a commercial lender might do by occasionally setting a lower rate for a very large loan, but as early as 1952 it had become so imbued with its primary role of assistance to small and medium-sized businesses that it was starting to reverse this practice.

Early in 1952, rising operating costs and an upward drift in market rates were again putting pressure on the IDB's rate. Action was taken in April to raise the rate to 6 per cent, but application was delayed until June of that year. Six per cent remained the Bank's lending rate until 1956.

Financing of the IDB

We shall now turn to the way in which the IDB raised its money. The original expectation was that the Bank of Canada would put up the money for the IDB equity capital and that issues of bonds and debentures by the IDB, perhaps to the public or other financial institutions, might then provide any additional amounts needed. Accordingly, the Bank of Canada subscribed for the full initial stock issue of $25 million and as funds were required drew it down and paid for it. By starting off with only equity money and no borrowed funds, the new Bank was to have a favourable start and develop some strength and attractiveness in its operating record before it should have to borrow and pay interest.

The first purchase of stock by the Bank of Canada was for $10 million on 2 October 1944 (the IDB's fiscal year-end was to be 30 September). By 30 September 1946, the Bank of Canada had paid for another $5 million of stock, and by 30 September 1947, the full $25 million had been taken down.[3] The purchase of shares in these large blocks meant that the IDB had surplus cash resources on hand for considerable periods of time. At the end of fiscal 1945 these amounted to more than $9 million; at the end of fiscal 1946, they were over $10 million; and on 30 September 1947, they were over $14 million. Surplus funds were invested in federal government securities, but there were many, sometimes rather acrimonious, discussions between the general management of the IDB (at GMO in Montreal) and head office officials (in the Bank of Canada in Ottawa) about decisions on these investments. The management of these surplus funds was ultimately left in the hands of head office in Ottawa, but the operational officers at GMO were naturally anxious that all matters should be handled in the way most advantageous to the IDB. This might mean buying and selling the federal government securities held by the IDB when market conditions were favourable to the one action or the other. Head office officials, however, who had a greater responsibility in their positions in the Bank of Canada, were unwilling to involve themselves in sharp trading of this sort lest it lead to false interpretations by the securities markets of the Bank of Canada's views on financial matters. These differences of opinion were never serious, and by 1951 the problem was disappearing, since by then virtually all the equity funds had been used up in the IDB's loans, and it was starting to look into ways of borrowing.

For the first few years, the IDB's revenues from the investment of surplus cash in government securities were quite considerable relative to its other revenues. In the three years to the end of fiscal 1947, by which time the full $25 million of authorized capital had been bought by the Bank of Canada, interest earned on surplus cash totalled approximately $600,000, as compared with income from loans and so on totalling $550,000. The income on surplus cash was, therefore, of importance in enabling the IDB to meet its operating expenses in these early years.

By 1951, it was apparent that the Bank would need to borrow soon. The amount estimated for the first borrowing was $2–$3 million. This sum was considered too small for public financing, and it was decided that, for the time being at least, the IDB would borrow its additional funds from the Bank of Canada. The latter continued, in fact, to be the IDB's source of borrowed money to the end. None the less, when Mr Marble, the secretary of the Bank (at head office in Ottawa), wrote to the Bank's outside legal advisers in 1951 for guidance in drafting debenture documents and resolutions to cover the borrowings from the Bank of Canada, he thought that there was a real possibility that in future years the IDB might borrow elsewhere for its further needs. In his letter to the lawyers, he said, 'It is probable that in the course of time the needs of the Bank will increase to the point which would justify consideration of a bond issue which could be sold directly to holders other than Bank of Canada or purchased by Bank of Canada and resold.'

The first borrowing was made in 1951 as part of an authorized issue of debentures in the amount of $5 million, the issue to have a three-year term and bear interest at the same rate as Canadian government three-year bonds. The proceeds of the authorized issue were to be drawn down by the IDB only as needed, and the interest rate at which drawings were made was changed every six months to conform to changes on the market in the rates on federal government bonds. At the end of fiscal 1951, debentures outstanding were $1,250,000.[4]

Discussions between the general management of the IDB in Montreal and the Bank of Canada as to the exact form and terms of such borrowings went on for a long time. The general manager, S.R. Noble, suggested at first some sort of overdraft account that would give desirable flexibility and could easily accommodate itself to the unpredictable outflow and inflow of cash in the Bank's loan disbursements and repayments. This was not agreed to by the Bank of Canada, which insisted on formal debentures being issued in fixed amounts. The IDB management in Montreal then tried to adapt this arrangement to its cash flow problems, first, by suggesting that, once a total debenture issue was approved, it should be purchased by the Bank of Canada, as needed, in units of $100,000; and second, by seeking flexible powers for the redemption of debentures. There were obviously fears that, if the IDB were required to receive the proceeds of debenture sales in units or multiples that were too large to adjust easily to its cash flow, the Bank would find itself involved again in the old problem of investing surplus cash for which it really had no need. The Bank of Canada at first insisted on units of $250,000, but in March 1952 it agreed that sales would be in units of $100,000.

Regarding redemption, the operational management of the IDB in Montreal wanted to be able to solve any short-term problems of excess cash by using it to redeem some debentures, expecting, of course, to sell more debentures later if its cash needs demanded it. If the IDB had a surplus of cash, it would redeem the higher-interest debentures among those outstanding and hope to replace them later, if more cash were needed, by selling new debentures at a rate more favourable to the IDB. Indeed, at one point the Bank of Canada became suspicious that, during a period in 1955 when government rates of interest had declined on the market by about 1 per cent, the general management of the IDB in Montreal was redeeming some old debentures, not because the Bank had a surplus of cash but because it could then replace them with fresh issues of new debentures at the lower rate of interest then prevailing on the market! Very complicated formulae were passed back and forth for several years to attempt to settle this issue. Through all these discussions Mr Towers was adamant that, while some recognition should be given in the terms of borrowing by the IDB to the difficulties and costs of operating in its assigned sphere, the Bank of Canada should 'stop short of an unbusinesslike arrangement which would amount to outright subsidization.'

During 1951 and early 1952, the Bank of Canada purchased a total of $2,750,000 of debentures of an authorized issue of $5 million, callable in whole or in part at the option of the IDB. In March 1952, the arrangement was revised with the cancellation of the unissued part of the old authorization and the authorizing of a new issue of $8 million, of which $2 million would mature on 1 April in each of the years 1955–8. These debentures were to be sold to the Bank of Canada by the IDB as needed in multiples of $100,000 and with equal representation from each of the maturities. The debentures could be redeemed by the IDB without notice at its option at any time prior to maturity, in whole or in part, 'at a price of par if the debentures were sold at par or at a discount, or at the purchase price if the debentures were sold at a premium over par.'

In April 1955 new arrangements were made. The Bank of Canada would purchase IDB debentures dated 1 April 1955 bearing a coupon rate of 2½ per cent per annum, in an amount not to exceed $10 million, of which $2½ million would mature on 1 April in each of the years 1958–61, i.e. they were to have maturities ranging from 3 to 6 years; later some debenture issues ran as long as 7 or 8 years. The price of these debentures was to be based on the average yield, to two places of decimals, on government of Canada bonds of the same maturities for the three preceding months, plus 0.10 per cent. Sales were to be made in amounts of $100,000 or multiples thereof and in rotation of maturity date. It was agreed also that, until further notice, any debentures outstanding then or later could be called for redemption, with premiums ranging from 1¾ per cent (for debentures with a remaining term of 5–6 years to maturity) to ¼ of 1 per cent (for those with a remaining term of six months).

These arrangements remained roughly the pattern for debentures until the end, and they introduced a new and very important element – the addition to the rate of interest of a fraction of a percentage point above the government yield. This step reflected an opinion on the part of Bank of Canada officials that it was not reasonable that federal crown corporations should have access to funds at just the same borrowing costs as the government itself. This additive was gradually increased to 0.60 per cent in 1961 and represented a substantial additional return to the Bank of Canada for the money it was supplying to the IDB.[5]

CHAPTER SEVEN

Operational developments

Economic background

During the period 1944–55, there were three major developments affecting operations that require particular consideration. The first had to do with the effect of several intervals of general credit stringency, and the second and third involved amendments in 1952 to the IDB Act, concerning loan ceilings and commercial air services, respectively.

The IDB started operations seven months before the end of hostilities in Europe, and so for several years it was functioning while the Canadian economy and society adjusted to peacetime conditions. This was accomplished more quickly and more successfully than had been expected. It had been feared that 'prices and costs would be distorted by post-war inflation resulting from temporary shortages of goods on one side and a great accumulation of demand, backed by war-time savings, on the other.' However, despite some material bottle-necks and pressure of demand on resources, the government was able to lift the wartime wage and salary controls in 1946 and most price ceilings in 1947.[1]

Apart from what was described at the time as a 'mild recession'[2] in 1954, the period was one of economic growth and was marked by relatively stable prices, fairly low rates of unemployment, and high levels of business activity. In 1948, the consumer price index rose by 14.4 per cent, but thereafter, although increases were recorded annually (except for a small decline in 1953), most were much smaller. From 1948 to 1955, the consumer price index rose by a total of 20 per cent, representing an average of less than 3 per cent per annum. Most of the increase occurred in the the years 1949–51 and probably reflected the impact of the start of the Korean War of 1950–3 and ancillary defence expenditures. From 1951 to 1955, the total increase in the consumer price index was only 2.4 per cent. Similarly, although the labour force was growing each year, the increases were largely taken into employment, and the proportion of the labour force that was unemployed remained constant and fairly low. Between 1946 and 1955 inclusive, the rate of unemployment ranged from 2.2 per cent to 4.6 per cent (in 1954). The annual average was 3.2 per cent. At the same time, there was steady growth in business activity. The gross national product (in constant 1971 dollars) increased by 50 per cent between 1945 and 1955, in spite of slight declines in 1946 and 1954.[3] The average annual increase was 4.3 per cent.

Policies for periods of credit restraint

Throughout the period, the government and the Bank of Canada were constantly alert for any developments that might overheat or distort the economy and perhaps provoke inflation. These apprehensions resulted, from time to time, in steps being taken, usually as a result of consultations between the Bank of Canada and the chartered banks, intended to hold the growth of bank credit to what were thought to be safe limits. These steps to restrain lending by chartered banks were taken as an aspect of monetary policy and on the initiative of the IDB's parent, the Bank of Canada, which also provided the IDB with its capital funds. The IDB therefore sought, on each such occasion, to follow policies that would respect the position of the chartered banks and at the same time be faithful to its own responsibilities.

The IDB wanted to be fair to the chartered banks by not making loans that they would probably have made had circumstances and their resources permitted them to do so. Any restraint on the ability of the banks to add to their loans was the result of monetary policy, and the IDB tried to respect such a policy by not taking over from the banks loans they might have liked to get rid of in order to improve their liquidity and their ability to make other, and perhaps better, loans. To have taken over such loans would have meant easing the discipline that monetary policy was intended to apply to the chartered banks and the credit system.

At the same time, such policies as the IDB adopted under these conditions viewed with particular sympathy the problem of small businesses caught up in these large issues, and sometimes, in dealing with individual proposals, these sympathies prevailed over other considerations. In this, it was consistent with the intentions expressed by the Bank of Canada in its talks with the banks that attention be given to the special problems of small businesses at times of a tightness of credit.[4]

One such occasion of credit stringency occurred early in 1948. The Bank of Canada became concerned that the strain on manpower and material resources, which had appeared in 1947 under pressure from heavy capital expenditure programs, would carry over into 1948 and push up prices. In fact, the consumer price index did rise in 1948 by a large percentage (14.4 per cent). Since much of the financing for these programs was coming from the newly developed practice on the part of the chartered banks of extending term accommodation to businesses through the purchase of corporate securities, in February 1948 the Bank of Canada suggested to the banks that term assistance of this sort should be discouraged whenever the amount involved was large enough to warrant the client's being directed to the security markets instead. As a result, the IDB established a policy, for the period of this concern, of taking the same attitude with any client of a chartered bank that had been guided by the latter in this manner. A year later these concerns had abated. The IDB was able to terminate the policy just described, and presumably the chartered banks also resumed normal lending practices. Whether these developments affected the operations of the IDB very much is hard to say. The restraints agreed on between the Bank of Canada and the chartered banks did not extend to businesses with needs too small to support an approach to the market, and it was with these businesses that the IDB was most active. In any event, as will be seen from Table 1, in each of the fiscal years ending 30 September 1948 and 1949, the number of loans and investments authorized by the IDB was lower than in the preceding fiscal year.[5]

Concerns of this sort next arose early in 1951 and this time were serious enough to result in a public statement by the Bank of Canada. Again pressure on available supplies of materials, arising from the Korean War and heavy defence expenditures, put pressure also on price levels. In February, the Bank of Canada met with the chartered banks to discuss the situation. The former had already taken steps to discourage credit expansion, and the chartered banks agreed that restraint in bank lending was desirable. They also agreed with the suggestion now made by the central bank that they should undertake 'a more rigorous scrutiny of applications for credit with a view to curtailing advances for less essential purposes and to encourage borrowers to go to the security market or elsewhere for their capital requirements.' By this means it was hoped to prevent an expansion of bank credit from creating and facilitating demands for goods and services beyond the aggregate capacity of the country and thereby tending to cause rising prices and conflicts with the defence program. In effect, except in the case of small amounts, the chartered banks would temporarily discontinue making term loans or purchasing corporate securities with a term of one year or longer.[6]

The IDB responded to this in several ways. It added to its appraisal criteria the possibility that a program could be postponed in view of urgent defence requirements and the necessity to restrict overall consumption as an anti-inflation measure. Its officers were instructed not to consider, except in very special circumstances, the refinancing of building or equipment programs already financed by a chartered bank. Sometimes a company's chartered bank would have temporarily financed such a program with short-term credit, expecting the borrower to replace it soon with longer-term loans obtained elsewhere; in other cases, a chartered bank might have agreed to provide itself such medium-term financing as was required. Businesses involved in such arrangements might subsequently apply to the IDB to have either type of financial arrangement replaced by a longer-term loan, but these requests were now to be declined.

In his instructions to the IDB supervisors, Mr Noble said: 'We shall probably receive an increased number of applications from industrialists who have already financed a capital programme through the commercial banks. Obviously to the extent we refinance such operations we will thereby relieve the pressure on the commercial banks, and to that extent defeat the purpose of the understanding between the commercial banks and the Bank of Canada, and such loans should not be considered unless the circumstances are such as to justify special treatment. In consideration of loans we must conform to the underlying principles which made the arrangement between the commercial banks and the Bank of Canada necessary.'

In addition, Mr Noble gave guidance on the general subject of inflationary pressures by adding to the considerations to be weighed in the appraisal of a loan application:

Should the proposed development or extension be postponed in view of the urgency of the defense programme and the necessity to restrict overall investment demand as an anti-inflation measure? The decision as to what recommendation to make in many cases will be difficult because it is obvious that the best means of preventing increased prices is to increase the supply of goods in relation to the demand. It would therefore seem that where a moderate expense on capital account would contribute to a substantial improvement in cost or volume of production, it would be desirable to assist. On the other hand, expensive developments with a delayed return in production should be avoided, except of course where such developments are needed in connection with the defense programme.

In its annual report for 1951, the Bank referred to its efforts 'to discourage applications for purposes which were not likely to contribute to the defense programme or to the general strength of the economy. Our policy in this respect was of course related to the general desirability of credit restraint at a time when the total demand for labour and materials threatened to outstrip the available supply.'[7]

The number of authorizations by the IDB fell somewhat in fiscal 1952, as in 1948 and 1949. These policies remained in force until May 1952.

Limit on loans over $200,000

The second development affecting operations was that the total of balances outstanding on loans of more than $200,000 was rapidly approaching the limit of $15 million set by the IDB Act on such loans. It may seem paradoxical that this problem should have arisen during a time when policies to restrain applications over that amount were from time to time introduced. Be that as it may, within four years of the start of operations the total of IDB loans in this category was close to the statutory limit. To avoid turning down applications for this reason an amendment to the act was required. A bill to raise the limit to $25 million was passed in 1949 and on 10 December given royal assent. This relief was not adequate for long, and by 1951 the IDB was looking for another amendment to raise the limit again. This came in 1952, when a bill was introduced to raise the limit to $50 million; after passage in Parliament, it received royal assent on 18 June 1952.[8]

Commercial air services

This 1952 bill contained another provision important enough to be regarded separately as the third major development affecting operations, namely the addition of commercial air services to businesses eligible to obtain assistance from the IDB. The possibility of such an amendment had been raised with the Bank by the Air Transport Board in September 1950. The air-service operators were going to have to replace, within a few years, the pre-war and war-surplus aircraft on which they had been depending. Apart from the two major carriers, Trans-Canada Airlines and CP Air, few, if any, were in a position to finance these replacements from their own resources or through the issue of stock to or loans from the normal backers of the companies. Of various means considered for helping the operators, including subsidies, special depreciation rates, and government ownership of new aircraft to be leased to the operators, the simplest solution was to make commercial air services eligible to apply to the IDB. There was some apprehension among the officers of the Bank that to acquiesce in this might mean exposure to other amendments from time to time at the behest of the government when some department was confronted with a special problem; however, it was recognized as a reasonable extension of the IDB.

The air service companies had a number of special financial problems. Any available financing was strictly limited and for a short term. Little or no aid was available from banks or licensed lending agencies, and equity capital was shy. Most financing was through private parties on a short-term basis and at very high interest rates, reported in one case to be 45 per cent per annum. Short-term payments on loans and high interest charges were preventing the operators from settling themselves down on a sound basis. With better financing arrangements such as the IDB might offer, it was believed that the financial health of the companies would improve, releasing money from earnings to increase insurance coverage, improve management, increase working capital, and generally upgrade the companies.

The magnitude of need, as seen by the Air Transport Board, was total credits of $5 million to finance 120 replacement aircraft costing $7 million for approximately 20 companies. Like almost all other forecasts about the IDB, this appraisal of the situation was ultimately surpassed by events. By the end of fiscal 1955, the Bank had authorized 25 loans to 16 commercial air services companies for a total of $4 million, quite well in line with expectations. It was estimated at the time that one out of ten commercial aircraft in Canada was pledged to the IDB and that a person could probably travel from one end of the country to the other on aircraft mortgaged to the Bank, being handed on from one borrowing company to the next. By the end of the Bank in 1975, it had authorized 504 loans to 302 companies for a total of $51 million.[9]

From the Bank's standpoint, apart from any concerns about the financial strength of the borrowing companies, there were serious legal problems in the taking of security from commercial air services. Most loans were secured principally by a charge on aircraft. A charge on equipment of this sort is normally taken by way of a chattel mortgage, debenture, or trust deed and registered in some local or limited jurisdiction such as a province, county, or district. An aircraft, however, could easily fly to other jurisdictions or even leave the country and so escape from the embrace of the security registration. Multiple registrations in many jurisdictions to cover all places that an aircraft might go were scarcely practical. Further, the ease and speed with which an aircraft could move from one jurisdiction to another made it difficult, and really quite impractical, to check for all possible prior encumbrances against aircraft to be pledged to the Bank. Such a check would have required a great number of registry searches. To overcome these difficulties in the way of obtaining a satisfactory charge on aircraft, the Bank recommended to the federal government that it set up a central system for registering encumbrances on aircraft that could be enforced in all parts of Canada.

At a meeting in June 1952 with the chairman and senior officials of the Air Transport Board, H.M. Scott, chief of the Bank's legal department, had formed an impression that the Board recognized the problems involved in taking security over aircraft and would at least give sympathetic support to any effort to obtain legislation to set up a central legal registry. This was encouraging, but the efforts of the Bank got nowhere. In fact, it was surprised to learn, in January 1954, that the chairman of the Air Transport Board did not really think the Board was particularly interested in the problem or that it ought to be. The issue did, of course, involve questions of provincial rights, and the Bank was left to find its own solutions.

With care and ingenuity on the part of the Bank's legal department, such aircraft security as it took never failed to protect it. The Bank did not consider itself to have the power to purchase an aircraft and sell it under a conditional sales contract, as a finance company might do, or to go through the fiction of purchasing an aircraft from the 'borrower' and selling it back to him. Accordingly, it generally followed the practice of registering a charge on aircraft in any jurisdictions where the head office of the borrowing business was located, where the borrower had a branch office, or where the business's aircraft were based.

In this unusual field, the Bank certainly had no expertise. That it was successful in financing air services was probably due to its treating the operators like any other applicants, asking them the same kind of questions, making the same kind of analysis, and forming a view as to an applicant's prospects of success. An early application to the Bank illustrates the simple approach taken. The applicant wanted to buy a de Havilland Otter to establish an operation in the north. This was to be the first Otter sold in Canada for commercial use. The credit officer, who knew little about aircraft, sought information on the proposed purchase just as if it had been a concrete-block-making machine or a lathe. What were the Otter's capacity, operating costs, fuel consumption, etc? Was the

TABLE 1

Loans approved 1945–55

	Number of loans authorized				Amount of loans authorized – total ($millions)	Average size of loan ($thousands)
	To manufacturers	To air services	To other	Total		
1945	98	–	5	103	4.2	40
1946	168	–	19	187	8.0	43
1947	193	–	21	214	11.7	55
1948	185	–	19	204	11.7	57
1949	142	–	11	153	7.4	48
1950	167	–	21	188	7.7	41
1951	184	–	18	202	18.8	93
1952	150	2	13	165	11.5	70
1953	195	8	15	218	13.0	60
1954	166	4	10	180	13.0	72
1955	201	11	9	221	17.5	79
Total	1,849	25	161	2,035	124.5	62

SOURCE: Brief, Tables 8 and 10.

aircraft suitable for the applicant's needs? Details on all such things were patiently supplied by the de Havilland Company, and finally C.H. (Punch) Dickins, then vice-president of de Havilland, invited the credit officer out to the plant to see how the Otter was made and to see that it really could fly! As it happened, the applicant himself was also of an analytical turn of mind, speaking of all financial elements of his plan on the basis of 'cents per mile' and planning all his moves in practical financial terms. The loan was made, much larger ones followed, and the borrowing company ultimately became one of the great air charter operators of the world.

Loans: volume, distribution, and purpose

Table 1 shows how the Bank's business developed between 1945 and 1955. In the first fiscal year, 1945, 103 loans were authorized; by 1947, annual authorizations were up to 214, and they remained around this level until 1955. However, without the loans to commercial air services following the 1952 amendment to the act, no other year in the period up to 1955 would have achieved the level of 1947.

It is not difficult to think of reasons for this slow growth – the time and effort required to develop policies and procedures, the slow spread in the business community of knowledge about the Bank, the limited field to which it was restricted by its act, and the welding together of a new staff operating in a new and hazardous field. Also, small businesses had to be taught to think of solutions to their financial problems, or some of them, in terms of long-term borrowing through what were, in effect, small mortgage debentures. This was a novel idea that spread slowly. Undoubtedly, the absence of advertising by the Bank and the small number of offices were also factors.

As Table 1 shows, most of the loans went to manufacturers. These included, for example, small machine shops, manufacturers of automobile parts, chemical plants, sawmills, planing mills, ceramic plants, textile and garment factories, makers of building products, soap manufacturers, furniture factories, flour mills, bakeries, and metal-casting companies; these are just a few of the wide range of industries helped by the IDB in these early years. Many businesses needed assistance to adjust to peacetime conditions, set up new activities, or apply new technology to industrial uses. For example, some of the earliest helicopter operations in both western and eastern Canada were financed by the IDB, as were new photographic air survey services and the purchase of short-takeoff aircraft for use in opening up the north. In Quebec, the first apple warehouses employing a new technique of controlled-atmosphere storage were financed. Fish plants in the Atlantic provinces and small meat packers were modernized with stainless steel equipment and convenient icing facilities to meet federal government regulations. In Quebec, a large plant was established to manufacture ethyl alcohol from waste sulphite liquor previously dumped into the Ottawa River. In the Atlantic provinces, small woodworking and shipbuilding businesses were assisted. In the prairie provinces, an important refinery was set up and community frozen-locker plants were financed in more than a score of towns, although as rural electrification spread these were ultimately replaced by domestic freezers.

A feature of lending in the post-war years was assistance to immigrants from Europe who wanted to establish new businesses in Canada. Lumber and plywood plants in British Columbia, a glass plant in Montreal, a meat packer in the prairies, a plant in Ontario to make dental burrs, sausage factories, and a shirting manufacturer are examples of new industries established by immigrants with the Bank's assistance. Since the principals in these businesses were usually unfamiliar with Canadian business methods, the Bank was often of great assistance in guiding and counselling them in their new homeland. One immigrant businessman, eager to apply the technical skills and apparatus of his native land, was saved from bringing to Canada a splendid new log carrier that could not climb a hill covered in snow![10]

Many of the loans made from 1945 to 1955 were associated with the construction industry. Small cement block plants, ready-mix concrete plants, a ceramic tile factory, plywood plants, and sawmills were prominent among loans in these years, and many grew to a substantial size. A ready-mix concrete plant in the prairies, started with only an outside personal guarantee for an investment, was later sold for several million dollars.

Many of the Bank's borrowers in these years grew to become large and important corporations. One company in Quebec became one of the world's leading producers of electronic equipment for the aviation industry. Another in Ontario, starting with an IDB loan of $25,000, developed an international market for heating equipment with subsidiaries in other countries. A small business on the west coast that started in a basement printing a college paper branched into other lines and became a multi-million dollar business. Associated with the 2,035 loans approved from 1945 to 1955 were 19 investments in equity for a total of $1 million, and the Bank also gave 32 guarantees for a total of $5 million. Generally speaking, the financing provided was for fixed asset programs, i.e. the purchase of equipment or the purchase or construction of buildings or building additions. A much smaller number of loans was made to improve working capital, particularly where the borrower's liquid position was strained as a result of capital expenditures already made but without proper term borrowing to finance them.

Although in its thirty-one years the Bank made some large loans, including one for $6 million and another 88 for $1 million or more, the intentions of the Bank's founders that it should serve small businesses particularly were fully realized. The average size of loan between 1945 and 1955 was $62,000. Fifty-one per cent of authorizations were for amounts of $25,000 or less, 73 per cent were for $50,000 or less, and 95 per cent were for $200,000 or less.

Provincial distribution of loans is given in Table 2. It shows Quebec in the lead by number of loans with 33.1 per cent, Ontario second with 30.0 per cent, British Columbia next with 15.3 per cent, the prairies with 14.8 per cent, and the Atlantic provinces with 6.8 per cent. The attempt to give increased attention to the Atlantic provinces by appointing, in 1952, a supervisor who operated from Montreal was not effective. In 1951, the number of loans approved in that area was 16; in 1954 it was 2; and in 1955 it was 11. It was an early demonstration of what was later recognized by the Bank, that to serve an area properly it was necessary to have an office on the spot.

Of course, at this stage only manufacturers and processors were, for the

TABLE 2

Regional comparison of loan authorizations, 1945−55, with employment in manufacturing

	Number of loans authorized		Amount of loans authorized		Share of manufacturing employment (percentage)
	Number	Percentage	Amount ($millions)	Percentage	
Atlantic	139	6.8	5.6	4.5	5.1
Quebec	674	33.1	45.4	36.5	33.4
Ontario	611	30.0	36.6	29.4	47.4
Prairie	301	14.8	18.7	15.0	6.6
British Columbia and Territories	310	15.3	18.2	14.6	7.5
Total	2,035	100.0	124.5	100.0	100.0

SOURCES: Brief, Table 12. Figures for manufacturing employment from M.C. Urquhart and K.A. Buckley, *Historical Statistics of Canada* (Toronto: Macmillan, 1965), Series Q12-29. This series has no figures for 1946 or 1947, for reasons given in the book. The figures used for manufacturing employment in Table 2 were obtained by averaging the annual percentages in Series Q12-29.

most part, eligible, and this definitely limited opportunities for the Bank in some areas such as the Atlantic provinces and the prairies. Table 2 indicates the percentage distribution of authorizations and the regional distribution of labour employed in manufacturing.

It is interesting to note that Ontario received fewer loans than the other regions proportional to numbers employed in manufacturing – virtually the only field of business eligible to apply for a loan. This distribution of loans was quite contrary to frequent complaints from the Atlantic and prairie provinces that the Bank favoured the central provinces.

Each year some authorizations were cancelled because the applicants decided not to use them; perhaps they had cancelled or changed their plans or got their money somewhere else. The proportion cancelled ranged between 6 and 14 per cent.

Trans-Canada Pipe Lines Ltd

We shall close this outline of operational developments from 1945 to 1955, rather paradoxically, with a brief account of a loan that the IDB did not make – a loan to assist in financing the trans-Canada pipeline.[11]

In 1951, Trans-Canada Pipe Lines Ltd, controlled by Delhi Oil Corp of Delaware, was incorporated to construct a pipeline to take natural gas from Alberta to eastern Canada as far as Montreal by an all-Canadian route. Earlier, in 1949, another company, Western Pipe Lines Ltd, representing Canadian interests had been formed to build a pipeline to carry Alberta gas eastwards, but only as far as Winnipeg, where the line was to turn south to the American border to serve Minnesota and nearby markets. In March 1953, the Hon. C.D. Howe, federal minister of trade and commerce, announced that the government favoured the all-Canadian route. The two companies merged, with the approval and encouragement of Premier E.C. Manning of Alberta and Mr Howe, because it was not considered economic to have two separate pipeline projects pursued. The merger took place under the charter of Trans-Canada Pipe Lines Ltd, and each of the two groups had an equal interest in it. The company now concentrated on the all-Canadian route, but work could not start until the Alberta oil and gas regulatory authorities decided that gas reserves were large enough to permit export of large quantities of gas to the east. This did not occur until late in 1953, and a permit to export gas from Alberta was granted in May 1954. In July the federal Board of Transport Commissioners approved in principle the company's application to construct the pipeline.

The project was considered a most formidable one, comparable to the construction of the Canadian Pacific Railway across Canada in the 1870s. The cost was estimated at $350 million, a huge sum in those days; the pipeline would be the largest and longest (2,400 miles) gas pipeline ever built up to that time and so was really a new concept. It would pass through sparsely populated areas, and so there was uncertainty whether it would be profitable; also, it had to cross a very difficult terrain of rock, lakes, rivers, and forest in northern Ontario where construction costs would be high.

Raising money to build the pipeline presented the company with a conundrum – it could not line up financing without showing that it had contracts to sell gas, but it was unable to negotiate all the sales contracts it needed unless the prospective purchasers of gas could be shown that the pipeline would be financed and built. The financial plan itself presented similar problems. Those responsible for raising money for the company believed that in order to attract purchasers of shares, the number offered for sale must not be too great and that approximately $280 million of the $350 million estimated as required would have to come from the sale of first mortgage bonds; of the $70 million remaining to be raised, only part, they believed, could be obtained from the sale of shares, and the remainder would have to be in some sort of junior securities. However, they were doubtful that as much as $280 million could be sold in first mortgage bonds because of the uncertainties surrounding the project.

On 21 October 1954 the principals of the company reported to Mr Howe that they had been unable to solve the financing problem. The possibility of some sort of support from the government was undoubtedly in their minds, but, although the possible remission of some duties and sales tax was discussed, there does not appear to have been any precise talk about other kinds of government support. Six days later, Mr Howe called on the governor of the Bank of Canada, Graham Towers, as someone who might have useful insights into the problem of raising the large sums needed. Mr Howe mentioned that the government might be asked to guarantee interest on the company's bonds in some way. Mr Towers wondered whether the government could properly make the deal possible without a quid pro quo in the form of a share in the equity. Mr Howe did not favour this, and Mr Towers then suggested that the IDB might come into the picture by buying convertible debentures backed by a second mortgage on the property as one element in the financing package. This was an extraordinary suggestion, because a pipeline was not eligible under the IDB Act, and the Bank's financial resources were completely inadequate to provide the sums involved. The IDB Act would require amendment in both respects to accommodate this transaction.

Mr Towers was unaware that the idea of applying to the IDB had occurred to others even before the company received approval for construction of the pipeline from the Board of Transport Commissioners. In June 1954, someone representing himself as speaking on behalf of the company contacted K.K. Hay-Roe, then a credit officer at the Bank's Toronto office, and asked if the IDB would lend $50 million to a company like theirs. Mr Hay-Roe gave the obvious answers that the Bank did not have enough money to lend $50 million to anyone and that the company was ineligible anyway. The discussion was so short and the proposal so far-fetched that he did not even record the conversation in the usual memorandum.

By the end of 1954, the company was no nearer success in its financing, and it then proposed a government guarantee of principal and interest payments on the bonds that the company would issue, effective until the company's earnings after depreciation and income tax equalled $1\frac{1}{2}$ times the bond interest requirements for two successive years. Mr Howe was sympathetic, but the Hon. W.E. Harris, the minister of finance, demurred, and the proposal was rejected. The idea first put forward by Mr Towers was revived, and Mr Harris suggested that the company should approach the IDB. This the company did in mid-January 1955. Although any loan from the IDB would require major amendments to its act, there was a certain attraction for the government in using it as the vehicle for dealing with the company's proposal, because it put the issue into a business-like context, removed to a degree from the government itself.

Understandably, the proposal was not dealt with through the field offices of the IDB in the usual way. Discussions were directly with the president of the Bank, J.E. Coyne, who had succeeded Mr Towers, and his senior officials at the Bank of Canada, assisted by W.C. Stuart, who had come to Ottawa for the purpose from the IDB's office in Montreal. In addition, Mr Harris was kept informed throughout the negotiations. Discussions between the company and the Bank went on from mid-January to mid-March. They were conducted under pressure, since the company had a number of deadlines to meet, for ordering materials, demonstrating to the Alberta and Canadian licensing authorities that the pipeline could be financed, and taking advantage of suitable weather to get construction under way in 1955.

From the beginning of the discussions, the representatives of the company and those negotiating for the IDB differed on how the total financing package should be made up. The company held strongly to the opinion that there should be $280 million or so of first mortgage bonds plus $70 million, partly in shares and partly in junior securities. This put the first mortgage bonds at a level that would require government support. The company suggested that this should take the form of a government guarantee of the bonds or a government undertaking to purchase the whole issue.

However, the management of the IDB felt that if the Bank was to be fitted into this package somewhere, the extent to which the enterprise would be leaning on governmental help would be much too favourable to the shareholders. Mr Towers, in his conversation with Mr Howe in October 1954, had suggested that the government should receive some share in the equity of the company in return for support then proposed to be given its financing. Mr Coyne now outlined how he felt this might be done. To dispense with any government guarantee of the bonds, he suggested that the total to be sold be reduced to $245 million; the IDB would buy $35 million of junior debentures convertible into stock; and $70 million would be raised through the sale of shares. In addition, the Bank would stand ready to buy up to $35 million further convertible debentures in the event the company was unable, in the first year, to sell the full amount of $70 million in shares. This would mean that if the IDB converted into shares any debentures it bought, the total of share equity would be $105 million, or 30 per cent of total financing, as Mr Coyne felt it ought to be.

Final negotiations settled on a scheme somewhat similar to this, except that the shares to be sold to the public were set at $40 million and the IDB was to buy $5 million in shares 'pour encourager les autres' and, instead of standing by to purchase debentures, would buy $60 million. This left the same amount of mortgage bonds – $245 million – to be sold.

Agreement along these lines was reached on 13 March. The following morning the company began checking with the prospective suppliers of gas who had been waiting to be shown that the pipeline could be financed and built. The most important of these was Canadian Gulf Oil, which controlled about one-third of the gas earmarked for the pipeline. W.K. Whiteford, president of the Gulf Oil Company of Pittsburgh (which controlled Canadian Gulf), was contacted by phone. He pointed out that the $60 million of debentures to be bought by the IDB would, if all were converted into shares by the Bank as was to be allowed in the terms of the debentures, give the Bank control of Trans-Canada Pipe Lines Ltd and said his company would not make a contract with Trans-Canada to supply gas if it could be controlled by a government agency. This made further negotiations on the basis of the terms agreed to pointless, and the IDB passed out of the Trans-Canada picture.

The government's ultimate solution to the problem of getting the pipeline financed and built developed gradually in the following months: the costly northern Ontario section would be constructed and owned by a specially created crown corporation, thus relieving Trans-Canada of the need to finance it, and a short-term loan would enable the company to start work on the western section of the pipeline that summer, i.e. in 1956. These plans do not seem to have caused difficulties with the gas suppliers, despite the government's involvement. As a result of a series of events having to do with Trans-Canada's efforts to obtain steel pipe, Canadian Gulf and two other American oil and gas corporations emerged with control of a majority of the shares of Trans-Canada.

This American control of Trans-Canada turned out to be a great handicap to the Canadian government when, in the spring of 1956, it introduced into Parliament legislation to incorporate a crown company to build the northern Ontario link in the pipeline and authorize a loan. A violent debate ensued; the government imposed closure on proceedings in the House of Commons; and the image of arrogance that it acquired in the process was a material factor in the Liberal party's defeat in elections of 1957 and 1958.

One is tempted to speculate on whether these later events would have been the same if a loan by the IDB had been made. Would there have been a big pipeline debate? Would the results of the 1957 elections have been the same? Would Mr Diefenbaker and Mr Pearson have been prime ministers in the late 1950s and the 1960s? Would Canada's political history have been the same? Perhaps the Industrial Development Bank influenced the country's affairs profoundly through a loan it did not make.

However, had the loan been made, it might have had a great impact on the history of the Bank itself. It would have meant that the Bank had been used outside its statutory limits to finance a huge program of national importance and of the government's desiring. The fact that a precedent for the IDB would have been created was recognized by Mr Coyne, but he felt that the national importance of the pipeline project would have been sufficient defence against some other applicant who felt that the rules should be bent for its benefit just as they would have been altered to accommodate Trans-Canada Pipe Lines Ltd. Considering that small and little-known precedents in the Bank's application of its policies often caused it great difficulty, one can certainly speculate as to the effect of a precedent on this massive scale.

CHAPTER EIGHT

Operating results

Revenues and profits

Table 3 gives operating results for 1945–55; Table 4 expresses these results as a percentage of average loans and investments outstanding. Each year the Bank earned a profit for transfer to the reserve fund, although in 1948 the amount was only $34,000. The Bank was favoured in its first years by being able to depend on equity capital for its funds rather than on borrowed money. Not until 1951 did the Bank sell debentures, and even by 1955 these were still a relatively small source of funds for the Bank; equity was $25 million, and the reserve fund (i.e. accumulated net profit) was $7,384,000, while debentures were only $9,500,000.

When the Bank was being planned, it was the opinion of Mr Towers that it should stand on its own feet to the extent of earning enough profits to return to the Bank of Canada, which held its shares, a yield equal to what the Bank of Canada could earn on long-term government securities; at the time, this was put at 4 per cent per annum. This opinion was based on estimates of income and expenses prepared while the Bank was still in the planning stage. These proved to be incorrect, and it could hardly be otherwise for an institution not yet in existence and with no parallel as an example. None the less, through the early years of the IDB the Bank of Canada clung to the idea of obtaining a satisfactory return on its share investment in the Bank, and this affected discussions between the two banks as to the terms on which the central bank would buy its subsidiary's debentures and what rate of interest the IDB should charge its borrowers on its loans.

TABLE 3

Operating results ($millions) 1945-55

	1945	1946	1947	1948	1949	1950	1951	1952	1953	1954	1955
Interest on loans	–	0.1	0.4	0.7	0.9	1.0	1.2	1.6	1.8	2.1	2.2
Other income	0.3	0.3	0.4	0.2	0.2	0.2	0.1	–	0.1	0.8	–
Total income	0.3	0.4	0.8	0.9	1.1	1.2	1.3	1.6	1.9	2.9	2.2
Operating expenses	0.1	0.2	0.3	0.4	0.5	0.5	0.6	0.6	0.6	0.7	0.7
Interest on debentures	–	–	–	–	–	–	–	0.1	0.2	0.4	0.3
Total costs	0.1	0.2	0.3	0.4	0.5	0.5	0.6	0.7	0.8	1.1	1.0
Net income	0.2	0.2	0.5	0.5	0.6	0.7	0.7	0.9	1.1	1.8	1.2
Adjustments*	–0.1	+0.1	–	–0.3	+0.2	+0.1	–	–	–	–	–
Net income after adjustments	0.1	0.3	0.5	0.2	0.8	0.8	0.7	0.9	1.1	1.8	1.2
Provision for losses	–	–	0.2	0.2	0.1	0.1	–	0.1	0.2	0.2	–
Transferred to reserve fund†	0.1	0.3	0.3	–	0.7	0.7	0.7	0.8	0.9	1.6	1.2
Percentage of return on capital (shares plus reserve fund)‡	1.0	2.7	1.5	–	2.8	2.6	2.4	2.9	2.9	5.6	3.7

*These were various adjustments for contingency reserves only provided for in 1945 and reversed in 1946, and a revaluation of government securities made in 1948 and reversed in 1949 and 1950.
†All the figures in the table have been taken to the nearest decimal. In 1948, the amount transferred to the reserve fund was $34,000, but it shows as nil because it was less than $50,000.
‡In all tables where the return on 'Shares plus reserve fund' is given, the figure used for the latter in each year is the average between the amount at the opening and the amount at the closing of the fiscal year, except for 1945.
SOURCE: Brief, Tables 2 and 3.

TABLE 4

Operating results, expressed as percentage of average loans and investments outstanding, 1945–55

	1945	1946	1947	1948	1949	1950	1951	1952	1953	1954	1955
Income as percentage of average loans and investments	3.12	4.09	4.88	3.48	4.30	4.42	4.51	5.03	5.05	7.15	5.34
Less:											
Debenture cost	–	–	–	–	–	–	0.01	0.25	0.54	0.87	0.73
Operating costs	1.12	1.77	1.77	1.55	1.82	1.98	2.11	1.90	1.61	1.79	1.74
Net profit before provision for losses	2.00	2.32	3.11	1.93	2.48	2.44	2.39	2.88	2.90	4.49	2.87

SOURCES: Brief, Table 4.

Up to 1951 (the year in which the Bank first sold debentures) it had earned net profits totalling $2,881,000. Of this, $1,286,000 came from interest earned on surplus cash. By 1955, the total accumulated net profits earned were $7,384,000. The average yield on equity, i.e. share capital plus the reserve fund, from 1945 to 1955 was 2.6 per cent. Only in one year, 1954, did the IDB come up to Mr Towers's hopes as to a return on the Bank of Canada's investment. In that year, the yield was 5.6 per cent on equity, but this was partly due to a fortuitous profit of $800,000 from the sale of shares acquired by the Bank as compensation for what seemed like particularly risky loans when they were made. Without this profit, the yield in 1954 would have been 2.9 per cent.

Loss experience

Of course, some borrowers got into trouble. During the period 1945–55, each year between 15 and 30 per cent of borrowers experienced difficulties sufficiently serious that at the time of the annual loan reviews their loans were regarded, even if only temporarily, as doubtful accounts. For some of these, there ultimately proved to be no way in which the money loaned by the Bank could be repaid to it other than by action on the part of the Bank to take over and sell the security that had been pledged. Sometimes even this action did not provide enough money to pay off the loan, and the unpaid balance was 'written off' as a loss to the Bank. For the first few years, there were no write-offs, since there had hardly been enough time for the first loans made to reach such a state. In fiscal 1947, however, the Bank made its first write-offs in the amount of $34,340, and an amount was written off each year thereafter. Of the 2,035 loans authorized up to 1955, 32 were ultimately written off in some amount as a loss. By the end of fiscal 1955, a total of $359,000 had been written off. Mr Towers's opinion, as expressed at the hearings of the standing committee of the House of Commons in 1944, was that annual loss experience should not exceed 1½ per cent of outstanding loan balances.[1] In the period 1945–55, the average annual relationship between write-offs and year-end outstanding loan balances was 0.15 per cent, far below Mr Towers's limit.

In reviewing the history of the IDB, it is questionable whether expressing write-offs or losses as a percentage of outstanding balances is the best way of measuring the loss experience of the Bank. This ratio is a common measure of the experience of the chartered banks, and the nature of their operations makes it appropriate. Their business loans are mostly for the short term, and the borrowings of a particular business may, in the course of a year, rise and fall several times and perhaps disappear completely for a while. It may be, then, quite appropriate, as well as convenient, to relate the amounts writen off by a chartered bank in any year to the total of loans remaining outstanding at the end of the year.

The position of the IDB was quite different. First, all of its loans were in the form of long-term contracts, and a loan might not get into trouble until it had been running for two or three years of its contract. Second, the IDB was usually very patient in dealing with borrowers that were in difficulties or fell into arrears of payments. An outstanding example of this was a veneer plant for which the IDB had financed a major modernization program. The company got into trouble through bad inventory management, and the chartered bank seized the assets. The IDB assumed the chartered bank's loan, hired a new manager for the company, and for three years the business was virtually run by the Bank under section 19 of its act, which gave it the power to finance on the support of inventories. The market for the company's products improved, and finally the new manager bought the business from its original owners for $1 million and the IDB's loans were all paid off.

In some cases, repayment schedules would be lengthened by formal amendment of the loan contracts so as to ease the pressure of payments on the IDB's loan. Many borrowers might pass through a period when they could make no payments at all. If they were able to improve their position and resume payments, they would not likely be expected to catch up on the payments missed but would have their schedule revised to give them, in effect, a moratorium for the period of difficulties. Such a formal revision would probably be made only if the borrower were able to demonstrate that it had now emerged from its troubles and could be expected to maintain payments thenceforth. Even if a borrower could not win its way to such a satisfactory position that the Bank would revise the repayment schedule formally, the Bank would not usually take action to recover its loan and seize its security until all hope for the recovery of the business had vanished. These practices helped many borrowers to survive and may well have kept down the amount written off from bad loans, though adding to the Bank's administrative costs.

A further circumstance affected the relationship between amounts written off and loan balances. Very early it became the practice of the Bank to write off the balance of a loan only when the tangible security for it had been disposed of and the loss the Bank faced established. This practice made comparisons with other lenders' experience difficult and almost meaningless since they might write off portions of a bad loan progressively year by year to reflect a debtor's deteriorating position. The

IDB's practice also meant that a write-off would often occur long after the relative loan 'went sour' and many years after it was made. As a result, a large part of the amounts written off in any one year would almost certainly relate to loans made several years earlier. For example, while there were net write-offs totalling $353,000 in the period 1945–55 of loans that originated in that period, a further net sum of $133,000 was written off in subsequent years on loans originating in the same period. The last write-off on a loan from 1945–55 occurred in 1971.

If the security for a loan included a personal guarantee, a write-off would not usually be delayed until this guarantee had been collected. Recovery under a guarantee was often difficult, protracted, and uncertain. Sometimes it would be decided that no action should be taken to collect under a guarantee or that a compromise should be agreed to because of the personal circumstances of the guarantor. As a result, action to write off the remaining balance of a loan would not usually be delayed until a guarantee was settled; if there were any subsequent recoveries from the guarantor, these would be shown in the Bank's annual financial statement as 'Recovery of amounts previously written off.'

Under all these circumstances, and particularly with the Bank's volume of business growing steadily as it did after 1955, it would be quite unsatisfactory to relate write-offs in one year to the outstanding balances at the end of that year as a measure of the Bank's loss experience. A better measure would be to relate write-offs to net authorizations for the year or years of origin of loans written off. By net authorizations is meant the total of loans approved in a fiscal year, less any cancellations or reductions prior to disbursement in that year. This figure represents roughly the amount that was finally actually borrowed by the Bank's customers and hence at risk. The figure is only approximate because some cancellations and reductions might be related to loans authorized in another year. Similarly, some changes affecting loans authorized in a particular year might be made later. If we assume that the qualifications just described largely balance one another out, we may take it that the figure for net authorizations is reasonably useful as a basis for measuring loss experience.

In the years 1945–55, net authorizations were $103 million.[2] Net write-offs of loans that originated in that period had totalled $486,000 by 1981, a loss ratio of 0.47 per cent. This is probably a fair indication of the Bank's actual loss experience on loans approved 1945–55.

A lending institution should recognize that some of its loans will inevitably turn into losses in future years and make provision from each year's earnings for these future losses. The amounts so provided by the

IDB each year were held in a reserve for losses account. It was the Bank's practice to charge write-offs to this reserve and, by an annual transfer from earnings, restore the reserve balance to a proper level to provide for future write-offs.

The first transfer to the reserve for losses was made in 1947 in the amount of $200,000. In the next fiscal year, a system was set up for the regular submission by the Bank's various offices of reports on loans in which there had been uncorrected unfavourable developments. Criteria for judging which loans might come within this description developed gradually. From fiscal 1949 each office was asked to submit, at 30 September each year, a review of all its loans, divided into various categories according to the state of each loan and of the affairs of each borrowing business. From this annual survey of the Bank's loans, the Bank's officers and the auditors made independent estimates of the possible loan write-offs in prospect. Although arrived at separately, these estimates were almost always very close to each other. On the basis of these estimates of possible write-offs, but also of general economic conditions and prospects, and a general view of the direction in which the Bank's affairs were moving, a conclusion was reached, following discussions with the auditors and with their concurrence, as to the level at which the reserve for losses should be established at each fiscal year-end and, hence, of the amount to be transferred to the reserve from earnings to bring it to that level.

It would be difficult to make a statistical presentation of the Bank's view of the state of its loans from year to year because the criteria for the various categories used in the annual review changed from time to time. However, at the end of fiscal 1955, by which time the review system was well established, 84 per cent of loan balances outstanding were regarded as in a satisfactory condition. Of the remainder, accounts totalling $2.4 million were considered as possibly subject to write-off. It was not expected, however, that they would be a total loss. The Bank estimated that write-offs on them might amount to $711,000. The auditors' estimate was much less, at $555,000. As between these two estimates it was considered reasonable and conservative to put the reserve for losses at $700,000. This proved to be a sound opinion. By the end of fiscal 1981, total net write-offs[3] on loans originating prior to the end of fiscal 1955 were $486,000, little more than two-thirds of the reserve at the end of that year.

In the years 1945-55, the balance in the reserve for losses was, on average, 46 per cent more than was needed to cover future loan losses on outstanding balances as estimated by the Bank's officers and 60 per cent more than was needed according to the auditors' estimates.

Forecasts of future growth

We are now at the end of the Bank's first period, from 1945 to 1955. In 1956, the act would be amended to increase greatly the number of businesses that could apply for assistance, which altered the role and scope of the Bank. However, before we move on to the second period of the Bank's history, we might pause for a moment, placing ourselves back in those early years to see how the prospects for the Bank then looked to those involved in its affairs.

In January 1949, when the IDB operational management in Montreal was engaged in one of its periodic arguments with head office in Ottawa and with the Bank of Canada about how surplus cash was to be invested and what rate of interest the IDB was to charge on its loans, a forecast was prepared. It was made on the basis of a number of assumptions – the Bank would 'level off' at $90 million of outstanding loans (they were around $20 million at the time); the average loan (which had ranged between $40,000 in 1945 and $57,000 in 1948) would increase to $100,000; 200 new loans would be made each year; and losses on bad loans would be about 1 per cent. As we have seen, the number of annual authorizations did run around 200 until 1955, but losses were far below 1 per cent; outstanding loans did not level off at all, let alone at $90 million; and the average size of loans was usually well below $100,000.

At the end of 1950, a second forecast was made. It was recognized that estimates of operating expenses had been too low and that debenture interest costs had risen considerably, and it was believed that the Bank's loans would not reach $100 million for a long time (they actually got there in 1960). It was assumed that the Bank's loans would level off for a period before it would have to sell debentures and that by the end of this period outstanding loans would rise to about $28 million. Rather sadly it was concluded that the chances that the Bank of Canada would receive a reasonable return on its equity investment were remote. It was not long before this forecast was overtaken by reality. Within six months, the IDB was discussing with the Bank of Canada the sale of debentures, and within a year outstanding loans were up to $30 million and still rising.

In March 1953, two more forecasts were prepared, one short-range and one long-range. For the former, covering the period to 1957, it was assumed that outstanding loans would increase at the annual rate of

$3–$5 million and that no new offices would be opened. In fact, however, two new offices (Halifax and Calgary) were opened in 1956, and outstanding loans increased annually up to 1957 by an average amount of $8 million.

The long-range forecast looked far into the future to envisage the Bank as it might be in the 1970s. It was expected that the Bank's outstanding loan balances would reach a maximum of $100 million by 1971 or perhaps, taking a more conservative view, by 1978. By 1971, debentures outstanding would amount to $52.0 million. The forecast did not, of course, allow for an amendment to the act to be made in 1956 and discussed through most of 1955 by which the types of businesses eligible to apply to the Bank for assistance were greatly augmented or for a further amendment in 1961 that made virtually all types of businesses eligible to apply. By 1971, debentures were actually $445.5 million. The Bank reached the level of outstanding loan balances forecast for 1971 (or 1978) by 1959! By 1975 (when the Bank was converted into the Federal Business Development Bank), the balances outstanding on its books were equal to twelve times the figure forecast for 1971–8. By 1975, the Bank was authorizing each year new loans for more than four times the dollar figure that had been forecast for 1971 or 1978 for outstanding balances alone!

The IDB was never kind to forecasters, and in these early years it was already reflecting the enormous and largely unsuspected potential of the field in which it operated – long-term financing for small and medium-sized businesses – and constantly outrunning carefully prepared forecasts.

PART III

A broadened field
1956–61

*This group of IDB officers apparently discussing a loan
application was posed for an article on the Bank that appeared
in the* Financial Post *6 August 1949. From left to right:
B. Heron, K.F. McNamee, E.A. McRae, and A.N.H. James.
Although only the largest applications would be discussed
in such an elaborate way, the picture does illustrate
the care with which proposals were studied.
Photo by Fraser Films Limited, Montreal;
courtesy of* Financial Post, *Toronto*

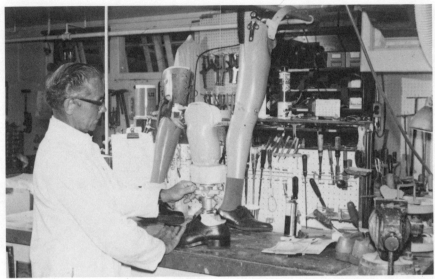

*An artificial leg is inspected (top). This long-established business,
which the IDB assisted with several small loans, was the only
manufacturer of artificial limbs in the Atlantic provinces.*

*This bus company (centre), which transported children to and from school,
became eligible under the 1956 amendments. It received several
loans and was finally servicing over thirty school routes.
Photo by John Evans Photography Ltd, Ottawa*

IDB loans helped this producer of chain-saw parts (top left) to grow until its annual sales had multiplied by ten to fifteen times and it was able to obtain term financing elsewhere.

The logs being drawn up to an eastern lumber mill (top right) that was assisted by the IDB are a contrast in size to those being processed in the western mill pictured earlier.

This prairie machine shop (centre) received several small loans to increase its productive capacity and improve its efficiency.

In addition to retailing and wholesaling tires, this Nova Scotia business retreaded them, as shown above left. The loan to this company reflects the broadening of eligibility for IDB loans that was accomplished by the 1956 amendments to the IDB Act. *Photo by Wamboldt-Waterfield Photography Limited, Halifax*

A plastic-injection moulding machine (top right). This business grew from small beginnings in the 1950s to be a world leader in the manufacture of these machines. Most of the company's output was exported. Following an initial small loan, the IDB made several loans to finance plant expansions, until the company was able to obtain term financing from commercial sources.

This paper mill (centre) is not large as paper mills go, but it carried on a successful business in the manufacture of specialty papers. It received several loans from the IDB to expand and improve its plant. *Photo by Studio Daniel, Enr*

*The Bank provided financing for some of the first helicopter businesses
in Canada, such as this one located in a western province.*

*This very successful northern Ontario company, a manufacturer
of wallboard from wood chips, was assisted by the* IDB. *The photograph
shows one of the large machines used for pressing the board.
Photo by Railton Studio of Photography,
North Bay, Ontario*

CHAPTER NINE

Political developments and legislation

In 1956, the Bank entered a phase that lasted until 1961. It started with an amendment to the IDB Act that increased greatly the number of businesses eligible to apply for assistance and ended with another amendment in 1961 that made virtually all types of businesses eligible. The period was marked by great growth and expansion. The number of offices, employees, and loans approved in a single year had remained relatively constant from 1947 to 1955. By 1961, however, the number of branch offices had increased from four to sixteen, the number of employees had grown from 99 to 402, and the number of loans approved in a year had increased sixfold from 221 to 1,365. The period was also characterized by complex questions of credit policy and by eligibility problems that were almost more troublesome than those of the past.

Changes in management personnel

Prior to the start of this new period, there were several changes in the senior management of the Bank. S.R. Noble, the first general manager, was appointed vice-president at the end of fiscal 1953 and retired in 1954. (This was the only time in the history of the IDB that the title vice-president was used.) He was succeeded as general manager by D.G. Marble, who had been secretary of the Bank of Canada and the IDB. With the appointment of Mr Marble as general manager, L.F. Mundy, who succeeded him as secretary of the Bank of Canada, was appointed secretary of the IDB. A.N.H. James, who as Mr Noble's assistant had borne the title executive assistant, was appointed assistant general manager, the first time this title was used. In January 1955, Graham Towers, the first president of the IDB, retired and was succeeded in that position as well as in the post of governor of the Bank of Canada by J.E. Coyne. Mr Coyne had followed Donald Gordon as deputy governor, an important post in relation to the IDB, and was now succeeded in that position by J.R. Beattie.

Fiscal 1956 was also marked by extensive changes in regional management. W.C. Stuart, who in the previous year had been appointed supervisor at GMO in Montreal, was appointed supervisor at Toronto to succeed J.C. Ingram, who resigned to take a position outside the Bank. F.M. Aykroyd, who had been supervisor for the Atlantic provinces, though stationed in Montreal, became supervisor for Alberta, the Yukon, and the Northwest Territories at a new regional office in Calgary. H.R. Stoker became supervisor for the Atlantic provinces at a new regional office opened in Halifax. The author became supervisor for Manitoba and Saskatchewan at the regional office in Winnipeg, succeeding D.T. Muskett, who resigned to take an outside position. In Vancouver, the regional office for British Columbia remained under the direction of N.C. Tompkins, who had opened the office, but his title was now changed to assistant general manager, British Columbia.

Thus there was a substantial change in management personnel as, in 1956, the Bank entered a new phase in its development. Undoubtedly these changes in management had their own effect on the way the Bank confronted the special problems that marked the ensuing years.

Amendments to the act in 1956

Some of these problems arose from the 1956 amendments to the IDB Act. The limitations placed on the Bank's scope by the definition of 'industrial enterprises' in the original act had created great problems. Indeed, decisions as to eligibility had produced some curious anomalies between businesses that could get assistance and others, scarcely differing from them, that were ineligible according to the definition. Although the Bank tried to become less legalistic in interpreting the definition, serious difficulties had remained. Some measure of the magnitude of these is indicated by the fact that in the fiscal years 1954 and 1955, during which time the Bank authorized a total of 270 loans for new clients, it also turned away 142 inquiries from businesses that were not eligible. Considering that the Bank had been operating for ten years and that there must have been some knowledge in the business world of the terms of the IDB Act, the fact that the number of ineligible businesses approaching the Bank for assistance was equal to half the number of new clients assisted indicates that the eligibility limitations were not well understood among small businesses.

In April 1955, a director of the Bank asked why the definition of industrial enterprise in the IDB Act was 'so restrictive as to exclude many kinds of businesses where assistance from the Bank, if extended without undue risk, should be very helpful.' During the balance of the year, the staff of the Bank was canvassed by management as to what types of business might be included in a new definition, with a view to approaching Parliament for an amendment to the act. When the matter was raised with the board of directors, it was agreed that the Bank should not get involved in 'corner grocers, tourist cabins, automobile dealers and a host of small service and repair shops,' because, quite apart from any merits of their cases, 'the investigation and supervision of loans would involve staff and office resources quite out of relationship to anything heretofore contemplated.' A mere six years later all these businesses were made eligible!

Great effort went into attempts to draft a new definition of 'industrial enterprise' that would embrace all the types of businesses that seemed to need help and which it was thought the IDB could handle, without including types for which existing sources of financing were believed to be adequate or that seemed likely to present the Bank with unfamiliar problems of investigation and administration. There appears to have been a feeling among senior management that where the Bank should operate and had developed some expertise was in businesses that were 'industrial' in some general way. Retail trade and hotels and motels were regarded as examples of the unfamiliar territory into which it would be better that the Bank not venture.

The general manager, Mr Marble, finally suggested that the Gordian knot be cut by the simple device of using the term 'industrial enterprise' in the Bank's legislation without any elaboration or explanation, very nearly anticipating the amendment of 1961 that made virtually all businesses eligible. The president, Mr Coyne, however, thought it unlikely that Parliament would be willing to open the door to the Bank quite so wide. By the autumn of 1955, a definition was agreed on within the Bank, and Mr Coyne was ready to discuss the proposal with the minister of finance. A bill to implement it was introduced in Parliament in March 1956 and, following passage in both houses, was given royal assent on 11 July.[1]

Section 1 of the act, giving the new definition, read as follows:

1. Paragraph (d) of Section 2 of the Industrial Development Bank Act is repealed and the following substituted therefor:

'(d) "industrial enterprise" means an enterprise in which is carried on the business of

(i) manufacturing, processing, assembling, installing, overhauling, reconditioning, altering, repairing, cleaning, packaging, transporting or warehousing of goods,

(ii) logging, operating a mine or quarry, drilling, construction, engineering, technical surveys or scientific research,

(iii) generating or distributing electricity or operating a commercial air service, or the transportation of persons, or

(iv) supplying premises, machinery or equipment for any business mentioned in subparagraph (i), (ii) or (iii) under a lease, contract or other arrangement whereby title to the premises, machinery or equipment is retained by the supplier.'[2]

In addition, other less important amendments were made. One empowered 'an officer authorized for that purpose by the Board' to reach the 'opinions' cited in the IDB Act upon which the extension of credit was to be based – that the applicant was an industrial enterprise, that credit would not otherwise be available on reasonable terms and conditions, and that the investment in the business provided the Bank with adequate protection. This was to permit delegation to officers of the Bank of authority to deal with applications in all their aspects. Also, the limit on the total amount permitted to be outstanding in loans over $200,000 was raised to $75 million.[3]

The bill did not provoke long debate in the House of Commons. There were comments to the effect that the Bank had not really made as much progress as might have been expected, that it was too slow in dealing with applications, that more authority to deal with applications should be delegated to the regional offices, that the Bank did not do enough to make itself known, and that the amendments still left unassisted some types of businesses, such as retail trade and hotels and motels, that needed help.[4]

At the hearings of the Standing Committee on Banking and Commerce Mr Coyne was asked why service businesses were omitted from the amendment; expressing inability to answer fully, he said that he thought it was 'a matter of government policy.' When pressed further, he said: 'I would personally think that the hotel, tourist home or restaurant business is quite different from the industrial operation ... in which we are engaged, and I think you might find that our particular experience ... and the skills we have would be much better displayed in the industrial sphere.' Another member asked about the possibility that the IDB might make loans to farms that did not qualify for help from such special institutions as were dealing in farm credit. To this Mr Coyne made a similar reply: 'Not right now. I think it will take some little time to deal with the added problems which will arise under this proposed bill. The approach we should make to lending for farm operations is, I am sure, different from what we make in regard to industrial operations, and this would probably be better handled by people who specialize in that field.'[5]

The general feeling of the House of Commons was expressed by Mr J.M. Macdonnell, a member of the opposition: 'To sum up, I think one can fairly say that up to the present the Bank has gone along the lines it was intended to follow, that it has been well run and has worked in harmony with the other agencies in the financial structure of this country ... As I listened to the Governor of the Bank I felt that it has been conducted in a sensible fashion.'[6] In retrospect, there is an appropriately climactic sound to these complimentary phrases, marking as they did the end of the Bank's first and formative phase.

Small business as an element in politics

The parliamentary session in 1956 that saw the passage of the IDB amendments also witnessed the bitter and uproarious debate in the House of Commons over the Trans-Canada Pipe Lines, terminated by resort to closure on the part of the government. An election ensued in June 1957: the Liberals, who had held office since 1935, were defeated, and the Progressive Conservatives took office as a minority government. In March 1958 there was another general election, and the Conservatives retained power with one of the greatest landslide victories in Canadian history.

The elections of 1957 and 1958 have a special significance for the history of the IDB since they marked the appearance of 'small business' as an important element in the political world. This is reflected quite strikingly in Hansard, the record of House of Commons debates. In Hansard for the parliamentary session of 1957–8, the first of the new Conservative government, the item 'Small Business' appeared in the index for the first time, and it has never been absent since.

When the bill to establish the IDB was introduced into Parliament in 1944, those opposed to it do not seem to have seen any political risks in expressing their opposition to it even though it was to assist small and medium-sized businesses. In the intervening years the operations of the Bank had attracted little attention in Parliament. A few questions might be asked in the House each year to find out how many loans were made in some part of the country or to urge that the Bank open more branches, and that was about all.

By 1957 all this was changed, and the political parties vied with each other to see who would be the best and earliest friend of 'small business.' The change may have been partly a reflection of developments in the United States, where 'small business' was making itself heard in the political world with the result that in 1958 Congress created the Small Business Administration to help small businesses in a variety of ways. More important, perhaps, were the efforts in Canada of two large groups of businesses – the tourist industry and retailers – not made eligible for IDB loans by the 1956 amendments; they carried on energetic campaigns for their inclusion in the IDB's scope or for government assistance in some other form. A member of the Canadian Tourist Association said in September 1956, 'A tourist operator is as much entitled to a loan from the Industrial Development Bank as a man who wants to start a mine in Northern Ontario or a person wanting to start a lobster factory in Prince Edward Island.'[7] The results of these efforts by the business groups may have been reflected in the budget debate of March 1957 in the House of Commons when J.M. Macdonnell, Conservative financial critic, took up the cause of small businesses, claimed that in periods of credit restraint they had more trouble obtaining credit than did large businesses, and suggested that special efforts be made on their behalf.[8]

In the general election carpaign that came shortly afterward, the platform of the Progressive Conservatives included a pledge of help of some kind for small business. Their leader, John Diefenbaker, was reported as saying that his party, if it formed the government, would set up a committee composed of members of the cabinet and representatives of 'small business' associations 'to take necessary effective action to assist small business, the backbone of our national business.' He was reported also as promising a loan fund for small business at low interest rates.[9] By 1958, following the Conservative victory in June 1957 and in preparation for the election campaign of March 1958, the Liberal party had a similar plank in its platform that declared that small business would get special assistance from a Liberal government, including extension of the facilities of the IDB to embrace the retail trade.[10]

The speech from the throne following the 1957 Conservative victory did not mention small business.[11] However, the Hon. Donald Fleming, minister of finance, during his periodic discussions with Mr Coyne about financial matters, referred frequently to the plight of small businesses in trying to get financing. When Parliament met on 12 May 1958 following the Conservatives' second victory, the speech from the throne stated the government's intention: 'In order to assist small business, there will be established a small business section within the administrative machinery of government. The functions of this organization will be to provide liaison between the government and small businesses, to study the problems of small business and to advise on measures necessary to meet them.'[12]

Legislation to implement this intention did not appear quickly, and the government came under strong pressure from opposition parties to live up to its campaign promises. Everyone wanted to help small business! For the Co-operative Commonwealth Federation (CCF), H.E. Winch, member for Vancouver East, stated that his party had 'always recognized the indispensable role' of small business and suggested a program including broadening the scope of the IDB to include 'service industries' and 'distributive trades' (including tourist and retail businesses) and providing chartered banks with a guarantee of 10 per cent of their losses on mortgage loans to small business. Erhart Regier, CCF member for Burnaby-Coquitlam, claimed that 'this problem of the small businessmen has been considered at considerable length by the CCF movement for a goodly number of years ... We have had a continuing committee studying this matter for many years.' He submitted a proposal for government-guaranteed loans taken from a submission made by the Retail Merchants Association of Canada a few months earlier. For the Liberals, G.J. McIlraith claimed that 'it was a definite part of the program of my party that there would be easier credit for small business, including the extension to the IDB Act in order to make its benefits available to retailers.'[13]

By September 1958 the government had set up a Small Business Section in the Department of Trade and Commerce to investigate and recommend measures to assist small business. To the end of 1959, no results from this had been announced, and in February 1960 C.W. Carter, Liberal member for Burin-Burgeo, introduced a private motion that the government 'give urgent consideration to the provision of some means whereby low interest loans may be made available to small business.' In the debate several members called for the amendment of the IDB Act. This motion was talked out, and in March W.M. Benidickson, Liberal member for Kenora-Rainy River, moved to amend the IDB Act in order to aid small business, particularly retail businesses 'presently crucified under an unprecedented tight money policy of the government,' but this motion also came to nothing.[14]

While all this political manoeuvring was going on, ample opportunity was provided to members of Parliament to criticize the IDB for sins of omission and commission. As the Halifax *Chronicle-Herald* said on 9 February in reporting the debate on Mr Carter's motion, 'The proposal received general support from all sides of the House. The members used the opportunity to hurl brickbats at the Industrial Development Bank and what was called "niggardly and tightwad treatment".' It may seem paradoxical that MPs should have been falling all over each other in their eagerness to be the strongest advocate of making fresh types of businesses such as tourist operators and retailers eligible to apply for loans to a bank that was condemned as niggardly and tightwad, but that was how it was.

While the debates on Mr Carter's and Mr Benidickson's resolutions were taking place, the government was developing plans for financial help for small business. Early in 1960 the Department of Finance asked the board of directors of the IDB to review the categories of business activities that did not appear to fall within the definition of 'industrial enterprise' in the IDB Act. In Mr Coyne's reply in April, the list given included farming, fishing, retail and wholesale trade, tourism, sports, radio, television, parking garages, and professional businesses such as doctors and lawyers. He pointed out that the first two already qualified for loans under other government legislation. Regarding retail, wholesale, and 'service' businesses, he inclined toward the uncertainty expressed by Mr Towers in 1943 that their credit needs suited the type of term financing provided by the Bank. By summer, however, it was reported in the press that the government was going to propose two measures – first, one to set up a system of governmental guarantees of chartered bank loans to retailers and wholesalers, and second, one to expand the operations of the IDB.

Legislation to provide guarantees
for chartered bank loans to small businesses

When the next session of Parliament opened on 17 November 1960, the throne speech contained reference to 'a bill authorizing government guarantees for bank loans to small businesses to finance additions and improvements to their business premises and equipment'; there was no reference to the IDB. A bill to provide for guaranteed loans was introduced on 21 November by the minister of finance.[15]

When the bill was introduced into the Senate, a question was raised as to why the responsibility for financing of this sort was not left to the IDB. R.A. Bell, parliamentary secretary to the minister of finance, said: 'It was thought the government or one of its agencies should not get into a position where it would be providing all necessary intermediate credit. If the IDB, as a subsidiary of the Bank of Canada, were to go into this field it would mean the Crown would be completely taking up the slack in intermediate credit.'[16] By this he probably had reference to the intent of the bill that the funds for the loans would come out of the chartered banks' own resources and to the fact that the IDB could not, at that time, make loans to retail and wholesale businesses.

In any event, the bill passed both houses of Parliament and on 20 December received royal assent. The loans to be made under the arrangement were limited to $25,000 per borrower and were to be extended only to manufacturing, wholesale, retail, and service businesses with gross revenues no greater than $250,000 per annum. Loans were not to extend beyond ten years and were to be used only for the purchase and improvement of equipment and the extension and renovation of business premises. A bank making such loans was to be guaranteed against loss up to 10 per cent of the aggregate of loans made by it under the act. There was to be a limit of $300 million for a period of three years on the total loans by all banks to which the guarantee would apply. Regulations were drawn up setting the rate of interest for such loans at $5\frac{1}{2}$ per cent.[17]

It was expected by some who supported the bill that it would result in a substantial reduction in the number of loans under $25,000 that the IDB would make. Even within the Bank there was some expectation that its operations might be affected. The departments of Trade and Commerce and of Finance saw this as an advantage to the IDB in that it would be relieved of the 'burden' of making unprofitable loans, which they assumed those under $25,000 must be. That to relieve the Bank of this 'burden' was desirable was an assumption they continued to make for some years, without considering the views of the Bank itself. For the Bank, these small loans seemed to have many advantages. While undoubtedly some did not yield a profit, they provided a good substance to the business of an IDB branch, giving its staff excellent training and experience, and helping to keep a branch's operation healthy and effective. Further, as Mr James, when general manager, pointed out in 1963, to avoid them or even to appear to avoid them would be inconsistent with the Bank's role and might support the criticism of some other lenders that the Bank was oriented to a commercial, profit-earning operation. The Bank found that many a business for which the first IDB loan was $25,000 or less grew and obtained several more loans, perhaps finally borrowing hundreds of thousands of dollars. These new arrangements to facilitate small business loans by the chartered banks had no apparent effect whatever on the IDB in the years immediately following the passage of the Small Business Loans Act. The volume of the Bank's small loans continued to expand as fast as that of larger loans, and sometimes even faster.

The next step taken by the government − the enlargement of the scope of the IDB − took place in 1961. It will be discussed in part IV since it marks the opening of the next phase in the Bank's history.

Proposal to separate the Bank from the Bank of Canada

The political developments of 1957−8 had another consequence for the IDB in that they resulted in changes in its board of directors. Directors of the Bank were appointed by the government for three-year terms. Resignations from time to time would require replacements, so that there was always a certain amount of change going on in the composition of the board. It was not, however, until fiscal 1960, or three years after the Conservatives' first victory, that the 'outside' directors, i.e. apart from ex-officio members from the departments of Finance and of Trade and Commerce and from the Bank of Canada, were all appointees of the new government.

A change among the directors of the Bank did not necessarily mean a sudden or drastic change in the oversight the board gave to the Bank's operations. Not only was some time needed to effect a change in the full board of a majority of its members, but it naturally took a new director some time to familiarize himself with how the IDB operated and what it did. Nevertheless, at a time when the world of small business was prominent in political life, it was to be expected that new appointees would bring fresh views of the Bank to board meetings. Early in 1959 one of the new directors suggested informally that the IDB should be separated from the Bank of Canada. He felt that as a subsidiary of the Bank of Canada it was not getting the direction necessary to be aggressive and imaginative in providing for the medium-term financing requirements of small business. In the autumn the matter was raised, at his request, at a board meeting. The board did not agree with him, although by that time a majority of the 'outside' directors were new appointees. However, there was, as a result, a marshalling of views for and against the Bank of Canada connection.

Basically, the director who raised the matter felt that the IDB gave more support than it ought to do to 'big business,' which he defined as businesses borrowing more than $200,000, although only 5 per cent of the loans made had been for more than $200,000. He also felt that its rate of interest, then 7 per cent, was too high and that the term of its loans, which was averaging six years, was too short. By inference, he attributed these practices to the connection with the Bank of Canada.

There was a certain irony in the appearance of these views during Mr Coyne's presidency of the IDB. Within the Bank's discussions and meetings, he was constantly pressing for more liberal responses to credit applications, for new and imaginative forms of financial assistance such as the purchase of equity, for freer interpretations of eligibility, for a more critical view of the terms offered by other lenders, and for increased readiness to accept risk in making loans. His views were well known to operational personnel.

Those supporting the connection with the Bank of Canada cited the recent growth of the IDB as indicating 'aggressive and imaginative' management. They also claimed that there were administration cost benefits from the connection with the Bank of Canada. It was pointed out that the ease with which the IDB financed itself through the Bank of Canada was possible only as long as it was a subsidiary. Finally, it was claimed that the connection protected the IDB against political influences so that it was able to develop a character as close as possible to that of private business enterprise in type of personnel, method of operation, criteria for loans, and so on.

Nothing more came out of the discussion at this time, but the question raised by the director surfaced again in the political discussions about the Bank that occurred in 1961, and these will be considered in part IV.

CHAPTER TEN

Policy problems

Economic background

The years from 1956 to 1961 were characterized by just about as much variety in the business environment as in that of politics. Although at times the economy seemed to renew its expansive trends (1956 and 1959), at others it relapsed into recession (1957–8 and 1960); unemployment reached post-war peaks (1958 and 1960), housing construction declined (1957 and 1960), inventories accumulated (1960), and investment in plant and equipment fell (1960). Underlying all developments were fears of inflation and persistent strains on credit facilities.[1]

The year 1955 closed with the Canadian economy operating at what was considered to be its full capacity.[2] The manner in which the country had progressed since the end of the war was viewed with satisfaction and pride. In its annual review of Canadian affairs, the *Britannica Book of the Year* said: 'As 1955 reached its close, the people of Canada could look back with wonder and humility on the most remarkable ten-year period in their history. It was a decade to stir the national pride and quicken the common pulse ... a decade of expansion and buoyancy.'[3]

It was a mood that did not last. Within little more than a year the annual growth in production had fallen to the lowest levels since the war, with the exception of the recession in 1954, and the rate of unemployment had risen close to a post-war record. The gross national product (in constant dollars) rose by 8.4 per cent in 1956, but increased by only 2.4 per cent in 1957; for the five years 1957–61 inclusive the annual increase averaged only 2.8 per cent. The rate of unemployment, which had averaged 3.2 per cent from 1945 to 1955, was up to 7.0 per cent by 1957, and apart from a modest drop to 6.0 per cent in 1959 remained at that level up to and including 1961. Prices remained relatively stable. From 1956 to 1961 inclusive the consumer price index rose by an average of only 1.7 per cent each year.[4]

The growth in 1955 had been accompanied in the last part of the year by accelerating expansion of chartered bank credit, partly to finance an upsurge in capital expenditures by businesses for resource development as well as for buildings and equipment. These expenditures, as in 1948 and 1951, were being financed to some extent by the banks through the unaccustomed medium of term loans. In addition, there had been substantial growth in consumer credit.[5]

Policies for periods of credit restraint

In November 1955, the Bank of Canada, believing that 'the very rapid increase in the use of bank credit to finance business and personal expenditures had been well in excess of the rate of growth in the country's production which was possible once a condition of virtually fully employment had been reached,' met with the chartered banks to discuss the situation. The result was an agreement by the banks to make no new commitments for term loans in excess of $250,000. In 1956, an attempt was even made by the Bank of Canada to arrange a voluntary agreement with the major instalment finance companies to restrain the growth of consumer credit, but 'agreement of all concerned could not be reached.' In November 1955 and in 1956, however, the chartered banks took 'special steps' to limit lines of credit available to the larger finance companies.[6]

As before, the understanding between the chartered banks and the Bank of Canada was accompanied by the expression by the latter of a desire that the credit needs of small businesses should be taken care of. This thought was repeated in the Bank of Canada's annual reports. Although it was recognized that there was 'no way in which the central bank's operations can induce lenders to take a more favourable view of loans to small business as distinct from large enterprises,' the Bank of Canada did consider 'the matter of providing adequate finance for small business ... to be one of great importance.'[7]

In February 1958 the term-loan agreement between the Bank of Canada and the chartered banks was reviewed, and the level of loan above which the agreed restraints were to be applied was raised from $250,000 to $1 million and 'the banks removed the limitations on lines of credit to instalment finance companies which had been put into effect in 1955 and 1956.'8

The IDB responded to the agreement between the Bank of Canada and the chartered banks. First, it established a policy of scrutinizing all credits with extra care, tending to expect a greater margin of security and better prospects than might have been the case previously; second, it applied this policy with particular emphasis on applications for over $200,000; third, it exercised 'particular care' where funds seemed to be requested to relieve pressure from other creditors or to permit the extension of increased credit to others or the carrying of larger inventories; fourth, it refrained from refinancing programs already wholly or partly financed by a chartered bank; and fifth, it entertained an application to finance a change in the ownership of a business only when it was clear that the business concerned would be benefited.

This last principle reflected recognition by the IDB's management that the money supplied to it by the Bank of Canada should be used for fruitful purposes and not merely to facilitate a fortuitous profit for someone. It became a permanent part of the Bank's lending policies, and a troublesome one at that. If the owner of a business claimed that he wanted to sell it so that he could retire, it was not hard to argue that the business would benefit from having a new and younger owner, and one could hardly follow the vendor after the sale took place to see that he really did retire. Nevertheless, the rule probably protected the IDB from the more obvious cases of simple profit-taking. Only a small proportion of the Bank's loans were affected at the time by this particular rule. In 1960, only 1 per cent of programs financed provided for a change of ownership.

During 1956 and 1957 the branches received six more sets of instructions (in addition to discussions at the annual supervisors' conferences and guidance by telephone) as the Bank's management strove to clarify its thoughts and modified them to meet changing circumstances.

Policies of a fundamental sort were regarded as the responsibility of the board of directors and / or the executive committee (which, under the IDB Act, had the full power of the board except in any matter that the board had specifically reserved to itself). In practice, policy questions that seemed not to be answered in directives that had been issued would be referred by the general manager to the president. He might deal with them himself, but, since the executive committee met weekly, it was not difficult for him to thrash out policy questions with his colleagues on the committee if he needed guidance and support. In 1955-6, Mr Marble (general manager), Mr Coyne (president), and the board and committee were all agreed that small businesses should not suffer excessively during the period of restraint. However, it was found difficult to formulate directives that would provide for this and reflect a proper attitude toward general economic and monetary conditions and at the same time distribute the weight of emphasis of policy among proposals of differing amounts so as to deal properly with all.

One example, taken from instructions of March 1956, will illustrate this. These instructions were communicated by phone to the branches, presumably because it was felt that only when accompanied by verbal explanations and exchanges could they be made clear: 'Be more ready to consider applications up to $50,000 than over $50,000. Be more ready to consider applications over $100,000 up to $200,000 than over $200,000. On applications over $200,000 all the principles set forth in the memorandum of December 22, 1955 to apply.' Even these instructions were more simple than clear, and they cannot have been much more successful than others as a means of communicating a very subtle message, because this particular pattern was not used again.

In November 1956 fresh instructions, basically modelled on those of December 1955, were issued. This time the figure above which applications 'should receive more than the usual careful scrutiny' was lowered to $100,000. Since about 90 per cent of the Bank's loans were below this figure, the policy still reflected a strong sympathy toward the problems faced by small businesses during a period of credit stringency. This was also emphasized in a new instruction that 'it is desirable that small firms should not be unduly hampered in making progress even under present conditions. Credit policy should not be regarded as an inhibiting factor on applications up to $100,000,' provided that the position of other sources of financing was respected. The Bank's constant anxiety to avoid becoming inflexible in its policies is reflected in a concluding sentence that followed a recital of the new instructions: 'It is not intended that the principles should be applied with such rigidity as to preclude consideration of cases where exceptional circumstances are involved.'

In June 1957, the figure for 'more than the usual careful scrutiny' was raised to $200,000; about 93 per cent of the Bank's loans were below this figure. In September, this limiting figure was moved to $500,000, and by December it was removed entirely. By 1958, monetary conditions were no longer regarded as an inhibiting factor in making loans.

The impact of policies of this sort on the Bank's operations is difficult to appraise. Since they were of a very subtle character that made their precise and definite expression difficult, they were, by the same token, hard to interpret and apply precisely. Their effectiveness depended on their being understood by the ordinary credit officer in the field offices.

Since he was several steps removed from the level within the Bank that formulated the policies concerned and drafted the relative instructions, his application of them was inevitably open to some uncertainty no matter how sincerely he tried to follow them.

Loans to foreign companies and subsidiaries

Apart from policy adjustments made during periods of credit restraint, three important policy issues were faced during 1956–61: loans to businesses having foreign ownership; the familiar bugbear of eligibility; and relations with other lenders, particularly the sales finance companies. This section deals with the first issue; the next two sections deal with the second and third issues respectively.

The instructions concerning foreign-owned businesses that were issued in November 1956 had included one to the effect that if an application were received from the subsidiary of a large Canadian or foreign parent company there should be a presumption that the subsidiary could finance its requirements from sources other than the IDB (presumably, from or with the support of the parent company) on reasonable terms and conditions. This was later modified to allow such applications to be considered if other financing proved impossible, but in that event the IDB was to explore the matter of support by the parent for any funds that the IDB might be asked to provide. This rule was basically a test as to the availability of financing elsewhere.

By 1960 and 1961, however, there was a great deal of public discussion in Canada about the extent to which Canadian business was controlled outside the country, and concern was expressed in many quarters about the sale of Canadian businesses to foreign control. In July 1960, an approach was made to the Bank for a loan of $1–$2 million to a Canadian company that had normally been supported financially by a foreign company; the latter was said to be willing to provide the money needed in this instance but only if it obtained control of the Canadian company. The amount requested was enormous by IDB standards and raised questions about policy that had been smouldering for some time. It subsequently transpired that the impression first formed of the Canadian company's situation was not correct. The foreign company either already controlled the Canadian company or had the contractual right to do so whenever it wished. The real purpose of the proposed loan from the IDB was discovered to be that of relieving the foreign company, which was very large and wealthy, of having to provide further money to the Canadian company because the former wished to invest large sums in projects of its own. This was considered an inappropriate situation for an IDB loan, and the proposal was not pursued.

It had, however, served to prompt Mr Coyne to express himself on the issues involved. His view was that the IDB should be prepared to consider appropriate financing in any case in which the only feasible alternative would require the Canadian owners of a business to give up control to a foreign group, or even perhaps to a larger Canadian group. The latter never became a live issue, but the former certainly did and in due course Mr Coyne's approach became Bank policy.

The following January the president suggested the establishment of two new policy principles dealing with foreign ownership. First, the IDB ought not to provide the funds with which a foreign company would make a takeover purchase of an existing Canadian company. Second, foreign companies should generally be regarded as able to obtain funds elsewhere on reasonable terms and conditions, for expansion of any operation they might have in Canada, without aid from the IDB. The general manager, Mr Marble, perhaps recalling the constant hair-splitting judgments required in eligibility questions, expressed apprehensions about the practicality of the second suggestion. Not only did he have doubts about the desirability of taking too strong a stand on the principle of regarding foreign-owned companies as being able to obtain elsewhere funds for expansion, but he foresaw problems arising where decisions would have to take into account various degrees of joint involvement in a Canadian company by both foreign and Canadian interests.

In the next few months various tentative principles were propounded within the Bank, some of which favoured a more severe attitude toward foreign owners than others did. The Bank seemed beset by the old problem of providing for the discouragement of some, not very well defined, proposals while leaving the way open for assisting others that were not much better identified. The problems of the field officers in coping with the principles in practice were very great.

Finally, in July 1961, instructions were issued. The Bank ought not to assist a non-resident to make a takeover or partial purchase of a Canadian business, and it should not be expected to assist businesses owned or controlled by large parent companies or wealthy individuals, particularly non-resident ones. Exceptions to this last principle could be considered if the expansion or establishment of a business to be financed would decrease imports to Canada or increase exports, if the loan was to assist Canadians to take over all or part of the equity in a business in which non-residents were involved, or if the Bank could, by a loan, prevent Canadian shareholders in a Canadian company, partly owned or financed outside the country, from having to diminish or impair their share in the company's equity.

Problems of eligibility

The second major area of policy that presented itself following the 1956 amendment to the IDB Act was the familiar one of eligibility, i.e. determining whether an applicant business was one of those to which, by its act, the IDB was permitted to extend assistance. The Bank started the period with great hopes that the amendment had put an end to the worst examples of this sort of problem. Repeatedly the president and the general manager announced the intention that these questions would now be dealt with in a way much less legalistic; applications were to be reviewed positively, not negatively; and the definition of an industrial enterprise was to be stretched to all reasonable limits. Even before the act had passed both houses of Parliament, Mr Coyne said at a meeting of the Bank's supervisors in May 1956 that the Bank had got away from the legalistic approach which he saw as associated with the Bank's history up to then: 'We can now make policy as we go along, and build up a body of precedents and principles.'

However, in due course the eligibility problems were almost worse than before. The amendment to the act had widened the Bank's scope very considerably but still left many types of business outside its range. These last included farming, fishing, retail and wholesale, hotels, entertainment, communication, professional, and, as was said at the supervisors' conference in the sort of question-begging phrase in which eligibility directives usually ended, 'services not of an industrial character.'

With many new types of business now embraced, the characteristic issue of the new eligibility problems was that of 'mixed' businesses, i.e. those that were a mixture of eligible and ineligible activities. At the supervisors' conference in May 1956 it was decided that in mixed businesses a business would be eligible when its eligible portion formed a 'substantial' part of the whole and the funds to be borrowed were to be devoted to the eligible part. The Achilles' heel of the first of these two criteria was, of course, the word 'substantial.' What did it mean? Fifty per cent of the business? Forty per cent? Thirty per cent? Twenty per cent? And what part of the business was to be measured in this way? Total revenues? Net revenues? Investment in building and equipment for the various parts of the business? Floor area devoted to each part? Number of employees? What if a business seemed to qualify on the basis of some criteria, but not others?

Many businesses raised problems of this sort: importers of food products that also carried on packaging activities; wholesalers and retailers that packaged foods or other products; country grain elevators that also stored and cleaned grain; bottling in cylinders of propane gas by a distributor; repair of vehicles by firms that also sold them – these and many other mixed businesses required difficult decisions. There was no way the Bank could escape from the language of the law. It could not back away from the issues, and it tried in every way to deal with them honestly and sincerely, favouring a decision that was, as far as possible, sympathetic to the needs of the applicant business.

In May 1957, Mr Coyne was still of the opinion that the Bank should decide cases on the basis of the facts in each case and attempt to work out consistent rules of 'application.' However, by November 1958 the view was rather sadly expressed that 'it is going to be difficult to know where to draw the line.'

Two types of business that were definitely not made eligible by the amendment of 1956 were retail and wholesale. In September 1957, a key decision involved a company that warehoused goods that it purchased from its parent company, but also warehoused goods for two affiliates that paid it a fee for this service. Because it received a fee, it was ruled eligible as a warehousing business. Subsequently, however, the requirement that the warehousing service must be paid for in order for the business to qualify was dropped, since a semblance of such arrangements could easily be set up simply to qualify. Accordingly, a company that stored goods on consignment from others, but without a fee for the service, was also ruled eligible; at the same time, a company that stored its own goods for sale or distribution was still ruled ineligible!

From such cases a new consideration emerged by which it was apparently hoped that hair-splitting and anomalous rulings could be avoided: if a service of any kind required a large amount of machinery or equipment, it would strengthen grounds for its being considered eligible because it would have the air and appearance of an industry. By this means scrap metal dealers employing heavy shears and large presses and equipment of that sort were ruled eligible; scrap dealers without this equipment were not eligible.

Fine distinctions were also made with respect to businesses transporting persons. A cable transport installation up a mountain or across a valley was eligible, but 'a ski tow providing a moving rope which drags skiers wearing their skis along the ground' was not. Inclined railways, cable cars, and similar forms of transport to a hotel or restaurant on a mountain were eligible if operated to carry the public generally but not if operated only for patrons of the hotel or restaurant. The principle was, of course, that the eligible activity had to have the nature of a business in its own right.

To keep all these careful decisions in balance and consistent with one another was difficult; to avoid their creating an impression of bureaucratic playing with words was virtually impossible.

In February 1959, the General Manager's Office prepared a circular to provide instructions for the Bank's staff on the whole question of eligibility, but the attempt made in it to clarify the position of wholesalers was not concurred in by all concerned in establishing policy, and it was withdrawn a week later. The system was clearly beginning to break down. In a letter of February 1959, Mr Marble, after summarizing the view of the board of directors as disclosed in previous rulings, said, 'I am not sure, however, that it is always going to be possible to give reasons that will stand up against arguments in decisions on marginal cases.'

In April 1959, another circular of instructions was issued in which the eligibility of mixed businesses was to be based on the eligible activities being 'of a magnitude to take on the character of a business'; on their employing at least 20 per cent 'of the whole of the business,' whether measured in sales, earnings, space occupied, or staff employed; and on the purpose of the proposed loans being for the needs of the eligible activities. This lasted about a year. By June 1960, the purposes of a loan were merely 'not to be used specifically for the ineligible activities' and the amount of a loan was to be in 'reasonable relation to the magnitude of the eligible portion and its expected contribution to overall earnings.' It is not to be wondered at that a year later the act was amended to make practically all types of business eligible to apply for assistance, and the problem of 'eligibility,' which had troubled the Bank from its founding, was virtually ended.

Relations with other lenders

The third policy area that concerned the Bank in the period 1956-61 was that of relations with other lenders, particularly in the application of the requirement in the IDB's Act that it should extend financial assistance only when it was of the opinion that it 'would not otherwise be available on reasonable terms and conditions.'[9] During the debate in Parliament in 1944, as we saw in chapter 2, a lot of discussion had centred around this requirement and the methods by which the Bank would comply with it. During the debate in 1956 on the amendment to the act, however, there was little reference to it. Neither during the parliamentary committee hearings on the original bill in 1944, nor during the committee hearings on the amending bill in 1956, did any commercial lenders, such as the chartered banks or finance companies, make any representations about the Bank or its operations.

The attitude of the chartered banks toward the IDB varied from time to time, from bank to bank, and even, within a bank, from officer to officer. At one point, in 1949, Mr Noble, then general manager of the IDB, commented to the president, Mr Towers, that some banks actually seemed to be trying to discourage their customers from applying to the IDB. Quite often, a chartered bank would intervene once the IDB had investigated an application and offered to make a loan and would make the loan itself. Occasionally, a chartered bank went to considerable lengths to turn a customer away from borrowing from the IDB, even in one instance persuading an insurance company to divide with the chartered bank the provision of the financing required by the client. The IDB had no great objection to all this, since in such cases the money required by the applicant was obviously 'available elsewhere.' It did, in these circumstances, however, feel a certain chagrin when the time and trouble it had spent on an application went unrewarded.

Nevertheless, on the whole, relations with other lenders were fairly harmonious in the early, formative years. Of course, the Bank was not operating at a level to concern other lenders very much. Each year the number of new loans authorized was about the same – 200. The volume was not great, and there was not much growth. With the passage of the 1956 amendments, however, the situation changed. The chartered banks began to make more term loans than before, even though the conditions and repayment schedule might not be set out in a written contract as was the case with an IDB loan. Finance companies, too, were gradually moving into a broader type of industrial term financing than before. Also, the Bank now served a much broader field and many more types of businesses. It tried to respond to the challenge of the larger and more varied field it now served by adopting a more open attitude toward the various types of program submitted to it. It opened new branches where it had not been represented before, and the number of loans approved in a single year increased rapidly. All these developments meant that the Bank's operations touched on those of other lenders more often than before and in new and different ways.

The Bank continued to check as to the availability of funds elsewhere in the case of every application for a loan. Every applicant made a declaration as to its inability to obtain from someone else the assistance needed; for each application, a letter was written to the manager of the applicant's bank to acquaint him with the application and ask for a report; applicants for larger amounts were required to provide letters of refusal from other lenders; any applicant, no matter how large the amount requested, whose proposal or financial position seemed likely to be of interest to another lender was directed to explore the possibility of getting a loan elsewhere; and so on. For the vast majority of applications to the Bank, these methods seemed to work well. Only in a relatively few cases did questions arise. However, the Bank could not ignore any of these. Even a single case could become a *cause célèbre*, and so each question of principle as it arose had to be considered carefully and conscientiously even though this often required an amount of time and effort quite disproportionate to the number of cases affected.

It was considered impossible to set up standard criteria or tests for deciding whether the terms and conditions offered by another lender were reasonable. Each case had to be decided on its own merits. Did the amount of financing offered meet the needs of the business, and were the terms of repayment within its earning ability? An affirmative answer to these questions generally led to a decision that the terms offered were reasonable; a negative answer, to the conclusion that they were not.

The Bank sometimes saw major differences between its approach to the needs of its applicants and that taken by other term lenders. Its loans were not made simply as an advance safely secured by a charge on a certain item or on certain items of security. The IDB made a decision on any application, no matter what the size or purpose, only after an exhaustive analysis of an applicant's financial statements covering a period of years, a visit to his place of business to study his operation in action, and an analysis of his marketing system, production flow, cost controls, working capital needs, quality of management, and future prospects. It described itself as lending 'on the strength of the whole business.'

This process was, of course, time-consuming, and the Bank was later obliged to streamline these methods in some respects in order to speed up things. Nevertheless, one of the great strengths of the Bank's procedures for handling applications was that a borrower got a great deal more than money with his loan. In many cases, he got his first introduction into the proper analysing of the problems of his business, and this was one of the greatest benefits that a loan from the IDB bestowed. Many, many borrowers testified to this, and often another lender would acknowledge the depth of understanding of an applicant's problems and needs developed by the IDB credit officers and engineers.

The Bank also saw as a characteristic of its approach to lending that it determined the repayment terms for a loan on very broad considerations.

It naturally considered the nature and life of the security pledged, but it gave first importance to the capacity of the borrower to pay, on the basis of the past earning record and future expectations of the borrowing business, and the general outlook for the industry. Often this approach would suggest a term of repayment longer than might be set by another lender. If the longer term seemed necessary for the borrowing business, this might, in the eyes of the Bank, justify its regarding the other lender's terms as unreasonable.

In 1950, the average term of repayment for IDB loans was 65 months and by 1961 it was 76 months.[10] During the period 1955–61, however, the Bank was recording in its internal policy memoranda arguments for longer terms, and in the next few years the average term lengthened considerably. When it seemed necessary, the Bank would stretch the repayment of a loan over ten years or so, and occasionally over a longer period.

Effect of differences in interest rates and the refinancing of loans made by others

As a rule, then, it was on the basis of a broad comparison of terms in the light of an applicant's needs that a decision on the reasonableness of alternative terms was reached. Between 1956 and 1961, however, when credit stringency was a live issue for much of the period, and the level of interest rates a sensitive issue, some consideration was given to the difference between the IDB's rate and that charged by others.

While the Bank was small and its field restricted, it tended to measure itself against the chartered banks and the mortgage companies, and, accordingly, its rate of interest was usually set above that of the former (by 1 per cent or so) and close to that of the latter. Now, however, with a much larger field and a greatly increased volume of business, the IDB found it had to range itself with many other types of financial institutions with interest rates sometimes much higher than those of the chartered banks or mortgage companies, and perhaps higher than the rate of the IDB. To have raised its interest rate above these rates would, in the view of the Bank, have been to stultify its role of helping small businesses.

The suspicion that a difference in interest rates might affect the Bank's opinion as to the reasonableness of the terms of alternative financing available to an applicant aroused some other lenders to strong criticism of the Bank. The finance companies in particular saw the IDB as obtaining its funds from a privileged source, the Bank of Canada, at a lower cost than they had to pay for their funds and as being free of the obligations they faced of earning a commercial return for their shareholders on their equity and of paying income tax. They felt it was unfair that a rate of interest they set to meet their circumstances might be stigmatized as unreasonable by comparison with the IDB's rate simply because their rate was the higher.

Another irritant in relations with other lenders was the occasional refinancing or prepayment of one of their loans from the proceeds of an IDB loan or as part of a program the Bank helped to finance. As we shall see, these cases also raised questions as to what should be the attitude of the Bank toward the interest rates of other lenders. There had always been a certain amount of refinancing, particularly to clear away an existing encumbrance on some asset to be included in the security to be given the IDB for a loan. In its later years the Bank was more willing than in its early years to accept a security position junior to an already existing charge in favour of another lender, but this did put the Bank in an uncomfortable position. If the borrower got into financial difficulties and was unable to maintain his loan payments, the Bank did not have complete freedom in deciding how to react. Its usual practice of exercising patience and trying to help the borrower to work his way out of his troubles might be compromised by the presence of another creditor secured on all or part of the borrower's fixed assets. This was particularly bothersome to the Bank if its security charge was a secondary one. In such a case the Bank felt that by accepting a junior position it had, in effect, guaranteed the other lender against loss in the event of some differences between them as to how to handle a bad loan or in the event of liquidation. This view sometimes led to the Bank's requiring that an existing debt be refinanced by the proceeds of any loan it might make. Such refinancing had not caused serious difficulty. In the early part of the period 1956–61, when the Bank was influenced by the general atmosphere of credit restraint, a number of refinancing proposals that came to the Bank seemed designed for the relief of the lender to whom the debt was owed, either to improve its own liquidity or to rescue it from a difficult situation, rather than for the relief of the applicant. Proposals of this character the Bank would usually decline.

The more expansive attitude adopted by the Bank after the period of restraint passed away, however, resulted in its having to consider more closely than it had previously done what its policy on refinancing should be, since the amount of refinancing was increasing. In fiscal 1955, only 1.6 per cent of the dollar amount of programs submitted to the Bank by applicants for assistance represented refinancing; by 1961, this proportion had risen to 10.4 per cent.

This increase did not necessarily mean that the IDB was itself refinancing the existing debts. There would usually be funds contributed to a program from other sources than the loan from the IDB. These funds might come from resources of the applicant business, from the owners or shareholders of the business, or from another outside lender, private or commercial. In 1961, IDB loans accounted for 75 per cent of the money needed to finance the programs with which they assisted. The balance of the money came from other sources and in many instances could well be regarded as having handled any refinancing that was done. There were other cases in which a loan from the Bank was specifically intended to refinance an existing debt. An applicant might seek to refinance a debt if he felt that the period provided for its repayment was too short for the earning power of the borrowing business. If the Bank agreed with this view and the other lender was unwilling to lengthen the time for repayment, and if other aspects of the proposal were satisfactory, the IDB might make a loan to retire the existing one. The Bank also continued its practice of sometimes providing funds to retire an existing debt in order to provide the Bank with a clear first charge on pledged assets.

These reasons for refinancing an existing loan were not difficult to explain to another lender even though it might not agree in every case that they were valid. Now, however, the issue was sharpened by the increase in the frequency of refinancing and complicated by the questions that the expansion of the Bank and the broadening of its field had raised about the relationship between its rate of interest and the rates of other lenders. If the IDB refinanced a loan or lien bearing a rate of interest higher than its own, it was difficult for the other lender to believe that the difference in interest rates was not the true reason for the refinancing. The Bank thus had to consider more closely its attitude toward the interest rates of other lenders.

In November 1957, at which time the IDB's rate was 6 per cent, the supervisor in Winnipeg asked the general manager whether funds offered by another lender at $7\frac{1}{2}$ per cent should be regarded as available on reasonable terms and conditions. The resulting exchanges between Mr Coyne and Mr Marble produced guidelines that lasted for several years. Mr Coyne's first views were expressed orally, but recorded in a letter Mr Marble wrote in reply to the supervisor who raised the question: 'there should be no disposition to intervene to make a loan where money is available at $7\frac{1}{2}$ under present conditions, and certainly we should avoid giving the appearance of seeking to displace such loans ... However, if the approach [in this case] is satisfactory on all other counts, we see no reason why under present circumstances we should not proceed with it notwithstanding that money is available from another source at 7½%.' The meaning of all this was interpreted as lying in the last sentence – a rate of interest 1½ percentage points over the IDB rate could, in some circumstances, be regarded as unreasonable.

Mr Coyne then followed up with a written expression of his views in a letter to Mr Marble:

I doubt if it is possible to make a hard and fast ruling as to whether the availability of money elsewhere at 7½% means that it is available on reasonable terms and conditions.

A great deal would depend upon such matters as the relation between the amount of the loan and the value of the property, the term and repayment provisions, the additional security or other advantages obtained by the lender, the question of whether the loan was made wholly on real estate security or partly on the profit prospects of the company, and so on.

We are not in the business of making straight mortgage loans, but where criteria are satisfied, I would not hesitate to make a loan at our regular rate of 6% merely because we thought the applicant could obtain a loan elsewhere at 7½.

The supervisor felt the need for further guidance and asked if a rate of 7 per cent set by another lender should be considered unreasonable. Mr Marble sent him a verbatim report of Mr Coyne's written views as outlined above. That there was some uncertainty about the matter is indicated by the decision not to circularize these views to the other supervisors but to let them, in Mr Coyne's term, 'percolate.' This latter process apparently included several conversations between Mr Coyne and Mr Marble and discussions at supervisors' conferences. These discussions served to simplify the policy down to considering anything above the Bank's rate (6 per cent) to be unreasonable, particularly if the financing involved the borrower in a longer term for repayment than desired.

This was a drastic view, and by the end of 1958 it was apparent that Mr Coyne's opinion was not as firm as it had seemed to be on the point of what was a reasonable rate of interest and what was not. Nevertheless, the Bank's policy remained along the lines described above.

By the spring of 1961, experience with actual cases was steering the Bank toward a milder attitude on the rates of interest attached to alternative financing. In April of that year, Mr Coyne expressed doubt that 'we have ever taken the stand that an interest rate 1% higher than our own is unreasonable, having regard to all the circumstances.' This prompted Mr Marble to refresh Mr Coyne's memory with a review of the exchanges of letters and the conversations of 1957 and 1958 as outlined above, and Mr Coyne then responded with a statement that came to be the general basis of the Bank's attitude toward the rates of interest offered by other lenders.

Acknowledging some earlier inconsistency, he wrote to Mr Marble: 'My starting point is that it is scarcely possible to say that the general rate of interest or range of rates of interest on first mortgage loans by private lenders can be regarded as unreasonable ... On the other hand, it may be that the borrowing enterprise desires a loan for a [different] term than would be acceptable to an ordinary mortgage lender, or desires a loan for an amount which exceeds the normal proportion of loan to asset value required by mortgage lenders, or has some other good reason for desiring to obtain funds on terms and conditions suitable to its circumstances but which would not be provided by ordinary mortgage lenders. In that event, there is a case for consideration by the Bank.'

The 'general' rate level on the market was to be considered reasonable, and thereafter the rate of interest charged by an alternative lender was rarely considered by the Bank in determining whether the conditions of advances to a business by the other lender should be regarded as unreasonable. It remained, however, a sensitive matter in the minds of other lenders, particularly the finance companies, and, as we shall see, it arose again in a few years.

More flexible attitude in general policy

In terms of general policy, the Bank was moving toward a freer and more flexible position in credit matters. At the supervisors' conference in May 1960, the president stressed the desirability of a more relaxed attitude on the part of the Bank toward applictions for credit. In June, Mr Marble issued fresh instructions to the branches to reflect these views: 'Loans for moderate amounts have been recommended and approved where the estimated value of the security has not provided any margin in excess of the loan, or where in fact it has been less than the loan. In such cases, it would be expected that the future prospects of the business would be regarded favourably, and that we should have full confidence in the character and capacity of the owners and management. In the application of this policy it will be necessary that good judgement be exercised. It would not be constructive if the Bank were to provide funds to facilitate ill-conceived projects unlikely to succeed or to attempt to rescue a business that seemed to be doomed.'

The terms used here show much diffidence and caution, and by September Mr Coyne and Mr Marble were discussing how the policy ideas might be better conveyed to the field. Mr Marble felt that 'while the written word could come back to haunt us, ... letters from me to Supervisors to lower any barriers there might be, while still retaining reasonable principles, would be better than a general talk at a meeting.' When drafted, the letters, although genuinely seeking to establish new lines of thought on which to appraise credit applications, still approached the matter in a somewhat roundabout way: 'We feel that even more can be done to expand the operations of the Bank for the general benefit of small businesses ... It is hoped that an overly cautious attitude towards enquiries for loans will not tend to nullify these greater efforts to make available to businessmen the facilities the Bank has to offer ... It occurs to us to wonder whether full advantage is being taken of the invitations to relax somewhat the standards previously followed which may have been somewhat conservative in the case of loans for smaller amounts ... In the exercise of a more liberal lending policy, we are prepared to see more losses but as long as they are confined to relatively small amounts in individual cases, the aggregate would be unlikely to cause concern.' These words were hardly a trumpet call to action, but the shift in general policy that they represented was genuinely felt. The problem lay in finding a proper and true expression of it.

A major problem in developing new policies was the difficulty of so wording instructions as to cover all the shades of meaning and ensure that no appropriate opportunities for a loan would be overlooked and no improper ones accepted. The language used in the various directives illustrates these problems: 'care will have to be exercised'; 'no hard and fast rules can be laid down'; 'but there may be deserving cases'; 'should not be unduly hampered'; 'unless circumstances are unusual'; 'may be considered in appropriate cases'; 'not too rigid'; 'should not be considered unless the circumstances are such as to justify exceptional treatment.' These are examples of phrases used to qualify instructions, to round off their corners, so that allowance could be made for the impossibility of anticipating all the situations that might be encountered and the likelihood that no two cases would be exactly the same. An experienced IDB credit officer, schooled in the unique circumstances in which the Bank had to operate, could usually interpret and apply the nuances of this sort of uncertain and qualified language almost as if it were as clear as day, but as the period wore on it would sometimes be uncertain that the intended policy in a particular case had been successfully communicated to the field officers.

Perhaps this review of some of the policy developments of the period 1956−61 might conclude with quotations from a letter from the general manager to the supervisor in Calgary in December 1957. The monetary stringency seemed to have passed, and the Bank was adjusting itself for more 'normal' conditions and moving toward a broader outlook on credit policy.

You have properly inferred that we now have greater freedom in lending, particularly in the case of smaller loans [not defined as to amount], *but while we are quite prepared to take reasonable risks, it certainly is not the intention to court losses for the purpose of expanding our business. There is a risk of loss in almost every loan and we are quite prepared to suffer losses which occur because of misfortune or error of judgement on the part of the Bank but we should not seek accounts in which losses are expected.*

One factor not mentioned is that I think we need not be so restrictive as we have [been] *in the past as to the purpose for which smaller loans may be required, as long as we do not stray too far from the general principles ... Our attitude should be constructive and not negative ... We would not rule out a case where other factors being favourable the value placed on the physical security was something less than the loan but ... we should have full confidence in the character and capacity of the management ... and feel that the future of the business is sound.*

CHAPTER ELEVEN

Operational developments

Growth in lending

Against this background of policy problems, the Bank recorded great growth and expansion. In the six years from 1956 to 1961 inclusive it approved 4,025 loans, 98 per cent more than in the preceding eleven years. The number of loans approved in 1961 was over 500 per cent greater than the number approved in 1955, the last year of the previous period, and 84 per cent greater than in 1960.

The 1956 amendment to the IDB Act, extending the Bank's scope far beyond the fields of manufacturing and commercial air services to which it had been virtually limited, was a major factor in this growth. Of the 4,025 loans approved from 1956 to 1961, 26 per cent were to businesses made eligible by the amendment. Borrowers in such newly eligible businesses as trucking, construction, passenger transportation, laundries, dry cleaners, repair garages, and warehousing were rapidly becoming almost as numerous as the manufacturers the Bank had originally been established to serve (see Table 5).

For the time being, however, manufacturing remained the largest category of loans. Fish plants in the Atlantic provinces, furniture and garment factories in Quebec, and sawmills in British Columbia were among those given material support. One of the most striking examples of assistance in the manufacturing field was that given to the hosiery industry, in which new technology, immigrant initiative and energy, and a great shift in market demand were all involved in switching the industry away from full-fashioned hosiery to seamless hosiery in the 1950s. Prior to

TABLE 5

Loans approved 1955–61

	1955	1956	1957	1958	1959	1960	1961
By number							
Manufacturing	201	308	319	430	442	500	870
Transportation and storage	18	26	41	50	60	83	137
Construction	1	5	13	32	37	59	143
Wholesale	–	1	4	4	8	16	28
Retail	–	1	6	2	8	18	52
Agriculture	–	–	–	–	4	2	8
Restaurants	–	–	–	–	–	–	–
Hotels and motels	–	–	–	–	–	–	–
Other	1	8	18	53	40	62	127
Total	221	349	401	571	599	740	1365
By amount							
Total ($millions)	17	39	30	36	31	39	71
Average ($thousands)	79	113	75	63	51	52	52

SOURCES: Brief, Tables 8 and 10.

the Second World War, the Canadian hosiery market was largely served by a few giant manufacturers producing full-fashioned stockings. The end of the war naturally brought a great upsurge in demand. The large profits that resulted drew new entrepreneurs into the industry and prices fell. At the same time the market was demanding stockings of an even finer gauge, and this required the producers to invest in new machinery. The post-war companies were able to meet this situation by acquiring the most modern machinery as they expanded. A great deal of this expansion was financed from earnings and the private resources of the owners, but the IDB assisted with loans totalling approximately $700,000 from 1948 to 1955, by which time the post-war companies were, almost without exception, borrowers from the IDB.

The Bank had extended this assistance with a degree of caution in regard to both security values and to the scale of expansion. It did not help any mill in process of formation or those that were under-capitalized. All the loans were subsequently justified by the strictest adherence to repayment schedules.

The market now experienced a revolutionary change. Partly as a result of a greatly improved product and perhaps partly because of the inscrutable ways of fashion, in 1955–6 demand for the previously quite rare seamless stockings began to rise abruptly, first in the United States and subsequently in Canada. While full-fashioned stockings were selling for $5 a dozen, seamless hosiery was fetching $10 to $12 a dozen.

This change in market taste had an enormous influence on the competitive situation. The seamless machines were much smaller than the full-fashioned ones, had about one-twelfth the productive capacity, and cost only $2,000 to $4,000 each, as compared with $20,000 or more for each of the full-fashioned machines. Capital requirements for equivalent production were comparable, but the size and price of the seamless machines made possible a fresh wave of new entrants into the industry.

At first the new machines were readily available, but demand was such that soon two or three years were required for delivery. The new entrants, more willing to risk quality of product than their better-established rivals, resorted to cheaper and rebuilt machines costing only $1,200 to $1,500 each. Small mills were set up with between 10 and 30 machines initially, occupying rented premises and with minimal overhead costs. Many of these were assisted by the IDB. At first, because of the uncertain state of the market, the Bank required quite good margins, lending between one-quarter and one-third of the total capital required for a new business. Later, when the industry became more stable, it might lend 45 per cent of the cost of machines. The term of the loans was kept relatively short, between two and four years. From 1956 to 1961, when the great burst of expansion pretty well ended, the Bank assisted some twenty companies with over forty loans for a total of approximately $3 million. By 1960, two-thirds of the seamless stocking market was supplied by the post-1956 manufacturers, and the price of the stockings had been cut in half.

The role of the Bank in these developments was described by A.H.C. Lewis, the credit officer at the Bank's Montreal office who handled almost all these loans, in a memorandum written in 1960, on which the above review is based: 'The part the Industrial Development Bank has played has been one of enabling the consumer to obtain goods of the type he [or she] wants at a reasonable price, still allowing a proper profit to competitive producers.'

New branches

The second development behind the growth in 1956–61 was the opening of more branch offices. In the first two years of the Bank it established four offices – in Montreal, Toronto, Winnipeg, and Vancouver. In the nine years following no offices were opened, and the number of employees, which had risen to 99 by 1948, was still 99 in 1955. During these years there were suggestions from outside the Bank that more offices should be opened. This was particularly so on the Atlantic provinces' behalf, and in 1948 Mr Towers engaged in an exchange of letters on the subject with a correspondent in New Brunswick. Mr Towers, though agreeing that additional offices should be established in due course, described the obstacles in the way of opening new offices as he, and the general management of the Bank, saw them: 'It is not practicable to open a branch unless the volume of business on hand and in prospect is such that the staff – even a very small staff – will be kept fully occupied ... There is also the point that good men are exceedingly hard to find.' Although Mr Towers also declared, somewhat ambiguously, that the absence of a branch should not be related to profit considerations, the cost of operating a new branch with inadequate revenues from a small number of loan accounts was undoubtedly borne in mind.

In response to the complaint that the volume of the Bank's business in the Atlantic provinces was less than it ought to be, Mr Towers pointed out, possibly with some exasperation, that 'if we don't get applications from the Maritime Provinces, we cannot authorize loans.' This was perhaps not quite fair to his correspondent; the later experience of the Bank showed very clearly that offering small and medium-sized businesses the convenience of a local branch of the Bank was the best way to lead them to make use of the Bank's services.

From fiscal 1956 up to and including fiscal 1961, the Bank opened twelve new offices – two in the summer of 1956, four in 1959, three in 1960, and three in 1961. This was a considerable achievement, following, as it did, a long period of no change in the number of branches or employees. The first new branch was opened in Halifax in June 1956, with H.R. Stoker as supervisor, to serve all of the Atlantic provinces as a regional office; in 1959, another regional office was opened in Saint John under R.H. Wheeler as supervisor, to serve New Brunswick and Prince Edward Island, and the Halifax office became responsible for Nova Scotia and Newfoundland alone.

Since 1952, the Atlantic area had been served by a supervisor, Atlantic provinces, situated in Montreal who would, in Mr Towers's words, 'visit that territory five or six times a year.' That this was not an adequate answer to the problem is indicated by the figures in Table 6 for annual loan authorizations in the Atlantic provinces. The change following the opening of a branch in Halifax in June 1956 (and the amending of the IDB Act about the same time), and another in Saint John in 1959, was remarkable.

A new regional office was opened in July 1956 in Calgary under Frank Aykroyd as supervisor for Alberta and the Northwest Territories. The Vancouver office had served this area, and though it had been most diligent in sending representatives into Alberta at frequent intervals, the

TABLE 6

Annual loan authorizations in the Atlantic provinces 1950–61

	Number of authorizations	Amount of authorizations ($)
1950	18	825,000
1951	16	822,000
1952	18	684,000
1953	12	363,000
1954	2	175,000
1955	11	458,000
1956*	22	7,310,000*
1957	38	2,561,000
1958	54	2,665,000
1959	71	2,526,000
1960	74	2,772,000
1961	135	5,665,000

*The large dollar figure for 1956 was affected by one large loan for several million dollars.
SOURCE: Brief, Table 12.

results had been only slightly better than those achieved in the Atlantic provinces while they were served from Montreal. Table 7 gives figures for annual authorizations in Alberta. The improvement following the opening of the Calgary branch was very similar to that experienced in the Atlantic provinces after branches were opened there.

The success of the Halifax and Calgary branches was an indication that the broadening effects of the 1956 amendments had opened up to the Bank real opportunities for service to small and medium-sized businesses in areas not strong in manufacturing. It also showed that one effective answer to the criticisms that the Bank was not active enough and not sufficiently well-known was to extend the branch office system. Three years later, in 1959, four more branches were opened: Saint John in April, London and Quebec City in June, and Regina in September. In the same year, a regional office, separate from the General Manager's Office, was set up in Montreal, with the author as supervisor to cover Quebec and eastern Ontario, formerly served directly by GMO. H.R. Stoker became supervisor of the Winnipeg office and was succeeded as supervisor at Halifax by E.A. Bell.

Offices were opened in 1960 in Ottawa, Sudbury, and Edmonton and in September 1961 in Hamilton, St John's, and at the Lakehead. Some of these new branches took the Bank right into the frontier and less-industrialized areas. This presented new problems in travelling to and serving distant communities. Engineers in the prairie region were quite

TABLE 7

Annual loan authorizations in Alberta 1950–61

	Number of authorizations	Amount of authorizations ($)
1950	11	346,000
1951	8	119,000
1952	8	1,578,000
1953	21	2,047,000
1954	8	931,000
1955	14	694,000
1956	25	2,232,000
1957	28	1,621,000
1958	58	2,796,000
1959	56	2,745,000
1960	76	3,465,000
1961	131	5,990,000

SOURCE: Brief, Table 12.

used to driving to an investigation through temperatures of −50°F along prairie roads hidden by a horizontally moving blanket of drifting snow.[1] In British Columbia all-night travel by bus had sometimes to be resorted to in serving the inland communities. In the early days of the Sudbury branch, visits to clients or the investigation of applications sometimes required travelling by small planes, four-wheel-drive trucks, or amphibian Canso aircraft.[2] Once GMO, after checking the travel expense accounts of the BC engineers and finding no hotel room billing for one night for J.E. Nordin, inquired very suspiciously, 'Where did Mr. Nordin spend the night of ... ?' As it happened, Mr Nordin had been investigating a small lumber operation in a remote part of the province and had had to be put up for the night by the applicant at no expense to the Bank.

Although the sudden outburst of branch openings reflected a changed concept of the Bank's potential, the full possibilities for growth were not yet clearly apprehended and each decision to open an office was reached slowly and cautiously. For example, the possibility of opening up in Newfoundland was raised in January 1960. There were only 9 loans on the books there, and the supervisor at Halifax and the general manager both held the view, as expressed by the latter, that 'the prospects of increasing the volume to a point where we could keep a competent person interested and suitably employed are somewhat remote.' As an alternative, Halifax branch stepped up the visits made by its officers to St John's to about one a month. By January 1961, these visits had stirred up enough inquiries that the supervisor talked of having occasionally to stretch out some of these visits to three weeks and cautioned against strengthening publicity efforts in the province as the burden of inquiries had reached such a point that to stimulate them further might do more harm than good 'if we are unable to follow up the flow of enquiries by a rapid processing of acceptable proposals.' He suggested renting desk space in the premises of a local trust company for the use of the visiting IDB officer, and this was done in April. In the summer it was decided to establish a full office, and it opened in September with N.J. Weedmark as manager. The results were almost instantaneous. Two loans had been made in the province each year from 1956 to 1958 inclusive; in 1959, 7 had been made, and in 1960, 8. The increased visits and publicity in 1960 and 1961 had resulted in 21 in 1961, but in 1962, the first year after the branch was opened, 60 were approved.

Each branch, as it was opened, was assigned a precisely defined area to be served. This practice had been started when the original four offices were opened as a natural way of describing the huge areas each served. The system was continued when the new smaller branches were opened, and each branch operated pretty strictly within the bounds of the area it covered. In practice this was very convenient as publicity efforts increased and each branch diligently cultivated its assigned area. It would have been confusing to local businessmen, and a useless duplication of expense, had representatives of several branches of the Bank presented its story in the same town.

As the branches vied for a good record of achievement, each manager and his staff regarded their area with great jealousy and resented any intrusion from neighbouring branches. A classic example was Lloyd-minister: down the centre of its main street ran the boundary between Saskatchewan and Alberta, which also formed the boundary between Calgary and Winnipeg branches. The staff of each branch watched with a wary eye the activities of the other branch on the other side of Main Street to be sure that its members stayed in their own part of town. In later years, when a branch had been opened in Saskatoon as well as Regina, the manager of the former, Frank Stewart, heard, with indignation, that the Regina manager, Harry Baker, had been talking about the Bank to bankers and businessmen in towns north of the invisible line that marked the boundary between the two branch territories. Deeply hurt by this clear breach of decent behaviour, he complained to his supervisor in Winnipeg, J.C. Ingram,[3] that he was 'being nibbled at by poachers,' and the over-zealous Mr Baker was instructed to stay in his own area.

By 1961, the Bank had at least one office in each province except Prince

Edward Island. Quebec, Ontario, and Alberta each had two or more. This last circumstance introduced a new element into the Bank's structure. The four original offices and those opened in Halifax, Calgary, and Saint John had been established as regional offices under the direction of supervisors. As other new offices were opened to serve smaller, localized areas, these were put under the direction of managers and placed under the supervision of the already established regional offices. For example, the new branch in Edmonton under a manager came under the oversight of the supervisor in charge of the Calgary branch office.

A curious feature of these arrangements as they evolved was that the regional offices continued to serve the local areas around them. The supervisors of these offices thus had dual responsibility – to oversee the direct lending activities of their own offices and to supervise the activities of other offices. Not for several years were the supervisors relieved of the first responsibility and confined to the role of supervising the work of a number of local managers' offices.

Change in attitude toward publicity

A third development bearing on the Bank's growth during the years 1956–61 was a gradual change in its attitude toward publicity. Up to 1955 the principal efforts in publicity had been in speeches made to service clubs and community groups, articles about the Bank in financial newspapers and professional and trade journals, and information pamphlets supplied to branches of chartered banks and to trade and business associations. These efforts were considered to be safe from any accusation of aggressive competition with commercial lenders and were credited with the great virtue of being relatively inexpensive. Annual expenditures on publicity had been approximately $2,000 until 1955, when the Bank's first series of display advertisements appeared in twenty-one business journals and papers, increasing expenditures that year to $12,500. This advertising program was continued. The number of journals and papers used changed from time to time, but annual expenditures remained around $12,000–$14,000 for several years.

While this was a rather modest venture into advertising, it represented a new attitude to publicity, and this stimulated and encouraged publicity efforts among the field officers of the Bank. They called on branch bank managers, chartered accountants, lawyers, boards of trade, municipal officials, and other leaders in the communities served by the Bank's branches to acquaint them directly with its role in the business world. These efforts had the advantage of still being quite inexpensive, and they also served to familiarize the branch officers with the territories they served. Branch officers became energetic in seeking opportunities to make speeches about the Bank to local service clubs and business groups. Visits to chartered bank branch managers and other business leaders helped, since often one of those called on would have the responsibility of finding speakers for a service club and be delighted to find that the visitor from the IDB was available.

The top management of the Bank deliberately encouraged a more expansive mood in the Bank, and this was stimulated by the enlarged scope resulting from the 1956 amendments, the opening of branches, the increasing volume of lending, the advertising programs, and visits by branch officers to community business leaders. In 1958, the Ontario supervisor, W.C. Stuart, initiated what was to develop into one of the Bank's most effective instruments for publicity and growth. He was invited to supply someone to speak about the Bank to a class of business students at the University of Western Ontario. He took advantage of an officer's being in London, Ontario, for this purpose to put an advertisement in the local newspapers of London and neighbouring towns inviting people to come and see the officer to find out about the Bank or to discuss business problems. This sort of thing had been done in the early years of the Bank when the regions of the Atlantic provinces and Alberta were being served by branches many hundreds of miles away, and this way of cultivating communities in the area served by a branch now became gradually the Bank's principal method of reaching businesses in the smaller centres.

More dramatic than this as a reflection of a changed attitude in the Bank toward publicity was a proposal made early in 1959 and adopted that a film about the Bank should be made. A script was prepared, built around the true story of a loan made by the Bank to a small manufacturer of dental burrs or drills, and by the fall of 1960 the film was finished. Using fictitious names, it told the story of a small business launching itself into the manufacture of a new product and needing a new plant. The film showed the way in which an approach to the Bank for financial assistance was processed. Copies of the film were supplied to the Bank's branches, which showed it on local television stations and to service clubs and business groups. Twenty years later the film was still being used by IDB officers to help new development banks in other countries to set up proper procedures.

The Bank was moving toward the view of publicity mentioned by Mr Marble in a letter to a supervisor in 1955 and quoted earlier, 'that we should make our existence known to those who might have need of our facilities.' It had, however, to consider its supplementary role, as in all matters of policy, and to recognize, as Mr Marble wrote in 1957, 'that an attempt to advertise our wares is always subject to the criticism of competition.' In addition, the management of the Bank was very concerned about costs. In June 1958, the view was taken that 'the cost of a semi-national advertising campaign would not be justified.' In March 1959, it was proposed that the Bank advertise in a daily newspaper in each of Montreal and Toronto on the grounds that 'both have a substantial circulation in the smaller communities in their areas,' but the proposal was turned down because the cost, put at $2,600 for a year, would be 'out of line with the business benefits.' Nevertheless, the Bank was definitely moving toward a freer attitude about advertising and other forms of publicity, and by the latter part of 1960 advertising in daily newspapers in the large metropolitan centres had begun, though on a somewhat smaller scale than in the dailies and weeklies of smaller communities. By fiscal 1961, annual expenditure on publicity had increased to $80,000, which included advertising in newspapers, printing a publicity brochure, 'advertised visits' by the branches to small communities, printing the annual report, and a charge for amortizing the cost of the new film.

Not all proposed new publicity initiatives were approved. A suggestion that the issuing of the annual report should be accompanied by a prepared press release was declined. Some years later, this became a regular practice; in fact, separate releases were later prepared for each region. In 1959, W.C. Stuart suggested that an IDB desk or booth be set up at suitable conventions or exhibitions, but the idea was rejected with the comment that it was 'not quite the type of publicity in which we should engage.' This, too, later became a regular means of publicity; collapsible booths were made that could be shipped from one exhibition to another, and a special slide show for use in the booths was prepared.

The recognition that publicity was necessary if the Bank was to do its job resulted in the appointment of J.W. Sivers as information officer in 1961. For the first time the Bank had professional knowledge and skill on its own staff to guide the development of publicity programs.

The changes in the Bank's attitude toward publicity and public relations that occurred in the years 1956 to 1961 can be well illustrated by a quotation from circular instructions sent by the general manager in the latter part of 1960: 'At the May [supervisors'] Conference, the desirability was stressed of IDB officers taking advantage of opportunities arising to publicize the Bank's facilities by means of addresses to business and professional groups, visits to bank managers, showing of the IDB film, etc. The Conference Notes requested that a monthly report be made to the General Manager covering activities of this nature.'

Not only were field officers permitted or encouraged to engage in publicity activities; they were now instructed to do so.

While publicity was now encouraged, one characteristic of the Bank's attitude to public relations that had a restraining influence deserves to be mentioned, namely, a certain wariness or prudence in contacts with politicians or newspapers. A good illustration of this occurred in 1958. The Manitoba government had decided to establish a lending agency of its own to be known as the Manitoba Development Fund. The proposal was supported in public discussions by claims that the IDB did not assist small businesses. In the *Winnipeg Free Press* for 28 October, the minister of industry and commerce, the Hon. Gurney Evans, was reported as making a statement to this effect in the legislature. A couple of days later the Winnipeg *Tribune* published an editorial with a similar claim, viz. that making loans for less than $25,000 was 'a field in which the Industrial Development Bank has not been active.'

The Winnipeg supervisor of the IDB wrote to Mr Evans and called on the editor of the *Tribune*, pointing out to both of them that the criticism of the Bank was not justified, since in the previous year nearly 40 per cent of the IDB's loans had been for $25,000 or less. Mr Evans acknowledged the correction in a courteous letter of reply, and the *Tribune* did the same in an editorial on 1 November. Nevertheless, Mr Marble, general manager of the IDB, was alarmed by these exchanges and expressed his views in a letter to the supervisor: 'We both agree that the Bank should not be expressing any opinion on the legislation [i.e. to set up the Manitoba Development Fund] and we both agree that it is quite appropriate for you to state facts and figures in any speech you might make or in response to any questions that might be addressed to you. I think the basic difference is that I take the view that if a newspaper or a politician chooses to take a stand that we might consider wrong even on a factual basis, it does not serve any useful purpose, and in fact may be harmful, to attempt to make corrections since with a newspaper or a politician it is always the case that they will have the last word.'

This posture was gradually modified by the Bank but never completely abandoned, and it sometimes led to the Bank's refraining from responding to public criticisms, even though these might be based on errors of fact.

Loans: volume and distribution

A circumstance that may have been partly a cause of the Bank's growth and partly a result was that the Bank seemed to reach out to smaller businesses to a greater extent than before. The size of loans made had been tending to increase, but it now became smaller again. From 1945 to 1950, the average size of loans approved had been approximately $50,000; the highest average was $57,000 in 1948. For the years 1951–5, however, the average size was $75,000, and in 1956, $113,000, the highest level ever reached. This last average figure was affected greatly by a few large loans to commercial air services and for warehousing and cold storage. From 1956 on, the average size of loans approved fell steadily to $52,000 in 1960 and 1961 as the primary role of the Bank to assist small and medium-sized businesses became preponderant.[4]

An increasing outreach by the Bank is also reflected in the proportion of loans that went to businesses that had not previously borrowed from the IDB. It was always a characteristic of the Bank's operations that a borrowing business might receive additional loans from the IDB as the business grew and needed financing for further expansion. Some borrowers received 4 or 5 loans over a period of years, and some of these might be approved even before the preceding ones had been paid off. Even in fiscal 1945, the Bank's first year of operation, 6 of the 103 loans approved were made to businesses that had received their first loan only a few months before.

The Bank was always happy (other lenders felt much too happy!) to assist further a borrower that had so prospered with earlier assistance that additional financing was required. It also regarded as an indication of its success in bringing its story to the business community the number of loans made each year to businesses that had not previously borrowed from the Bank. By 1948 the proportion of loans going to existing borrowers was up to 30 per cent. For the next eight years it never fell below that level, and in fiscal 1951 it was 37 per cent. However, this proportion fell to 22 per cent in 1961, while the proportion of loans going to new customers rose to 78 per cent.[5] The Bank was making many more loans than before to both groups, but the group of new customers was growing more rapidly.

A great deal of the growth took place in Ontario. Up to fiscal 1955 Quebec had led in the number and total dollar amount of loans approved, but from 1956 to 1961 Ontario was well out in front as is seen in Table 8 (figures are given for 1955, for comparison).

TABLE 8

Regional comparison of number of loans authorized 1955–61

Region	1955*		1956	1957	1958	1959	1960	1961*		Population 1961 (percentage)
Atlantic	11	(5)	22	38	54	71	74	135	(10)	10
Quebec	71	(32)	96	98	147	140	147	258	(19)	29
Ontario	61	(28)	121	129	169	193	264	538	(39)	35
Prairies	34	(15)	48	54	111	107	141	301	(22)	17
British Columbia	43	(20)	60	80	89	86	110	128	(10)	9
Territories	1	–	2	2	1	2	4	5		–
Total	221	(100)	349	401	571	599	740	1,365	(100)	100

*Percentages in parentheses.
SOURCE: Brief, Table 12.

TABLE 9

Regional comparison of amount of loans authorized ($millions) 1955–61

Region	1955*		1956	1957	1958	1959	1960	1961*	
Atlantic	0.5	(3)	7.3	2.6	2.6	2.5	2.8	5.7	(8)
Quebec	5.3	(30)	11.9	7.1	10.4	7.6	9.4	16.9	(24)
Ontario	5.6	(32)	9.1	9.1	10.5	9.9	12.4	24.9	(35)
Prairies	1.9	(11)	4.8	3.8	5.9	5.8	6.8	14.6	(21)
British Columbia	4.1	(24)	6.2	6.9	6.2	4.7	7.1	9.0	(12)
Territories	0.1	–	0.1	0.6	0.3	0.1	0.1	0.1	–
Total	17.5	(100)	39.4	30.1	35.9	30.6	38.6	71.2	(100)

*Percentages in parentheses.
SOURCE: Brief, Table 12.

Table 9 gives dollar amounts for the same regional comparison.

In Table 8 a comparison is made with the distribution of population instead of with manufacturing employment, as in Table 2. With the broadening of the IDB Act the population figures are more suitable for comparative purposes. The distribution of loans matches population quite well in most cases except that in numbers of loans Quebec was well below the population percentage; in both tables the loans in the prairies and British Columbia are higher.

The biggest percentage gains in loans both in numbers and in amount were in the Atlantic and prairie regions. By 1961, as compared with 1955, the former had nearly tripled its share of the dollars loaned and doubled its share of the number of loans. The prairie share also increased substantially.

New departments at GMO

The 1956 amendments to the IDB Act and the growth that followed put pressure on both organization and procedures. In that year the first steps were taken to crystallize a clearer departmental structure. Those in charge of legal and insurance work, H.M. Scott and W.L. Mundy respectively, became 'chiefs' of their departments. (The title was adopted from Bank of Canada practice and provoked the obvious remarks about the relative shortage of ordinary Indians). There was some strengthening of the general oversight of operations by the appointment of an administrative assistant, A.M. Swan. His duties were not defined, however, and consisted of his taking on any tasks (including the processing of credits) assigned to him by the general manager or assistant general manager.

In 1957, the Bank modified slightly the system that had existed since the beginning by which GMO doubled as a regional office. A new department of branch credits, with G.R. Elliott as 'chief,'[6] was set up to process credits received from offices outside Montreal. Even this modification of structure had an anomalous aspect to it in that credits originating in GMO in its role as a regional office in Montreal did not have to pass the scrutiny of the new department but were processed under the supervision of the general manager, assistant general manager, or administrative assistant. This was changed in 1959, when a separate regional office for Quebec and eastern Ontario was created, and GMO devoted itself exclusively to overseeing the operations of the Bank as a whole.

Development of the Bank's structure continued along these rather simple lines. By 1960, there were at GMO four departments headed by appointed chiefs – with the addition of loan accounting under Hugh Duncan – and two administrative assistants without defined duties. In this evolutionary process there emerged two features that, though unusual, were, in some degree, an unshakeable tradition of GMO. First, the ultimate disposal of credit submissions was spread among a number of people who had other important duties. While all incoming credit proposals were processed by the branch credits department under its chief after 1959, once the processing of an incoming credit was completed, it would be taken to any one of a number of officers – general manager, assistant general managers, executive assistant, or, for a few years, an administrative assistant – for a decision. As the Bank grew, officers' titles changed, and ultimately a general manager for credits and a superintendent for credits were appointed, but the principle of dispersing the responsibility for credit decisions remained. Second, while the reaching of a decision on a credit involved discussions among those taking part in the processing of it, the final decision was the responsibility of an individual, not of a group or committee.

Delegation of authority to approve loans
and other efforts to shorten processing time

The 1956 amendments permitted the board to go ahead that year with previous plans to delegate authority to the general manager, assistant general manager, and supervisors along the lines projected in 1954. This was not done without some apprehension since the Bank was believed to be operating in a risky field, and there was uncertainty that uniformity of judgment and decision in credit and policy matters could be maintained. These apprehensions reflected two basic concepts in the approach of the Bank's management to its responsibilities. One was that there was a more than normal risk in lending in the area in which the Bank operated. That this view was shared by others was certainly apparent in the parliamentary debate in 1944, and it would seem a reasonable view considering that the Bank was to provide assistance only when it was of the opinion that financing would not otherwise be available on reasonable terms and conditions. The risk was enhanced by the extent to which the Bank's operations concentrated on small businesses, where management might be inexperienced and prospects of success difficult to assess.

A basic concept was that in matters of credit policy there should be uniformity in all parts of the Bank so far as possible. All applicants should be treated in the same way, and policy, whether dealing with eligibility, alternative sources of financing, the acceptability of proposals for loans for working capital or changes of ownership, the terms offered by other lenders, or other matters, should be uniformly applied. The experience of the Bank confirmed the desirability of this. Many times it found that a decision on a particular loan or application, whether that decision was to grant a loan or to refuse one, to take certain security, to set a certain interest rate, or to behave in some particular way in the administration of a loan, would soon be known to other owners of businesses, particularly in the same industry and even in another part of the country. As a crown corporation, it felt it had to be consistent in all dealings.

A member of Parliament once spoke to the general manager of the Bank about a prepayment indemnity that one of his constituents was being asked to pay. When the Bank's policy was explained to him, he had no quarrel with it. He was most anxious, however, to know whether the policy was applied invariably and uniformly. He did not want his constituent to be in a position of paying the indemnity and then hearing of someone who had not had to pay. When assured all were treated the same, he was quite satisfied.

These considerations led to GMO's continuing to receive copies of some of the documents involved in the processing of credits whether or not the credits were of a size to require submission to the general manager. For example, copies of all initial interview memoranda, records of subsequent interviews with an applicant, and copies of all investigation reports were sent to GMO. This was done to enable GMO to monitor what was happening in the field. It may have affected the processing time for an application, since the knowledge that a memo or report was to go to senior officers at GMO may have resulted in these documents being written with more care and style than was necessary. Certainly these practices did contribute to the flow of paper pouring into GMO to be read.

Various means of shortening procedures were tried, and the regular supervisors' conferences discussed the question over and over again. In 1958–9, a preprinted form for use as a 'short form' of investigation report for small and simple proposals was introduced but received general use only in Ontario branches. In 1954, it had been suggested to the branch offices that credit officers should work in teams, presumably so that discussions of an application between the junior and senior members of a team would, in some cases, obviate the need to involve the supervisor of the branch until the last stages of an application. This device was not used extensively. In 1957, a step was taken in the opposite direction with the introduction of the practice of sending to all branches copies of 'summaries' for all loans made throughout the Bank as a means of letting all parts of the Bank see what was being done elsewhere. By fiscal 1961 the Bank was approving over 1,300 loans per year and had sixteen branch offices, and the amount of paper handled for this alone, without considering the 'summary' copies required for each director and for filing, was very large. It was becoming clear that revision of procedures was not keeping pace with the growth that was taking place.

CHAPTER TWELVE

Operating results

Revenues and profits

Table 10 gives operating results for 1956–61 inclusive, with 1955 given for comparison. In the six fiscal years 1956–61, the Bank earned net profits (after provision for transfers to the reserve for losses) totalling $8,127,000 – slightly more than the $7,383,000 earned in the preceding eleven years. The average annual yield on the Bank's capital (share investment plus the accumulated reserve fund) was 3.7 per cent. This did not quite reach Mr Towers's hopes of a yield equal to what the Bank of Canada could have earned by investing in long-term Government of Canada securities. In the six-year period, these securities, with a term of ten or more years, yielded on the average approximately 4.5 per cent per annum.[1]

Interest rates on loans and debentures

The main source of revenue for the Bank was interest on its loans, although other income, relatively small in itself, was important when compared with the net profits to which it contributed. From 1956 to 1961, there was no drastic change in the Bank's lending rate of interest, as shown in Table 11.[2] For part of 1960 it rose as high as 7 per cent, but generally it ranged from 6 to 6½ per cent.

The intention, as expressed by Dr W.C. Clark when the original IDB Act was being considered in Parliament, that the Bank should be a 'non-profit-making institution' earning a 'modest or relatively moderate

TABLE 10

Operating results ($millions) 1955–61

	1955	1956	1957	1958	1959	1960	1961
Interest on loans	2.2	2.6	3.5	4.5	5.5	6.3	7.1
Other income	–	0.1	0.1	0.2	0.4	0.2	0.3
Total income	2.2	2.7	3.6	4.7	5.9	6.5	7.4
Operating expenses	0.7	0.9	1.1	1.3	1.6	2.0	2.8
Interest on debentures	0.3	0.3	0.9	1.5	2.0	2.5	3.0
Total costs	1.0	1.2	2.0	2.8	3.6	4.5	5.8
Net income	1.2	1.5	1.6	1.9	2.3	2.0	1.6
Provision for losses	–	0.2	0.3	0.7	0.7	0.5	0.4
Transferred to reserve fund	1.2	1.3	1.3	1.2	1.6	1.5	1.2
Percentage rate of return on capital (shares plus reserve fund)	3.7	4.0	3.9	3.5	4.1	3.9	3.0

SOURCE: Brief, Tables 2 and 3.

profit,' was a narrow target at which to aim.[3] F. Aykroyd, supervisor at Calgary, stated the Bank's problem in this regard in a letter to Mr Marble in May 1961, when the Bank was wrestling with its interest rate policy: 'Under all circumstances this Bank will have to continue to walk a "tight rope". If we make too much money, we will be described as gouging the public. If in any single year we showed a loss, we would be described as an incompetent government enterprise.'

Much of the discussion in Parliament that resulted from the new wave of sympathy for small businesses dwelt on the need for low-interest-rate loans.[4] Since the annual cash cost to a business, after tax, of an extra ½ per cent on a loan of $25,000 would be only about $100, a business, even a small one, that depended on a margin of safety of this magnitude for its survival might seem in a perilous state indeed. Nevertheless, when in March 1959 the executive committee of the Bank raised the IDB's lending rate by ½ per cent because of an urgent need to respond to market conditions, one of the newly appointed directors said that this meant that the Bank would be 'charging small business at least 1% more and big business can get accommodation at a chartered bank,' and he added that this was not his idea of the way the IDB should operate.

TABLE 11

Average rates of interest on new loans made and on new debentures issued 1955–61

	Average interest rate (percentage) on new loans made	Average interest rate (percentage) on new debentures issued	Difference, or 'spread'
1955	6.00	2.34	3.66
1956	6.04	3.35	2.69
1957	6.50	4.55	1.95
1958	6.00	3.79	2.21
1959	6.34	4.81	1.53
1960	6.96	5.33	1.63
1961	6.50	4.71	1.79

SOURCE: Brief, p. 47-A.

Dependence on debenture financing

Although the times appear not to have favoured prompt action by the management or the board to raise the lending rate whenever market rates rose, the Bank was increasingly concerned about the market rate of interest in another way through its growing dependence on the sale of debentures. At the end of fiscal 1955 (i.e. at the start of the period now under review), share capital was $25 million and outstanding debentures were only $9,500,000. By the end of fiscal 1961, share capital had risen to $26 million, because amendments to the IDB Act passed that summer had increased the permitted share capital beyond the previous limit of $25 million. Debentures outstanding, however, had risen in the same interval by $69,400,000 to $78,900,000.[5] The rates of interest on debentures were automatically determined according to a formula agreed on with the Bank of Canada based on the yield on Canada government securities of the same maturities and so were very responsive to changes in the money markets. Not only was the Bank becoming dependent on the sale of debentures, but the rate of interest on them was rising more rapidly than the lending rate, as Table 11 shows. (The Bank's lending rate was usually changed by ½ per cent at a time. In 1956, 1959, and 1960 the fractional averages shown in Table 11 resulted from changes made in the course of each of these years.)

The increases in debenture rates shown in the table were partly due to the additional fraction of 1 per cent added to the rate on government securities. Starting at 0.10 per cent in 1955, this additional fraction was

TABLE 12

Operating results expressed as percentage of average loans and investments outstanding
1955-61

	1955	1956	1957	1958	1959	1960	1961
Income as percentage of average loans and investments	5.34	5.72	5.69	5.87	6.27	6.41	6.61
Less:							
Debenture cost	0.73	0.68	1.45	1.92	2.13	2.45	2.68
Operating costs	1.74	1.82	1.73	1.56	1.74	1.98	2.47
Net profit before provision for losses	2.87	3.22	2.51	2.39	2.40	1.98	1.46

SOURCE: Brief, Table 4.

increased to 0.15 per cent in 1958; then, first to 0.25 per cent and later to
0.50 per cent in 1960, and finally to 0.60 per cent in 1961.

The automatic changes in the debenture rates were not necessarily
accompanied by changes in the lending rate, which usually occurred at
much longer intervals. From the standpoint of the operational management in Montreal, the increasing dependence of the IDB on debenture
financing for its funds introduced a new and important element into the
Bank's operating costs that had to be taken care of. GMO was anxious to
operate the Bank on a business-like basis and keep it out of an operating
loss position. As a result it was now more inclined than previously to
favour raising the Bank's rate promptly when the market showed an
upward trend. However, the Board and head office officials, who in
earlier years had been interested in moving the lending rate up in order to
provide a satisfactory return on the IDB's equity, seem now to have
inclined toward slower or more moderate increases more in line with the
economic and political climate of the day and to have placed less emphasis
than previously on the return on equity represented by the Bank's profits.
As a result, as shown in Table 11, while the lending rate increased by 1/2 of
1 per cent from 1955 to 1961, the average rate on new debentures
increased by 2.37 per cent.

The importance of debenture interest as a cost is also reflected in Table
12 in which revenues and costs are related to a common base, viz. average
loans and investments outstanding. In 1955, debenture cost was 0.73 per
cent of average loan and investments. In 1961, it was 2.68 per cent, an
increase of 1.95 per cent. In the same interval operating costs rose 0.73
per cent. Debenture cost was eating rapidly into the margin between
income and operating costs.

It will be recalled that when the IDB was founded it had been thought possible that whenever debenture financing was needed the debentures might be sold to the public. The idea had surfaced briefly in 1951 when a draft prospectus had been prepared. The subject now emerged again. In 1960, the president, Mr Coyne, made a speech in Vancouver in which he referred to hopes that the IDB might be able to sell its debentures to the public. This aroused the interest of several brokerage firms. Discussions went on for several months, the board of directors approved the idea in principle, and a draft prospectus was prepared. No serious difficulty seems to have arisen over the possible terms of an issue. Conversations with financial houses seemed to contemplate a term of five years and a coupon rate of interest close to what the Bank was paying on new debentures being sold to the Bank of Canada. The amount contemplated for the first year's issue was only $5 million. Considering that outstanding debentures at the time (1960) were $63,600,000, that in 1961 they increased by $15,300,000, and that in 1962 they increased by $36,400,000, the contemplated venture into the public market was modest.

However, problems soon arose. The debentures would not have qualified as legal investments for Canadian insurance companies because the IDB's earnings record would not have met the requirements for this. The minister of finance, Donald Fleming, expressed himself as cool toward the idea with the obscure and cryptic comment that any indication that the IDB could get funds from the public would play into 'the hands of those who want expansion of plans involving IDB.' In any event, nothing came of the idea of selling debentures in the public market.

Operating costs

While the Bank was faced with an increasing expense from debenture interest, it was able to control its ordinary costs of operation fairly well. Between 1956 and 1961, annual operating costs per customer fell slightly, from $1,050 to $1,000. Success in controlling costs may have been partly the result of a decision by the executive committee in June 1954 to have credits of up to $25,000 authorized at the branch level and credits of up to $100,000 authorized by the general manager. Following the 1956 amendments, these arrangements were converted into full delegation in the interests of reducing costs and expediting the processing of credit applications.

A variety of other efforts were made to speed up the procedures for handling applications and disbursing loans and so reduce costs. These included partial disbursements before the security for a loan was completed, abbreviated reports by investigating engineers, and the forgoing of the investigation of a proposal by one of the Bank's engineers, leaving this to the credit officer handling the application. Some of these measures ultimately became part of normal procedures, and the original system under which all applications were processed in the same way was gradually modified in the interests of reducing costs and saving time.

All items of expense, in fact, were closely scrutinized with a view to their being kept down. R. Prokopetz, now assistant, office services, for the Federal Business Development Bank, has recalled a good example of this. In 1955 or 1956, one of his duties as a messenger at GMO was to take loan contract documents to the office of the notary concerned to have the notarial seal put on them. The office was near Place St Henri, three to four miles from the Bank's offices on Victoria Square. C.I. Stuart, deputy-secretary, who would dispatch Mr Prokopetz on this errand, was torn between recognition of the considerable distance to be travelled and a desire to hold down the Bank's costs. Balancing the two, he reached what seemed to him a satisfactory compromise: he gave Mr Prokopetz one car-ticket. He was free to choose which way he would walk (or run), but rain, snow, or storm it was all the same – one car-ticket!

Policies on prepayment of loans and various fees

Of increasing importance in the Bank's revenues were those received from various fees such as the prepayment indemnity and the commitment fee. From 1949, prepayments on a loan had required the payment of an indemnity of six months' interest on the amount of the prepayment. This requirement did not rouse many objections when loans were being negotiated, but in some cases strenuous complaints were made when a prepayment was actually made. Most of the objections dwelt on the fact that the IDB was a 'government' bank, and it was claimed that the indemnity was 'unfair' or 'unjust' or 'contrary to the intent and purpose of the IDB.' As one complainant put it, 'This amount ... is exorbitant, particularly when it is paid to a Government bank set up for the sole purpose of encouraging industrial expansion.'

Often the objections arose when the business of one of the Bank's borrowers was sold to other interests, perhaps at a substantial gain to the vendors, and retirement of the Bank's loan was a condition of the sale. In one case only two instalments on the Bank's loan had been made when the business was sold, so that the indemnity was calculated on virtually the whole loan. This prompted strong objections.

The Bank continued to take the position that in permitting all or any part of a loan to be prepaid at any time without any consent from the Bank being required, it was offering its borrowers an option that few commercial lenders then gave. Some protection for its position as a lender was needed, and the indemnity called for by its loan contracts was considered quite modest and reasonable by comparison with the requirements of other lenders. Nevertheless, it was decided in October 1956 to calculate the indemnity on a sliding scale related to the length of time remaining in the life of the loan when the prepayment was made. This was intended to apply the highest indemnity to any prepayment made shortly after the IDB loan was disbursed and ultimately to establish a point in the term of a loan after which only a small indemnity would be required.

In June 1960, a formula was adopted providing for an indemnity of 6 per cent of the amount of the prepayment (the Bank's lending rate was then 7 per cent) for the first three years of a loan, after which the indemnity fell by 1 per cent a year to a minimum of 2 per cent. This was by no means the last attempt at a satisfactory formula, but the progressive aspect was permanently retained.

The basis for commitment fees was also reviewed. In April 1957, the general manager, Mr Marble, proposed that a commitment fee should be paid by a customer at the time that he accepted the terms of a credit; if the credit was actually drawn down in due course, so that no commitment fee was needed, the amount paid would be applied on the first amount of interest due. This idea had been proposed by Mr Marble in 1946 when he was secretary of the Bank, apparently with the support of Mr Towers. It had been opposed by the then general manager, Mr Noble, who felt it would expose the Bank to a great deal of criticism. It was now opposed by the supervisors. They felt that, since a borrower had already to pay legal fees, sometimes trustee fees, and in many cases travel expenses to get to a branch of the Bank to discuss his proposal, another expense would be going too far. Accordingly, the proposal was dropped, and the commitment fee continued to be collected only if, after acceptance of the terms of a credit, the borrower did not make use of it. However, in June 1957, the rate was changed from 1 per cent to $50 plus 2 per cent of the amount by which the credit exceeded $25,000, representing an increased charge over the previous basis of 1 per cent per annum for the period the credit was unused before it was cancelled.

The same instructions of June 1957 introduced a 'stand-by' fee. It was assumed that for most credits a period of four or five months after the borrower had accepted the terms offered by the Bank would suffice to complete security and pay out the proceeds of a loan. If any amount remained undisbursed after that time, the Bank considered it was 'standing by' with its money until it was needed. It felt that this gave the borrower protection for his financing for which the Bank should receive some compensation by way of a stand-by fee. A fee of this sort had been levied in the past in special cases. It was now applied to virtually all credits. It required the payment of a fee of 2 per cent per annum on any portions of a credit remaining undisbursed later than four or five months after acceptance of the Bank's letter of offer.

In the six years 1956−61 the total amount collected from these three fees was $789,000, equal to 10 per cent of the total amount of net profits (after provision for a transfer to the reserve for losses) in those years. This was a significant contribution to the Bank's earnings, and in later years the amounts received from these fees were sometimes even more important.

In 1959, $258,000 was earned from an unusual source. This represented the profit received by the Bank from disposing of shares in two borrowing companies the loans to which had been considered large enough and risky enough to warrant the Bank's participating in the equity of the companies.

In 1960, net profits were also affected, although indirectly, by an unusual occurrence. It had been the practice to place in a special reserve, included in 'Other Liabilities' in the balance sheet, any interest paid by borrowers of which the affairs had reached such a state that there were fears that their loan accounts would develop into losses and have to be written off in part at least. The theory behind the practice was that it would not be sensible to show earnings that, while received as interest payments, might from a practical standpoint have to be regarded later as a partial offset to losses. In fiscal 1960, this practice ceased, and, as explained in the annual report of the Bank for that year, the balance of $315,000 in this special reserve account was transferred to the reserve for losses. This, of course, diminished the amount that had to be transferred to the reserve from 1960 earnings.

One further measure that affected income was the adoption of the practice of setting the rate of interest on any new loan that absorbed the outstanding balance of an old loan at the full current rate of interest if this were higher than that on the old loan. Many borrowers prospered to the point that they needed an additional loan to finance more expansion before any previous loans were paid off. In the years 1956−61, one out of every four loans was made to an existing borrower.[6] Often the new loan was made in an amount to absorb the balance of the old loans so that there would be just one loan contract. This made payments simpler for the borrower and made administration of the account easier for the Bank, particularly in the event of liquidation, since the Bank could then proceed on only one contract embracing all the security. New loans of this character were called 'superseding' loans.

To apply the current higher rate of interest on the full amount of such a new loan contract had the appearance of raising the rate on the outstanding balances of the previous loans that were absorbed into the new contract, and customers objected to the practice on this score. The general manager, Mr Marble, however, argued that this view was not correct and claimed that, in effect, the old loans had simply been retired by a new larger loan that naturally bore the higher current rate of interest. It was even hinted that there was a certain generosity in the Bank's terms because the borrower was not asked to pay the Bank a prepayment indemnity on the old loans that had been 'prepaid' by the new loan from the Bank, as the borrower would have had to do if the new financing had been obtained elsewhere.

The practice described was ultimately dropped and the rate for a 'superseding' loan established by combining the current rate for the newly provided money with the old rates for the existing loans to be absorbed, resulting in a blended rate. Formulae and paperwork of a horrendous character were used to perform the arithmetic required for this exercise. Gradually this was avoided in most cases by making a new loan for only the amount of new money required, called a 'supplementary' loan, and allowing the old loans to continue under their original contracts.

Loss experience

Two elements of the Bank's operating picture during the period 1956–61 remain to be considered: write-offs and transfers of funds to the reserve for losses. Loan balances outstanding at the end of the 1956–61 period were considered to be in a somewhat better condition than was the case at the end of the previous period. On 31 August (the new date used for the annual review of loans) 1961, the proportion of loan balances considered satisfactory was 86 per cent, as compared with 84 per cent on 30 September 1955, while 14 per cent were considered as open to possible write-offs. These latter totalled $17 million, but both the auditors and the Bank's officers estimated the write-offs on these loans to be only $2 million.

At the end of September, the balance in the reserve for losses account was raised to $2,700,000. This represented a margin of 38 per cent over estimates of possible losses. During the period 1956–61, the reserve did not have quite the same margin of protection that it had had in the previous period, 1945–55. In the earlier period, the balance had been on average 46 per cent greater than possible loan losses as estimated by the Bank's officers and 60 per cent greater than estimates by the outside auditors. From 1956 to 1961, however, the margin over the Bank's estimates of possible loan losses averaged only 26 per cent, as compared with a margin of 27 per cent over the auditors' estimates. In three years – 1958, 1959, and 1960 – the balance in the reserve for losses account just about covered exactly the Bank's estimate and the outside auditors' estimate of possible losses, with no margin. Part of the explanation for the apparent decrease in the margin probably is that during these years there developed a very large loss on one 1956 loan ending in a large write-off in 1959, and this single case distorted the usual provision for margins.

If no more money had been transferred to the reserve from the earnings of the years after fiscal 1961, the balance in the account at that time would have been approximately $600,000 over the amount required to take care of all the write-offs of loans authorized up to then that did actually materialize later, up to and including fiscal 1981 of the successor bank, the Federal Business Development Bank.

As was pointed out in chapter 8, figures of write-offs have to be used carefully in determining the Bank's loss experience with its loans because of the long period that would usually intervene before a 'bad' loan terminated in a write-off. One loan authorized in 1952 was not written off until 1971, and in each fiscal year up to 1976 at least one of the loans authorized in 1961 was written off. Of all the loans approved between 1956 and 1961, 13 were written off in those years, but 78 were written off after 1961, including 2 written off after the IDB was absorbed in 1975 into the Federal Business Development Bank. If we gather together all the write-offs on loans originating 1956–61, we have to 1980 a total of $2,531,000 (net after recoveries), representing 1.18 per cent of the net authorizations 1956–61. The corresponding figure for 1945–55 was 0.47 per cent. It would appear, then, that the various elements affecting the Bank's activities in those years – the 1956 amendment to the act, the various periods of credit restraint, the efforts to be more responsive to applications for assistance, and the increased number of branches and new efforts at publicity – produced a relative increase in losses as well as an enormous increase in loan volume.

Although it was not intended that the Bank's operations should be oriented to profit-making, the Bank had now passed through a very profitable period. For eight successive years, 1954–61 inclusive, net profits after provision for a transfer to the reserve for losses were over $1 million per annum. They did not surpass that figure again until the Bank's final five years, 1971–5. This makes a fitting note on which to end our review of the years 1956–61. The Bank was now about to enter a completely new phase in its history, confronting new circumstances and fresh problems – as well as some old problems in new guises.

PART IV

A still broader field
1962–7

*The assistance given this general store in the Northwest Territories (top)
by IDB financing illustrates the broad scope opened up to the Bank
by the 1961 amendments.*

*Many of the agricultural loans made by the IDB went to highly specialized
enterprises, such as this hog farm in Alberta (centre) financed by the Bank.
Photo by Foto-Arts Studios, Red Deer, Alberta*

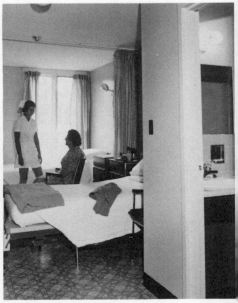

A broad view of machines used to manufacture plastic bags (top left). A series of loans, some of which were quite small, helped this company to multiply its sales tenfold and to become a major element in the packaging industry.

The Bank made many loans to nursing homes such as the Ontario home pictured above right.

Following the 1961 amendments to the IDB Act, tourism became an important field for the IDB. Pictured here (centre) is a major resort complex in British Columbia that the Bank financed.

An IDB loan to this Manitoba manufacturer of men's trousers (top) enabled
it to construct a new building and double its productive capacity.

This greenhouse (centre) received assistance from the Bank at a time
when this kind of 'agricultural' operation was not eligible for loans
from the Farm Credit Corporation.

The IDB helped to finance the construction of this large car ferry (top) for use on the lower St Lawrence. Much careful planning on the part of local businessmen went into the establishment of the business, which was very successful.

Ranches such as this one (centre), needing assistance to purchase land or make improvements, often appeared among the Bank's specialized agricultural borrowers.
Photo by Vic La Vica, Calgary

What appears to be a fence in this picture (top) is one wall
of a lobster pound being built, with the help of an IDB loan,
in a small Nova Scotia port.

On the West Coast logs have often to be transported great distances
by water to a sawmill. Barges sometimes were used in place
of the traditional booms towed by tugs. This barge (centre), financed
by the IDB, was an improved type: logs were loaded by a crane
mounted on the barge and unloaded, as here, by simply tipping the barge.
Photo by Commercial Illustrators Ltd, Vancouver

*The Bank assisted in the financing of this major,
and very successful, ski hill in eastern Canada.*

CHAPTER THIRTEEN

Legislation again

We now enter the next period into which this history of the Bank is divided. It starts in 1962, following the final major amendment to the IDB Act in the summer of 1961 by which virtually all types of business became eligible to apply to the Bank for assistance, and it ends in 1967, when formal restructuring of the Bank into a regional system was completed.

Economic and political background

In contrast to the period we have just reviewed, the years 1962–7 inclusive were ones of steady economic growth and expansion. In 1961, the country had started to climb slowly out of the recession of 1960, and this trend continued until 1967 when, in the latter part of the year, there was a slowing down. Contemporary comments reflect the satisfaction with which the economic statistics were reviewed from year to year. In 1963, the 'economy moved forward at a high level.' In 1964, 'economic activity ... reached its highest level' and gave its 'most effective ... performance in seven years.' In 1965, the country 'continued to enjoy long and vigorous business expansion.' The year 1966 was welcomed as 'another prosperous' year, with 'the pace of economic activity ... at a high level.' These comments are reflected in the annual figures for the country's gross national product. From 1957 to 1961 inclusive, the annual increase (in constant 1971 dollars) had averaged only 2.8 per cent. In 1962, however, the GNP increased by 6.8 per cent, and from 1962 to 1966 inclusive the annual increase averaged 6.5 per cent; in 1967, a decline in activity was signalled by a reduction in the increase to 3.3 per cent.[1]

Intermingled with this generally expansive trend, however, were problems, some of long-term significance. First, in May and June 1962, a large decline in official exchange reserves precipitated an emergency. The government took a number of restrictive measures to control the demand for foreign currencies, and the Bank of Canada, which had followed a relaxed monetary policy in 1961 and early 1962, took action to stimulate a rise in interest rates in order to check the flow of funds out of the country. With the crisis safely surmounted, the central bank reverted to an easier monetary policy through 1963 and 1964. Second, while unemployment declined, it did so only very gradually; not until 1966, when it represented 3.6 per cent of the labour force, was it as low as it had been in 1956 and during most of the post-war period up to that year. Third, although prices had been fairly steady through 1962-4, in 1965-7 they began to rise. From 1962 to 1964 inclusive, the consumer price index rose by an average of 1.6 per cent per annum, whereas from 1965 to 1967, the annual increases mounted so that in those three years there was a total increase of 10.1 per cent, representing an average annual increase of 3.2 per cent. These increases in prices (and, therefore, in production costs) were not considered as having been reflected in greater productivity, and by 1965-6 fears of serious inflation had been aroused.[2]

The expansion in the economy had been accompanied by large capital investment programs and high levels of expenditure on plant and equipment. The resulting pressure on credit facilities had been apparent in 1965 and 1966. When, however, in 1967 the pace of expansion slackened, as reflected in a falling away in capital investment programs, in a reduced rate of increase in the gross national product, and in lagging construction activity, the threat of inflation from the continued 'upward push of costs and prices' made it difficult to adopt stimulating policies to maintain economic expansion and hold down unemployment. In its report for 1967, the Bank of Canada, after referring to 'the recent behaviour of costs, and in particular the very high rates of increase in wages and salaries,' said: 'The delay in returning to reasonable stability in prices and costs inevitably impedes a return to a more vigorous rate of expansion of the economy on a non-inflationary basis.'[3]

In spite of these problems, however, the general trend in the economy in the period was one of steady expansion and prosperity. The political scene, in contrast, was very troubled. Early in 1961, the government, claiming a difference of views on economic policy between itself and the governor of the Bank of Canada, J.E. Coyne, had sought to have the post of governor declared vacant by Parliament. These efforts were defeated in the Senate, but in July 1961 Mr Coyne resigned. Parliament was dissolved in April 1962 and an election called for 18 July. The opposition dwelt on the high rate of unemployment (7.5 per cent in April and 5.1 per cent in May)[4] and economic difficulties. The foreign exchange crisis broke just a few weeks before polling day, seeming to add weight to these criticisms, and, although the government held on to office, it did so with a minority. Thrown into disarray by this result, by dissension in the cabinet over the acquisition of nuclear weapons, and by the retirement of several ministers, the government went to the country again in February 1963. This time it was defeated, and the Liberals, led by Lester Pearson, took office – also as a minority government. In 1965, they too, dissatisfied with this situation, tried their luck at the polls, only to be returned to office, with much the same number of seats.

Proposals for expansion of the IDB

We shall now consider those developments that particularly affected the IDB. All political parties were united, as we saw in chapter 9, in an eagerness to promote measures to assist small businesses with their finances. In November 1960, Parliament had approved the Small Business Loans Act providing government guarantees of chartered bank term loans to small businesses. The act was somewhat limited in its range. Businesses with gross annual revenues of over $250,000 were excluded; borrowings by one business were limited to $25,000 at any one time; loans could be used only for the 'purchase and improvement of equipment' and 'the extension and renovation of business premises'; only businesses engaged in manufacturing, the service industry, or wholesale or retail trade qualified; and the term of a loan was limited to ten years. It was likely, then, that these arrangements would leave many small businesses unaffected.

Even before that act was passed, the management of the IDB had indications, such as Mr Fleming's inquiry in April 1959 as to which businesses were ineligible to apply to the IDB and conversations with departmental officials, that the government was considering enlarging the scope of the IDB. In November 1960, just a few days before the bill to set up the system of guaranteed small business loans was introduced into Parliament, it was reported in the Toronto *Globe and Mail* (17 November) that the IDB Act was to be amended. In mid-March 1961 the Progressive Conservative Association at its annual meeting passed a resolution that 'consideration be given to an expansion of the activities of the Industrial Development Bank with particular reference to credit assistance for businesses creating new employment.'[5]

The board of directors of the Bank had begun in February 1961 to discuss how the activities of the Bank might be expanded, and by the last week in March Mr Coyne was in correspondence with Mr Fleming on the subject at the latter's request. Mr Coyne described some possible amendments to the IDB Act that might be helpful in increasing the Bank's usefulness, although he was at pains to explain in each case that the Board itself had not come to a firm conclusion one way or another about it. The suggestions called for a widening of 'eligibility' to embrace all types of business, an increase in the Bank's financial resources, a higher limit on loans over $200,000, a national registry for liens and chattel mortgages on aircraft, and power for the Bank to finance equipment purchases by conditional sales agreements. He also suggested that consideration be given to empowering the IDB to participate in small local investment corporations; the Small Business Administration in the United States had initiated such a program, and the idea had a lot of glamour for those interested in helping small businesses in Canada. In addition, he described various ways in which the IDB expected to increase its activity, quite apart from possible amendments to its act – by seeking opportunities to enter into underwriting agreements and purchase shares, decreasing its reliance on the value of physical assets as a criterion for making loans, placing more emphasis on the earnings prospects of an applicant business, and making loans for working capital.

In April, Mr Marble issued to the Bank new instructions on lending policy and principles and on repayment of loans, trying to take into account the various public criticisms that had been made of the Bank and reflecting the more relaxed attitudes on lending implicit in the views as to the further evolution of the Bank passed on to Mr Fleming by Mr Coyne. For example, it was said that 'the owners of the business must, of course, have a reasonable investment in it themselves. This is a matter of judgement on the part of the officers of the Bank and a flexible attitude should be taken ... There is no bias against making a loan which is greater than the investment by others ... The value of the security is only one of the factors to be taken into account. Of greater importance are such factors as the needs of the business, quality of management, market prospects, and the prospective profits available to facilitate repayment.'

That the change in policy direction was significant is shown by the response to it of the supervisor at Vancouver, Frank Aykroyd. On 12 April 1960, he wrote to Mr Marble: 'It [the circular on lending policy] seems to me to be a somewhat inflammatory document in the hands of inexperienced credit officers. I am, for the time being, taking the attitude with the staff that the key to the understanding of the circular is in paragraph (1) reading: "The following is a statement of principles (as distinct from credit criteria) to be observed in respect of lending policy ..." Meanwhile, however, we will be busy making loans which, after all, is the purpose of the Bank.' Mr Marble replied: 'I see clearly from your remark that this is to be regarded as "a statement of principles (as distinct from credit criteria)" that ... we were confused when we attempted the distinction. Actually the statements include both principles and credit criteria ... I note that you will continue to be busy making loans which you say, after all, is the purpose of the Bank but the policy might also be interpreted that the purpose is not only to make loans, but not to decline applications!'

A conference of supervisors to discuss policy was called for May. At the conference Mr Coyne, in commenting on the rapid growth the Bank had been experiencing, said: 'Here we have an organization which was very soundly based to start with, which had great potential for growth and which worked its way carefully for some years, working out procedures and ideas and becoming accustomed to this kind of operation and getting the business world accustomed to it. It is now enjoying a period of fruition such as comes to any organization at intervals if it is lively and aggressive.'

Regarding lending policy, he said: 'When it comes to authorizing a credit within delegated limits, if it is felt that the business fulfills all reasonable requirements, if it appears to be soundly based, has good market prospects for its products, if there is appropriate risk capital ahead of us and keenness and ability on the part of management and they appear to have a good chance of earning a profit in the future, we should not worry too much about the realizable value of the security, even though we may have a higher loss experience than we have had so far.'

Amendment to the act in 1961, and discussion in Parliament

On 20 June 1960, the government's intention to amend the IDB Act was announced by the minister of finance as 'the next link in the financial chain that the government is forging,' and on 23 June the bill was introduced into the House of Commons.[7]

The main amendments to the IDB Act were as follows. 1 / The detailed listing of eligible businesses was replaced by a definition of 'industrial enterprise' as 'an enterprise in which is carried on any industry, trade or other business undertaking of any kind.' 2 / The deputy minister of trade and commerce was added to the board of directors and also to the executive committee. 3 / In addition, another 'outside' director was to be chosen by the board to act on the executive committee, bringing to two the number of 'outside' directors on the committee. 4 / The share capital of the Bank was increased to $50 million, and the Bank's borrowing power, previously limited to three times the sum of the paid-up capital and the reserve fund, was raised to five times this sum. This increased the Bank's financial resources from $160 million to about $400 million. 5 / The Bank was given power to purchase equipment trust certificates for financing the purchase of transportation equipment and to assist in the purchase of 'moveable property' (such as machinery or equipment) through conditional sales agreements. 6 / The limit on loans outstanding in amounts over $200,000 was increased from $75 million to $150 million.[8]

The amendments were very similar to those outlined in Mr Coyne's earlier letter to Mr Fleming, apart from the changes in the board of directors and the executive committee and the provision for purchasing equipment trust certificates. The last-mentioned power was never used by the Bank.

In introducing the bill, Mr Fleming described the Bank as having furnished 'a valuable service in providing for the financial needs of small and medium-sized businesses' and spoke of new avenues of service now to be open to the Bank. In particular, he expected the Bank to assist small family enterprises with estate tax problems in the hope that 'in this way the Industrial Development Bank can also contribute to the retention in Canada of the ownership and control of Canadian businesses.' In the debate that followed, although most members concurred in Mr Fleming's reference to the IDB's 'valuable service,' there was much criticism of the Bank. Several felt it was too 'restrictive' and not 'flexible' enough. One member said he had 'heard it is much easier for companies to get loans from the commercial banks than it ever was to get them from the Industrial Development Bank in the past' and added that 'the view of the public in general toward this institution' was that 'it was easier to get teeth out of a hen than it was to get a loan from the Industrial Development Bank.' Another member expressed the opinion that if the Bank were to be governed by commercial criteria 'practically all its lending will be done in Central Canada'; while eschewing 'recklessness or imprudence,' the Bank, he felt, should be willing to take a greater degree of 'calculated' risk.[9]

It is perhaps only fair to say that among the operational management staff of the Bank, the extreme criticisms that were sometimes expressed in the parliamentary debates were not always taken seriously. In some cases an MP would illustrate his criticism with one or two 'examples.' It was usually possible for people on the Bank's staff to identify the cases mentioned, and as a rule they had no doubts about the decisions reached in these cases and no doubts that, if they had been free to disclose details, an objective outside person would generally have agreed with them.

In addition they were receiving scores of letters of thanks and gratitude from borrowers, and even from some whose applications had been turned down, as is shown in the following extracts from some of these letters. 'The company has had problems of various kinds, and to the credit of the Industrial Development Bank these have always been met with understanding,' 'I wish to express my thanks for the profound interest that you and your Bank have shown in my case.' 'The cordial reception which I received from you was so kind that even if I consider abandoning my project now, I wish to take this opportunity of thanking you for your courtesy.' 'Would like to take this opportunity to thank you for the splendid cooperation and help you have given us the past three years.' 'We did find that dealing with you has been a great experience.' 'Through our association, we have found that those who are entrusted with administering the Bank's policies are worthy of the highest commendation for the job they are doing in assisting the small business community.' 'Directors of the company by means of a resolution wish to record with you their vote of thanks and deem it a privilege to have been able to deal with such a cooperative group as you represent.' 'We have had much experience with banks and were amazed with the courtesy received from all your officers and with your friendly way of conducting business.'

Some criticisms seemed to be based on an imprecise understanding of the Bank's operations. An example occurred in a debate in the House of Commons in February 1960 on a private motion that the government give urgent consideration to the provision of some means whereby low-interest loans be made available to small business. An MP from the Atlantic provinces, claiming that people in his area had found the Bank 'rather snooty,' said:

A constituent of mine ... applied for a small loan to assist in constructing a salt-fish–processing plant. The Bank [the IDB] required that an appraiser drive some 90 miles from Sydney to appraise the building and fixtures. They required a special audit. They required long-range forecasts of prices and markets and practically wanted a guarantee of the price of fish five years from now. They wanted an architect's drawing of a $7,000 or $8,000 one-storey building, and so on. If and when my constituent does obtain his small loan ... he will have paid heavily for all this appraising and information and I doubt whether the loan is worth the trouble.[10]

The basic elements of this story were probably correct. The appraiser was probably the Bank's engineering investigation officer, and, in addition to driving from Sydney, he must first have driven or flown to Sydney from Halifax. This cost the applicant nothing. The 'special' audit was probably asked for to procure proper financial statements. While a guarantee of the price of fish in five years would not have been asked for, the possible trend in fish prices would undoubtedly have been discussed. As a result of the Bank's investigation, the applicant almost certainly had a better understanding of his business, its potential problems, and his ability to solve them.

The member continued: 'I am sure the local bank manager would have processed that loan in one quarter of the time that was required by the office of the IDB, some 250 miles away in Halifax. The banker would know at a glance whether the proposition was sound and feasible. He knows the man's history and character. He would know whether or not he is a good credit risk.'[11]

Without realizing it, the MP had here put his finger on the very essence of the IDB's operations. No matter how fast or slow the local chartered bank manager would have been in reaching a decision, he obviously would not advance the money in this case since otherwise the man would not have had to apply to the IDB. It was partly to rescue the small business from dependence on a credit decision based on a 'glance' that the IDB's operations were designed. Because it made a careful study of a proposal, financial needs, production costs, plant layout, markets, and so on and depended on much more than a 'glance' or knowing a person's 'history and character,' the Bank was able to assist those who could not get help elsewhere and generally do so safely and soundly from the standpoint of both the borrower and the Bank.

One of the few criticisms of the bill itself came from a member who feared that the broader field opened up to the Bank would lead to loans to racetracks and other types of amusement places 'which do not meet the requirements of most taxpayers in this country.' His objection was partly based on his impression that the Bank would use 'taxpayers' money' for these undesirable purposes. In fact, the Bank never used money derived from taxes. In commenting on these criticisms, Mr Fleming said: 'Now sir, it should not be thought, either, that the Bank in exercising the wide powers conferred upon it under this measure is going to throw to the winds those proper considerations and that discretion which any banker ought to observe ... The Bank must still use a banker's judgement and decide whether or not applicants are really creditworthy. In this regard, let me say that there is here no thought of just casting away the proper restraint.'[12]

The leader of the opposition, Lester Pearson, said that the Bank had performed very useful services. In supporting the bill, he claimed to see in it many proposals already put forward by his party. He noted the omission of one of these proposals – the separation of the IDB from the Bank of Canada – and in reply to this comment, Mr Fleming said that this had been considered by the government and would continue to be under consideration. A good deal would 'depend upon the views of management and the Bank authorities.'[13]

The bill was not referred to the House of Commons Standing Committee on Banking and Commerce, although much of the debate in the House was devoted to efforts by the Liberal members to have it referred to this committee. No doubt they expected that they would then be able to have Mr Coyne, president of the IDB, called as a witness. Mr Coyne was also, of course, governor of the Bank of Canada, and the opposition may have hoped to find ways of slanting questions to him in that capacity. The government would not agree to referring the bill, no doubt to prevent this from happening. The bill was passed by the House on 6 July and, after passing the Senate, received royal assent on 13 July.[14]

Criticisms of the Bank, and replies of Mr Coyne and Mr Marble

Had the bill to amend the IDB Act been referred to the standing committee, the management of the Bank would have been given a chance to answer criticisms made during the debate. Since it did not have this opportunity, it will only be fair if we hear its members speak for themselves and the Bank now by setting down the answers they gave to similar criticisms that came to them by other means.

In November 1960, just about when Parliament was opening for a new session, Mr Coyne had passed on to him by its recipient a letter in which a member of Parliament (in fact, a cabinet minister) criticized the performance of the IDB on several counts. He claimed that the Bank was not aggressive enough, was too conservative, and allowed the fear of loss to dominate over any desire to encourage expansion and growth. Before hearing Mr Coyne's reply, it is worth noting that this complaint was made when the Bank had just completed a fiscal year (1960) in which the number of loans authorized (740) was four times the average number authorized annually (185) in the eleven years preceding the 1956 amendment to the IDB Act and was 20 per cent greater than the number approved (599) in the preceding year (1959). Also, the Bank was in the early months of a fiscal year (1961) in which the number of loans approved would surpass the record year of 1960 by 88 per cent and reach the new record figure of 1,365!

To the criticism, Mr Coyne replied:

I can assure you that fear of loss has not dominated the desire to encourage expansion and growth ... I do not think you can operate a lending business with the deliberate intention of making losses or of incurring a predetermined loss ratio. It is true that the loss ratio actually experienced by the Bank to date has been a satisfactory one from a businesslike point of view. One reason is that, where a borrower gets into trouble the Bank and its officers make great efforts, by deferring payments due and by providing expert analysis and advice to help him work out of his difficulty in a constructive way. It must be remembered, too, that on the whole this has been a period of rising prices, when the value of a company's physical assets was increasing fairly steadily ...

The policy of the Bank has always been to follow the injunction in the statute, namely, to make loans wherever it appears that the borrowing business has a good chance to succeed in conditions where a high level of national income and employment is maintained.

Mr Coyne's correspondent also complained that the Bank had followed a policy of maximizing profits and minimizing the possibility of losses. Recollecting Mr Tower's disappointed hopes that the IDB would earn a profit comparable with the yield on long-term government bonds, Mr Coyne replied:

This net revenue has run between 3% and 4% per annum on the amount of the capital and reserves employed in the business ... considerably less than the rate which every private institution would consider it necessary to earn ...

In the view of the management of the Bank, and of its directors, it was the clear intention of Parliament that the Bank should not be operated with a view to incurring overall losses, as this would amount to subsidization of the borrowing businesses at the expense of their competitors ... So far as I can recall, all the public discussion in Parliament and outside Parliament in the past fifteen years has been based on the assumption that the Bank should endeavour to earn some moderate rate of return on the capital employed.

Mr Coyne closed with a statement of the Bank's attitude toward risk that expresses very well the Bank's view on this matter from beginning to end:

Finally, and most important, I should like to express the view that it is of no assistance to a man to make him a loan in order to enable him to go ahead with a venture which cannot succeed, in which he will lose all of his own money as well as bring a loss to the Bank. In any lending institution someone must exercise his judgement on the question whether the borrowing company is likely to succeed. Subject to human fallibility, it is our desire to make loans to all those eligible enterprises which satisfy the requirements of the statute and which in the opinion of competent credit appraisers are likely to succeed in their proposed projects, and be able to pay off their loans within a period of time which is reasonable having regard to the nature of the enterprise, under conditions in which a high level of national income and employment is being maintained.

In March 1961, when Mr Coyne was writing to Mr Fleming to suggest how the activities of the IDB might be expanded, a government department submitted to the Bank a report recording comments on the Bank received during a small survey of medium-sized manufacturers in Toronto. Mr Marble, the general manager, responded. First, the Bank was said to be too slow. To this Mr Marble replied that, while the time that elapsed between the initiating of a loan application and the disbursement of the proceeds was an embarrassment,

Many borrowers do not appreciate the reasons for the difference between the time consumed in obtaining a demand or short-term loan from a chartered bank for working capital purposes, secured perhaps by an assignment of inventory and receivables where procedures are routine, and a term loan relating to fixed assets and secured by mortgages, chattel mortgages, etc.

In the case of a term loan to a borrower previously unknown to a lender, there must be a great deal more investigation and the legal procedures relating to mortgages, frequently time-consuming, are beyond the control of the lender. Our own checks have shown that a high percentage of delays are caused by the borrowers themselves, sometimes arising out of a vagueness of plans and frequently in providing documentation without which the security cannot be completed.

Second, it was said that the costs of engineering studies, increased life insurance, and accounting and legal work made the cost of borrowing heavy. In reply, Mr Marble pointed out that the Bank made no charge for its engineering investigation, that the Bank did not always require the pledge of life insurance and even less often required an increase in life insurance, that special accounting work was rarely required unless the applicant could not otherwise provide properly audited statements, and that legal costs were what a borrower would have to pay for a mortgage loan from any lender.

Third, the most serious cause of concern was said to be that, in order to obtain a loan from the IDB, manufacturers had to place a mortgage on all their assets, including their homes and property held by their wives. This was, of course, quite untrue. Mr Marble said:

During the sixteen years of the Bank's existence, when it has authorized more than 5,000 loans, there are less than half a dozen cases where mortgages have been taken on the homes of borrowers, since this is a form of security we strongly prefer to avoid. There have been cases where we have taken mortgage security on property held by the wives of owners of businesses, but almost without exception, this would be where the property occupied by the business is registered in the name of the wife of the owner.

In the case of automobiles, we generally try to avoid including them ...

The implication that we take security on everything that is lying around loose is absolutely untrue.

Fourth and finally, the Bank was reported as demanding security worth several times the amount of the loan obtained. To this, Mr Marble replied: 'In the eyes of the owner, the value of his assets usually greatly exceeds the value that might be placed on them by any lender who depended upon them for security. This must be a matter of judgement.'

CHAPTER FOURTEEN

The Bank under study – organization and procedures

Changes in senior management personnel

Following the resignation of Mr Coyne as governor of the Bank of Canada in July 1961, Louis Rasminsky, deputy governor, was appointed governor and so became also president of the IDB. In the following years, there were other changes in the management of the Bank. At the end of 1961, the writer was appointed an assistant general manager at GMO, and C.E. DeAthe was appointed executive assistant. H.R. Stoker was appointed supervisor at Montreal, and J.C. Ingram returned to the IDB as supervisor at Winnipeg. In July 1962, D.G. Marble, who had been general manager since 1953, resigned because of ill health. He was appointed special consultant to the Bank, but his health prevented him from serving in this capacity for long, and unfortunately a short time later he died. His service to the IDB as secretary and general manager covered eighteen years, and he contributed to every aspect of the Bank's policy, organization, and operation. Mr Marble was succeeded as general manager by A.N.H. James, who had been the 'No. 2' man in the operational management of the Bank since its establishment and had held the title of assistant general manager since 1953. Also, early in 1961 a third administrative assistant, K.K. Hay-Roe, was added to the staff at GMO, and E.C. Scott was appointed personnel officer to establish a Personnel Department at GMO for the first time.

At the end of the fiscal 1960, N.C. Tompkins, assistant general manager, British Columbia, retired. He had been in charge of the Bank's office in Vancouver since it was opened in 1945 and had directed the growth of the Bank's business in British Columbia and, until 1956, in Alberta. He was replaced as supervisor by F.M. Aykroyd, who was succeeded as supervisor at Calgary by H.J.C. Russell, at that time executive assistant at GMO.

These changes in the management team took place as the Bank was about to pass through a series of examinations of its operations. In 1961, along with other crown corporations and agencies and federal government departments, it came under the scrutiny of the Royal Commission on Government Organization, known as the Glassco Commission after its chairman, J. Grant Glassco, an eminent chartered accountant. In 1962, it was studied by the Royal Commission on Banking and Finance – named the Porter Commission after its chairman, David Porter, chief justice of Ontario. In the same year, it was examined by a firm of management consultants retained by the Bank itself. The Glassco Commission and the management consultants concerned themselves mostly with organization and procedures, while the Porter Commission, which had a broader mandate, was mainly interested in the way the IDB fitted into the general financial structure of Canada and in the relationship between its operations and those of other lenders.

Study of the Bank by the Glassco Commission

We shall look first at the work of the Glassco Commission.[1] It was set up in September 1960 to study the operation of federal government departments and agencies with a view to improving their efficiency and management. By March 1961 it had organized its staff, selected those who were to study the various departments, crown corporations, and agencies, and started its examination of the IDB.

At this time the Bank was trying to convert itself from a relatively small institution to a much larger one. Its organization and procedures were in a state of flux as it made adjustments required by the growth that had followed the 1956 amendments and in anticipation of the further growth expected from the 1961 amendments. From 1955 (prior to the 1956 amendments) to 1962 (after the 1961 amendments), the number of loans approved in a single year increased from 221 to 2,085, the number of customers with loans on the Bank's books increased from 692 to 4,083, and the number of branch offices increased from 4 to 22.

Because of this large increase in the scale of activity, the Bank's personnel regarded as unjust the implications of some comments made during the parliamentary debates of 1960 and 1961 that the Bank lacked drive and had achieved little. The growth had required the rapid recruitment of additional staff, and the preponderance of inexperienced staff affected efforts to change organization or procedures. From 1955 to 1962, the number of employees increased from 99 to 472,[2] and over half of these had joined the Bank in the last two years. The staff of credit officers and engineering officers who actually processed credit applications had an even greater proportion of inexperienced people. In December 1961, 75 per cent of credit officers had been with the Bank for less than two years, and 36 per cent had been with the Bank for less than six months. For engineering officers, the corresponding figures were 83 per cent and 43 per cent.

The adjustments already made to accommodate this growth had taken various forms. The delegation of power to authorize loans had been extended, and by 1961 over 85 per cent of loans made were authorized in the field without any reference to GMO unless difficult matters of policy were involved.[3] This extension of authority had been intended, along with measures previously mentioned (such as field investigations by credit officers, 'short-form' investigation reports, pre-printed forms for quick field investigations, and one-page summaries for credit submissions) to reduce paperwork, cut loan processing time, and lower expenses. In May 1961, operating procedures were revised to diminish the role of GMO in reviewing credits authorized in the field. Until then, GMO had given about the same amount of attention to all credits regardless of amount or where they were authorized. All disbursements of loan proceeds had been checked by GMO. All credit summaries were checked and examined there. From authorization to repayment, the progress of all loans was followed at GMO through regular reports from branches analysing the borrower's financial statements. This last routine was rapidly becoming more honoured in the breach than in the observance because the amount of time-consuming work required to comply with it was simply too great for the branches to handle.

In May 1961, it was announced that these established procedures were being changed. In future, GMO would concentrate on credits in excess of supervisors' authorizing limits and on loans in difficulty. Full responsibility for loan accounts in good shape within supervisors' or branch manager's limits would rest with the supervisors. Disbursement of proceeds of loans within supervisors' and branch limits would be handled by supervisors, not by GMO.

These changes were made 'with a view to streamlining operations and increasing the productivity of the staff,' but they were expressed in qualified language. While full responsibility for loans operating satisfactorily and within supervisors' limits was to rest on the supervisors, GMO would 'review credits newly authorized by branches to whatever extent is considered appropriate.' (The word 'appropriate' was a favourite in the IDB to round out instructions or a statement of policy when it was felt that a small escape hatch should be provided from a position that might turn out to be too firm!) Also, while supervisors were to attend to the disbursement of loans within their limits, the disbursement sheets recording and analysing the disbursements would be reviewed later by GMO.

An effort was made to cut down on the size of investigation reports. The attempts previously and persistently made to this end had apparently been unsuccessful, for it was now said that 'as a general observation, investigation reports for applications up to $100,000 are undesirably and unnecessarily lengthy. Too many investigation reports of 12 or sometimes 15 pages or more plus appendices are submitted for smaller credits.' The concern can be appreciated when it is realized that in 1961 well over 1,200 investigation reports were written for credit proposals for under $100,000. Short-form reports were to be used more extensively. This was not really as drastic a reform as it sounds since it merely meant that headings used in a standard form of report that were not relevant to a particular application could be omitted, that an effort should be made to be concise, and that the report could, if considered 'appropriate,' be prepared by a credit officer. For applications of up to $50,000, however, a target of three pages for the report was suggested.

It was while the Bank was in this state of re-appraising and revising its procedures that the Glassco Commission made its investigation. A 'project team' of the commission interviewed many officers of the Bank, visited branch offices, and studied the operations of the Bank in detail over many months. The Bank supplied the team with numerous memoranda describing its policy principles and methods of operation. This team then made a long report to the commission itself.

The team regarded the Bank's policies and operations as reflecting a progressive concept of the special responsibilities resting on the Bank as an agent of government functioning in the role of a residual lender of capital funds. It considered that its management had given faithful but not unduly rigid effect to the statutory principles on which it should operate. It also concluded that, in a relatively hazardous lending field, the Bank did not seem to take unwarranted risks, and it commented on the Bank's evident readiness to give full and sympathetic consideration to the less attractive loan applications. For the Bank, these views, coming from outside people who had studied it closely, were a refreshing change from some of those expressed in Parliament.

Regarding procedures, the general tenor of the team's comments was that the Bank had earned inadequate profits and that the General Manager's Office still exercised too close a control over the lending activities of the branches as a result of which too much paper passed around the Bank. Unfortunately it did not say what rate of profit would have been considered adequate. Nevertheless, that the Bank should be charged with earning inadequate profits, just after parliamentary debates in which it had been accused of not losing enough money, was, for the personnel of the Bank, at least a change. The senior operational officers at GMO felt that the conclusion that GMO was too active in supervising the branches gave insufficient consideration to the unique character of the Bank. They believed that GMO had to know what was going on in the Bank, first, because of the high degree of risk in the field in which the Bank operated, and second, because it was considered necessary that policy should be applied as uniformly as possible in all parts of the Bank. To them the study seemed to have used chartered bank concepts for judging the methods of a very different institution, the IDB. As G.D. Coates, an administrative assistant at GMO, expressed it, the investigators seemed to think that 'what is good for the chartered banks, would be good for the IDB.'

The formal report of the commission was issued in July 1962. It did not go into the details commented on by the project team. It was devoted mostly to principles and concepts to govern the organization and operation of crown corporations and agencies and government departments generally. Regarding the IDB, the commission recommended that 'Steps be taken to give greater independence to the management of the Industrial Development Bank and to bring the activities of the Bank more appropriately under the general control of the Minister of Finance.' On the face of it, the recommendation appears self-contradictory. It would hardly seem reasonable to see the path to independence of management as lying in control by a minister. It was made clear in the report, however, that by 'independence' was meant independence from the Bank of Canada and that the general intention was that the Bank should be brought under closer control by the minister of finance. The absence of such control as a result of the Bank's being a subsidiary of 'another agency which, by statute enjoys exceptional independence' was decried.[4]

The report described the governor of the Bank of Canada as the chief executive officer of both banks.[5] This was technically incorrect; the IDB Act did not name a chief executive officer, and, as was explained earlier, this omission had been deliberate. The comment would seem to suggest that the commission had not fully grasped the exact nature of the relationship between the president and the general manager as it had evolved since the Bank was founded. While the former held a title at least as elevated and significant as that of chief executive officer, the fact that this last phrase was not added to it meant that the general manager was able to exercise authority and initiative in the directing of operations that he might not have done so easily had the president's title been enlarged upon.

The commission appears to have dismissed the role of the IDB as a supplementary lender. It referred to the Bank as competing with other lenders, as if this were unavoidable: 'The legislation still treats the Bank as a special residual source of credit, to be tapped only when money is not otherwise available on reasonable terms and conditions, but it has become impracticable to police this statutory injunction ... Today, when industrial financing is available for virtually any worth-while venture, at a price determined in the marketplace and based on the risks involved, the Industrial Development Bank almost inevitably competes with other lenders.'[6]

The report did not give the reasons for the commission's reaching this sweeping conclusion. The statement was just a rephrasing of the original argument by which the setting up of the Bank was opposed by some back in 1944 − if a business is creditworthy, it can get whatever financing it is entitled to in the market-place.

Study of the Bank by management consultants

The report of the Glassco Commission had little influence on the Bank, but the work of the project team did make it aware of the importance of reducing paperwork and of the need to overhaul its procedures. In the mean time, discussions had been going on within the board as to the desirability of retaining a firm of management consultants to give guidance in matters of organization and procedures and to help the Bank make the transition from a small to a large institution. The matter was first raised by a director at a meeting of the board in March 1961, just as the Glassco Commission was starting its work. It was suggested that consultants might evaluate staff responsibilities and duties and review the methods used for processing and supervising credits and routine practices generally. In February 1962, when the work of the Glassco Commission was ended, a firm of management consultants was retained.

In preparation for the consultants' work, the management of the Bank drew up an outline of the matters upon which it desired guidance. These included the questions raised by the Glassco Commission about relations between GMO and the field offices and about paperwork within the Bank. In addition, management prepared an outline of plans it had already tentatively formulated for changes in organization and procedures. The principal ones among these were: 1 / a more formally structured regional system with the supervisors relieved of the responsibilities of managing branches of their own and occupied solely in supervising the branches in their respective regions (Mr Marble had written to the president in November 1961 to make this suggestion.); 2 / the assignment of specific duties to each of the senior officers at GMO; 3 / the appointment of an inspector of branches who would spend the greater part of his time among the branch offices; 4 / the appointment at GMO of someone to keep under study the most suitable operating procedures for the Bank; and 5 / the establishment of a staff training program. Other matters listed for consideration included the possible transfer of all staff administration to the new Personnel Department at GMO, the transfer of the general ledger (as distinct from loan accounts which were always maintained at GMO) from head office in Ottawa to GMO, a changed format for various reports, and the necessity of other kinds of paperwork.

The consultants made their report in June 1962. Their recommendations, which were very numerous and detailed, included all of the tentative ideas of the Bank's management listed above and rested on the view that, whereas since 1944 senior operating management had been concerned primarily with credits, the Bank had now reached a size that required that operational general management devote more time to administration. To achieve proper administrative control those functions performed by the Bank of Canada in Ottawa, such as personnel records and maintenance of accounting for administrative expenses, should be transferred to the General Manager's Office in Montreal. Since senior management would then have less time for credits, there would have to be further decentralization of the credit function, and this would require stronger regional offices, freed from the burden of having also to manage a branch office. Less involvement by GMO in reviewing credits would require some other means of overseeing the credit function and branch operations, and for this the appointment of an inspector of branches to visit the field offices was suggested; it would also mean reducing very greatly the reports and credit information sent by branches to GMO. At GMO, the increased emphasis on administration would require the appointment of a controller and the establishment of proper systems of costing and budgeting for the Bank's operations.

The report was referred by the board of directors to the general manager for his views. Some of the proposals were accepted for immediate implementation, some were accepted but left to be introduced later, and some were rejected. The plan that emerged was then approved by the board of directors and presented in November to a conference of supervisors and senior officers from GMO. Although it is clear from the Bank's files that the plan of reorganization based on the consultants' report was regarded as a major step in the Bank's evolution, it seems in retrospect that some of the drastic reforms in procedures intended by the consultants were not achieved to any substantial degree and that even those reforms that were accepted in principle were considerably watered down.

The basic idea of the consultants was that GMO should leave the bulk of the credit work to the regional supervisors and spend more time simply administering the Bank. A big element in this change was the setting up of a more formal regional structure. This was in the original tentative list of management's ideas for the future, and the recommendation was, of course, accepted by management. It did not seem a long step from the structure the Bank already had, but it took a long time to accomplish. It proved difficult to choose areas to be grouped into regions, decide on the responsibilities to be shifted to the regional supervisors, determine what oversight of credit work should continue to be exercised by GMO, lay down rules for identifying such 'exceptional' cases as might not fit new streamlined procedures, determine how to reflect changed responsibilities in changed routines, and to reassign senior personnel to new positions in the new structure.

In 1962, when the consultants made their report, there were seven major offices managed by supervisors, each of whom also supervised one or more other branches run by managers. It was felt that to set up a separate regional office in each case could not be justified. Three – Calgary, Saint John, and Halifax – would have supervised only two branches each. Accordingly, although the consultants believed that five regions would be needed eventually, management decided on three to start with on the grounds that each region would then have about the same number of loan accounts and represent about the same workload for each supervisor. Planning for only three regions then presented special personnel problems; since there were already seven supervisors in the field and there were now to be only three, some suitable roles would have to be found for the other four.

The three regions were to be called Eastern, based in Montreal and comprising eastern Ontario, Quebec, and the Atlantic provinces; Central, based in Toronto and comprising most of Ontario; and Western, based in

Winnipeg and comprising northwestern Ontario, the four western provinces, and the two territories. The Eastern Region (without the Atlantic provinces) and the Central Region were quickly set up in 1962, since this merely required converting the supervisors' offices already established in Montreal and Toronto. The next year, a step was taken toward setting up the Western Region by establishing a Prairie Region, based in Winnipeg and including northwestern Ontario, Manitoba, and Saskatchewan, i.e. the area served by the old Winnipeg office. These steps were relatively easy, but there the process bogged down. Management hesitated to attach the Atlantic provinces to Quebec as an appendage, as it were, and to put them under a supervisor in far-away Montreal. Accordingly, the supervisor in Halifax was temporarily left to look after the four Atlantic branches while still managing Halifax branch. A similar hesitation arose about placing British Columbia and Alberta under a regional supervisor in the distant prairie city of Winnipeg. Thus, the supervisors in Calgary and Vancouver were left in the same position as the supervisor in Halifax. Not until the latter part of 1966 were these problems resolved. Then, four regions were established – Atlantic, Quebec, Central (i.e. Ontario), and Western, the last comprising a Prairie Division and a British Columbia Division. The title of the supervisors in charge of the four new regions was changed to assistant general manager, partly to reflect their new responsibilities and partly to match better the titles of their local counterparts in the chartered banks.

The new assistant general managers were H.R. Stoker (Atlantic), L. Viau (Quebec), W.C. Stuart (Central), and J.C. Ingram (Western). E.A. Bell, who had been supervisor at Halifax, became supervisor at Central Region, and R.H. Wheeler, who had been supervisor at Saint John, became supervisor at Prairie Region or Division. C.E. DeAthe, who had been executive assistant, became an assistant general manager at GMO as did H.J. Russell, who had been supervisor at Calgary. The writer was appointed deputy general manager.

One refinement remained to be made. Although this regional structure was published in the annual reports for both 1966 and 1967, the BC divisional office was never actually required in practice to report to the assistant general manager in Winnipeg, and in 1968, British Columbia, with the Yukon, became a separate region, and the balance of the Western Region became the Prairie Region. J.E. Millard became assistant general manager of BC Region. At Halifax, Mr Stoker, who retired, was succeeded as assistant general manager of the Atlantic Region by K.A. Powers. In the next few years, three other regional assistant general managers retired –

L. Viau in 1972, J.C. Ingram in 1973, and W.C. Stuart in 1974. They were succeeded respectively by J.E. Nordin, R.H. Wheeler, and K.A. Powers, who was replaced by I.D. MacLaren.

The regional structure of the Bank was not altered further, except that in due course all parts of Ontario were taken into Central Region. Also, the name of Central Region was changed in 1972. This name was the only surviving vestige of the original three-region plan. In 1972, another regional assistant general manager complained that the name 'Central' might imply to those outside the Bank (and even perhaps to some inside it!) a somewhat superior status to that of the other regions that had provincial or geographical names. Accordingly, 'Central' was changed to 'Ontario' Region.

The purpose of the more formal regional structure recommended by the consultants was, as previously explained, to put the regional offices in a position to take over a large amount of credit work from GMO in order to leave the latter free to devote more time to administration, planning, and policy. This depended on three further recommendations being implemented. First, there was to be a drastic reduction in the amount of reporting to GMO by field offices on credits within their limits; in particular, no copies of memoranda recording the initial discussion with an applicant (known as Form 58) for amounts within field limits were to be sent to GMO, and details of credits authorized in the field were to be supplied for accounting purposes only. Since the branch offices were producing 11−12,000 interview memoranda per year, and since about 1,600 loans within supervisors and branch managers' limits were authorized each year, the flow of paper that the consultants were seeking to dam was considerable. Second, GMO was to review only credits over supervisors' limits, all checking of smaller credits being done at the supervisors' offices. Third, the ultimate responsibility of GMO for the quality of these smaller credits and for field operations generally was to be exercised through an inspector of branches who would visit field offices to check on their procedures and examine their credits. The first two of these recommendations were implemented only partially, and the third was not done for many years.

The setting up of a formal regional system was expected to increase the proportion of loans that would be approved in the field, because the new regional supervisors would all have the same relatively high authorizing limit, which was to be higher than that exercised previously by some supervisors. It was estimated that when the new structure was completed 92.5 per cent of all loans would be approved in the field, either by a branch manager or by a regional supervisor. The cutting off of all information on credits within supervisors' limits would have meant that GMO would receive full information on only the 7.5 per cent of a year's authorizations above this level. While operational management at GMO accepted the idea that less attention should be given by them to the smaller credits, it was unwilling to be cut off to such a large extent from full information on the greater part of the Bank's activities. The experience of the Bank was regarded as showing that the difficult policies that governed the Bank's activities had to be followed as uniformly as possible across the country, and that, as a crown corporation, the Bank had to ensure that the exercise of credit judgment at all the Bank's offices should also be held at a uniform level. The difficulties invariably experienced in phrasing written instructions on these matters seemed to make it impractical to depend on instructions alone to achieve uniformity in these areas. Direct communication on specific cases was the best way of maintaining a proper understanding between the overall operational management of the Bank and the field offices. Indeed, quite apart from the problems of keeping the application of Bank policies and practices uniform, it was believed that it would be difficult to formulate future operating policies at GMO on the basis of familiarity with only the 7.5 per cent or so of credits that might exceed supervisors' limits, because this would not give GMO a view of a full mix of the Bank's business.

Adherence to this attitude in spite of a genuine desire to implement these parts of the consultants' report may have been reinforced by the fact that the Bank was under vigorous attack by the sales finance companies, which claimed that it was improperly taking business away from them. This is discussed in the next chapter. In an attempt to ensure that the Bank had a good position to defend in this regard, all interview memoranda – 10,000 in a single year! – were in 1961–2 being read at GMO by an assistant general manager with particular care to catch at an early stage any cases that seemed likely to breach the Bank's policies. From this review, three letters per day on the average were going out to branch offices questioning the policy aspects of some proposal.

The views of operational management on the amount of credit information it should receive were tersely expressed in notes prepared for the general manager, A.N.H. James, for a conference held in November 1962 to tell the supervisors about the consultants' report and to explain what steps were to be taken on the basis of it: 'Easy to curtail flow of credit material to GMO but not advisable to do so – essential for management to maintain a close feeling of lending activities – assess adequacy and suitability of policy − ... be in a position to provide guidance as may be necessary − objective − uniform application and interpretation of policy throughout the country.'

Because of these views, operational management at GMO went along only to a limited extent with the consultants' recommendation that GMO diminish its involvement in credit work. The documents that were not to be sent to GMO after 1962 for credits within supervisors' limits were a copy of the letter by which a credit was offered to an applicant after authorization, notification of an applicant's acceptance of a credit, and the sheets recording the disbursement of loan proceeds. Not receiving these documents made little difference to GMO's workload. Interview memoranda and credit summaries for credits within supervisors' limits were still to be sent to GMO. The examination of them by the Credit Department was indeed to be reduced, and only those of special interest were to be sent on to the general manager; nevertheless, since they were to be studied by the department 'from the point of view of policy and credit judgement,' which covered just about everything but arithmetical errors, the withdrawal of GMO from involvement in credits approved in the field fell well short of the consultants' intentions.

That these attitudes on the part of operational management prevailed for many years is shown by the following extract from a memorandum written in 1966 to describe the responsibilities of the Credit Department, and reciting again the plans formulated in 1962: 'Experienced credit officers at GMO would continue to examine all credits authorized in the field. In the case of credits up to the Regional Supervisors' limits, this examination would be limited to a scrutiny to ensure conformity with credit policy, loan terms, presentation, etc. Credits between Regional Supervisors' limits and the Regional AGM's limits would receive closer examination at GMO and prompt action would be taken in the case of any departure from credit policy or lowering of standards.'

The retention by GMO of more oversight of credit operations than the consultants had proposed was tied to a decision not to adopt another recommendation, the appointment of an inspector of branches. The consultants had intended that this officer, in a newly created post, would, through regular visits to field offices, provide a new method of controlling field operations by examining every aspect of a branch office's activity. His examination of a branch's work was to take the place of any review by GMO of credits within supervisors' limits. With this review, however, still maintained at GMO to a substantial degree, the need for an inspector was diminished. A memorandum of July 1962 summed up the views of operational management as follows: 'The primary means of control over the lending activity of the branches within their authorizing limits is to be the review of enquiries (i.e. memos on initial interviews with applicants), applications and new authorizations at GMO by the Superintendent of Credits rather than a review in the field by an Inspector of Branches. This, then, eliminates the primary function of the Inspector as envisaged by the consultants.'

There were considered to be practical objections to the appointment of an inspector as well. If he were to visit each of the twenty-two branch offices and two new regional offices once each year for several days in each case, prepare fully for each inspection, and write reports on what he found, it would probably be impossible for him to review properly the 11,000 interview memoranda and 1,800 loans that would be his annual responsibility. In any event, experience had made it clear that any policy review of interviews or loans must be prompt to be effective and could not await the visit of an inspector once a year.

Further, the operational management of the Bank foresaw awkward situations arising in the event that the inspector gave a branch different guidance from that given by the regional supervisor or regional assistant general manager. These were all officers of long service and superior ability and with a tradition of a high degree of independence in the way they managed their regions. An inspector would have had to be very close to the highest seniority in the Bank if he were to intervene between a regional office and a branch with a contrary view to that of the former on some matter of branch administration or credit judgment. This raised the final practical problem, because it was most unlikely that an officer of the required seniority and ability would accept such a post as that foreseen for the inspector, at least while the Bank was of such a size that he himself might have to be away a great deal of the time.

A gesture toward the consultants' recommendation was made by setting up a system of inspections by regional supervisors (and later by assistant general managers) of the branches in their own regions. These inspections were to be concerned with how efficiently and how effectively a branch functioned and the manner in which it generally followed policy and procedural directives; they were not to involve a review of loans, which was still to be done on a continual basis at the regional offices and GMO. The consultants' comment acquiescing in this counter-proposal was, 'Preliminary indications are that the Regional Supervisors will perform effective branch inspections.' This proved to be an over-optimistic view. The system was quite unsatisfactory for the purposes of GMO. No matter how objective a regional supervisor tried to be, he was, after all, reporting to a degree on his own supervision, so that the reports were not usually very critical. In addition, they proved to be too bulky to be easily absorbed and not sharply enough focused to be informative.

The management of the Bank recognized the validity of the consultants' recommendation that more attention be paid to administration. The proposal that a controller be appointed was implemented with the appointment, in 1962, of G.D. Coates, who, as administrative assistant, had early in 1961 been made head of an administrative and planning group. This group was to cover a wide range of administrative matters – personnel, planning, premises, equipment, publicity, expense control, new branches, and operating procedures – but had not been fully effective because of preoccupations with the various investigations of the Bank that were being made. The position of controller really continued these responsibilities. In 1965, Mr Coates resigned from the Bank to take an outside position, and the responsibilities of subsequent controllers covered accounting, finance, budgeting, and statistics.

Some of the other recommendations by the consultants merit comment. One was that the general manager should attend the weekly meetings of the executive committee in Ottawa. This suggestion was adopted, although, since it meant an absence by the general manager from his office one day out of five, it was followed only when his presence at a meeting was particularly desirable.

Another proposal was for 'flexible' authorizing limits for branch managers. It had been the practice of the Bank to establish authorizing limits as considered appropriate for certain positions – general manager, assistant general manager, managers of large branches, managers of smaller branches, and so on. The consultants' proposal was that each manager should have an individual limit assigned to him personally, reflecting the degree of confidence placed in him. This was not adopted. It was seen as potentially reducing the proportion of credit applications that could be disposed of at the branch level because it would probably have resulted in a reduction in the limit employed at some branches if ever the branch managers were replaced. The Bank found that the staff of an office came to regard the limit of the manager of the office as being, in a sense, their limit. If a new manager was appointed with a lower limit than that exercised by his more experienced predecessor, this put him in a poor light with his staff, who found themselves suddenly burdened with the greater amount of work required to present to a higher authority credits formerly authorized by their previous manager. The general practice of assigning an authorizing limit to a particular post, rather than to an individual, was continued.

The problems arising from varying the authorizing limit exercised at a branch were well illustrated at the Calgary branch when it was incorporated into the Prairie Region and the supervisor who had directed the branch was replaced by a manager with a lower limit. Not only did the staff suffer a let-down from losing the responsibility of sharing with the supervisor the oversight of another branch (Edmonton), but it now found itself involved in the same procedural burdens as the branch that had formerly 'come under' them. This was because the submitting of a credit beyond a branch manager's limit and therefore requiring the consideration of a senior level within the Bank required more material to be supplied in support of the proposal.

Another minor recommendation that was not adopted was for some system of 'productivity indices' to assess the performance of individual branches and make comparisons between the branches within a given region. Many months were spent in the Bank trying to establish an index of activity or productivity for branches, but the attempt was finally abandoned. Too many imponderables were involved in weighing the effort expended on a particular inquiry, application, or loan to permit a standard yardstick of work effort to be arrived at that could, with confidence in its justice and accuracy, be imposed on the branches. Figures were maintained at CMO of the number of inquiries, applications, and loans per credit officer at each branch. These showed an extraordinary range among the branches and a significant tendency for a branch to remain in the same spot relative to other branches with respect to some activity being measured. Nevertheless, there were so many differences between the communities and areas served by each branch that could affect these figures that management hesitated to use them in any open administrative routine. The consultants went further than this and proposed a system for costing the work of branches based on time sheets and standard costs for engineers, credit officers, and legal officers. To this idea the objections mentioned above were even more strongly opposed, and the idea was not adopted. Branch expenses were reported in detail regularly, and management of the Bank believed it had no difficulty in spotting any branches where some item of cost deviated from the norm or the acceptable.

From the few proposals by the consultants that we have touched on, it would appear that, although their general concepts were accepted, they were only partially applied. Although this was the case, the consultants' report remained in the background of the management of the Bank's affairs for many years and provided goals which, if not always attained, at least gave something at which to aim. Further, their report brought into focus a fundamental problem for the Bank – how to leave the field offices the amount of room desirable for their exercise of initiative and imagination, while still protecting the Bank against varied lines of decision across the Bank in the very delicate areas of credit policy and credit judgment.

CHAPTER FIFTEEN

The Bank under study – policy

The Porter Commission

In 1962, the Bank was examined by a third body, the Royal Commission on Banking and Finance, known as the Porter Commission. Its appointment was announced in October 1961,[1] and it started work in April 1962. After holding public hearings in all parts of the country, it submitted its report in February 1964. Its task was to examine the whole system of banking and finance in Canada, so that the IDB was not one of its major concerns. Nevertheless, many of the briefs submitted had references to the IDB in them. These references to the Bank usually reflected the special interests of those presenting them, and so the comments reflected just about every possible attitude to the Bank. Some felt that the Bank was not nearly active enough despite the growth it had experienced in the preceding few years, while others regarded this growth with alarm as a clear sign that the Bank was becoming much too active. One of the latter, the Canadian Bankers' Association, said that some of the IDB's 'lending business in the last year or two would appear to have been directly competitive with the chartered banks.'[2] The association claimed that, were the chartered banks able to take mortgage security as collateral on loans, and were they not subject to a ceiling on the rate of interest they could charge, they would be able to handle a large proportion of the business being done by the IDB.[3] The Retail Merchants' Association considered that the IDB had an excellent record of performance and had made an important contribution to the growth of Canadian industry, but it wanted the Bank to make more working capital loans to finance inventories and receivables.[4]

The Canadian Federation of Agriculture did not think 'that in principle the IDB should be making loans for agricultural production purposes.'[5] Agriculture had just become eligible for IDB loans, but in 1961–4 nearly 400 were made. These loans were mostly to commercial types of agricultural endeavour and to specialized operations such as poultry raising and egg production which were not eligible for loans from the Farm Credit Corporation. The Federation of Agriculture felt the Farm Credit Corporation was a much more suitable source of loans; it made smaller loans than the IDB and so encouraged family farms rather than large units of production.[6]

The Canadian Manufacturers' Association reported that a survey of its members showed the IDB to be the third most frequently reported source of expansion money and said that it had been 'very valuable in filling gaps in the financial facilities available to industry.' It complained, however, of the Bank's loan conditions.[7] The Investment Dealers Association said that, in general, the operations of the IDB were satisfactory. 'In spite of ... criticisms, it appears to us that the IDB is doing a good job.' It described the Bank as Canada's best answer so far to the particular problems faced by the entrepreneur seeking to obtain less than $50,000 in financing. However, it felt that perhaps the Bank encouraged debt financing in cases where an issue of shares might have been more suitable.[8]

Several provinces referred to the Bank in their briefs, with the usual wide range of opinions. Premier Robert Stanfield of Nova Scotia said that the Bank had been very active in recent years and was 'quite helpful' in the industrial field. New Brunswick said that the Bank had done a very good job regionally in the field of small business. The Atlantic Provinces Economic Council said that during the previous few years the Bank had not left itself open to complaints that it was too cautious and, with new offices in the Atlantic provinces (the branch in Halifax had been opened in 1956 and the branch in Saint John in 1959), appeared to be performing its particular role with increasing satisfaction.[9]

Ontario lambasted the Bank. The scale of operations was far too small. It had only 'scratched the surface' of the problem of longer-term finance to small business. It had 'outbanked the bankers in caution.' While the province's brief did not say that the IDB should be separated from the Bank of Canada, it hinted at it with the comment: 'It is not clear whether the reason for the meagre scale of operations of the IDB is the close connection of the institution with the Bank of Canada.'[10]

Ontario's views seem a bit severe when one considers that the province's share of the total number of loans approved by the Bank had increased from 28 per cent in 1955 to 39 per cent in 1962. Previously, the Ontario Department of Planning and Development had been the Bank's strongest supporter among the provinces; in November 1955 the director of the Trade and Industry Branch of the department had written to Mr Marble, general manager of the Bank: 'We have always found the Toronto office [of the IDB] to be most cooperative and gave [sic] sympathetic hearing and action to any people we have taken to them. We consider your Bank to fill a gap in industrial development work to which there is no alternative amongst private financial organizations.'

Perhaps it should be noted that at the time that the province's views were given to the Porter Commission, the provincial minister of economics and development, Robert Macaulay, was considering whether to recommend to his government that Ontario set up its own loan fund. From comments made by him in his testimony before the commission, it would appear that his complaints were partly based, as so often with critics of the Bank, on a rejection or misunderstanding of the role assigned to the Bank by its act. Questioned by the commission as to the reason for his criticism, Mr Macaulay said: 'All we are saying is that if the IDB exists to aid small business, that is fine. If it exists to aid regional development, then that is fine. If it exists to bring industrial development to less wealthy provinces, that is fine. But let us have everybody dealing with them, including those dishing out the money, know what they are doing, because I do not think they do.'[11] The fact was that the last two possible reasons he gave for the existence of the Bank were not mentioned in the act at all, and even his first was valid only to the extent that the preamble to the act said that the Bank was to have 'special consideration for the needs of small and medium-sized businesses.' The mandate was quite simple, and those working in the Bank certainly thought it clear — to consider applications for financial assistance from businesses unable to obtain it elsewhere on reasonable terms and conditions.

Manitoba was also critical. The criticism in its brief to the Porter Commission suggested that the province saw the Bank in a different role from that given it by its act of incorporation. The province felt that the IDB should be not just a provider of financing but rather a sort of super-promoter of industrial development or, as Premier Duff Roblin put it in his evidence, 'an agency which is responsible for this whole phase of the creation and development of economic opportunity rather than just another source of obtaining money.'[12]

Manitoba thought that the Bank should concentrate its efforts on balanced regional growth. More decentralization was needed in the

Bank's organization since the branch personnel tended to be 'directed from the centre with uncertain local influence on judgment or policy.' Also, separation of the Bank from the Bank of Canada might be considered, not only because of the policies that came out of head office (and which were apparently presumed to be of a restraining character), but because the IDB might be used as an arm of monetary policy, which cut down its effectiveness. To be seen as an arm of monetary policy was almost a flattering role for the Bank, considering that its assets were only around $140 million as compared with the assets of the chartered banks, which were well over 100 times greater. To implement Mr Roblin's views would have required major changes in the nature of the IDB. Set up to fill a gap in the financial structure of Canada, it had neither the legal basis nor the structure to act as a 'creator of economic opportunity' or as a 'promoter' of any form of development, and, of course, it was not an 'arm of monetary policy.'[13]

Manitoba had set up its own loan fund, the Manitoba Development Fund, a few years before. Prominent among the arguments for doing so was a claim by Mr Roblin's government that the IDB was not doing a proper job for Manitoba. During his testimony to the Porter Commission, Mr Roblin suggested that perhaps the IDB could help the province by putting money into the Manitoba Development Fund.[14]

Saskatchewan combined compliments and criticisms, but, like Manitoba, felt the Bank should be more oriented toward promoting, and not merely financing, industrial development. It suggested that the Bank's 'credit committee' might well include representatives of the provinces 'who may bring a sort of eagerness for industries which the IDB officials do not feel.'[15]

More important to the IDB than these presentations to the Porter Commission were those of the sales finance companies. These had become quite concerned about the Bank's increased activity and what they regarded as its growing aggressiveness reflected in the new publicity efforts. To the finance companies, the increasing volume of loans made the Bank an open competitor with them in spite of the stipulation in the IDB Act that it should lend only when it was of the opinion that money would not otherwise be available on reasonable terms and conditions.

Attempts by the IDB to be more responsive to requests for loans

Up to this time, the principal public criticisms of the Bank were that it was not as active as it ought to be, that it was too conservative in its credit judgments, and that it did not lose enough money. As we saw in chapter

10, the Bank had responded to this by moving toward a freer and more flexible position in credit matters, and in 1960 instructions had been issued to this end. As 1961 opened, the reassessment of the Bank's lending policies was reflected in a memorandum by Mr Marble of a discussion with Mr Coyne. One sentence summed up Mr Coyne's views – 'The whole objective is to do more business.'

Shortly afterward, Mr Marble described some of the ways in which the Bank was trying to do this: 'We have just embarked on a new, enlarged and more intensive advertising campaign, and offices have been urged not only to take advantage of opportunities as they arise but to become more active in developing occasions to make speeches, exhibit the new IDB film, and visit bank managers, accountants, lawyers, etc.'

A more relaxed attitude toward credit proposals was reflected in a policy circular issued to the Bank's staff in April 1961 and at the conference of supervisors in May. This trend developed rapidly, and in August fresh instructions on lending policy were issued. It may be recalled that the Vancouver supervisor had described the April circular as a 'somewhat inflammatory document' and had been tempted to keep it away from inexperienced credit officers.[16] He must have felt like hiding the new one altogether. It repeated the instructions of April and gave even stronger encouragement to more receptive attitudes:

Under no circumstances should the impression be given that the Bank applies any rule-of-thumb based on percentages [regarding security or investment] ... unless there are factors obviously unfavourable or unacceptable, the reaction [to a credit application] ought to be positive and a willingness to consider the proposal displayed ... There is no bias against making a loan which is greater than the investment by others ... so [also] may the amount of a loan exceed even the original cost of the assets to be mortgaged as security ... The value of the security is only one of the factors to be taken into account. Of greater importance are such factors as the needs of the business, quality of management, market prospects and the prospective profits ... The borrower should be given no reason to feel that he is being bound hand and foot.

Complaints of finance companies about the IDB

However, the efforts of the Bank to respond to criticisms that it was not active enough understandably alarmed those who thought it was becoming far too active, viz. the sales finance companies. With the prospect appearing early in 1961 of even greater activity on the part of the Bank as a result of the expected enlargement of its field by an amendment to the IDB Act, the finance companies were thoroughly roused.

During the summer of 1961 – even before the bill amending the IDB Act was passed – and in the autumn, the officials of one finance company made strong representations about the IDB to the president of the Bank both by letter and by personal visits. They complained that the Bank was making loans that they were willing to make and refinancing some they had already made. They believed that this resulted from a newly aggressive attitude on the part of the IDB as reflected in its new and energetic publicity activities. The size and content of the Bank's new advertisements seemed to the finance companies to be designed to create business for the IDB rather than to serve the more modest purpose, which they thought appropriate to a non-competitive lender, of simply informing a reader where credit that was not available elsewhere might be obtained. They also attributed the Bank's ability to take business away from them (as they claimed it did) to some extent to certain operational advantages that the IDB enjoyed: it paid no income taxes, obtained its money easily and at lower rates of interest than commercial lenders had to pay in the public markets, and did not have to earn a commercial return on its capital as the finance companies had to do to satisfy shareholders and facilitate the raising of capital.

In March 1962, one of the largest of the companies, Industrial Acceptance Corporation Ltd, in its annual report for 1961, which received wide coverage in the press,[17] singled out 'increased competition from the Crown-owned Industrial Development Bank' as being 'not the least important' in the keen competition in the field of instalment credit offered by banks and credit unions. IAC was a substantial company with total assets of over $600 million and net profits after taxes of $11,700,000 in 1961.

Two aspects of the Bank's lending practices were of particular concern to the finance companies. The first was the occasional refinancing of a debt already owed by an IDB applicant to a finance company. The second was the basis on which the IDB determined that the terms for borrowing offered by another lender were unreasonable. They strongly suspected that the fact that their rates of interest were higher than the IDB's was often the determining factor in these matters. That their rate of interest was usually the higher was due, they argued, to the commercial necessities described above to which the IDB was not subject.

Policy instructions issued by the Bank regarding availability of funds elsewhere

As we have seen, the major preoccupation of the Bank regarding policy during fiscal 1960 and early 1961 had been with relaxing its attitudes to credit proposals. However, the position of other lenders had not been overlooked. The policy circular issued in April 1961 had had in it three paragraphs relating to other lenders recording what had become the established policies in this regard. These had been incorporated without change in the circular of August. The first paragraph dealt with the refinancing of debts owed to others. Applications for loans for this purpose could be considered if the debt to be refinanced were a demand or maturing obligation that the lender was unwilling to continue or renew and if a term loan were the proper answer to the applicant's need and could not be obtained elsewhere on reasonable terms and conditions. The Bank should not prepay a term debt except where necessary to remove a prior charge on assets pledged to the Bank so as to improve the Bank's security position, or where the terms of the existing debt put an unduly onerous burden on the debtor business.

The second paragraph dealt specifically with financing the purchase of machinery and equipment, a field in which the finance companies were particularly interested. It said that the Bank should be prepared to assist in these purchases even if financing were available elsewhere if it was at rates and on terms that appeared unreasonable.

The third paragraph had to do with working capital loans and therefore concerned the chartered banks rather than the finance companies. The IDB did not want to assume the normal role of the chartered banks of providing financing for a business's daily operations. Such loans to assist businesses to finance operations could be made 'to enable a business to expand or to place itself in a better financial position' (which pretty well covered everything), but the Bank would have to be satisfied that the chartered bank was doing as much as might be expected 'in the circumstances' through an operating line of credit. Unusual cases were allowed for in the closing instruction that, nevertheless, the Bank should be prepared in 'appropriate' (again!) cases to provide working capital where such was refused by a chartered bank; in such an event, the applicant's situation should be investigated very carefully.

Only the first two paragraphs concerned the finance companies. However, special circular instructions were issued in October 1961, again in November, and again in February 1962, dealing specifically with the refinancing of lien contracts. First, it was made clear that there was an onus on an applicant seeking a loan to refinance liens to demonstrate that their terms were unduly burdensome. Any opinion by the Bank in this respect should be based mainly on the relationship of the required lien payments to the prospective earnings of the business. Second, it was suggested that there would be cases where the liens could be left outstanding and whatever burden they might be thought to put on earnings could be accommodated by keeping principal payments on any further loan from the IDB at a low level until the liens were paid off; as time went on, this device was resorted to more and more.

These instructions provided for somewhat different procedures for loans of above and below $25,000. A division of this sort was often used by the Bank in policy instructions, partly to reduce the burden placed on its field staff by the instructions, partly to fit serious cases the Bank might encounter, and partly to extend more consideration to the smaller businesses. Whatever the policy was, it would be expected to be a much more important issue in larger than in smaller loans. The Bank's credit officer, before agreeing to consider a proposal for lien refinancing in excess of $25,000, was to ascertain whether an approach for repayment terms in better relationship to the applicant's earning power had been made to the lien holders, and what the response had been. In February 1962, the rule was strengthened to require that an approach to the lien holders had actually been made and refused. This seemed like a very useful sort of check on the availability of financing elsewhere, but it was not always easy to apply. Sometimes it seemed to suggest to the finance company concerned that the IDB was telling it to ease the terms of its liens under a threat to refinance them if it did not. Also, the limiting of this check to the refinancing of liens over $25,000 seemed to imply that refinancing under that level was not a matter to be seriously concerned about. There was nothing in the finance companies' representations or in the Bank's own experience to support this view. A study by the Bank the following year, in 1962, showed that approximately 75 per cent of finance company liens refinanced were under $25,000 and represented 33 per cent of the dollar total.

These circular instructions closed with a paragraph typical of the 'escape' phraseology in which IDB policy instructions often ended: 'The above should not be interpreted as indicating that any policy decision has been taken which would preclude lien refinancing in appropriate cases.' Although this would seem to open up the whole subject of the instructions all over again, it was consistent with the practice regarding policy directives that the management of IDB nearly always followed and that affected operations, organization, and procedures. It was found impossible to draft simple rules that could be mechanically applied to meet every situation. There had to be room in instructions for considering the nuances of general policy statements as they related to individual cases. This required the exercise of individual judgment at all levels in the Bank and either some sort of oversight by GMO or references to it for decisions in difficult cases in order to maintain a consistent policy across the Bank.

Further instructions were issued in November 1961 dealing with the general attitude to be adopted toward the availability of financing from other sources, quite apart from cases involving refinancing, and the same device was adopted of issuing slightly different guidelines for larger than for smaller loans. In this case, the dividing line was $100,000, but for both groups of loans the language used avoided rigidity and left room to vary the severity of the tests applied to suit the different sets of circumstances that might be encountered. For approaches in excess of $100,000, and 'particularly those which appear, on the basis of usual credit criteria, to measure up well enough that they might be regarded as appropriate lending situations for regular mortgage lenders or other conventional sources of financing,' the Bank would require 'specific assurances and, if possible, some supporting evidence that real efforts had been made to obtain the required financing elsewhere.' For proposals under $100,000, the instructions said it 'may' be a 'justifiable presumption, in most instances, that prospects of satisfactory alternate sources of term loan funds being available to the applicant are at least limited.' Accordingly, a declaration on the Bank's application form that the financing sought was not available from other sources on reasonable terms and conditions, supplemented by 'the exercise of good judgement on the part of the Bank's officers,' could be regarded as satisfying the requirements of the IDB Act in this regard. The desire of the Bank's management to ensure that all possibilities and variations in circumstances were somehow provided for was crowned by the final paragraph, which said that some proposals under $100,000 would have to be dealt with like proposals over $100,000, but this would have to be a matter of 'careful judgement on the part of branch officers.'

At about the same time as these instructions were going out, a system was set up for following from month to month the amount of refinancing being done by the Bank. Table 13 shows the dollar amount of refinancing of equipment liens held by the finance companies that was included in programs financed by the Bank between 1959 and 1967. The liens were not all refinanced by the proceeds of IDB loans, because funds from other sources would nearly always be associated with a loan from the Bank in financing a program. However, the table also shows the liens refinanced expressed as a percentage of IDB loan authorizations for each year, without considering other funds used to finance the programs, in order to give the most extreme measure of the relative magnitude of this particular aspect of the Bank's operations.

After 1961, refinancing of equipment liens held by finance companies

TABLE 13

Refinancing of liens 1959–67

	Annual total authorizations ($millions)	Part of programs used for financing of equipment liens held by finance companies ($millions)	Column 2 as percentage of total authorizations
1959	30.6	1.2	3.9
1960	38.6	2.2	5.7
1961	71.2	4.8	6.7
1962	92.0	3.3	3.6
1963	79.8	2.0	2.5
1964	88.1	n/a	n/a
1965	96.1	1.4	1.5
1966	122.6	1.5	1.2
1967	113.1	1.3	1.1

declined markedly both in dollars and as a percentage of total authorizations, undoubtedly as a result of the special instructions issued in the fall of 1961 and subsequent monitoring.

Early in 1962, the monitoring of the application of policy principles by the Bank's branches was strengthened. It was the practice for a copy of every memorandum recording the initial discussion with a prospective applicant (called an 'enquiry' within the Bank) to be sent to GMO as a matter of normal routine. These were being read by an assistant general manager with an eye to forestalling policy problems, and for a year or two letters went out to field offices just about every day about applications or proposals received that seemed to have the seeds of policy trouble in them.

The following long extract from a letter written to a regional office by the assistant general manager in 1964 is a good example of the kind of guidance that was given and of the sincerity with which the Bank tried to deal with these difficult matters:

Where liens have been recently incurred, there are several very good reasons why we should hesitate to refinance them or even, in some cases, to ask that the lienholders be approached to revise them. It really hardly seems fair to a lienholder with which a company has recently entered in a contract, that it should, while the contract is still fresh, be asked to extend its terms under threat of finding itself displaced by ourselves. We understand that some of the liens held by ... [the finance company] were actually refinanced by them in 1963 ... to give the company some payment relief. To be asked now, within a relatively short time, to revise these all over again or else have them paid off by ourselves could quite justifiably be regarded by them as unreasonable.

The liens ... include some which must have arisen within the past few months ... It must hardly seem justifiable to the lienholder that he should be threatened with displacement if he does not revise contracts so newly established. To ask that these be refinanced so soon, the company would have to represent either that it entered into the contracts with no intention of living up to them or that it had made a very serious error in judgement in undertaking them. Neither representation would reflect credit on the company. The liens could certainly hardly have run for long enough for the company to be able to argue that it had 'found' their terms to be too onerous.

There is implicit in these comments a strong suggestion that a request for the refinancing of recently contracted liens reflects very seriously on the judgement of the management involved. In this particular case, the reflection of this nature is very strong. The management is not only in a position now of having erred in estimating its capacity to carry liens assumed in the past few months, but must actually argue that it has erred in the revisions in certain liens which it negotiated within the past year with the same end in view as that now sought with part of the proceeds of our loan!

The Bank was in the throes of re-examining its policies, as well as its structures and procedures, as required by the expanded field opened up by the amendments of 1956 and 1961 and by the decision to relax its credit assessments somewhat. The increased volume of loans that these developments had produced had been augmented further by the opening of branches and a more energetic publicity program. All these things naturally had a very stimulating effect on the Bank's staff, and it took time and discussion to work out, for the Bank's staff, the proper but somewhat incongruous combination expected from them of eagerness to help those who were entitled to it, with wariness and caution on matters of policy, and particularly those involving other lenders.

Ultimately, the responsibility for reconciling these two somewhat contradictory views in their practical application to individual cases fell on the staff in the Bank's branches. It was not easily done. The diligence with which applicants would seek alternative sources of funds when asked to do so would vary widely, and the validity and sincerity of any 'letters of refusal' supplied were hard to establish. It was sometimes suspected that an astute applicant would avoid approaching the most promising sources of financing so as to ensure that he obtained refusals. It was also reported that in some cases lenders were reacting unfavourably to requests for letters of refusal and declining to supply them. Since this was now becoming a common requirement on the part of the IDB for applications for large amounts, such a reaction created difficulties. Perhaps the worst result of all, at least for the IDB, of its efforts to follow its policies regarding other lenders was that some applicants seemed to regard the Bank's caution in this matter as just an exercise in 'red tape,' and the Bank's image suffered from its attempts to do things properly. In the eyes of some applicants and of the Bank's branches, there was more involved than merely financial accommodation. In a letter written in 1963, J.E. Nordin, manager of the Bank's Montreal branch, explained the thoughts that led some businesses to approach the Bank for financial help: 'The Bank has, in its nineteen years of existence, established a reputation in Canadian business, of a specialized and understanding knowledge of the problems faced by small and medium size businesses in obtaining term financing. Therefore, many existing and potential borrowers wish to deal with the Bank to take advantage of this knowledge and have no desire to seek alternative sources of financing.'

Perhaps the most difficult policy to communicate, even internally, was that having to do with the interest rates of other lenders. Only in 1961 had it been established as a matter of policy that a rate offered by another lender, higher than the IDB's rate but within the normal commercial range, was not to be considered unreasonable per se, and in 1962, and even later, the precedents and judgments to make this effective at the field level were still being established. One supervisor put the problem as the field officers saw it: 'A 12–15% rate of interest and a two-year repayment term might not be at all unreasonable in the case of a new trucking business in which the investment of shareholders is relatively small and the experience of management somewhat limited. On the other hand, an established trucking company with a good record of earnings wishing to borrow an amount in keeping with its ability to repay and in line with the investment by others should not be required to pay interest rates of 12–15%.' A branch manager put it more succinctly: 'Why should we make a good customer pay someone else 10% when we can lend the money to him at 7%?'

In 1962, instructions were issued that, where an appraisal of the reasonableness of the terms of alternative financing depended upon the rate of interest itself, the matter should be referred to the general manager for a ruling in any case where the rate was more than 10 per cent; the IDB's rate at the time was 7 per cent. This was not intended to establish 10 per cent as the dividing line between reasonable and unreasonable rates. It was to reduce the number of cases referred to GMO for a ruling by eliminating those that, having a rate below 10 per cent, were considered unlikely to raise doubts as to their reasonableness.

Although an account of the evolution of the Bank's policies regarding other lenders makes the process sound quite formidable, constant correspondence and repeated rulings on individual cases gradually established a broad grasp of and adherence to these policies, and they were followed and applied by the Bank's staff with care and discretion. The heads of some of the chartered banks continued, from time to time, to use alleged misdemeanours on the part of the IDB in its role as a supplementary lender as conversation pieces when they would meet the Bank's president in his capacity of governor of the Bank of Canada. Relations with the banks at the branch level, however, and in actual operations were usually excellent.

Further complaints by finance companies

The federal government had announced the appointment of the Royal Commission on Banking and Finance (the Porter Commission) in October 1961. Almost at once the IDB received requests from finance companies, chartered banks, and the Canadian Bankers' Association for information about the IDB and its policies, presumably to help them prepare their briefs. The association of the major finance companies – the Federated Council of Sales Finance Companies – gave itself a dry run in the latter part of 1961 by submitting a brief to the government severely criticizing the IDB along the lines outlined previously. This council was the national association of the sales finance industry, with a membership of thirty-nine companies that together handled 70 per cent of the industry's total volume. Industrial Acceptance and another large finance company, Laurentide Financial Corporation of Vancouver, and the Federated Council all submitted briefs to the commission. The two companies appeared before the commission in May, and the council appeared in September. All made the same complaints – the Bank was not observing the restriction placed on it that it should provide financial assistance only where it was of the opinion that it would not otherwise be available on reasonable terms and conditions; it was using the advantages of a less expensive source of funds than was available to the finance companies, and of freedom from taxes, to lend at lower rates of interest than the finance companies could do; by these means and an aggressive advertising campaign, it was strenuously competing with the finance companies and making inroads into their business.[18]

These representations prompted the *Financial Times* of Montreal on 28 May 1962 to suggest as a motto for the IDB: 'Be like Caesar's wife.' Presumably the thought behind the suggestion was that the Bank should so conduct its operations as to place itself beyond criticism. However, Caesar's wife had the advantage of knowing what criticism to place herself beyond. The IDB was often criticized for opposite and contradictory reasons so that it could hardly have found guidance in her example.

Officials of the finance companies also made public speeches against the IDB, even to the point of calling for its eventual discontinuance. One that received wide coverage was given in Fredericton by K.M. MacDonald, vice-president and general sales manager of IAC. As reported in the Montreal *Gazette* on 10 January 1963, Mr MacDonald, apart from claiming that the IDB had many times overstepped the legal limits put on its operations, attacked the basic concept of a government-sponsored lending institution that extended assistance to businesses unable to get financing elsewhere. He questioned if a business proposal would prove both sound and profitable if it had been refused by all of the commercial sources of credit available. If this sort of government intrusion into the business world were accepted, no industry would be immune. He expressed the belief that a basic principle was at stake by which the private enterprise system might stand or fall.

This last doctrinal view perhaps helps to explain the vigour with which the finance companies criticized the IDB. Perhaps another circumstance should also be borne in mind. The chartered banks had moved into consumer credit in a big way. This was an important field for the finance companies, and it had been increasing. The brief submitted to the Porter Commission by the Federated Council estimated that in 1961 there was, in Canada, a total of $4,630 million of consumer credit of various kinds outstanding. The finance companies were estimated to provide $800 million of this total. The chartered banks were said to be providing $1,030 million, and the resources they commanded must have foreshadowed an ever larger share of the market for them in the future.[19] This development must have caused great apprehension on the part of the finance companies about the future growth of one of their major activities. In any event, the companies were apparently concerned about the IDB's rate of expansion.

In 1964, the same year in which the Porter Commission issued its report, the finance companies took the initiative to improve relations with the IDB. Through B. London of Niagara Finance and K.M. MacDonald of IAC, the Federated Council of Sales Finance Companies invited the writer, the assistant general manager of the IDB, to address one of its meetings. This went a long way to improve permanently relations between the Bank and the finance companies. Field officers of the finance companies and the IDB were instructed to cultivate a friendly acquaintance with each other, and one finance company sent 200 copies of the address to its branches to improve their understanding of the IDB's operations.

IDB brief to the Porter Commission, and the report by the commission

The IDB's turn to appear before the Porter Commission came in January 1963. Louis Rasminsky, president of the Bank, J.R. Beattie, senior deputy governor of the Bank of Canada, a member of the IDB's board of directors and executive committee, and Mr Rasminsky's alternate as president of the IDB, and A.N.H. James, general manager, gave testimony on behalf of the IDB. The Bank had previously submitted a brief that is still an excellent reference source on the Bank's history, operations, and policies up to that time. The commission also had available to help it in its deliberations a long study on the financing of small business prepared by one of its staff, F.X. Wildgen. This had in it a chapter on the IDB.[20]

The commission issued its report in 1964,[21] and it is clear from it, as well as from the questions the commissioners put to the Bank's representatives during the public hearing, that the commission had accepted, to some degree, the complaints of the finance companies. Although the commission said in its report that it believed the IDB had performed a valuable role in Canada's financial system and would continue to do so, it also felt that the system was evolving and that the IDB should take account of that evolution by encouraging, as an 'active agent ... constructive private developments,' presumably in the field of financing small businesses. No indication was given as to how this hazily expressed role was to be performed beyond the equally vague injunction that the Bank 'should cooperate to the fullest extent with other agencies – insofar as it can without favouring particular institutions – in order to encourage the development of additional financing facilities for small businesses and to ensure that small businesses are in a position to make the fullest use of existing sources.'[22]

Regarding the 'insofar as' clause, it is interesting to note that the IDB was asked from time to time by some other lender to simplify the administration of the Bank's policy toward other sources of financing by referring all inquiries received by the Bank first to it – the other lender!

As for the encouragement of 'additional financing facilities,' the Bank believed that it had itself been largely responsible for the evolution in Canada's financial system that had already seen the appearance of new sources of term financing for small businesses. It regarded this as one of its greatest accomplishments, even though it was achieved without overt efforts or elaborate programs. When the Bank was founded in 1944 to provide term financing largely for small businesses, there was no place that these businesses could go for such financing. Nevertheless, many observers in the commercial lending world saw no need for the Bank. In their opinion, if a small business could not get all the money it needed from one of the existing sources, and in such form as then provided, it was simply because the business was not creditworthy. And yet, by 1962-3, when the Porter Commission was making its investigations, the chartered banks had begun to make term loans and were clamouring for the power to lend against mortgage security so that they could make more, some of the major finance companies were setting up special departments to make broadly based industrial loans to small businesses, several provinces had set up special agencies to do the same, a number of companies had been set up to specialize in term or equity financing for small businesses, and a leading one of these had even been largely staffed in its senior positions by employees drawn from the IDB. To some extent these developments reflected world trends, but Canada's Industrial Development Bank helped to establish those trends. Within Canada, the mere example of its successful operation must have been a major factor in the emergence of new initiatives toward providing sources of financing for small business.

Equally important must have been the Bank's role in educating the owners of small businesses to see broadly based bond mortgage financing not as the exclusive privilege of large corporations but as a natural way for a small business to handle some of its financial needs. Private lenders all over Canada must have benefited from this. Indeed, other lenders very likely learned the same message from the IDB. A study made in 1972 showed that of the 8 per cent or so of IDB loan authorizations that later were cancelled, one-third were replaced by financing from other lenders, offered after the IDB's willingness to make a loan had been indicated.

During the hearings of the Porter Commission, one of the commissioners asked to what extent the 'gap' in the financial structure of Canada that the IDB was intended to fill still existed. Mr Rasminsky made the natural reply that the entry of commercial lenders into the field of small business financing had probably reduced the gap percentage-wise.[23] In later years, the Bank's experience suggested, however, that the process by which the IDB's operations were educating both lenders and borrowers was creating a whole new world of financing and, in effect, making a new gap to add to the old one.

The commission appeared to share with the finance companies the opinion that the most important factor in the relationship between the IDB's operations and those of other lenders was the rate of interest charged by each on their loans. In its brief and its testimony, the IDB stressed that an opinion of its officers as to the reasonableness of the terms of another lender generally rested on a broad range of circumstances such as the time allowed for the repayment of a loan, the prospective earnings of a business relative to annual debt payments, the security required, and the extent to which a loan met the needs of the borrower; rarely was a difference in interest rates a critical factor. However, the commission seemed unconvinced. It pointed out in its report that the Bank's early practice of setting its rate above that of the chartered banks was consistent with the fact that at that time the chartered banks were in practice the only alternative source of financing. There were few specialized small business lenders, and the finance companies were less active in the field. However, the situation had altered, and the IDB had now to take account of all these lenders.[24]

These views would seem to imply that the commission thought that the IDB's rate of interest was too low. In fact, however, the closest it came to saying so in its report was the comment that, when comparable credit was available from private sources at rates ranging upward from 7 per cent, the IDB rate of 7 per cent was 'perhaps' too low. The matter was explored during the commissioners' questioning of the Bank's representatives. J.D. Gibson, one of the commissioners, expressed puzzlement that the IDB's rate should be below that of some other lenders. In replying, Mr Rasminsky described one consideration very delicately: 'I think, Mr. Gibson, one would have to say that the reason for this is that given the whole background of the establishment of the IDB and its legislative history, and the type of discussion that took place when it was set up, the view that has been taken by the Directors of the Bank in fixing the rate from time to time has been that the rate should not be fixed at the levels that would be involved if the principle that you have just stated were to be followed.' To this Mr Gibson replied: 'I see your point.' In his report to the commission, Mr Wildgen spoke more plainly: 'It seems, however, extremely doubtful whether Parliament would condone the imposition of interest rates of, say, 9% to 12% by a publicly sponsored institution.'[25]

Commissioner W. Thomas Brown suggested that for the Bank's rate of interest to be below that of some other lenders was to favour the inefficient (as he considered those who came to the Bank because they could not get financial support from normal sources) over the efficient (i.e. those who could get support from other sources).[26] This view was just a new version of the old argument that there was no gap for the Bank to fill – a creditworthy business could get what money it needed from commercial sources.

At the time of the Porter Commission hearings, the IDB's lending rate was 7 per cent. As will be seen from Appendix I, while this was below some rates of interest in the market, it was not below all. The Bank believed its rate was within the range of variation of commercial rates and saw itself as assisting businesses that had good promise but were not yet strong enough to stand all the burdens and buffets of the business world. The Bank made loans to assist such businesses to survive and prosper. In due course, such a business would be able to stand in the business world as a borrower on normal terms and no longer qualify for aid from the Bank.

The commission made three general recommendations about the IDB's interest rate policy. First, the Bank should not restrict itself to a single rate for all loans. The Bank had occasionally departed from this practice, particularly in its early years, in what were characteristically known as 'special circumstances' − usually large transactions of an unusual character, which had occurred only rarely. In such cases, the rate might have been set above or below the Bank's standard rate. Also, the Bank had started, in 1962, setting a rate above the standard when its security was in the form of a second mortgage. However, the commission's view was that for every loan the rate of interest should give recognition to differing costs and risks as between one loan and another, with an overall range of perhaps 2 per cent.[27] The Bank did later establish a schedule of 'standard' rates with a range, in practice, of 2 per cent, with the rate varying according to the size of a loan, but for a government institution to fix the rate for each individual loan on the basis of the Bank's judgment as to the cost and risk of each loan would, in the eyes of the Bank's management, have been impractical.

Second, the commission suggested that the IDB keep its rates more in line with comparable private rates than it had been. Third, the commission said that, in setting its rate, the Bank should be 'wary of inhibiting developments in the private lending system,' which might result from its lending actively at relatively low rates.[28]

The commission seemed to think that the Bank was not too conservative and that its procedures were not too slow. It said: 'There are undoubtedly cases in which these criticisms are justified and the loss ratio of 1/2 of 1%, while not negligible, is moderate for an institution deemed to operate in areas beyond the risk-taking ability of conventional lenders. However, care is essential in all lending to smaller businesses. Moreover, the time taken for investigations reported to us by the IDB does not seem excessive and has been shortened.'[29]

The commission recorded its view that the Bank should remain a subsidiary of the Bank of Canada, because this appeared to shield it from interference with its exercise of sound business judgment. It also thought that the IDB should continue to be financed through the Bank of Canada.[30] The Glassco Commission had recommended that the IDB be separated from the Bank of Canada and placed under the minister of finance. The Porter Commission may have felt that, since it held a different opinion, it should place it on the record.

The commission recommended that the board and executive committee of the IDB 'should be made up of Directors suited to the IDB's quite different functions' rather than to the functions of the Bank of Canada.[31] This suggestion must have rested on some more abstruse thought than knowledge of who the directors of the IDB (and the Bank of Canada) were. At the time, the outside directors (those who were not ex officio directors as officials of the Bank of Canada or deputy ministers) included a former president of a chartered bank, a proprietor of a small wood-working business, a chartered accountant with many small businesses among his clients, a druggist, a principal in a medium-sized manufacturing company, the manager of a board of trade in a small city, the proprietor of a food-processing business that had grown from small beginnings to a medium size, the principal in another medium-sized manufacturing enterprise, and a small businessman in the wholesale trade. One might wonder what better qualifications for directors of the IDB the royal commission had in mind.

The commission also suggested that the IDB should have its own full-time chief executive officer to free the governor of the Bank of Canada from direct responsibility in this connection. A bill to achieve this had been introduced into Parliament in January 1963 at the suggestion of Mr Rasminsky. This bill would have introduced the term *chief executive officer* into the IDB's hierarchy for the first time. A full-time president was to be appointed to this position, and it was understood that the governor of the Bank of Canada would be chairman of the board. Mr Rasminsky had been appointed governor of the Bank of Canada in mid-1961 following Mr Coyne's resignation. The problems Mr Rasminsky faced as governor were serious enough without his having to pick up the reins of a bank, relatively unfamiliar to him, itself in the midst of controversy and rapid growth and change. On top of this, Mr Marble, who had been general manager of IDB since 1953, had retired in mid-1962. Accordingly, the plan to relieve Mr Rasminsky of presidential responsibility for the IDB seemed like a reasonable step in the evolution of the Bank. However, the bill died with the dissolution of Parliament in February 1963. It was not revived, and Mr Rasminsky went on to be an excellent and sympathetic president of the Bank.[32]

Examples of decisions by the IDB involving other lenders

The prestige of the commission as an important and serious investigatory body gave its recommendations, or at least some of them, great acceptability in government departmental circles. This probably had an effect on the development of departmental attitudes toward the Bank's future evolution, and we shall see signs of this when we come to study the final years of the Bank in the 1970s. At the time of the report's issuance, however, its recommendations had little immediate impact on the Bank. Perhaps this was because the Bank saw itself as operating, to a large extent and as best as it could, in the spirit in which the commission thought it should operate. In its report, the commission, when discussing the IDB's relations with other lenders, said that the Bank should take account of all these lenders and 'its decisions must reflect a continuing series of judgements about the level at which the cost and other terms of private funds justifies its intervening.'[33] A 'continuing series of judgements' was just what the Bank had been making since 1944, and with particular intensity in recent years. Here are a number of examples of these judgments drawn from the Bank's files to illustrate how conscientiously the Bank had been doing this as a matter of regular practice.

In the first case to be described, the Bank concluded that financing offered at 11 per cent, a rate of interest 4 percentage points above its own rate of 7 per cent, should be regarded as reasonable. Early in 1962, the Bank declined an application from company M for a loan of $311,000 on the grounds that financing was available elsewhere. One of the sources was finance company A. In October of the same year, company M approached the IDB again, this time for $425,000 on the grounds that the financing offered by finance company A was not on reasonable terms. These called for repayment over 4 or 5 years, at 11 per cent interest. The Bank declined the application on the grounds that the funds were available on reasonable terms and conditions.

In the second example, the Bank directed an applicant that wanted a loan to refinance liens to discuss its problem with the lien holders. Company N applied to the IDB for a $40,000 loan for working capital, new equipment, and refinancing liens held by finance company A and others. When it was referred to the lien holders, finance company A, the largest lien creditor, lengthened the repayment schedule and reduced the payments of most of the contracts. The Bank felt that this took care of the applicant's needs in a reasonable way and declined the application.

The third case is a somewhat different version of the same sort of situation. Company O was referred to the Bank in 1961 by finance company A to see if the IDB would refinance outstanding liens and put them on a manageable basis. The application was declined, but the company returned at the suggestion of its auditor in December 1962 to ask for refinancing of liens of $179,000, of which $121,000 was due before the end of March 1963. A large new investment in the company was in the offing. GMO wrote to the IDB branch concerned that, since the investment would reduce the liens considerably, the company could undoubtedly work out a new arrangement with finance company A, and the proposal was not suitable for the IDB.

Two more examples should suffice to complete this illustration of the kinds of judgments that the Bank had been making. One was of an IDB borrower that was required by the Bank to accept further financing from another lender at a much higher rate than that of the IDB. Company T had had several loans from the Bank and had become an extremely profitable business. In 1962, it approached the IDB for another loan of $40,000 for more equipment. It was asked to seek the money elsewhere first. An offer was received from finance company C for one year at 14 per cent. The principal of company T did not quarrel with the term of one year, but claimed that the interest was too high. (At the time the IDB's rate was $6\frac{1}{2}$ per cent.) The IDB did not regard the terms offered as unreasonable and declined to accept an application. The company ultimately financed the purchase through another finance company. The principal of company T was very angry with the IDB – understandably.

The other case also involved a borrower of the IDB's that needed an additional large loan and was directed by his bank manager to a lending corporation specializing in loans to small businesses. This lender offered a loan of $300,000 at an interest rate not very different from that of the IDB, the proceeds of the loan to include the prepayment of the IDB loan, then outstanding at $145,000. However, this loan had been running for only two years. As a result, the prepayment indemnity required to be paid to the IDB was fairly substantial, amounting to $8,000 or more. Both the borrower and the other lender asked IDB to forgo the indemnity since the company's cash position was not strong. The general manager of the Bank, A.N.H. James, was unwilling to do this since it would have established a precedent regarding the collection of prepayment indemnities that would have been difficult for the IDB to escape from, and which would, in his eyes and those of the other senior officers of the Bank, have exposed the IDB to being virtually a shopping centre for the other lender.

The IDB suggested that the other lender provide a loan for the amount only of the new money required, secured by a first charge on the new equipment to be bought, and a second charge on the assets securing the IDB's loan. This the other lender declined to do, and it continued, at the highest level, to press the IDB to waive its indemnity. Since a new loan from the other lender could be expected to involve rather heavy legal fees if the amount included enough to retire the IDB loan, the IDB decided that this, plus the prepayment fee on its own loan, would put an 'unreasonable' strain on the already weak working capital position of the company and on these grounds authorized an additional loan itself. This action created great excitement on all sides, but very soon, as a result, the other lender approved a loan for only the amount of new money required, as the Bank had suggested, leaving the original IDB loan to run its course, and with the added feature that no principal payments were to be made on the new loan until the IDB loan was fully retired.

In 1964 and 1965, supervisors' conferences gave some reflection of the mood of the Bank following several difficult years of rapid growth and investigation by two royal commissions. From the records of discussions at the two meetings, one can see that the operational staff of the Bank was feeling the strain of the controversies and investigations it had passed through and the adjustments it was having to make in its organization and procedures; the records give an impression of irritability and edginess where there was normally high good humour.

The 1964 conference took place in April, just before the official report of the Porter Commission was released. The supervisors saw the commission's views as raising major questions about the Bank's future, and they feared that the implications of these would have a bad effect on the Bank's staff. One of the supervisors expressed the view that what the Bank was already doing was not very different from what the commission said it ought to do. The president, Mr Rasminsky, assured the supervisors that it was not the wish of the government that the IDB should be curtailed. He expected the Bank to continue to grow even on its existing basis. In addition, there was still much to be done in reaching the many businesses that did not yet know about the Bank and in searching out fresh areas of risk to develop.

At the 1965 conference, held in October, Mr Rasminsky repeated more strongly his comments about the Bank's future role and took the opportunity to comment on a related matter of concern, the Bank's relationship with the government itself. He did this by quoting the following passage from a speech delivered in September by the minister of finance to the Canadian Institute of Actuaries in which the minister dismissed concerns about excessive influence by government on the then-proposed Canada Development Corporation. In doing so, the minister had cited the freedom of the IDB from governmental interference: 'In this connection it may be useful to recall that the Industrial Development Bank, in 20 years of existence, has operated quite independently of the government. I think it fair to say that the IDB has earned the respect and esteem of the business community.'

CHAPTER SIXTEEN

Operational developments

Loans: volume, distribution, and purpose

Against the favourable economic background that prevailed from 1962 to 1967, the IDB recorded a big jump in new loan authorizations in 1962, principally reflecting the enlargement of eligibility by the amendments of 1961. New loan approvals then settled down to a fairly level volume for each year from 1963 to 1967. As Mr Rasminsky said at the supervisors' conference in 1964, 'The surge in IDB's volume resulting from the 1961 amendment has come to an end – volume has flattened out and is now on a plateau.' The expansion of the Canadian economy in the years 1962–7 was not otherwise substantially reflected in the volume of business done by the Bank. In 1967, the number of new loans approved was just 83 (4 percentage points) above the number approved in 1962. Preoccupations with the various investigations by royal commissions and management consultants, with the revision of organization and procedures required, and with the development of policies to fit the types of business made eligible by the 1961 amendments tended to occupy management and to restrain the Bank from steps toward broad expansion, such as major programs of branch openings would have represented. In any event, the volume of business handled was pretty steady from year to year. Each year from 1962 to 1967 inclusive, the Bank received between 10,000 and 11,000 inquiries from businesses wanting to find out about the Bank and to discuss their financial needs, and each year 2,000–2,300 loans were authorized.

Table 14 gives the number of new loans approved, by business

TABLE 14

Loans approved 1961−7

	1961	1962	1963	1964	1965	1966	1967
By number							
Manufacturing	870	805	768	733	801	842	692
Transportation and storage	137	120	115	91	125	100	98
Construction	143	159	123	117	132	144	130
Wholesale	28	153	120	151	196	197	160
Retail	52	239	225	291	319	338	344
Agriculture	8	106	175	201	205	185	169
Restaurants	−	59	64	82	76	95	91
Hotels and motels	−	145	127	145	104	130	147
Other	127	299	269	272	251	303	337
Total	1,365	2,085	1,986	2,083	2,209	2,334	2,168
By amount							
Total ($millions)	$71	$92	$80	$88	$96	$123	$113
Average ($thousands)	$52	$44	$40	$42	$44	$53	$52

SOURCE: For 1961, Brief, Table 10; for later years, *Annual Report*, 1967.

categories and dollar totals in each fiscal year from 1961 to 1967 inclusive. The table makes clear the change in the character of the Bank that resulted from the 1961 amendments which were made near the end of that fiscal year.

Generally speaking, the categories of wholesale, retail, agriculture, restaurants, and hotels and motels all became eligible in 1961. Some small categories of businesses made eligible that year are also included in the table under 'Other.' Manufacturing businesses, although they continued to be an important sector for the Bank, received an ever smaller share of its loans. In 1967, less than one-third of all loans went to manufacturers. A greater number of loans went to agriculture, wholesale and retail businesses, and hotels and restaurants, which had been viewed with such apprehension by Mr Towers and Mr Coyne.

The increase in loans in 1962 was almost entirely due to the 1961 amendments to the act. Of the total number of 2,085 loans, 770 were identified as going to newly eligible businesses and 1,315 to businesses eligible before 1961. This is the only year for which the Bank's records give precise figures for loan authorizations for newly eligible businesses, but from them and the distribution of categories in Table 14 reasonable estimates can be made for later years. These have been used to make up Chart 1.

The bank was now into kinds of businesses with which it had had no

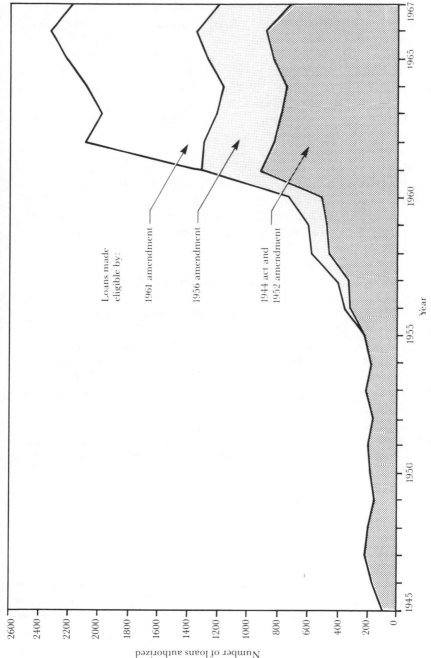

CHART 1   Effect of eligibility amendments on loan authorizations 1945–67

previous experience, but it stuck with the methods for analysing a proposal that it had always used. Was the applicant business likely to cope with the various problems facing it and earn a profit? Dave Macrae, later the regional engineer for the Prairie Region, has recalled his approach to the first farming application he investigated around Winnipeg. Having little knowledge of farming, he started at the beginning in the IDB tradition and, taking advantage of his training in the Royal Canadian Air Force during the war, hired an aircraft and flew over the farmer's land to see its condition, sloughs, and so on. He used the same device to break a log-jam of other investigations and astonished everyone by making five investigations in one week. Agricultural loans were also made in considerable numbers in Ontario and British Columbia. In the latter province, the Bank financed some of the first vineyards to serve the new wine industry. These were unusual loans in that several years were needed to bring the grape production to maturity so that money could be earned to make payments on the loans.

The new industries now opened up to the Bank brought many opportunities to finance innovations in one field or another. In southwestern Ontario, it financed many huge greenhouses to grow tomatoes. One farmer had 20 acres under glass, and the IDB financed another 20 acres. In the same province, new turkey and broiler chicken operations were financed on a big scale. In the Atlantic provinces, the Bank helped to set up lobster pounds and small shipbuilding yards. In the same area, road contractors were financed to serve the growing tourist traffic, and, in Prince Edward Island particularly, old motels were upgraded and new ones built.

In northern Ontario and in the west, fly-in fishing camps were financed. In Quebec, many goelettes (the small wooden vessels that served the north shore of the St Lawrence) were assisted. In British Columbia, the Bank financed newly developed self-loading and self-dumping barges for transporting logs, by which work that previously required many hours was done in a few minutes. In New Brunswick and northern Ontario, lumber mills now received, in addition to the usual IDB loans for expansion, loans for new chipping facilities to supply pulp mills with their raw material.

Companies supplying building materials received loans, particularly in Ontario and the Prairie Region. In Toronto, the Bank was involved with many of the major producers of concrete blocks. In Saskatchewan, producers of ready-mix concrete, blocks, and gravel were prominent among borrowers.

In addition, of course, manufacturers of metal products, food products, furniture, clothing, and so on continued to receive loans. A typical week's roster of loans in 1966 included a poultry hatchery, a door manufacturer, an optical lens manufacturer, a feed lot, an egg grader, a funeral home, a restaurant, a beef wholesaler, an air service, a retail building, a steel fabricator, a company that specialized in cleaning and maintaining parking lots and shopping malls, a motel and ski resort, a tomato greenhouse, and an automobile dealership.

In spite of the virtual elimination of eligibility problems, some remarkable proposals were turned down because they were simply not realistic. In its early years, the Bank had received requests from individuals for loans to construct the St Lawrence Seaway or retire the national debt! Now it received approaches for loans to construct a car to sell for $85 or to write a book to stamp out communism. Perhaps the most intriguing proposal of this type was one received in 1966 by T. Measham while a credit officer at Calgary branch. The request was for a loan of $50 million to irrigate the whole of the three prairie provinces. At the suggestion of the branch manager, Frank Stewart, Mr Measham tried to discourage the applicant with courtesy by telling him that such proposals had to be supported by complete engineering plans, fully expecting to hear no more from him. The sequel is described by Mr Measham: 'Two weeks later he entered my office staggering under the weight of the largest set of drawings ever seen. These turned out to be many large scale maps of various portions of Alberta, Saskatchewan and Manitoba, stapled and scotch-taped together, on which every lake, stream and river had been painstakingly joined together in an enormous irrigation system ... with literally thousands of dams, pipes, waterwheels, etc. It was only with considerable difficulty that Mr. Stewart and myself were finally able to persuade our visitor that the Bank was unable to help him.'

The distribution across the country of the numbers of yearly loan authorizations in the period is shown in Table 15. Figures are also shown for 1961, the last year of the previous period, for comparative purposes.

Authorizations in Quebec, Ontario, and the prairies increased between 1961 and 1967 to about the same extent as the national total, and so the percentage share of each remained about the same. Loan approvals in British Columbia increased to a greater extent and in 1967 were 15 per cent of the total number.

In the Atlantic provinces, the number of loans approved in 1967 was slightly more than in 1961, but the share of the total was down. In 1962, when the full effect of the new amendments was felt, the number of approvals in the Atlantic Region rose to 226. However, it declined steadily thereafter, even though there were four branches in the region which, for

TABLE 15

Regional comparison of number of loans authorized 1961–7

Region	1961*		1962	1963	1964	1965	1966	1967*		Population (percentage) 1967
Atlantic	135	(10)	226	181	178	166	170	144	(7)	9
Quebec	258	(19)	423	396	440	485	450	404	(18)	29
Ontario	538	(39)	810	675	674	684	752	824	(38)	35
Prairie	301	(22)	445	543	556	574	594	451	(21)	17
British Columbia	128	(10)	170	181	230	293	358	330	(15)	10
Territories	5	–	11	10	5	7	10	15	(1)	–
Total	1,365	(100)	2,085	1,986	2,083	2,209	2,334	2,168	(100)	100

*Percentage in parentheses.
SOURCES: For 1961, Brief, Table 12; for later years, *Annual Report*, 1967.

TABLE 16

Regional comparison of amount of loans authorized ($millions) 1961–7

Region	1961*		1962	1963	1964	1965	1966	1967*	
Atlantic	5.7	(8)	7.4	6.0	5.9	6.0	7.0	6.2	(5)
Quebec	16.9	(24)	24.3	22.5	24.9	25.5	31.9	20.8	(19)
Ontario	24.9	(35)	33.7	27.9	28.1	30.1	42.6	39.0	(34)
Prairie	14.6	(21)	17.4	16.3	18.4	19.6	23.7	25.8	(23)
British Columbia	9.0	(12)	8.6	6.7	10.6	14.7	16.9	19.9	(18)
Territories	0.1	–	0.6	0.4	0.2	0.2	0.5	1.4	(1)
Total	71.2	(100)	92.0	79.8	88.1	96.1	122.6	113.1	(100)

*Percentage in parentheses.
SOURCES: For 1961, Brief, Table 12; for later years, *Annual Report*, 1967.

most of the period, represented a larger number of branches relative to population than any other region had. In 1967, the 144 loans approved in the Atlantic Region were only 64 per cent of the number approved in 1962, and only 9 more than the number approved in 1961 before the act was amended.

Table 16 makes similar comparisons in terms of the dollar amount of loans authorized each year, and shows similar results.

A dollar figure for the Bank's volume of business provides a measure of the IDB's relative significance in the country's banking world. As loans were authorized each year and gradually disbursed, the dollar amount of loan balances outstanding naturally grew from year to year. By comparing these total balances with outstanding loan balances of the chartered banks, we can see to what relative stature the IDB attained. One has to remember that the chartered bank loans were largely amounts borrowed under revolving lines of credit, whereas the IDB loans were made under contracts by which balances were reduced steadily as payments were made. If we use the total of chartered bank business loans outstanding, however, we can make a comparison with IDB loan balances outstanding. At the end of 1962, this chartered bank figure was $4,038 million. The IDB loan balances outstanding at the end of fiscal 1962 were $165 million, or 4 per cent of the chartered bank figure. By the end of fiscal 1967, the IDB figure was $334 million, while the chartered bank figure was $6,929 million. The IDB figure was now 4.8 per cent of the chartered bank total. The IDB seemed to be growing faster than the chartered banks, but it was still a pretty small part of the whole banking picture.[1]

In spite of the IDB's having made persistent efforts for many years to cater to a broader range of the financial needs of those applying to it than

TABLE 17

Composition (percentage) of programs financed by the Bank 1955 and 1962-7

	1955	1962	1963	1964	1965	1966	1967
Land, buildings, machinery, and equipment	80	74	70	69	71	77	79
Working capital	12	13	15	15	13	10	9
Refinance debts owed to others	2	11	8	10	9	7	8
Changes of ownership	6	1	5	5	5	4	3
Other	–	1	2	1	2	2	1
Total	100	100	100	100	100	100	100
Proportion covered by IDB loans	65	74	68	74	76	70	68

SOURCES: For 1955, figures from the Bank's files; for 1962, figures from Brief, p. 16-A; for other years, from respective *Annual Reports*.

its usual role of financing buildings and equipment (and in particular to be more willing to consider requests for working capital loans), and in spite of its being accessible to all types of business after 1961, the purposes served by its loans had, by 1967, changed very little from the 1950s. This is illustrated in Table 17, which compares the make-up of programs financed by the Bank's loans 1962–7 with the distribution in 1955, prior to the first major amendment in 1956. The year 1955 is used for comparison because a breakdown of this sort is not available for 1961.

In the period 1962–7, as the Bank entered the new fields opened up to it by the 1961 amendments, such program elements as working capital, refinancing, and changes of ownership were, in most years, more important than they had been in the 1950s. In 1964, they totalled 30 per cent of programs as compared with 20 per cent in 1955, while building and equipment projects fell to 69 per cent, as compared with 80 per cent in 1955. Nevertheless, by 1967, the distribution was pretty well back to the 1955 pattern; there had been an increase in the amount of refinancing, but even this percentage was below 1962.

Policies for periods of credit restraint

Although the 1961 amendments to the IDB act were a most important influence on the Bank's subsequent operations, the state of the Canadian economy from 1962 to 1967 was also a factor. In 1962, a number of businesses calling on the Bank reported that their chartered banks had declined requests for financing because of 'austerity measures' introduced by the federal government as a result of the foreign exchange crisis that summer. These measures included some that did not affect the banks directly, such as import surcharges, reduced foreign currency allowances for tourists, and reduced government spending, but there was also a degree of monetary restraint applied by the Bank of Canada that did affect the banks directly. The chartered banks had become quite interested in making term loans, but because they did not, until 1967, have the power to take mortgages as security for new loans, those they made were often different from those made by the IDB in that their terms were not necessarily covered by a written contract. They fell into the category of term loans rather because they involved an understanding with a borrower – probably informal and possibly only oral – as to the term for the repayment of a loan. This type of loan they were now sometimes reported as declining. The IDB followed its established policy of not, under these conditions, substituting, in the case of large loans at least, for chartered bank assistance that might normally have been available.

The economic conditions that prompted this development in 1962 were short-lived, but at the end of 1965, when there was considerable pressure on commercial credit facilities, a similar but somewhat stronger situation arose. At the supervisors' conference in October of that year, notice was taken of the fact that the chartered banks seemed quite 'loaned up' and that conventional mortgage and other term lenders were experiencing a shortage of funds. Further, the view was expressed that, if over an extended period conventional lenders were to decline applications through a lack of resources, the IDB should not do what the conventional lenders could not. Once more, the IDB fell back on its normal policy in such circumstances: no restrictions were imposed on the quantity of lending by the IDB, but it was to avoid making larger loans (i.e. those over $200,000) that other lenders would normally have made but could not because of their own tight liquidity position. Instructions were issued to the Bank's branches along these lines in February 1966.

An example of the application of these policies is provided by an approach by a textile plant for a loan of $250,000 to finance capital expenditures of $150,000 and provide working capital of $100,000. The company's chartered bank had, in the past, financed the company's capital expenditures and would, according to the chartered bank branch manager, have done so again had money market conditions been normal. It seemed obvious to the IDB that the company's request for money for working capital arose from this past practice, from the consequences of which the company and chartered bank now, with the money markets strained, wanted relief. Although the financing of capital expenditures had been done ostensibly on a term basis, the chartered bank's shortage of loan funds had led it, as often seemed to happen in such circumstances, to lump its 'term' loan with its working capital risk in assessing the latter.

The amount requested from the IDB for capital expenditures in this case was not over $200,000 and therefore was within the limit set by the Bank's policy as being admissible without special difficulty in such a situation, but the working capital portion was another matter. The Bank took the view that it was not its role to relieve either the company or the chartered bank from the situation into which it had gotten, and the proposal was declined. The chartered bank then eased the terms for the repayment of the term financing still outstanding, and the company came back to the IDB, this time for $200,000 for capital expenditures and $50,000 for working capital. The Bank was still willing to consider a loan for the building and equipment program, but once more refused to consider the working capital portion. The latter clearly arose from the previous financing of capital expenditures by the chartered bank, and it was felt that it was in that bank's power to give such relief, in the way of delayed payments or in some other way, as might be needed.

This view was reflected in fresh instructions issued to the Bank's branches in November 1966 that repeated those of February, emphasized the importance of examining carefully any proposals over $200,000, and concluded: 'A proposal to pay off other creditors who could normally be expected to continue their accommodation or to extend loan contracts where necessary should not be entertained'; as was customary, the door was opened a little at the end of the instructions by adding the standard IDB qualification 'except in unusual circumstances.'

It required very careful judgment for the Bank's officers to form an honest opinion on individual cases because 'tight money' might some-times be given by some lender as an excuse for not making an unattractive loan. In any event, the Bank estimated that between February, when the instructions were first issued, and November, when they were reissued, approximately $16 million of proposals were discouraged where credit stringency was the prime factor in the decision.

It may be that the economic conditions in the business world damped down borrowing from the Bank in the years immediately following 1965−6, but the Bank's figures suggest that the strictures it imposed on loans over $200,000 also had an effect. From 1966 to 1967, annual loan authorizations over $200,000 fell from $26 million to $25 million, while loan approvals for $200,000 or less fell from $96 million to $88 million. In 1968, however, loans over $200,000 continued to fall and declined to $17 million, while loans for $200,000 or less rose to $103 million. Even in 1971, loan approvals over $200,000 were still only $30 million, whereas loans for $200,000 or less were now $166 million.[2] It is also possible that the increased activity of conventional term lenders, which was recognized by the policy and seemed most apparent in loans of a larger size, may have accounted for the check to loan authorizations over $200,000.

New branches

At all times an important influence on the Bank's operations was the opening of branches. Up to 1956, the Bank had functioned through 4 offices. However, an institution intended to give special consideration to the needs of small and medium-sized businesses in a country 4,000 miles wide could hardly function through 4 offices. In 1956, 2 more were opened, and from 1959 on branch openings were a permanent part of the Bank's evolution.

From 1959 to 1961, 10 branches were opened in a deliberate program to improve the Bank's coverage of the country. In 1962, 6 more were opened, giving the Bank 22 branch offices. So much enthusiasm for opening offices had been aroused that, apart from the 6 opened in 1962, 10 more locations were cited at the time by Mr Marble as suitable places for opening offices soon, if not in that year. However, as it turned out, it took from 1963 to 1967 inclusive to open just 5 more offices, and some of those listed by Mr Marble were not established until the 1970s.

At the supervisors' conference in 1964, Mr James, the general manager, included the opening of branches among things the Bank could do that would have an effect on its volume of business. Apart from Rimouski, however, where an office was due to open the next month, and Montreal and Toronto, where the offices might, he thought, be divided into two, he felt that there were few possibilities for further new branches and added: 'We should be reluctant to open any more branches at the present time unless and until a strong case can be made for a particular location.'

The Bank had gradually evolved criteria for deciding whether to open a branch. Was the number of loans in the area smaller, in relation to population or industrial concentration, than in other areas? If so, the convenience of a local office might be necessary to acquaint local businessmen with the Bank's services. Was there enough potential business to make a branch profitable? It was felt that a branch should earn at least enough of an interest margin on its loans to cover its own operating costs. Did the Bank have experienced personnel available for the staffing and management of a new branch? Was there enough business available to occupy a branch staff? It was thought that there ought to be a big enough workload to keep at least two credit officers busy. Mr Towers had stated this view in 1948, and it was repeated again and again. In a memorandum of December 1961, Mr Marble said: 'A location is undesirable ... if there is insufficient business or insufficient potential to keep a competent staff interested and occupied. If this is not done, we spoil the staff or may even lose them. While we cannot overlook the question of cost (or possibly of earnings) this is not disconnected with the point of sufficient volume and potential to keep staff interested.'

Mr Marble did not have fixed ideas as to how many loan accounts a branch should have when it was opened. The branch at Saint John had only 52 customers on its books when it opened in 1959; London branch had only 54, and Regina 22. Sudbury branch, opened in 1960, had 42 customers, and St John's opened in 1961 with 40. The branches opened in the early 1960s also started with a small list of customers. Of the six established 1962-4, one had more than 90 customers (Moncton), and one (Victoria) had only 31. Prince George was opened in 1965 with 129 customers, but no more branches outside metropolitan areas were opened until 1968. The single branches opened in 1966-7 were only splits of the big main branches in Toronto and Montreal.

A most important consideration in deciding whether to set up a branch was the possibility of its improving the accessibility of the Bank to small businesses. In chapter 11, the results of opening up branches in Halifax and Calgary in the 1950s were given as illustrations of what happened when offices were opened in places previously far from any branch. Even more striking results followed from adding a second branch to each of Saskatchewan and Alberta in the 1960s, as shown in Table 18.

Like the Bank as a whole, the number of authorizations in these provinces remained relatively stable for the latter part of the 1962-7 period, but opening up second branches in these large areas had lifted the Bank's activity there to a new level.

In 1963, a new device was employed to meet the need for improved accessibility. A part-time branch was opened that year at Sherbrooke, Quebec, as a sub-branch of the Montreal branch. An office was rented in Sherbrooke and furnished and opened up one or two days every fortnight or so when a credit officer from Montreal would go to Sherbrooke to operate it. This was regarded as an initial step toward a permanent office where the amount of local business was thought not to have reached a point where it could support one. It was adopted several times later in other places, but it was not a very successful idea. The cost

TABLE 18

Number of loans authorized in Saskatchewan and
Alberta 1960–7

	Saskatchewan	Alberta
1960	28*	76†
1961	64	131‡
1962	86§	216
1963	79	306
1964	122	282
1965	153	256
1966	150	300
1967	111	257

*First branch opened at Regina.
†Only Calgary branch operating.
‡Edmonton branch opening.
§Second branch opened, in Saskatoon.
SOURCE: For 1960–2, figures from Brief, Table 12;
for later years, figures from *Annual Report*, 1967.

was not much less than that of a permanent office, since rent, telephone, and furniture had to be paid for anyway, plus constant travelling expenses. In addition, although it did establish a presence for the Bank, it created a rather uninterested image as the office was unoccupied most of the time. Generally speaking, sub-branches did not result in any growth over and above whatever growth was experienced in the region as a whole, whereas new, full-time branches usually experienced very rapid growth, particularly during their first four years of operation.

By the end of the period, another reason for opening a branch had appeared, viz. to improve the administration of existing loan accounts. In fiscal 1965, the Toronto branch, which had over 1,000 loan customers, was divided into two branches known as Metro-Toronto, to serve the metropolitan area, and Mid-Ontario, to serve the central parts of the province previously served by the Toronto branch and not covered by the Ottawa, Hamilton, and newly created Metro-Toronto branches. Both the Metro-Toronto and Mid-Ontario offices were located in Toronto, in the same building, across the hall from each other, but the division was expected to improve supervision and general management. In the following year, the Montreal branch, which also had over 1,000 loan customers, was divided into Montreal South and Montreal North, but the offices were separated and located in their respective areas in the southern and northern parts of Montreal Island.

It would seem reasonable that the number of branches in operation should have a bearing on the number of loans made; that, for eight years after 1962, few new branches were added to the list was undoubtedly a factor in keeping the number of new loans fairly steady from year to year.

There are several possible explanations for this slowdown in branch openings. First, the management of the Bank was preoccupied with two royal commissions and with management consultants and later with developing revised procedures and structures based on the report of the consultants. Second, the sudden upsurge of business in 1961 and 1962 following the amendments to the IDB Act had required the rapid addition of staff whose level of experience may not have been able to support a continuation of a large branch program. Third, the Bank's volume of business was not yet large enough to provide an adequate portfolio of loans for many new offices. Only when the Bank had developed a larger list of accounts to distribute among new branches could a major program of openings be sustained.

Enlarged publicity program

Another factor affecting operations was the Bank's publicity program. By 1964, the IDB was advertising regularly in dailies, weeklies, and trade and business journals at an annual cost of approximately $100,000, as compared with an expenditure of $13,000 for this sort of thing just five years before. These advertisements were very carefully worded so as to make clear that the Bank could lend only when financing was not available elsewhere 'on reasonable terms and conditions.' At least one finance company took advantage of this by inserting in a paper, right beside the IDB's notice, an advertisement offering loans 'on reasonable terms and conditions.' In 1963, the Bank omitted this phrase because it felt it might discourage approaches from businesses it could legitimately help. This created a small and brief furore as other lenders took alarm at the apparent abandonment by the Bank of this fundamental principle, and the Bank put the phrase back into its advertisements.

By now there was a strong emphasis on publicity, and the branches and regional offices were very ingenious in devising new ways of accomplishing it. Mr Stuart, supervisor of the Ontario Region, wrote small playlets showing the Bank at work. These were presented at meetings of service clubs or business groups. Bank managers, accountants, and others were called on diligently, and speeches were made by the score. Booths and displays at trade fairs and business gatherings, which had once been frowned upon, were now quite commonplace and almost passé. The London branch even set up a booth at a ploughing match!

Particularly effective were 'advertised visits.' A branch would advertise that a credit officer would be in a particular town on a certain date to receive inquiries or applications. In 1961, 99 such visits were made; in 1967, 696 were made which meant that, on average, each branch was conducting such a visit every fortnight. By 1967, approximately 10 per cent of loans being made were the result of advertised visits.

One branch manager, caught up by the enthusiasm for publicity, suggested that the Bank should distribute to bank managers and others glass ashtrays bearing the Bank's name. The idea was that, for example, a bank manager, as he extinguished his cigarette, would be silently reminded, through the ashes, of where his customers could find term financing. This seemed to be going a bit far, and at GMO in Montreal the suggestion earned the comment from one senior officer: 'I am afraid that I cannot by any stretch of the imagination believe that this sort of "promotion stunt" would be appropriate for IDB!'

The idea was probably considered a bit 'pushy' because, whatever other lenders thought, the Bank, when designing its advertisements or planning publicity efforts, did remain sensitive to its position as a residual or complementary lender. In 1962, a supervisor suggested that the Bank should join with a contractor and others that had participated in a large industrial project financed by the Bank in making up a display advertisement extending good wishes to the owners. The proposal was turned down with the comment: 'It could be construed as an undue effort of the Bank to promote its services. Being an emanation of the Crown our advertising and publicity endeavours must, like Caesar's wife, be beyond reproach.' The *Financial Times* would have been pleased with the simile.

In 1965, it was thought that the Bank's film should be brought up-to-date by drawing attention to the much larger chain of branches now in operation with the insertion in the film of the statement that 'IDB offices are conveniently located from coast to coast.' The idea was rejected because it was thought it would smack of a 'plug for business.'

The cost of advertising was always carefully considered. Even while they were being encouraged to greater efforts to spread information about the IDB, its officers managed to retain the strongly economical instincts that had been drilled into them from the first day they joined the Bank. An earlier attempt to update the film, in 1961, had resulted in a proposal to add an epilogue to deal with the changes in the Bank arising from the 1961 amendments. The cost was put at $1,985 plus $490 for fresh prints. This was considered too expensive; it was thought that an officer presenting the film could easily add a word of explanation afterwards at no expense to the Bank. In 1963, the manager of the Trois-Rivières branch, G. Bourbonnière, unsuccessfully sought approval for spending $185 to get a fifteen-minute exposure for the Bank's film on a local television station; he was told to try and get it done for nothing, as others had done!

Attempts to increase responsiveness to loan applications

The Bank continued to encourage a more flexible responsiveness to loan applications − to set easier terms for loans and to assume greater risks. The injunctions in this direction previously issued were reiterated and emphasized in new policy circular instructions issued in 1964. Credit officers were encouraged to give out application forms at the first interview with an applicant, and statistics on this were reported to GMO. Longer repayment periods were encouraged, although by 1967 the average term, eighty-eight months, was only three months longer than the average for 1964. The security conditions for loans were eased with respect to the assignment of life insurance and personal guarantees. Finally, authorizing limits for the various levels within the Bank were gradually raised. In 1967, 45 per cent of loans made were authorized at the branches without reference to a higher authority, 45 per cent were approved at the regional offices, 8 per cent were approved at GMO, and 2 per cent were sent on to the board of directors or executive committee for authorization.

It was made clear that modifying loan terms and security requirements and assuming greater risks were not expected to produce greater losses. At the supervisors' conference in April 1964, the president said: 'On this matter of taking risks, we want to continue to feel our way. We now take considerable risk ... The important thing is that our own minds should be flexible and that we should be open-minded.' He made it clear, however, that he did not have in mind any general lowering of credit standards, and Mr James, the general manager, summed up the line to be taken: 'The approach should be open-minded − but with discretion.'

In spite of the efforts to increase responsiveness, the proportion of applications for assistance that resulted in loans declined between 1962 and 1967. In 1962, the proportion of formal applications processed that received approval was 72 per cent; in 1967, the proportion was 69 per cent. For the whole period, the average was 71 per cent. That 71 per cent of formal applications were approved on the average from 1962 to 1967 did not mean that the other 29 per cent were turned down by the Bank. Many applications were withdrawn after they had been lodged with the Bank and perhaps been partly investigated. In some cases, the applicant would decide not to proceed with his plans; in others, some transaction upon which his plan depended might fall through; in still others, market trends might turn against his project. Some 14 per cent of the applications received would be withdrawn for such reasons, and around 15 per cent would be declined by the Bank.

Starting from 1963, there are available other means of measuring the Bank's responsiveness to requests for assistance. In that year the Bank started keeping track of the number of inquiries received each year. For several years, the proportion resulting in loans was remarkably steady. In 1963, 19 per cent of inquiries resulted in loans; in 1964, 1965, and 1967, the proportion was 20 per cent; and in 1966, it was 19 per cent. There were signs, however, of a change in the willingness of the Bank's branches to accept formal applications from those who came to see them. In 1963, 25 per cent of inquiries were taken under full investigation as formal applications. This increased to 30 per cent by 1965 and remained in that area until 1969. It would appear that the process of 'feeling our way ... in the matter of taking risks,' as Mr Rasminsky had put it, had started with the Bank's branches' taking in formal applications from a higher proportion of those coming to see them.

A figure that also remained relatively steady was the proportion of authorized loans cancelled and not drawn down by the 'borrower.' As explained above, some applications would be withdrawn before they had been fully processed. There were also cases in which an application was processed and approved but the 'borrowing' business did not proceed with its plan. The plan might have been changed, there might have been some part of the security that the business found it could not provide, market conditions might have changed, or some other reason could have persuaded the business to ask that the credit be cancelled. For the years 1962–7, the number cancelled was 10 per cent of authorized loans. From 1962 to 1975 this proportion averaged 10 per cent and never fell outside the range of 9–12 per cent.

Processing time

An important aspect of the Bank's work was the time taken to process an application. This affected every part of operations – operating costs and profits, the size of the staff, the volume of applications handled and loans authorized, the public image of the Bank, and even, indirectly, the spirit and zest of its staff. The problem of how to expedite the Bank's work plagued the Bank for years. All kinds of procedures were devised to shorten the time needed to deal with an application. By the 1960s, credit officers were investigating small, simple proposals themselves to avoid their having to brief an investigation officer. Some investigation reports were written on a pre-printed form that required only the filling in of answers to printed questions; this was used with great enthusiasm in some branches, but ignored in others because it was thought to discourage penetrating thought or analysis. In addition, short forms of reports prepared in a narrative form were also encouraged. In the larger branches in Ontario, some credit officers and investigation officers were paired off in teams to work quickly together on a proposal. Authorizing limits in the field were raised until by 1967 90 per cent of loans were approved in the branches or the regional offices without reference to GMO at Montreal, except on policy.

One could hardly say, however, that any of these devices made much difference up to 1967. There are few records of the Bank's experience with processing times until 1964, but from then on statistics were regularly maintained. The average processing time from receipt of application to authorization was 41 days in 1964, 41 in 1965, 49 in 1966, and 46 in 1967. Such statistics have to be regarded with caution since they depend on a decision as to when the time for processing an application might be considered to have started. Sometimes the date used was that on which the application was received, and most of the figures cited were made up on this basis. Later, the date used for starting to measure the processing time was that by which the information required to support an application had been supplied to the Bank. Sometimes this would be later than the receipt of the formal application itself. However, considering that an applicant probably counted processing time from the date of his or her first visit to the Bank, the average time taken to deal with an application must have seemed very long.

By 1967 processing time was longer than in 1964 – on average 46 days. To disburse a loan required a further period, since it had to await the completion of the security documents. For about one-quarter of the loans, 2 months or so might suffice, but some took 3 or 4 months or more, depending on the complexity of the loan agreement and the promptness with which the borrower supplied the required information. For about half of the loans, 3 months would be enough, and the other half would take longer. In the late 1960s, the Bank's legal staff extended what had previously been an occasional practice and drafted the security documents for the smaller loans before sending them to an outside lawyer for formalization, completion, execution, and registration. This was thought to save time, and in 1962–5 they experimented with taking the security for loans of up to $25,000 or so themselves. This meant meeting with the customer and doing all the detailed and formal work formerly done outside. However, this new practice did not develop because the large staff of lawyers required would have presented a real staffing problem. By 1967, little progress had been made in reducing the average time taken to prepare security.

Other sources of term financing for small businesses

A factor that had a general influence on operations between 1962 and 1967 was the growing number of other sources of term financing for small or medium-sized businesses. When the IDB was founded, there were virtually no sources of funds of this sort. By 1967, all the provinces except Alberta and British Columbia had set up such agencies, the chartered banks had entered the field to a degree, some specialized private lenders had appeared, and at least one new agency of the federal government could be identified as operating in the same field.

The functions of the provincial agencies varied slightly. Their scope was different from or more restricted than that of the IDB, and they all had a strong developmental leaning. In some cases arguments presented to support the creation of a provincial agency were based on alleged shortcomings of the IDB. The comments of the Ontario minister of development before the Porter Commission were a natural prelude to the setting up of the Ontario Development Corporation later the same year. Similarly, in Manitoba the establishment of the Manitoba Development Fund in 1958 was supported by the government of the day with claims that the IDB did little for small business;[3] this disregarded the fact that half the Bank's loans were for under $25,000.

From time to time one or another of these agencies would set a policy of requiring that any business applying to them must first apply to the IDB, but this policy was not adhered to permanently in any instance. One agency moved so far toward withdrawing from active operation that it entered into negotiations with the IDB to sell its portfolio of loans to the Bank. The negotiations were stopped only by the opinion of the Bank's legal advisers that it did not have the legal power to make such a deal. Generally, however, the provincial lending funds were quite energetic, and their activity must have affected the volume of loans made by the IDB.[4]

The chartered banks had become increasingly interested in term loans, particularly after 1967, when the Bank Act was amended to allow them to take mortgage security for new loans and make loans against it free of the restrictions on the rate of interest that applied to their ordinary loans. No figures are available for term loans made by the banks in the 1960s, but it is not likely that the total was large by 1967.

The banks were also active in term loans made with the federal government's guarantee under the Small Business Loans Act (SBLA) passed in 1960. From 1961 to 1967, the banks made around 18,000 loans under the SBLA for a total of $168 million. There was a $25,000 limit on these loans. In the same period, the IDB made 7,100 loans of $25,000 or less for a total of $106 million. Although the banks' figures are much larger, IDB loans in this category followed just the same growth pattern as other size categories, which suggests that the IDB's operations were not greatly affected by SBLA loans. Some of these loans might have been made anyway without the special provisions of the SBLA. From 1961 to 1967, there was no sign of developing growth in SBLA loans by the chartered banks. In 1967, the number of such loans made was only 70 per cent of the number made in the first year of the scheme, 1961.[5]

This absence of growth in SBLA loans prompted the government to make major amendments to the act when it came up for renewal in 1966-7. Previously, where the purpose of a loan involved the improvement or extension of premises, the loan had been restricted to the purchase or construction of alternative premises where the premises being used would no longer be available. The amendments, made in February 1967,[6] permitted the financing of the purchase and construction of premises without this restriction. Also, whereas the act had previously been limited to small businesses engaged in manufacturing, wholesale and retail trade, and the service industry, now businesses engaged in construction, transportation, or communication were added. The definition of a small business enterprise now was to embrace any business with an estimated gross revenue of $500,000, instead of $250,000 as previously. Up to 1967, however, the act does not appear to have been a significant influence on the operations of the IDB.

A federal government program of financial assistance that did affect the IDB directly, if not substantially, was the Automotive Adjustment Assistance Board, set up in 1965 as a result of the Automobile Pact between the United States and Canada.[7] This pact removed all tariffs and other impediments to trade between the two countries in motor vehicles and original equipment parts used in the assembly of vehicles by automobile manufacturers. It was expected that the pact would give the automobile industry in Canada a larger share of the North American market, and the car manufacturers gave certain undertakings as to their future output that were intended to bring this about. It was estimated that by the 1968 model year production of vehicles and parts used in their manufacture would be one-third greater than the 1965 level, apart from normal growth. This meant that automobile manufacturers and many parts manufacturers would have to expand their production facilities. This was expected to require large expenditures on buildings and equipment, and it was thought that some smaller companies manufacturing car parts might find these difficult to finance. There was also the possibility that some parts manufacturers would not be able to fit into the new structure of the industry that would emerge and would have to switch to other products and markets. This also might require the financing of buildings and equipment.

Since these various financial needs were the result of government policy as represented by the pact, the government felt that it should provide financial assistance where needed to make these adjustments. The IDB seemed a source of assistance ready to hand, and in January 1965, in announcing the pact, the minister of industry said: 'The management of the Industrial Development Bank has been informed of the nature and purpose of the automotive program so that it will be in a position to consider promptly, under the terms of its Act, any application for financing which may be forthcoming.'[8] This really said nothing more than that the IDB was ready to consider any proposal made to it 'under the terms of its Act,' which it was ready to do at all times in any case. Some people interpreted it to mean that the Bank was going to provide some form of special assistance, and one outside observer complained, after some months, that the IDB had not made any new policy at all and still considered each application on its merit – which was undoubtedly true!

The government moved rapidly to set up a special fund for 'adjustment assistance' and in June 1965 announced the creation of such a fund to 'make loans available to those automotive products producers who have a reasonable prospect of profitable operation but who would otherwise be prevented from doing so through lack of financing.' An Adjustment Assistance Board (AAB) would be responsible for administering the programs, but the IDB would 'be cooperating with the Board ... and be responsible for the day-to-day administration of the loans.'[9] The Bank, however, had not agreed to do this and declined the assignment.

The management of the Bank did not think it practical or desirable for the IDB to operate, as an instrument of some government policy, a loan fund serving different goals and charging lower rates of interest than characterized the IDB's normal operations. For one thing, such a special role might have seemed in the eyes of businessmen and of the Bank's own staff to diminish the IDB's independence from governmental influence in the exercise of its credit and business judgment. Further, it might have been difficult for the Bank to justify to its regular applicants the credit judgment that guided it to decisions and set the terms of loans in its regular operations if at the same time it were also involved in a program served by different credit judgments and setting different terms and rates of interest for loans made to another group of businesses. The Bank could not perform the role given it by its act of incorporation and at the same time be a catch-all for special programs of financial aid that might be introduced by the government from time to time.

This unwillingness on the part of the IDB to become involved in a government scheme to provide some special type of financial assistance to a particular industry or to take on functions outside its parliamentary mandate was consistent with its earlier positions. In 1959, a royal commission on coasting trade had proposed that the Bank 'give serious study to the needs of the operators of small ships in the coasting trade to ensure that adequate credit facilities are properly available to them.' Mr Marble, the Bank's general manager, responded: 'If we were to adopt such an attitude in respect of any particular group, we would soon find ourselves in serious difficulties with others.'

The Bank did lend an officer to the AAB, however, to give guidance in dealing with loan applications, and for several months the staff of the Bank's Ottawa branch assisted the board by doing financial analysis of proposals that it received. In addition, the Bank provided a great deal of help in setting up procedures and forms. By the end of 1965, the board was operating completely on its own.

The creation of the AAB introduced a new and unusual element into the IDB's operating situation. The federal government had set up a special fund and agency to do for one sector of industry what the IDB had been set up to do for all, i.e. to assist with financing not otherwise available those businesses with reasonable prospects of being profitable. The requirement set out in the order-in-council creating the board was that it could make a loan 'if in the opinion of the Board the loan would provide the eligible manufacturer with a reasonable prospect of a profitable operation that is not available through other sources of financing.' The IDB had many loans to car parts manufacturers outstanding on its books, and when the board was set up the Bank had before it applications for additional loans from some of these as well as from new applicants in the automobile industry. However, since the board's rate of interest was lower than the Bank's, some of these applicants were anxious to switch their requests over to the new board.

At first, in order to avoid any overlapping of the responsibilities of the Bank and the board, it was the policy of the board that any applicant business should first have had its request for financing refused by the IDB and should submit evidence of this in the form of a 'letter of refusal' from the IDB. The Bank was unwilling to put itself in the position of providing written formal evidence of a turndown on a proposal without giving it full consideration, which required that the proposal be processed like any application in the normal way. This took time. Also, the Bank's decision was often in the form not of a simple 'no' but of a counter-suggestion as to how the proposal might be made acceptable to the Bank in amount, security, term of repayment, and so on. As a result, when the Bank did finally give such an applicant business an answer on its proposal, it might not be in the simple negative form that was wanted. Since the business was probably anxious, in any event, to finance through the AAB because of its lower rate of interest, having to approach the IDB first did not make its officers any happier and did not expedite the work of the board. Accordingly, the practice of asking an applicant to the board to apply first to the IDB was not invariably followed.

This created a certain amount of coolness between operational staffs of the Bank and the board at the field level, which was, perhaps understandably, compounded by the fact that many of the field staff of the board had previously been credit officers with the IDB in branches catering to the needs of car parts manufacturers. At one time the managers of these branches suggested that protests should be lodged with the board about the activities of their former colleagues whom they saw as 'soliciting' business from clients or applicants of the IDB's. No protest was made, however, since it was felt that, as Mr Rasminsky said, 'We can hardly take exception to officers of the Automotive Adjustment Assistance Board taking the initiative in calling on firms in the automotive industry.' The finance companies would undoubtedly have seen poetic justice in the IDB's finding itself confronted with a lender of which the main attraction was a lower rate of interest.

The volume of loans made by the board 1965–8 was not large: loans to 11 firms 1965–6 worth $9,617,000, to 31 firms 1966–7 for $24,481,000, and to 9 firms 1967–8 for $8,155,000. However, the role of the board was so similar to that of the IDB that, in its own sector of industry, it undoubtedly did reduce the IDB's loan activity.

As for the newly emerging private specialized lenders, it is difficult to determine to what extent they affected the operations of the IDB. There were, of course, individual cases of inquiries or proposals received by the IDB that were also submitted to one of these lenders and that resulted in financing being obtained. Certainly, they appeared to develop a satisfactory level of operations, but they were mostly active in making the larger loans. Whereas the IDB's average loan authorization was for around $50,000, a private lender might have an average of $150,000–$200,000. Each emerging source of term financing or investment for small and medium-sized businesses seemed to result in more applications to the IDB. One new specialized lending corporation, RoyNat Ltd, was established by the Royal Bank of Canada, the Banque canadienne nationale, the Montreal Trust Company, and the Canada Trust Company. It would not have been surprising if there had been a decrease in the proportion of the IDB's applicants that dealt with these banks, but not merely was there no decrease; in the case of the Royal Bank there was an increase. Each new lender in the field in which the IDB had pioneered seemed to give the Bank indirect publicity since it would often describe its operations by likening them to those of the IDB. In addition, the business world was probably still passing through the evolutionary process started by the IDB of educating small and medium-sized businesses to the appropriateness of term loans or bond mortgage financing, previously the privilege of large corporations, for their much smaller needs. In other words, the market for this kind of financing was constantly growing and seemed able to contain the new lenders, the chartered banks, and the IDB.

The period closed in 1967 with amendments to the IDB Act. First, the Bank's capacity to raise capital was increased. Its authorized share issue was changed from $50 million to $75 million, and the limit on direct liabilities, which regulated the ability of the Bank to sell debentures, was raised from five times paid-up shares plus the reserve fund to ten times. Second, the deputy minister of industry was added to the board of directors and replaced the deputy minister of trade and commerce on the executive committee. The Department of Industry was now principally responsible in the federal government for industrial development within the country, and it was considered appropriate that its deputy minister should sit on the Bank's board.[10]

CHAPTER SEVENTEEN

Some policy issues

Problems of eligibility

The amendments of 1961 to the IDB Act had greatly reduced but not entirely eliminated problems of the 'eligibility' of applicants. Determining qualification of an applicant business under the terms of the act was now confined to deciding merely whether it was a 'business undertaking' operated for the purpose of making a profit. A great variety of businesses could now apply. Retail and wholesale trade, restaurants, hotels, motels, hospitals, nursing homes, agricultural businesses, trade schools, skating rinks, curling rinks, trailer parks, camping grounds, theatres, and many kinds of recreational and entertainment facilities are examples of the new fields of business with which the Bank had now to deal.

With every kind of business now eligible to apply for a loan, however, the Bank found itself faced with new questions as to the appropriateness of its assisting a particular kind of business. The federal government now had functioning several special arrangements to provide financial assistance for some types of businesses, and the Bank had to decide what its attitude was to be if a company in one of these sectors of industry applied to it for a loan. Should the IDB make a loan and, in effect, compete with the other government program? Also, it was now being brought into touch with businesses of a kind that, for one reason or another, might not be considered as suitable for assistance by an IDB loan. The Bank was lending money having, as it were, a public character, and doing so on fairly reasonable terms. The mere fact that the IDB would make a loan when another lender would not was in itself a kind of liberality of accommodation quite apart from the rate of interest it charged and the other terms and conditions of its loans. There might be legitimate questions as to whether some types of businesses should receive accommodation of this character.

Once the principles for deciding these matters were established, the vast majority of cases were dealt with fairly readily. In 1962, 36 cases of eligibility were ruled on by GMO and/or head office, while in 1963 only 7 cases required rulings.

Some of these decisions involved recreational clubs. The Bank considered that to be eligible under the act as a 'business undertaking,' a club had to be operated as a commercial enterprise with a view to making a profit. This eliminated as potential borrowers all private clubs operated for the pleasure of their members only. However, some private clubs rented out their facilities occasionally and claimed that they were, therefore, carrying on a commercial operation. This argument was not accepted by the Bank; the earning of a profit had to be the fundamental intent of the operation. Also, the club's facilities had to be open to the public generally. An exclusive private club might be operated by a proprietor or company for profit, but the Bank felt that it was inappropriate that it should finance recreational facilities for the exclusive use of a favoured few.

This distinction was not always easily made. Clubs open both to members paying an annual fee and to pay-as-you-play players were ruled eligible only if the former group did not enjoy privileges not open to the casual players. The exclusive use of a swimming pool or dining room or playing facilities on weekends was enough to make a club private in the eyes of the Bank. Sometimes a golf club would argue that the annual membership fee required from members was only a way of prepaying green fees; in such a case it would have to be shown that the fee was not so high as effectively to bar the general public.

Charitable or religious organizations were not eligible, but commercial, profit-oriented businesses owned by them were. A religious order was not eligible, but a small business that was a separate company owned by an order and sold, at the gateway to the order's property, an 'elixir of life' based on a secret formula was ruled eligible.

Hospitals and nursing homes presented problems. Even if they were ostensibly operated for profit, the Bank considered them inappropriate for a loan if they were dependent on government grants. Partly this reflected the Bank's traditional desire to avoid entanglement with governments; even though such an institution might regard itself as profit-oriented, the Bank would not want to get involved if the success of the enterprise depended on the readiness of some government to make a grant toward the operation. Receipt of per diem payments from a government for welfare cases or under a medical care plan was regarded in a different light and did not affect the eligibility of a profit-oriented hospital or nursing home.

More difficult problems arose when a decision had to be made as to whether a so-called nursing home was not really a senior citizens' residence. It was the Bank's policy not to lend to provide housing, since the Central Mortgage and Housing Corporation was considered to be the instrument intended by Parliament to provide assistance in this field. It was finally ruled that, for the Bank's purposes, a 'nursing home' could be eligible only if medical or professional nursing care was constantly available.

The policy regarding housing involved other tricky cases. A trailer court would be regarded as appropriate only if it were used for casual or short occupancies, not for long leases. Motels sometimes provided housing for a manager, but financing this was not objected to where such an arrangement was necessary to make the motel operation practicable. More difficult cases involved buildings with some commercial occupancy such as stores on the ground floor and residential apartments above. Where the apartments occupied only one or two floors, one could argue that they were merely a necessary adjunct to the commercial space to make it viable. But how many storeys of apartments would be needed to turn the view around and make the commercial space merely an adjunct to the provision of residential accommodation? This question was never supplied with a simple answer, and each such case was dealt with as seemed 'appropriate.'

The policy adopted toward some other government-sponsored programs was slightly different. There were three acts under which loans guaranteed by the federal government in some degree could be obtained from chartered banks for special purposes. These were the Small Business Loans Act, the Farm Improvement Loans Act, and the Fisheries Improvement Loans Act. They were very similar to each other, providing for government guarantees of chartered bank loans in special areas. The general terms of the SBLA were given earlier; the other two were rarely encountered by the IDB. The Bank did not see these acts as having as significant a role assigned to them by Parliament, unlike the case with the Central Mortgage and Housing Corporation. They were regarded simply as measures intended to make it easier for businesses to obtain accommodation from a chartered bank for the special purposes set out in the respective act. Whether the credit was granted was entirely a matter for decision by a chartered bank. It was the IDB's view that a negative decision should not bar a business from obtaining a loan from the IDB if it met the Bank's criteria, any more than would a refusal by a chartered bank for any other kind of accommodation. A business that seemed to fit the terms of these acts would be informed of them, but if it did not want to apply to a chartered bank for assistance under them it was not required to do so. In any event, if its application to the IDB were taken under consideration, its chartered bank was notified as part of normal routine, which gave it an opportunity to consider offering assistance under these acts if it wished to do so.

A somewhat different policy was adopted toward the Farm Credit Act and the Coal Production Assistance Act. In these cases, separate bodies had been set up by the federal government to extend credit as provided in the respective acts, and these were regarded as Parliament's intended instrument within the limits of their legislation and regulations. The Farm Credit Act was the more important from the IDB's standpoint, and the Bank's policy and practice with respect to it will illustrate its relationship to these acts.

The Farm Credit Act was administered by the Farm Credit Corporation (FCC). Any applicant to the IDB in the field of agriculture that qualified under the regulations of the FCC was directed to the latter. Such a person would probably go to the FCC anyway because its rate of interest was much lower than that of the IDB and the terms for repayment could be as long as thirty years. If the proposal were eligible for consideration by the FCC and were turned down, it was considered that the IDB should not get involved, just as it stayed out of the housing field in which the Central Mortgage and Housing Corporation operated; accordingly, the applicant could not then turn to the IDB to try his luck. There were also practical reasons for the IDB's taking this position. Within the limits of its regulations, the FCC was presumably expert in appraising farm credit proposals, more so than the IDB. It was not likely that a proposal that met its rules and was turned down would be an attractive credit risk.

However, the regulations of the FCC were rather restrictive, particularly in the early 1960s. It was intended to help family farms, and it would lend only for certain types of agriculture for certain purposes and up to a certain amount. In 1962, the largest loan permitted was $27,500;[1] in 1964, the limit was raised to $55,000. The regulations even required that for certain types of loans the farmer must not be more than forty-five years old. There was obviously a great deal of scope for lending outside the regulations of the FCC. It was the IDB's policy to be willing to consider any proposal excluded from consideration by the FCC by the latter's rules. The Bank's loans covered almost every conceivable aspect of agriculture.

In one year, it made loans for a cranberry farm, a turkey farm, greenhouses, cattle ranches, commercial hog production, a wildlife park, sod growing, potato farming, a feedlot and riding academy, egg hatcheries, a mink ranch, mushroom growing, dairy farms, mixed farms, a tree farm, breeding rats for laboratories, and many other types of agricultural activity.

IDB agriculture loans tended to be larger than FCC loans. When the IDB Act was amended in 1961, loans by the FCC were averaging \$11,000[2] in amount, while in 1962, the IDB's first year of making agricultural loans, IDB's loans for agriculture averaged \$39,000. In later years, the Farm Credit Act was amended and the regulations of the FCC were modified to raise the limit on loan size and to take in some specialized types of agriculture previously excluded. Perhaps these changes were partly the result of the IDB's demonstrated ability to operate successfully in these areas.

One curious feature of relations between the FCC and the IDB resulted from the practice of the former of lending only when it was possible to check the fertility of the applicant's land because it was not covered with snow. This led to applications being made to the IDB during the winter by farmers who at other seasons would have applied to the Farm Credit Corporation. If a loan were granted by the Bank, the farmer would sometimes turn later to the FCC for a loan when the snow was gone and want to pay off the IDB with the proceeds so that he could take advantage of the FCC's lower rate of interest. The IDB took a dim view of this sort of thing, and long arguments ensued over the Bank's opinion that it was entitled to a prepayment indemnity in such cases.

The desire of farmers to get the benefit, so far as possible, of the FCC's relatively low rate of interest led some, who needed financing beyond the maximum permitted by the corporation's regulations, to suggest to the IDB that the needs of such applicants should be met partly by an FCC first mortgage loan for the largest amount the corporation could lend under its regulations and partly by a second mortgage loan from the IDB for the rest. The Bank rejected such proposals. It did not see itself as having the job of mitigating the effects of the FCC's rules. Whatever these were, they were no doubt drawn up to reflect the role and goals of the FCC. If a farmer needed more than the FCC's limit, he and/or his program were presumably in different categories from those served by the FCC, and the Bank felt free to lend to him the full amount he required if it wished to do so.

Money lending and investing institutions, although eligible for IDB loans under the 1961 amendments as 'business undertakings,' were ruled out as inappropriate for loans from the IDB. Also, the Bank continued to regard in the same light daily newspapers and breweries and distilleries. The eligibility of restaurants, hotels, and motels, as a result of the 1961 amendments, however, compelled the Bank to rethink its attitude toward alcoholic beverages. It was obvious that the Bank would not be able to help many restaurants if it ruled out all that sold alcoholic drinks. Accordingly, at first it tried to apply the percentage principle that had been used for job printing; any licensed premises with a 'substantial portion' of gross revenues coming from the sale of alcoholic beverages were to be regarded as 'inappropriate.' Internally, this proportion was set at $33\frac{1}{3}$ per cent. This, of course, created the old familiar problems of dealing with borderline cases; a restaurant estimating future beverage sales at 35 per cent was actually ruled inappropriate. The critical percentage was supposed to be kept secret, but inevitably the industry deduced what the Bank's policy was. The Canadian Association of Hotelmen, meeting in 1964, complained openly of the $33\frac{1}{3}$ per cent rule.[3]

The Bank's policy was partly based on the attitude inherited from its early days that it was not suitable that the kind of money loaned by the Bank, having a public character and available on reasonable terms and conditions, should finance breweries and distilleries, and partly based on concerns about getting involved in any business which, because of its dependence on sales of alcoholic beverages, was so subject to regulation and licensing as to make it difficult to predict its future or to estimate the prospects of selling its assets in the event of liquidation. However, these concerns gradually faded, the rule was found difficult to apply with justice in all cases, and, in December 1967, the $33\frac{1}{3}$ per cent rule and all restrictions regarding alcoholic beverages were rescinded. In the mean time, the Bank had been able to approve 1,200 loans for $54 millions to hotels, motels, and restaurants anyway.[4]

The revision of the Bank's instructions on eligible and appropriate businesses that followed the 1961 amendments listed one more group that was to be regarded as inappropriate. These were 'race tracks, night-clubs, and cabarets, dance halls, and gambling or betting establishments.' Racetracks may well have been included because of their having been referred to directly by a member of Parliament during the debate on the 1961 amendments in the House of Commons.[5] The other businesses may have been the kind that the same member had in mind when he expressed fears that the Bank might lend to types of amusement places 'which do not meet the requirements of most taxpayers in this country.' In any event, the rule against racetracks was applied quite firmly. Tracks for any kind of racing – horses, automobiles, go-karts, motorcycles – were ruled inappropriate. In 1964, however, the rule was qualified to exclude only racetracks 'at which there are facilities for betting.'

The ruling against loans to 'night-clubs and cabarets' produced the usual cases of difficult borderline decisions. At what point did a restaurant that provided entertainment become a night-club or cabaret? Would one pianist be enough to do it? If not, would the addition of a singer be enough? Or the addition of another act? Might a restaurant escape disqualification if such entertainment as was provided took place on the floor-level and not on a stage? One proposal was put forward by a credit officer, obviously well trained in making fine policy distinctions, on the grounds that, though the applicant business was called a night-club, it was really more of a supper-club. He was unsuccessful, but a regional supervisor, R.H. Wheeler, obtained a favourable ruling for a night-club at which entertainment was described as intended only 'as an inducement for people to dine' and as constituting a 'refined theatrical performance.' Not so successful was C. Pineau, manager of the Ottawa branch. After describing the extraordinarily abstemious habits of the clientele of an applicant restaurant, he tried to obtain a favourable ruling by concluding, 'To give atmosphere and to attract the dollars of mildly sophisticated, cultured and artistic people, emphasis will be given to the present policy to display and sell Canadian paintings, sculpture and handicraft and imported wares. While the total volume sold here may not be large, the relatively high cost of these items should make them weigh heavily as a source of revenue.' However, GMO turned a cold eye on this one.

When restrictions on loans to businesses that sold or manufactured alcoholic beverages were lifted in December 1967, the Bank was placed in a position that implied, as it was put in a somewhat scornful internal memorandum, that the Bank considered that 'dancing was more evil than drinking.' In January 1968, the prohibition against loans to cabarets and night-clubs was lifted.

The IDB's concern about loans to such establishments was not quite as quixotic as it may appear to have been. Apart from any opinion about the kinds of industrial development for which its resources should be employed, the Bank had a practical concern about the view that might be taken by some disappointed applicant, who was running a small machine shop or manufacturing business, of the Bank's putting money into a night-club instead. A businessman whose application for a $15,000 loan to buy a new machine had been turned down might be puzzled, if nothing else, to see a much larger loan go to a noisy tavern or cabaret down the street. By 1968, society had presumably evolved to the point that this consideration was not as serious as the unhappy position the Bank was in through having to make the difficult and peculiar decisions these policies required and through having to endure the stuffy impression they created.

Policies on prepayment of loans and various fees

Another area of policy affected by the amendments of 1961, and by the increased activity and loan potential that resulted, had to do with the various fees levied by the Bank – the prepayment indemnity and the commitment and stand-by fees. These had become important sources of revenue, yielding $174,000 in 1961 for little additional direct expense.[6]

We shall look first at the prepayment indemnity. The terms of the Bank's loan contracts gave a borrower the right to prepay a loan in whole or in part at any time. Since 1947, most prepayments had required the payment to the Bank of an indemnity, although as the policy developed prepayments from certain sources were exempt. The formula used for calculating the indemnity and the basis for distinguishing between prepayments subject to it and those that were exempt varied from time to time. In 1960, a formula was established that required, for any prepayment in the first three years of a loan, an indemnity equal to 6 per cent of the amount of the prepayment; for any made in the fourth, fifth, and sixth years, an amount equal to 5 per cent, 4 per cent, and 3 per cent respectively; and for any made thereafter, an indemnity of 2 per cent. At that time, the Bank's lending rate of interest was 7 per cent, and a few months later it was reduced to 6½ per cent, and so the indemnity payable for the first three years of a loan was roughly equivalent to ten or eleven months' interest. Prepayments were accepted without indemnity from the proceeds of assigned insurance, the expropriation of property, or incidental sales of machinery or equipment, or if the prepayment was made after the borrower had been adjudged bankrupt.

As commercial sources of term financing emerged into greater prominence in the late 1950s and early 1960s, and as the number and types of businesses dealing with the Bank increased, prepayments seemed to occur more frequently and created some problems. We will now consider these, but it should be understood, first, that the actual number of difficult cases was not great. For example, of 327 prepayments made in 1963 and 1964, only 8 provoked serious complaints. However, although small in number, they touched on fundamental issues, and their settlement was essential for the establishment of defensible and fair principles and practices that could be consistently followed.

One problem had to do with customers of the Bank who, needing

additional money, found it with another lender who wished to prepay the
IDB's loan. Sometimes this happened because the Bank honoured its role
as a complementary lender by directing an IDB borrower needing more
money to look elsewhere first. Several such cases arose in 1963 and 1964.
One example will illustrate the problem. A loan for $100,000 at $6\frac{1}{2}$ per
cent interest was made to a company by the IDB in 1961. A year or so later,
the company contemplated adding more machinery to its plant and
constructing a building. After it had considered different ways of
financing the cost of all this, it was told by the IDB that, if it intended to
approach the Bank, it would have to explore other sources first. When it
did so, it received an offer of a loan for five years at 8 per cent on condition
that the IDB's loan should be prepaid. This required an indemnity of
$4,500, and the company, intending to accept the outside financing,
asked if the indemnity could be waived.

The Bank considered itself constrained from providing the additional
financing since it regarded the terms offered by the other lender to be
reasonable. As for the prepayment indemnity, it was well within the
customer's ability to pay, and so, on the Bank's insistence, it was paid. This
could have been avoided if the other lender had been willing to make a
second mortgage loan for only enough to finance the new expenditures
on machinery and building, but this it declined to do.

By 1964, enough such cases had occurred, even without complaints, to
cause the Bank to re-examine its position and its indemnity formula. The
operational management of the Bank felt it was entitled to an indemnity
in these cases as much as for any other prepayment. Only in this way
would it be compensated for the loss of the interest revenue that was to
have covered the cost of processing the loan application and authorizing
and disbursing the loan. Further, as Mr James, the general manager, said
in a letter to the president in 1964: 'It would, of course, be anomalous if
the Bank, which is authorized by Parliament to lend only where financing
is not available elsewhere on reasonable terms and conditions, were to
operate on a basis markedly more favourable to borrowers than conventional lenders in this respect ... [i.e. without requiring an indemnity for a
prepayment]. A possible alternative would be to charge an investigation
or processing fee for [all] loan applications, but this is not considered
appropriate for an institution of the character of IDB.'

Also, the Bank believed that to waive the indemnity in such cases as
were described above would lay the Bank's portfolio of loans open to
raiding by other lenders and mean, in effect, doing their investigating
work for them; this would not be in their long-term interests and would
not foster a stable and sound operation for the Bank. It was obvious,

however, that the Bank was going to have trouble maintaining this position unless it could modify the terms of its prepayment indemnities. Complicated ways to do so were tossed around, but, finally, the simple device was adopted of reducing the indemnities to be paid. Beginning in March 1965, a prepayment indemnity was to be 5 per cent for the first two years of a loan and then decrease by 1 per cent in each succeeding year until it reached nil at the end of the sixth year. This formula was used until the end, and this particular problem with prepayment indemnities was not serious again.

A departure from the principle that an indemnity should always accompany a prepayment was made in 1965 in the case of prepayments from the proceeds of loans by the FCC: 'What was really happening was that the financing was being transferred from one Federal lending agency, IDB, to another Federal lending agency, FCC, which specializes in loans to farmers and which, at the time IDB made the loan[,] was unable by statute to provide the funds required.'

The loans concerned were invariably small, and it was recognized that, due to its specialized nature, the FCC was really better equipped than the IDB to make farm loans. In addition, the FCC was engaged, at the time, in a broadening of its regulations to permit loans to types of operations not previously considered eligible for its assistance. This enabled the FCC to finance things that it had had to refuse before; in some cases, the IDB had financed these programs, and it was decided that the Bank would not stand in the way of the FCC's catching up, as it were, by refinancing some of these IDB loans. Accordingly, in May 1965, it was decided that prepayments from FCC loans would be accepted without an indemnity. The operational management of the IDB was not comfortable with this position; in 1967 it was concluded that the passage of time had weakened the original reasons for the position and this departure from normal policy was terminated.

In due course, the (Automotive) Adjustment Assistance Board, which had started operations in the summer of 1965, heard of this concession, and in January 1966 it asked the Bank to apply the same principle to prepayments from AAB loans. This the Bank firmly declined to do. In the view of the IDB, there was no similarity between the two cases at all. Any existing IDB loans to companies in the automotive industry had been made in the ordinary course of doing exactly the kind of thing the Bank was created to do. It did not consider the AAB as having any special expertise in the field to which the IDB should defer. There was always open to the AAB the making of a second mortgage loan behind the IDB in any case where the payment of a prepayment indemnity might present serious problems.

With respect to commitment and stand-by fees, the only change made in them was that, from 1962 on, no stand-by fee was charged on loans for $25,000 or less or on undisbursed balances that had been reduced to $25,000 or less.

Inquiries and criticisms by MPs

Another consequence of the 1961 amendments was that the IDB had to take more account than previously of the relationship of a crown corporation to the political milieu. The parliamentary debates on the Small Business Loans Act and the amendments to the IDB Act had drawn attention to the IDB in parliamentary and governmental circles. The rise of small business as a significant element in the political world, the increased visibility of the Bank as a result of its growth, and the much more extensive contacts of the Bank with every kind of business in all parts of the country following the amendments to the IDB Act gave the Bank an increased prominence in the politicians' view.

Members of Parliament took much more interest than they previously had done in the success businesses in their constituencies had in obtaining loans from the Bank. Never did this interest descend to serious pressure on the Bank to make a loan. Rarely did it go beyond recommending an applicant to the Bank (which was treated by the Bank as nothing more than a normal courtesy by an MP toward a constituent) or inquiring as to the success of an application or why one was declined. Where inquiries of this sort had previously occurred in dozens each year, however, they now occurred at a rate of over 200 per year. Of course, in relation to 11,000 annual inquiries to the Bank by businesses, and loan authorizations of over 2,000 per year, this number was not large. Nevertheless, dealing with inquiries from MPs with proper courtesy did involve time and effort on the part of the secretary of the Bank in Ottawa and a senior officer at GMO.

Another reflection of increased interest in the Bank by politicians was a continuation in Parliament from time to time of the kind of criticisms that had featured the debate on the amendments: the Bank was 'inadequate'; its rates of interest were too high; its repayment terms were too short; it was subject to too strict regulations (whatever that meant); it should operate as a 'development agency'; it always wanted everything in 'black and white' (which was true); it refused 90 per cent of applications; it had become a 'money-making machine.' One member capped all by claiming that when the Bank made a loan it held back $2,500 from the proceeds as a reserve that would be paid to the borrower after ten years! This was one dodge the Bank never thought of.[7]

The interest of members of Parliament as shown in these frequently unfavourable comments seemed more likely to be aroused by the failure of a business in a member's riding to obtain a loan than by any successful applications. Presumably, successful applicants would have no reason to inform their MP of their success in getting a loan in which, in any event, he would have had no part. An unsuccessful applicant, however, might appeal to his MP to see if by this means the Bank's decision might be reversed. Since an MP's intervention would not influence the Bank, beyond perhaps its reviewing the case again with the applicant, the applicant's disappointment would be sharper and shared now to some extent by his MP.

Choice of lawyers to prepare security

More important to the Bank in its relations with the political world than the picturesque, although no doubt sincere, comments made in Parliament was the maintenance of its independence in choosing lawyers who would act for it in preparing security documents for loans. Legal work for governmental activities was a traditional field for political patronage, and early in its history the Bank took steps to ensure that its operations were not embraced by it. The management and personnel of the Bank considered it most important not only that the Bank should be entirely free to make all its decisions on loan applications and administration on a business basis but also that it should appear free.

The position of the Bank was summed up by Mr Rasminsky early in his presidency in a memorandum on the Bank's policy prepared for the minister of finance: 'It is clear that the intention of Parliament in the original IDB Act was to give the institution a character as close as possible to that of private enterprise and to have it operate independently of political influence either in relation to the loans it makes or in relation to its internal organization, personnel and administration.'

At the same time, since the Bank was a crown corporation, management recognized that its integrity in this respect would appear stronger if it avoided using lawyers who were prominently active on behalf of a political party. As early as 1948 and 1949, it was made clear by Mr Towers, president of the Bank, and by Donald Gordon, deputy governor of the Bank of Canada, and concurred in by the government, that lawyers who would be asked to prepare security for the Bank's loans should be selected independently and only on the basis of their competence to do satisfactory work promptly. They would include neither those identified as active adherents to the political party in office nor those active in opposition to it.

The prime consideration in selecting lawyers or notaries to whom work would be referred was that they should be competent professionally and give prompt service in their work for the Bank. It was also considered to be an argument against using any other criteria in the choice of a lawyer that the legal fees for a loan were paid by the borrower, not by the Bank. Since the security work for an IDB loan was highly technical and often of an unusual character, it was considered that it would be improper to choose professional services for which the borrower paid on other than a business-like basis. Up to 1955, the Bank would sometimes use the borrower's solicitor if the loan involved were for a modest amount, but Mr Coyne, when he became president, thought this practice unwise as potentially involving the lawyer in a conflict of interest, and in 1955 it was stopped.

It became clear with experience that something more precise than good intentions was needed to maintain a proper policy. In some parts of the country it seemed almost impossible to find a lawyer who was not possessed of such an intense political commitment, inherited perhaps in a direct line of succession from his great-grandfather, as to be ruled out by the Bank's criteria as to political activity. Also, the number of lawyers whose services were used in the course of a year increased rapidly as the Bank expanded. In 1955, before the first major amendment to the IDB Act, the Bank used 60 lawyers and notaries; in 1962, following the second major amendment, it used 248. In 1959, guidelines were laid down to guide field offices, and, in 1963, the Bank introduced a form to be used by branches in reporting on choices of lawyers and notaries made or recommended; henceforth the whole issue was kept under satisfactory control.

The attention given the Bank by the 1961 amendments and by public comments during the early 1960s had extended very far. In 1965 the Bank's accounting department was astonished to receive for payment from one of the chartered banks a $280 cheque drawn on the IDB by a private individual and deposited in the chartered bank. Since the IDB did not accept deposits or carry ordinary banking accounts, the cheque was sent back as fraudulent. On the back of it was the intriguing endorsement: '2 billets voyage en Floride qui comprend l'autobus et les couchers.'

Change in interest policy

An area of policy that reflected the expanded activity following the amendments of 1956 and 1961 was that by which the rate of interest charged on one of the Bank's loans was decided. The traditional policy had been to charge one rate of interest on all loans. However, early in 1962 there were a number of cases in which a rate higher than the normal or standard rate was set, either because the IDB's loan was going to rest on a second or third mortgage position for security, or because the loan concerned was a very large one, perhaps representing a somewhat greater risk than usual. Both sets of circumstances arose to some extent from the fact that the IDB's rate of interest was sometimes below that of some lenders. The more frequent appearance of loans against junior security may have resulted from the Bank's reluctance to refinance existing debts in view of the controversy about such cases or may have reflected the growing activity of commercial sources in term financing for small businesses. Presumably these sources were unwilling to increase their loans when further assistance might later be required. Some of these loans bore a rate of interest higher than the IDB's, and it struck the Bank as unsatisfactory that its second mortgage loan should be at a rate below that of the first mortgage. In such cases, the Bank began to set a rate above its normal rate. The appearance of higher rates for larger loans arose from a feeling that, whatever sympathy should be shown to a small business in the way of a rate of interest that was liberal compared to some rates in the market-place, there was less justification for expressing sympathy in the same fashion for a larger business that would probably be used to paying higher rates on the market-place for other financial needs.

Since these developments were contrary to the Bank's normal practices, they created great uncertainty at the branch level as to what the Bank's policy really was. Accordingly, instructions were issued in June 1963 that for an IDB loan secured 'principally or substantially' by a second mortgage the suitability of the Bank's charging $\frac{1}{2}$ to 1 per cent over the normal rate was to be considered, and in due course setting this higher rate for second mortgage loans became the invariable practice.

Guidance on the rate of interest on large loans was less easily established. These loans were authorized by the board of directors or the executive committee. There was not always unanimity among the directors as to how the risk in a large loan might most properly be reflected by some addition to the Bank's normal rate of interest. As a result, their decisions did not seem to follow any clear guidelines, and the Bank's officers in the field felt uncertain, when discussing a proposal with an applicant or explaining the terms of an authorized loan, as to how to explain the Bank's policy on rates of interest.

The general manager, Mr James, and the operational officers generally argued for some firm basis on which the growing practice of setting higher rates for large loans might be fixed. An internal memorandum summarized their views in 1964: 'We should have some clear definite and explainable policy on interest rates, being, as we are, a public institution which carries a greater obligation than a chartered bank does to explain its policy and operations to those with whom it deals.'

The president, however, was reluctant to establish as an invariable principle that interest rates on large loans should be established only by some rule. He did not consider it suitable that he, as president, and the board of directors should have no prerogative to diverge from some interest formula or rule in special circumstances. The board seemed to feel that its ultimate responsibility for the Bank's credit operations was quite properly reflected in the area, even if only a small one, of loans for large amounts by exercising its own judgment as to the rate of interest to be applied in such cases. Indeed, the suggestion was even made that interest rates as a whole could well be determined by judgment more often than was the Bank's practice. This suggestion had some support from the report of the Porter Commission, which recommended that the Bank charge various rates for its loans to reflect different risks[8] – based, presumably, on someone's judgment of the relative risks. Mr James, however, was cool toward depending on judgment as a basis for interest rates in a public institution such as the IDB. To quote the same memorandum: 'If we were to accept "judgement" as the basis for interest rates, one would have to decide whose "judgement" was to be involved. It would be quite impossible to leave such a decision to Managers scattered from coast to coast. There would undoubtedly be great inconsistency and variations in such an event ... All rate decisions would have to be concentrated in one place ... and the time factor and administrative problems involved would certainly rule out such a practice.'

The two points of view were not reconciled until early in 1966, when the tradition of a single rate was finally and permanently abandoned. From then on, the Bank applied a table of rates that varied according to the size of a loan. The first such table, established in February 1966, called for a normal or 'standard' rate, $7\frac{1}{2}$ per cent, on all loans of up to $300,000; $7\frac{3}{4}$ per cent from $300,000 to $600,000; and 8 per cent from $600,000 to $1 million. A discretionary rate was to be set by the board for any loan over $1 million, with a minimum of 8 per cent; but the number of cases involved was small and the borrowers were thought to be sufficiently sophisticated to accept the explanations about risk and so on on which a higher rate would be based. This pattern, with variations in categories and rates, was followed from then on.

CHAPTER EIGHTEEN

Operating results

Revenues and profits

Results from operations 1962–7 are summarized in Table 19, which also shows, for comparative purposes, figures for the last year of the preceding period, 1961. The table shows that, although revenues tripled between 1961 and 1967, there was a great drop in the final annual net profit transferred to the general reserve fund after provision for anticipated loan losses. The decline in profits was actually greater than the table shows; in 1954 they had reached a peak of $1,688,000. The low point was reached in 1962. The net profit of $415,000 earned that year was lower than any since 1948, when a net profit of $34,000 was recorded. In no year did the Bank record a loss, but the percentage return on capital fell to very low levels.

There were many reasons for the falling off in profits. The Bank was doing more business, but in smaller loans; its dependence on debentures to finance its loans was increasing; and the rate of interest paid on the debentures had risen without a compensating rise in the Bank's lending rate. This last fact meant that the proportion of revenues available to meet operating expenses and provide a profit had become much smaller.

The trend toward smaller loans had started in 1957, following the amendments of 1956, and continued after the amendments of 1961. In 1956, the average size of loan approvals was $113,000, whereas in 1967 it was $52,000.[1] Since the cost of processing an application was not necessarily affected greatly by the amount involved, a fall in the average size of approvals reduced interest income without a similar reduction in

TABLE 19

Operating results ($millions) 1961–7

	1961	1962	1963	1964	1965	1966	1967
Interest on loans	7.1	9.4	12.2	14.2	16.6	19.3	22.8
Other income	0.3	0.3	0.4	0.5	0.5	0.5	0.6
Total income	7.4	9.7	12.6	14.7	17.1	19.8	23.4
Operating expenses	2.8	4.1	4.6	4.9	5.3	6.4	7.0
Interest on debentures	3.0	4.5	6.6	7.9	9.5	11.5	13.9
Total costs	5.8	8.6	11.2	12.8	14.8	17.9	20.9
Net income	1.6	1.1	1.4	1.9	2.3	1.9	2.5
Provision for losses	0.4	0.7	0.7	1.0	1.3	1.4	1.9
Transferred to reserve fund	1.2	0.4	0.7	0.9	1.0	0.5	0.6
Percentage rate of return on capital (shares plus reserve fund)	3.0	0.9	1.5	1.7	1.7	0.9	1.0

SOURCE: *Annual Reports.*

operating expenses. The effects of this development showed themselves slowly as the larger loans of an earlier day were gradually replaced on the Bank's books by the ever-smaller loans authorized in each successive year and as the average size of individual account balances outstanding on the Bank's books, on which interest was collected, gradually declined. In 1956, the average size of customers' accounts outstanding had been $63,000; in 1967, it was $39,000.

Dependence on debenture financing

The Bank's costs were rising as it became more dependent on borrowed money to finance its lending operations. At the end of 1961, 66 per cent of the capital funds at the Bank's disposal were in debentures, 22 per cent in share capital, and 12 per cent in the reserve fund.[2] The 1961 amendments increased the permitted share capital from $25 million to $50 million and raised the limit on direct liabilities (largely debentures issued by the Bank) from three times paid-up shares plus reserve fund to five times. This contemplated a maximum issue of debentures of approximately $325 million, as compared to $78.9 million outstanding at the end of 1961. Shortly after the amendments were passed, the board of directors decided to issue the new shares relative to new debentures sales in the ratio of 1:10; the Bank of Canada purchased $1 million in shares in the summer of 1961 and then bought no more until it had purchased $10 million in debentures. This policy was intended to bring the ratio between direct liabilities and equity, as shown on the Bank's balance sheet, gradually to the new legal ratio of 5:1. Also, it was thought that, if all the capital were drawn down by the Bank of Canada at once, it would artificially and temporarily inflate the profits of the IDB in the year of drawing. This might give rise to pressure to adjust the IDB lending rate to an extent that would have to be reversed in the years following. The 1967 amendments raising the ratio between direct liabilities and equity to 10:1 received royal assent on 21 December 1967 and had no effect on operations in the 1962–7 period, the review of which we are now completing.

Share capital had grown from $26 million in 1961 to $44 million in 1967, while debentures had increased from $78.9 million to $262.5 million and represented 80 per cent of the capital resources employed by the Bank.[3] This increased the proportion of the Bank's total expenses represented by debenture interest. In 1961, it was 52 per cent of total annual costs, while in 1967 it was 67 per cent. To the extent that debenture interest expense increased in relative importance, the costs to be covered out of earnings were becoming more rigid and to a large extent not subject to managerial control.

Interest rates on loans and debentures

Table 20 gives the annual 'weighted' average rates of interest on new loans made each year and on new capital funds, i.e. on new debentures plus new issues of share capital 1962–7. These figures are made up on a different basis than those given for interest rates in earlier years in Table 11. The latter table gave simply averages for rates on new loans and debentures. For the years from 1962 on, the figures available give a better idea of the effect on income and costs of new loans made and debentures issued because the rates have been 'weighted' according to the dollar total of transactions at each rate, and the average has then been arrived at. Further, in the case of the rate for 'new debentures issued and new share capital,' the figures in Table 20 take into account any new issues of shares on which, of course, no interest was payable. As a result this rate represents the interest cost of all new funds made available to the Bank and is slightly below – perhaps 0.4 per cent below – what would be the average rate on debentures alone.

To understand the interest rate situation 1962–7, it is necessary first to

TABLE 20

Weighted average rates of interest on new loans made and on new capital funds 1962–7

	Weighted average rate (percentage) on new loans made	Weighted average rate (percentage) on new debentures issued plus new share capital	Difference or spread (percentage)
1962	6.62	4.44	2.18
1963	7.01	4.53	2.48
1964	7.03	4.63	2.40
1965	7.09	4.70	2.39
1966	7.56	5.53	2.03
1967	8.03	5.50	2.53

go back to the years preceding. Between 1955 and 1961, the average interest rate on new debentures doubled, rising from 2.34 per cent to 4.71 per cent, but the average rate on new loans rose by only ½ of 1 per cent, from 6.00 per cent to 6.50 per cent.[4] That lending rates lagged behind rising debenture rates between 1955 and 1961 at a time when debentures were becoming the main source of funds meant that the Bank's portfolio of loans was having built into it a growing block of loans yielding a shrinking margin of return.

When, in early 1962, interest rates on the market increased, the unsatisfactory level of IDB's rate was sharply focused.[5] By this time, the average debenture rate (i.e. without taking into account issues of shares as is done in Table 20) was 2.5 per cent higher than in 1955, while the lending rate was only 0.5 per cent higher. The Bank's board of directors and executive committee concluded that the lending rate should be raised. There was a question as to whether it should be increased by ½ of 1 per cent to 7 per cent or by 1 per cent to 7½ per cent, with the weight of opinion inclining to the latter. However, there were grounds for believing that the government would be unhappy to see any increase at all, and so the lending rate was raised by only ½ of 1 per cent to 7 per cent at the end of August 1962.

Since the Bank's lending rate was not raised again for four years, the decision in 1962 to limit the increase to ½ of 1 per cent proved to be an important one. In the interval, a net amount of $275 million in new loans was authorized; an additional ½ of 1 per cent on these loans would, over a period of years, have produced substantial revenues.

Although the board of directors held back in 1962 from as large an increase in lending rates as some felt would have been justifiable, within a few months it began to try to compensate for this decision by setting rates for large loans at a higher figure than the normal rate, as explained previously. In February 1963, Mr James, the general manager, suggested that this inclination on the part of the board be incorporated formally in the Bank's policy instructions to field offices by setting a two-tiered system of interest rates, with a rate above the standard for loans over a certain amount. It was not until three years later, however, in February 1966, that such a device was adopted. At that time, as described in chapter 17, the 'standard' rate was raised to $7\frac{1}{2}$ per cent. This was to apply to loans up to $300,000. From $300,000 to $600,000 the rate was to be $7\frac{3}{4}$ per cent; from $600,000 to $1,000,000, 8 per cent; and over $1,000,000, a minimum of 8 per cent.

In September of that year, this schedule was replaced. The $7\frac{1}{2}$ per cent rate was to be applied only up to $75,000. From there to $150,000, the rate was to be 8 per cent; from $150,000 to $350,000, $8\frac{1}{2}$ per cent; and over $350,000, a minimum of $8\frac{1}{2}$ per cent. This was, in its effects, a drastic and important revision. It enabled the Bank to increase its revenues and to charge higher rates closer to the market on those larger loans in which other lenders were principally interested, and yet it appeared to serve the Bank's basic role of helping small and medium-sized businesses by favouring them with a lower rate of interest. On the basis of loans made in 1966, this schedule meant that the lowest rate would apply to about 80 per cent of loans by number, but to only 45 per cent by amount. The highest rates of $8\frac{1}{2}$ per cent or more would apply only to 5 per cent of loans by number, but to 30 per cent by amount. This increase, at the beginning of 1967, in the proportion of new loans paying a rate of interest above the lowest or 'standard' rate of $7\frac{1}{2}$ per cent, which had been set early in 1966, resulted in the average rate on new loans for 1967 actually being nearly 0.5 per cent higher than the 'standard' rate of $7\frac{1}{2}$ per cent, as shown in Table 20, without any change in the rates themselves as used in the schedule.

One more aspect of debenture costs should be noted. The rate of interest on new debentures was based on the current rate for government bonds of a like term, plus an additional fraction of 1 per cent. From 1961 on, the additional amount was 0.60 per cent. This accounts for some of the rise in debenture rates from earlier years. Since debentures normally matured serially in one to six years, virtually all the debentures outstanding at the end of 1967 had the additional 0.60 per cent in their interest rates. On the average, approximately $250 million was outstanding during that year, so that the 0.60 per cent added on must have accounted for close to $1,500,000 or so of debenture cost in that year.

The effect of all these developments on the Bank's earnings is reflected in Table 21 in which the various elements of the operating statement are expressed as percentages of the average loans and investments outstand-

TABLE 21

Operating results expressed as percentage of average loans and investments outstanding
1961–7

	1961	1962	1963	1964	1965	1966	1967
Income as percentage of average loans and investments	6.61	6.62	6.79	6.95	7.07	7.18	7.40
Less:							
Debenture cost	2.68	3.06	3.53	3.74	3.95	4.16	4.38
Operating costs	2.47	2.83	2.50	2.33	2.19	2.32	2.22
Net profit before provision for losses	1.46	0.73	0.76	0.88	0.93	0.70	0.80

SOURCE: Brief, Table 4; *Annual Report*, 1967.

ing in each fiscal year. As the table shows, the potential for a profit surplus out of earnings was now greatly reduced. Whereas in 1961 debenture interest costs were 2.68 per cent of average loans and investments, by 1967, they were 4.38 per cent. The return on loans and investments available to provide for possible losses and leave a profit had fallen from 1.46 per cent in 1961 to 0.80 per cent in 1967; in 1956, the profit return had been 3.22 per cent of average loans and investments.

Operating costs and loss experience

The figure for operating costs in the table suggests that these were still being kept under control in relation to the growing volume of business being handled. Actual annual staff costs were greater in the years 1962–7 than in 1956–61, rising from an average of $6,400 per employee to $7,500 per employee. Nevertheless, total operating costs per customer on the Bank's books fell from an average of $1,132 in 1956–61 to an average of $939 in 1962–7, as the number of loans under administration increased.

With net earnings greatly reduced between 1962 and 1967, revenues from the various fees collected by the Bank – prepayment indemnity, stand-by fee, commitment fee – took on a new importance. For the period 1962–7, the revenues from these fees totalled $2,600,000, more than half the total of net profits after provision for a reserve for losses. In 1962, 1966, and 1967, the amounts transferred to the reserve fund came almost entirely from these fees.

The final step in determining the profit at the end of a fiscal year was to transfer from earnings into the reserve for losses an amount sufficient to bring it up to a reasonable level to protect against future write-offs on loans then outstanding. At the end of 1961, the balance in the reserve for losses was $2,700,000; by the end of 1967, it was $7,500,000. For 1962−7, the total of annual transfers to the reserve came to $6,984,000. The total net income before provision for losses earned during these six years was $11,066,000, so that, after the transfers to the reserve for losses, little more than $4 million was left as the final net profit from operations to be added to the general reserve fund.

The condition of the Bank's loans remained pretty steady. At the end of each of the two previous periods, 1945−55 and 1956−61, the annual review of outstanding loans had shown around 85 per cent to be in a satisfactory state.[6] At the end of the 1962−7 period, the proportion was the same. The reserve for losses was being gradually built up to a level providing a much greater margin of protection against write-offs. For 1956−61, the reserve at the end of each year was, on average, 26 per cent more than was needed to cover foreseen write-offs. In the years 1962−7, however, this margin of protection averaged 52 per cent. In fact, by the end of 1967, the reserve for losses was 79 per cent greater than was needed to cover estimated probable losses. A margin was necessary, because no matter how carefully a review of the Bank's loans might be made, there were sure to be some unsuspected future write-offs among the outstanding loans. The reserve at the end of 1967, however, proved in the long run (i.e. up to 1981) to have been ample to take care of all write-offs of loans then on the Bank's books or authorized.

The balance in the reserve for losses was usually expressed, for convenience, as a percentage of the sum of outstanding loan balances and undisbursed amounts of new loans. For 1945−55, this had averaged 1.37 per cent. For 1956−61, it had averaged 1.56 per cent, and for 1962−7, 1.72 per cent. At the end of 1967, the only year in the six-year period with a reserve for losses account balance that proved in the long run to be greater than write-offs of loans then outstanding or authorized, the reserve was 1.94 per cent of outstanding loan balances and undisbursed commitments.

For a view of the Bank's loss experience, however, we have been considering the actual history of the loans approved in each year by following, through the records of the Bank, the various amounts written off each year and then relating these write-offs back to the total of net loan authorizations of the years in which the loans that were written off had been approved. Up to 1981, actual loss experience for loans in the first period we have studied, 1945−55, was 0.47 per cent of net authorizations; for the second period, 1956−61, it was 1.18 per cent; and for the third period, 1962−7, net losses were 1.34 per cent of net authorizations.

PART V

The final years
1968–75

F.M. Aykroyd
Joined Bank 1947;
supervisor, Atlantic Provinces,
1952–6; supervisor, Calgary,
1956–61; supervisor, Vancouver,
1961–3; retired 1963

C.E. De Athe
Joined Bank 1949;
administrative assistant 1959–62;
executive assistant 1962–6;
assistant general manager, GMO,
1966–73; died 1973
Photo by Milne Studios Limited,
Toronto

H.R. Stoker
Joined Bank 1948;
supervisor, Halifax, 1956–9;
supervisor, Winnipeg, 1959–62;
supervisor, Eastern
(later Quebec) Region, 1962–6;
assistant general manager,
Atlantic Region, 1966–8;
retired 1968

H.J.C. Russell
Joined Bank 1950;
administrative assistant 1958–9;
executive assistant 1959–61;
supervisor, Calgary, 1961–6;
assistant general manager,
GMO, 1966–73; general manager,
Loans, 1973–5
Photo by Arnott Rogers
Batten Ltd

R.W. Wheeler
Joined Bank 1948;
supervisor, Saint John, 1959–63;
assistant supervisor, Prairie
Region, 1963–6; supervisor,
Prairie Region, 1966–73;
general manager, Prairie
Region, 1973–5
Photo by McTavish / Point A,
Winnipeg

E.A. Bell
Joined Bank 1953;
supervisor, Halifax, 1959–66;
supervisor, Central (later
Ontario) Region, 1966–73;
general manager, Branch
Operations, 1973–5
Photo by David Bier, Montreal

The second staff administration training seminar, held in Montreal,
18–22 November 1968.
Seated (l to r): W.H. Jay, J.A. McKee, E.C. Scott, André Côté, J.Y. Milette;
middle row: J.A. Sutherland, F.G. Stewart, E.A. Duddle, T.F. Ching, H.D. Ramsey;
back row: I.D. MacLaren, M.D. Rudkin, C.V. Spielman, G.L. Vézina

Mobile office (top left) on tour in the Atlantic provinces at Plastic Rock, New Brunswick. On the left is J.E. McNulty, then a credit officer with Saint John branch, greeting Mr Pugh, the town clerk.

An IDB exhibit at a trade show (top right). At the back is the portable display booth, with a centre space for the continuous display of an automatic slide-show.

This branch office in Terrace, British Columbia (centre), illustrates the new approach taken to branch openings in the seventies. At street level, in a shopping centre, with a prominent electric sign, it projects an attractive and accessible image. The photo also illustrates the buoyant spirit of those days. Members of the staff (l to r): L. Pollard, N. Windsor, and M. Kartasheff (manager), with steelhead caught in the Copper River near Terrace

*An employee works on a mobile home (top left) This borrower (top right) manufactured women's
in a plant partly owned by a band of sweaters. A knitting machine is shown
western Indians and financed by the IDB. being set up with the required yarns.*

*A hotel is constructed (centre) in the northern part of Baffin Island
with the help of an IDB loan.*

Another unusual borrower – a producer of leaded art glass (top)
Photo by John Evans Photography Ltd, Ottawa

Seaweed is dumped into a hopper (centre) for drying and processing into
a gelling agent for use in custard powders. The output of this company
in the Atlantic provinces was all exported.

*This is another of the unusual agricultural operations
financed by the Bank – a nut grove.*

CHAPTER NINETEEN

Growth and expansion

We now come to the last of the periods into which this account of the Bank's history has been divided. The period starts in 1968, following the completion of the formal structuring of field operations in five regions. It ends in 1975 with the separation of the Bank from the Bank of Canada and its conversion into the Federal Business Development Bank owned directly by the federal government.

Changes in senior management personnel

Within the Bank, there were a number of changes in management. In 1973, Louis Rasminsky, the president, retired and was succeeded by G.K. Bouey on the latter's appointment as governor of the Bank of Canada. L.F. Mundy, secretary since 1953, retired in 1970 and was succeeded by Gray Hamilton. At the end of 1969, A.N.H. James, who had been involved in the overall direction of the Bank's affairs from the beginning, retired as general manager for reasons of ill-health and was succeeded by the writer. Mr James then served for a year as special consultant, handling relations with foreign development banks in which he had had a great deal of experience. In addition, a large number of senior officers with long service retired. Four of the five regional assistant general managers, the general solicitor, the chief of the Insurance Department, the superintendent, credits, and two deputy secretaries all retired in the years 1968–74.[1] They had all contributed significantly to the Bank's development. Some of them had served in the Bank from its first year. Their positions were all filled from within the Bank.

Economic and political background

Viewed broadly, in the eight years from 1968 to 1975 inclusive, the Canadian economy continued the expansion that had distinguished the period 1962–7. Between 1962 and 1967 the gross national product (in constant 1971 dollars) increased by 41.3 per cent overall, and annual increases averaged 5.8 per cent. In the eight years from 1968 to 1975 inclusive, the overall increase was 43.5 per cent, and annual growth averaged 4.6 per cent. A closer view shows, however, that the pace of the earlier period was maintained only for the six years immediately following, i.e. 1968–73 inclusive. In those six years, the overall growth was 38.1 per cent, and annual increases averaged 5.5 per cent. These figures are very close to those recorded for 1962–7. In 1973, the gross national product recorded the largest year's increase, 7.2 per cent, since 1956. In 1974 and 1975, however, the rate of growth fell off drastically. By the end of 1974, the economy was considered by some to be in the early stages of a recession, and in 1975, the last year of the IDB's operations, the gross national product remained virtually at a standstill. The increase that year was 0.1 per cent, the smallest since the recession of 1954.[2]

Although the period 1968–75 was, on the whole, one of economic growth, it was also one troubled by persistent and apparently intractable problems. Clouds, which had hovered on the horizon in 1967, steadily grew darker and gradually spread their shadows over the whole of the economic landscape. It is the intention not to analyse here the complex situations created by these problems or the attempts to solve them, but simply to identify and describe them as elements in the background to the IDB's operations.

First, inflation, which had not been a serious matter from 1951 to 1965 but had shown some early muscle in 1966 and 1967 with increases in the consumer price index of 3.7 per cent and 3.6 per cent respectively, became an almost permanent feature of life. In his report for 1968, the governor of the Bank of Canada referred to 'the development of an inflation psychology' and said that 'inflationary expectations have now become very strong.' In 1969, the government, presumably to counter such tendencies, appointed a Prices and Incomes Commission, not to control or regulate, but to analyse price and cost developments, make policy recommendations, and educate public opinion on actions and policies influencing price stability.[3]

The consumer price index rose in 1968 by 4.0 per cent, and in 1969, by 4.6 per cent. Smaller increases in 1970 (3.3 per cent) and 1971 (2.9 per cent) were followed by rapid and substantial rises; in 1972, the index rose by 4.8 per cent; in 1973, by 7.5 per cent; in 1974, by 10.9 per cent; and in 1975, by 10.8 per cent. In the last 3 years, the index rose by just about as much as it had risen in the 15 years from 1950 to 1965. In the autumn of 1975, wages, salaries, and prices were brought under regulatory control by the Prices and Incomes Commission.[4]

Second, the growth in the gross national product was accompanied by high and increasing rates of unemployment. The amount of employment available was growing, but not as fast as the labour force itself. From 3.6 per cent of the labour force in 1966, the rate of unemployment rose to 4.1 per cent in 1967 and 4.8 per cent in 1968. By 1970, it was 6.4 per cent, the highest level in ten years, and for the year 1975 it was 6.9 per cent.[5]

Third, there were drastic changes in the pattern of interest rates on the money markets, in that they rose steeply and fluctuated widely. From the chart in Appendix I it will be seen that from 1948 to 1965, a period of 17 years, the average yield on industrial bonds rose from approximately $3\frac{1}{2}$ per cent to approximately $5\frac{1}{2}$ per cent, with occasional gentle dips and rises of around $\frac{1}{2}$ of 1 per cent below or above the gradual upward trend. In the next 5 years, it rose steeply from 4 per cent to $9\frac{1}{2}$ per cent; within 2 years it had fallen 1 per cent; within another 2 years it was up to 11 per cent, a rise of about $2\frac{1}{2}$ per cent; and within twelve months it first dropped 1 per cent and then climbed back up to a new peak of $11\frac{1}{2}$ per cent.

The combination of business expansion, accelerating inflation, growing rates of unemployment, and rapidly changing interest rates presented conflicting problems in economic management to which, in the words of the Bank of Canada annual report for 1966, 'no country has found a completely satisfactory solution.' Measures intended as a corrective to one circumstance might aggravate one of the others.[6]

These uncertainties in economic life naturally affected the political world. Here there had been changes in the leadership of the federal parties. In September 1967 Robert Stanfield had been chosen to succeed John Diefenbaker as leader of the Progressive Conservative party. Early in 1968 Lester Pearson, leader of the Liberal party and prime minister, announced his retirement, and in April he was replaced by Pierre Elliott Trudeau. Almost immediately Mr Trudeau called a general election, and in June his government was returned to office with a clear majority in the House of Commons. It was the first time this had been accomplished since the victory of the Conservatives under Mr Diefenbaker in 1958.

The new government faced some difficult and contentious issues – the encouragement of the use of the French language in all parts of the country, the increasing strength of the provincial governments, constitutional problems, and the growth of the separatist movement in Quebec, culminating, in 1970, in a year of 'violence and terror.' In spite of the seriousness of these issues, however, and also in spite of a generally impressive performance of the Canadian economy in 1968 and 1969, the government's main preoccupations in its first years of office were with unemployment and inflation. Indeed, these two problems aroused so much controversy and critical comment that through most of 1971 and 1972 there was speculation as to how soon the government would respond by calling an election. As the *Canadian Annual Review* put it: 'In the uncertainty over when an election would be called, the government's legislative program ground virtually to a halt.'[7]

Finally, on 31 August 1972, an election was announced for 30 October. Economic issues dominated the campaign. Even the *Toronto Star*, normally a staunch supporter of Liberal governments, officially supported the Conservative party for the first time in fifty years, partly because of the government's performance on unemployment. The election results were the closest in Canadian history. The Liberals obtained 109 seats and the Conservatives 107, with 47 seats held by other parties. The Liberals had retained office, but the country had a minority government again.

The Canadian people were once more living on 'the brink of an election.'[8] Finally, in 1974, an election was called for 8 July. Rising rates of unemployment and accelerating inflation, now accompanied by a falling off in the rate of growth of the gross national product, were the principal topics of the campaign. The Liberal government retained office, and this time obtained a clear majority in the House of Commons.

Loans: volume

Through these years of economic expansion, mixed with economic problems, from 1968 to 1975, the IDB grew to a size and developed a volume of business that can hardly have been anticipated by those who founded it in 1944. In that eight-year period it opened nearly twice as many new branches, authorized more than three and a half times as many loans, and earned just about as much net profit for transfer to the reserve fund as in all the preceding twenty-three years taken together. At the same time, there were great changes in the types of business with which the Bank dealt, in the geographical distribution of its loans, in the kinds of programs it financed, in its own inner structures and procedures, and in its responsiveness to credit proposals.

The growth between 1967 and 1975 was reflected in almost every statistic. In the year with which the previous period ended, 1967, the Bank approved about 2,100 loans, for approximately $100 million. Just eight

TABLE 22

Loans approved 1967–75

	1967	1968	1969	1970	1971	1972	1973	1974	1975
By number									
Manufacturing	692	735	800	837	991	1,294	1,495	1,689	1,639
Transportation and storage	98	103	109	126	166	177	267	280	325
Construction	130	160	176	194	239	298	422	521	561
Wholesale	160	153	205	220	262	338	390	547	471
Retail	344	430	501	639	819	1,247	1,759	2,329	2,519
Agriculture	169	199	194	246	338	416	545	844	639
Restaurants	91	110	174	254	356	599	834	1,051	1,088
Hotels and motels	147	184	298	374	431	511	680	691	494
Other	337	441	531	694	847	1,009	1,467	1,760	1,725
Total	2,168	2,515	2,988	3,584	4,449	5,889	7,859	9,712	9,461
Percentage change from previous year	−7	+16	+19	+20	+24	+32	+33	+24	−3
By amount									
Total ($millions)	113	120	153	165	196	262	345	470	401
Average ($thousands)	52	48	51	46	44	45	44	48	42

SOURCE: *Annual Reports*, 1969 and 1975.

years later, the Bank approved in one year, 1975, more than 9,400 loans, for $400 million. The Bank started the period with 8,600 customers who had loans on the Bank's books or awaiting disbursement totalling $388 million. By the end of 1975, the Bank had 27,500 customers with loans on the Bank's books or awaiting disbursement totalling $1,300 million. The staff also grew rapidly. Between the end of fiscal 1967 and the end of fiscal 1975 the number of employees increased from 619 to 1,547.

Table 22 shows the growth in loan authorizations and changes in the types of businesses assisted after 1967. Figures are given for 1968–75 and for comparison purposes for 1967, the last year of the previous period. Apart from 1975, when a decline in the number of loan approvals probably reflected in part the difficulties that the Canadian economy was experiencing at that time, the number of loan approvals grew steadily. Between 1968 and 1974, annual increases ranged from 16 per cent in 1968 to 33 per cent in 1973.

A quotation from a letter written by a branch manager about half-way through 1970 illustrates the difficulty that even those close to the Bank's operation had in realizing the growth that still lay ahead of it. (Note the use of 'we': it was a curious IDB tradition often to use the first person plural for internal correspondence!) 'We think ... that attracting and maintaining a high calibre staff is one of the most serious problems facing the Bank at the present time. Unless there is some major change in the scope of the Bank or in its operations, the recent period of rapid growth, with frequent opening of new branches, appears to be over.' And yet little more than four years later, in 1974, the Bank authorized in a single year more than three times the number of loans approved in the year that had just ended when this observation was made. In fact, that manager's branch had more than doubled its own authorizations in the same period and in addition had spawned two new branches which, between them, approved more loans in 1974 than his own branch had done in 1969, just prior to his comment!

Loans: by others

There was at the same time an increase in the amount of term lending to small and medium-sized businesses by others. The chartered banks were becoming more active, although the arrangements by which one of their loans might be repaid over a period of time were probably still informal for the most part. In addition, the ceiling on chartered bank loans guaranteed by the federal government under the Small Business Loans Act had been raised to $50,000, and the amount of such loans made in a year had increased from $20 million in calendar 1967 to $35 million in calendar 1974. In calendar 1975, the total shot up to $73 million. The loans were usually quite small; in 1975, they averaged $15,000. The increase in volume in 1975 may have included some that would otherwise have been made by the IDB, but it is difficult to know to what extent this might have been the case. Possibly some of the 'Small Business' loans would have been made by the banks in the ordinary course, even without the government guarantee. The fact that the accumulated losses on the 'Small Business' loans were invariably each year below ½ of 1 per cent of the cumulative total of loans made suggests that some of them represented a normal credit risk for the banks and therefore proposals that would not have come to the IDB in any event. Nevertheless, the volume of 'Small Business' loans probably reduced the IDB's volume of loans to some extent.[9]

Loans by the Adjustment Assistance Board probably continued to take the place of possible loans by the IDB, particularly when the board's interest rate was well below that of the IDB. Demand for adjustment loans, however, probably decreased as the automobile industry adjusted to the effects of the Auto Pact with the United States. In 1973, the board's program of loans was replaced by another government program involving federal government guarantees of chartered bank loans. It would be difficult to determine whether this new program had any effect on IDB operations.

From 1965, when the AAB started, to 1973, 128 automobile assistance loans for a total of $115 million were approved.[10] In approximately the same period, the IDB approved 34,000 loans for a total of $1,573 million, so it is not likely that the AAB affected the IDB very much. The loans of the AAB were usually much larger than those of the IDB, averaging $900,000, as compared with the Bank's average from 1965 to 1973 of $46,000.

Provincial lending agencies were also active. By 1975 each province had a development fund or institution of some kind, although that in British Columbia (the BC Development Corporation) was new and not yet very active in lending. In 1975, these provincial agencies approved approximately $320 million in loans, compared with $400 million approved by the IDB. Their activity must have affected that of the IDB, although their loans tended to be much larger: on average well over $100,000, and for some as high as $300,000 or $500,000, whereas the IDB's average in 1975 was $42,000. However, regardless of any effect that the operations of the provincial agencies and the IDB might have had on each other, the Bank now had good operating relations with them all.[11]

Loans: distribution by industry

The types of businesses assisted by the IDB reflected the continuing effects of the amendments of 1961. When the Bank started in 1944, manufacturing was virtually the only field of business served. By 1967, manufacturers were receiving only 32 per cent of new loans, and in 1975 only 17 per cent. The number of loans to manufacturers actually increased steadily, but other types of businesses came to the Bank in even greater numbers. More numerous now were loans to tourist-oriented businesses. In 1968–75 inclusive, the Bank approved approximately 3,700 loans to motels and hotels for a total of $240 million and 4,500 loans to restaurants for a total of $179 million.[12] In fact, during these years the IDB was probably the principal source of financing for the expansion or construction of motels other than those connected with the large international chains. This was particularly true for motels built in national parks which were subject to land-lease restrictions as to use and to requirements about future expansion that were not attractive to commercial lenders. In some parts of the country, such as the Arctic or the interior of British Columbia, it would have been difficult to find a modern motel to stay at, or a modern restaurant to eat in, that was not financed by the IDB.

The Bank also financed other kinds of tourist attractions. It assisted with the early development of the Gastown area in Vancouver – a major revitalization of an old downtown area into a collection of boutiques, restaurants, and other attractions. It also helped to set up large major ski hill operations in Alberta, Ontario, and Quebec.

The growth in loans to retailers was even greater than that in loans to motels, hotels, and restaurants. In the period 1968–75, the Bank approved over 10,000 loans to retailers for $335 million.[13] In 1975 alone, the number was greater than the number of loans made to all kinds of businesses in 1968. The individual loans to retailers were often fairly small – in 1975, the average was $31,700 – whereas the average loan to all other businesses was $46,300. The smaller retail loans helped to reduce the overall average for all loans to $42,000 for that year.

Loans to commercial air services, although not as large in absolute numbers as some other industry categories, were important to the development of travel and transportation. In the northern parts of the country aircraft are essential for this. Up to the end of 1967, the Bank approved 217 loans to 132 companies. By the end of 1975, these figures had been increased to 504 loans to 302 companies for a total of $51 million. Considering that between 1957 (the earliest year for which figures are available) and 1975 the number of commercial air services holding licences in Canada is estimated to have ranged from 225 to 700,[14] it is obvious that the IDB gave financial support to a high proportion of air services in Canada.

Shifts in the distribution of loans, whether among the various types of business or among geographical regions, were often seen by some outside observers as reflecting a deliberate policy on the part of the Bank. The decreasing proportion of loans to manufacturers led some to conclude, erroneously, that the Bank was consciously de-emphasizing assistance in that field. Other observers felt the Bank was deliberately avoiding loans to recreational businesses. For example, in December 1970, an MP said in the House of Commons that 'when the IDB is approached for a loan for this purpose [recreational facilities] it replies, "We are really concerned about manufacturing" ... When someone approaches it about a recreation facility, it expresses great reservations.' As a matter of fact, in the fiscal year that had just ended, loans to manufacturers were only 23 per cent of the total number, and loans to recreational and tourist businesses were 19 per cent, so that they were very close to each other in importance.

The Bank did not either emphasize or de-emphasize assistance to any particular type of business. It saw its role as that set out in its act of incorporation – to assist those businesses that could not get assistance elsewhere on reasonable terms and conditions – and it wanted to help as many such businesses as it could.

Loans: distribution by province and by purpose

The regional distribution of new loan authorizations also changed greatly between 1967 and 1975, as is illustrated in Table 23. Of the intervening years, only alternate years are given due to limitations of space.

The greatest growth occurred in the extreme eastern and western regions – the Atlantic provinces and British Columbia. Quebec was next, while Ontario and the prairie provinces grew less and about the same amount in each case. These differences were not the result of any deliberate policy on the part of the Bank. There was no attempt to favour one area over another, and there was no rationing or allocating of funds as between regions. All offices of the Bank were expected to do all they could to fulfil its role in the areas assigned to them, and whatever funds were needed to finance the loans that resulted were supplied. Undoubtedly, variations in the energy, initiative, and imagination of branches and regional offices were reflected in the achievements of particular regions, but there were also differences in the conditions encountered. In Ontario and Quebec, there were probably more alternative and commercial sources of funds which would diminish the need for IDB assistance. In the prairie provinces and Quebec, the lending agencies of the provincial governments were very active. There were also such agencies in the Atlantic provinces, but their activity fluctuated. In British Columbia, there was no similar agency and loan activity was favoured by the great prosperity of the local economy and by the unlikelihood that commercial sources of term financing would be strongly attracted to the interior and frontier areas, where business expansion was in the early stages of development. Of the 3,000 loans authorized in British Columbia in 1975, about 40 per cent were made through branches in frontier or interior locations such as Prince George, Terrace, Campbell River, Cranbrook, Kelowna, and Kamloops.

Although British Columbia established itself during the period as the most active region in terms of the number of loan approvals each year, it was dropping from this position during the last two years. From 1968 to 1973, the number of loans approved in the province increased from year to year by a greater percentage than the rate of increase for the Bank as a whole. In 1973, the percentage increase for British Columbia was 47 per cent, compared with 27 per cent for the rest of the Bank. The next year,

TABLE 23

Regional comparison of number of loans authorized 1967–75

	1967*		1968	1970	1972	1974	1975*		Distribution of population (percentage) 1975
Atlantic	144	(7)	155	316	523	868	1,026	(11)	10
Quebec	404	(18)	461	601	1,085	1,652	1,459	(15)	27
Ontario	824	(38)	833	978	1,568	2,391	2,507	(26)	36
Prairies	451	(21)	545	543	727	1,561	1,370	(15)	16
British Columbia	330	(15)	493	1,094	1,928	3,159	3,019	(32)	11
Territories	15	(1)	28	52	58	81	80	(1)	
Total	2,168	(100)	2,515	3,584	5,889	9,712	9,461	(100)	100

*Percentage in parentheses.
SOURCES: *Annual Reports*, 1969 and 1975; population figures from Statistics Canada, *Estimated Population of Canada by Province*.

TABLE 24

Population per IDB customer as at 30 September 1975, by region

	Population (000s)	Number of IDB customers	Population per IDB customer
Atlantic	2,165	2,577	840
Quebec	6,198	4,899	1,265
Ontario	8,212	7,255	1,132
Prairies	3,729	4,430	842
British Columbia	2,448	8,094	302
Territories	64	253	253
Canada	22,816	27,508	829

SOURCE: *Annual Report*, 1975; population figures as for Table 23.

however, British Columbia increased by only 11 per cent, compared with 30.0 per cent for the rest of the Bank, and in 1975 it fell by 4 per cent as compared with a decline for the balance of the Bank of 2 per cent. Only the Atlantic Region maintained a high rate of growth to the end.

Perhaps as a result of the tremendous expansion in the Bank's loans in British Columbia, the demand there for the kind of assistance provided by the Bank had reached, at least temporarily, the limits of growth. This is suggested if one relates the number of loans made to population. This device was often used by the Bank to compare its activity in different areas and was called the 'penetration' achieved. Table 24 relates the population in each region to the numbers of IDB customers with loans outstanding on 30 September 1975.

The table demonstrates the enormous penetration recorded in British Columbia and in the Yukon and the Northwest Territories. Many loans had been made and paid off before 30 September 1975, when the figures were made up, and so one would have to conclude that the penetration in terms of all loans made was undoubtedly greater than shown in the table. This would imply that a high proportion of businesses in British Columbia and the Territories had been helped by the Bank at one time or another. Even in the Atlantic provinces and on the prairies, whence came regular complaints that the Bank favoured the central provinces, there was a much greater degree of penetration than in Quebec or Ontario. In these cases, also, allowance for customers with loans paid off before 30 September 1975 would make the degree of penetration higher than indicated in the table.

Table 25 gives the dollar amount of loans authorized, with the regional distribution, from 1967 to 1975; figures for 1969, 1971, and 1973 are

TABLE 25

Regional comparison of amount of loans authorized ($millions) 1967–75

	1967*		1968	1970	1972	1974	1975*	
Atlantic	6.2	(5)	5.4	10.2	16.8	31.8	31.6	(8)
Quebec	20.8	(19)	24.5	31.9	59.0	85.7	70.5	(18)
Ontario	39.0	(34)	41.6	46.5	65.2	110.9	102.3	(25)
Prairies	25.8	(23)	24.4	24.4	31.6	71.4	60.1	(15)
British Columbia	19.9	(18)	22.0	48.6	85.7	165.7	132.7	(33)
Territories	1.4	(1)	2.4	3.0	4.0	4.5	4.2	(1)
Total	113.1	(100)	120.3	164.6	262.3	470.0	401.4	(100)

*Percentage in parentheses.
SOURCES: As for Table 23.

omitted for lack of space, but this does not interfere with a clear picture of trends during the period.

The regional figures do not reflect fully the extent to which the Bank was now assisting businesses in the less well-developed parts of the country. If one were to regard the Atlantic provinces as falling generally within this category, and add to loans made there figures for northern Quebec, northern Ontario, the northern parts of the prairie provinces, the interior of British Columbia, the Yukon, and the Northwest Territories, one would reach a total of 34 per cent of all loans approved in 1975 by number and close to 30 per cent by amount. Among the distant communities in which loans were made were Inuvik, Tuktoyuktuk, the Queen Charlotte Islands, Fort McMurray, Cambridge Bay, Labrador City, Old Crow, Dawson City, Frobisher Bay, and Pangnirtung in the far north of Baffin Island. Loans to service businesses, particularly those related to the tourist trade such as hotels or motels and restaurants, were important among loans in the north.

Operations in the more remote areas had their own flavour. Land titles were not always in the usual form. In one case the only evidence offered that the borrower owned the land to be mortgaged to the Bank was a small piece of paper containing a handwritten and undated statement that a 'piece of land' had been sold by one person to another. In another case, as part of the liquidation of the security for a loan, the Bank was about to auction off a parcel of land mortgaged to it; the neighbours attending the sale, by a general discussion among themselves, persuaded all concerned that the mortgagor had also owned another plot of land that formed part of the Bank's security. The same sort of interest on the part of the community in the business affairs of all was displayed when a credit officer went to a small town in northern Saskatchewan to open and consider tenders for some equipment the sale of which the Bank had advertised in order to liquidate a delinquent loan.[15] When he arrived he was astonished to find several hundred people waiting for him. The mayor told him quietly that the people were expecting an auction and would not be satisfied with less. The credit officer, displaying the adaptability to the unforeseen expected of an IDB credit officer, declined the few tenders that had been submitted, borrowed a table and hammer, and embarked on his first experience as an auctioneer. He was rewarded with a greater intake than any of the tenders would have provided.

The Bank's officers had many experiences that revealed the energy and forceful directness of the owners of small businesses in these areas. For the construction of a motel financed in Dawson City, Yukon, it was necessary to ship portable room units from Portland, Oregon, up the Pacific coast to Alaska, and over the mountains by narrow gauge railway to Dawson. At one of the Bank's western branches, an application was received for a loan to assist in establishing a funeral home in a new town created to house the workers on a huge construction project in the north country. The applicant had observed the workers driving home up a long hill from the local tavern and had concluded that a funeral home would have lots of business! Another borrower in northern British Columbia whose loan had been long in default responded in a simple and direct way to word that the assets he had pledged to the Bank were to be placed in the hands of a receiver. He crashed his truck into a ravine, set his boat on fire, and finally, with a chain-saw, carefully and laboriously sawed in half a mobile home that formed part of the Bank's security. More drastic was the action taken by a borrower who operated a motel using individual units that rested on skids. He learned one day that the motel was to be seized the next day, but when the IDB officer arrived in the morning, there was nothing to be seen but the marks of the skids in the mud. The units had disappeared and were never found![16]

Of course, experiences such as these could be matched in all parts of the Bank. In one case in Ontario, a borrower whose loan had reached the point that foreclosure proceedings against his plant were begun threatened the regional supervisor so convincingly that the latter was given a guard of Royal Canadian Mounted Policemen for a time. In another unusual case, the regional office learned that a vessel representing the principal security for a loan had started down the Trent Canal en route to a purchaser in the United States. By innumerable phone calls to the various lockmasters on the canal, the course of the vessel was followed until finally it was seized by a bailiff as it entered a lock. Even the bailiff

TABLE 26

Percentage composition of programs financed by the Bank 1967–75

	1967	1968	1969	1970	1971	1972	1973	1974	1975
Land, buildings, machinery, and equipment	79	79	78	76	69	70	67	66	61
Working capital	9	9	9	11	13	11	10	11	15
Refinance debts owed to others	8	7	6	6	9	8	7	5	5
Changes in ownership	3	4	6	6	8	10	15	17	18
Other	1	1	1	1	1	1	1	1	1
Total	100	100	100	100	100	100	100	100	100
Proportion covered by IDB loans	68	69	69	68	71	70	70	67	66

SOURCES: To 1972, *Annual Reports*; thereafter, internal reports.

had problems: his efforts to nail the order for seizure to the mast in the traditional way were frustrated by the discovery that the mast was steel. The debtor claimed he had arranged accommodation to make the large reduction in the loan required by the Bank, and this now proved to be the case. The vessel continued to its new home, and the loan was ultimately retired in full. The Bank then found itself in a dispute in court over the bailiff's fee![17]

The figures in Table 25 show that the growth in all loans made by the Bank was substantial from 1968 to 1975, with the amount of new loans authorized in a year increasing from $113 million in 1967 to $470 million in 1974 and $401 million in 1975. Nevertheless, the Bank was doing little more than keeping up with the general growth in the country's economy and in its financial fabric. In 1967 the IDB's outstanding loan balances of $334 million were 4.8 per cent of outstanding business loans of the chartered banks. In 1975, the Bank's loan balances of $1,200 million were 5.2 per cent of chartered bank business loans.[18]

The makeup of the programs financed by the Bank's loans between 1968 and 1975 also reflected a major change in the character of the Bank's business. This is illustrated in Table 26. The proportion of programs directed toward the acquisition of buildings, machinery, or equipment, which had risen to 77 per cent in 1966 and 79 per cent in 1967, gradually declined to 61 per cent in 1975. The proportions for working capital and for changes in ownership increased, from 9 per cent to 15 per cent in the first case, and from 3 per cent to 18 per cent in the second. In 1975, these two items represented one-third of the programs financed by the Bank.

The increasing proportion of assistance for working capital aroused concern; an internal memorandum of April 1975 noted: 'We also discussed the matter of our policy with respect to working capital loans, and in particular those intended to refinance chartered bank loans. If a chartered bank has already advanced money to the applicant we should be very wary of an application whose sole or virtually sole purpose would be to refinance that loan. After all, in such cases, the applicant already has the money he needs and the chartered bank can take any security that we can take. Similar wariness should be exercised towards loans for refinancing of other debts.' However, while the kind of program in which the Bank was becoming involved was changing, and perhaps in directions presenting greater risk to the IDB, the Bank's share in the cost of financing these programs declined from the fairly high level of 76 per cent in 1965 (see Table 17) to 66 per cent in 1975. The share put up by the borrowing businesses themselves, by their owners or by others, increased correspondingly. In 1974, of 9,700 loans approved, only 65 involved the refinancing of equipment liens held by finance companies.

That the Bank was approving more loans than ever in the period 1968–75 meant, of course, that more businesses were coming to it each year to inquire about financial assistance. In 1963, the first year for which figures are available, the number of such inquiries had been close to 11,000, and in 1967 it was still 11,000. Starting in 1968, however, it increased steadily each year until it reached 35,000 in 1975.

Increasing responsiveness to loan applications

In addition, there was at last a substantial increase in the Bank's responsiveness to such inquiries, so that the increase in the number of inquiries was accompanied by an increase in the proportion of them that resulted in formal applications. In 1963, this proportion had been 25 per cent, and by 1965 it had risen to 29 per cent. For the next four years, i.e. from 1966 to 1969 inclusive, the proportion did not change but remained at or near 29 per cent each year. In 1970, however, a rise started, and it continued until in 1974 the proportion was 39 per cent, an increase of one-third over 1969. In 1975, when there was a marked check in the rise in loan authorizations that had been going on since 1968, the proportion fell back to 34 per cent.

In addition to the Bank's accepting formal applications from a higher proportion of those inquiring about assistance during the years 1968–75, a greater percentage of these formal applications was actually being approved. Since figures for the number of applications received and the number approved are available for each fiscal year right back to the

TABLE 27

Percentage of formal applications processed that were approved 1950–75

	1950	1955	1960	1965	1967	1970	1975
Number approved	53	62	73	70	69	78	81
Number declined	28	19	10	15	16	11	7
Number withdrawn	19	19	17	15	15	11	12
Total	100	100	100	100	100	100	100

Bank's beginnings, we can actually get a long perspective on the changes that took place in this particular aspect of responsiveness, i.e. the proportion of formal applications that resulted in loans. The figures in Table 27 show the change in the period 1968–75 and show also how the Bank moved steadily through its whole history toward a more responsive attitude to applications. For the latter purpose, the figures are given at five-year intervals, and 1967 is given as the last year before the period we are now reviewing.

In 1967, the proportion approved was 69 per cent; 15 per cent were withdrawn and 16 per cent turned down by the Bank. The proportion of approvals rose steadily to an all-time high of 84 per cent in 1972 and 1973, and fell slightly to 81 per cent in 1975. Of the 19 per cent of applications not approved in 1975, 12 per cent were withdrawn and 7 per cent declined by the Bank. The latter percentage was half the proportion turned down in 1967. In interpreting the figures in the table, one has to allow for the likelihood that, for the Bank as a whole, the readiness with which application forms were given out did not remain constant. Nevertheless, the change from 53 per cent to 81 per cent between 1950 and 1975 certainly reflects a considerably increased willingness to make loans. The most common reason for an application's being declined was doubt that the business would earn enough to repay the proposed loan. In more than half the cases this was a factor. The next most common reason was inadequate security, followed by inadequate equity investment in the applicant business, and then doubts about management.

These various changes in the way inquiries and applications were dealt with were very important. They meant that the chances that an inquirer might get a loan had increased tremendously. Not only were a higher proportion of inquiries resulting in formal applications, but a higher proportion of the latter were approved. Chart 2 shows loans authorized each year from 1963 expressed as a percentage of the number of inquiries received each year.

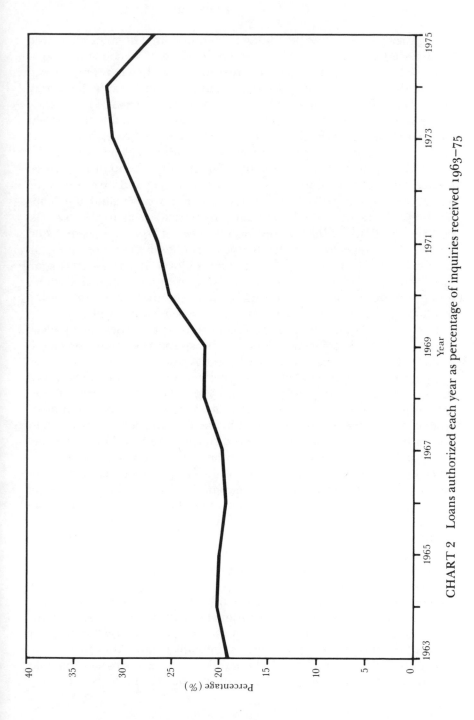

CHART 2   Loans authorized each year as percentage of inquiries received 1963–75

From 1963 to 1967, the percentage of inquiries that ultimately received loans varied between 19 per cent and 20 per cent. In 1968 and 1969, it increased to 22 per cent, and it then rose to a peak of 32 per cent in 1974; in 1975 the proportion dropped drastically to 27 per cent, the same as in 1971. The difference of 12 percentage points between 1967 and 1974 suggests that in the latter year 3,700 more loans were made than might have been made had the Bank's response to inquiries been what it was in 1967 and that in the full period 13,000 or so additional loans were made.

The decline in 1975 is noteworthy. The number of inquiries reached the record level of 35,000, 5,000 more than in 1974 and three times the number received in 1968. Nevertheless, the proportion resulting in loans fell back to the 1971 level. One can only speculate as to the reasons. Perhaps the Bank's officers drew back somewhat from the heady trend toward more relaxed attitudes to credit proposals. Perhaps recession conditions in 1974 and 1975 cast shadows over the prospects of an increased proportion of applicants. In any event, more and more businesses were coming to the Bank; more of them were submitting formal applications; and more of these were being approved.

The Bank was becoming more receptive to approaches for financial assistance, but it is difficult to identify those aspects of credit proposals toward which it had become more tolerant. A study made within the FBDB in later years of loans made by representative branches in all regions of the IDB during the last quarter of fiscal 1973 and the first quarter of fiscal 1974 does, however, indicate the extent of security protection and the type of management being accepted by the IDB. Of the loans covered by the study, 52 per cent were considered fully secured, and in 27 per cent any shortfall in security was believed to range from zero to 25 per cent. In other words, 79 per cent of the loans were thought to be fully secured or nearly so. In 69 per cent, the management of the borrowing business was experienced; in 31 per cent, it was not. Loans to new businesses represented 47 per cent of the loans, and in 66 per cent the tangible net worth of the borrowing business was equal to or greater than the total amount of term debt owed by the business.

That there was, over the years, a change in the Bank's responsiveness to applications was not so much the sudden result of specific instructions issued as the gradual consequence of constant correspondence and comment by both the central operational management at Montreal and regional and branch management in the field, and the final fruits, as it were, of the training and maturing of the Bank's staff. After many years of experience in the IDB's field of operations, its members had complete confidence in their ability to cope with its special problems. They saw themselves as just about the best in the world at their job and believed that they could now with safety and discretion take a more responsive position toward credit proposals.

A revision of the general manager's circular of instructions on policy had been made in 1964 and remained virtually unchanged for the duration of the Bank as the definitive directive on general policy. It introduced for almost the first time language bearing on the general posture to be adopted toward an applicant: 'There is ... a responsibility on us to establish, before declining an application, that no mutually acceptable basis for a loan from ourselves can be found ... No proposal should be declined because the effort and cost required to process it would be disproportionate to the financial return to be earned ... It is desirable to offer some constructive suggestions ... The reaction should be positive.'

These and other similar phrases, introduced in 1964, became a permanent part of instructions. Nothing more was formally said on the subject apart from a circular letter issued by the general manager in August 1973 dealing with the terms on which loans might be made. This letter encouraged 'balloon' payments, i.e. the maturing of a loan before the principal was fully repaid, seasonal repayment schedules for seasonal businesses, the avoidance of excessive security, equity financing when this seemed appropriate to the needs of the applicant business and the owner was of the same mind, longer terms of payment when necessary, and so on. The average term of repayment of a loan had steadily increased; 65 months in 1950, 77 in 1955, 69 in 1960, 87 in 1965, 92 in 1970, and 101 in 1975. From a little more than five years in 1950, it had lengthened to nearly nine years by 1975.

Policies for periods of credit restraint

Although the growth of the IDB between 1968 and 1975 occurred during a period of relatively favourable economic conditions, it encountered certain obstacles. In the opening years, there was still, in the financial world, the shortage of liquidity on the part of the chartered banks as well as of other lenders that had prompted the IDB to issue in February and November 1966 instructions described previously. These had enjoined the Bank's officers to be careful not to make loans of over $200,000 that conventional lenders would normally make but could not because of their tight liquidity position; indeed, any proposal for over $200,000 was to be scrutinized with particular care. Such instructions were felt necessary in order to be fair to other lenders. The instructions used $200,000 as a dividing line because larger amounts were usually of interest to commercial term lenders on industrial mortgages. It was not considered necessary to be as concerned about smaller loans; in fact, the governor of the Bank of Canada had asked the chartered banks not to allow liquidity problems to interfere with their financing of small businesses.

As part of its efforts to cope with the sometimes conflicting problems facing the country's economy, the Bank of Canada maintained policies of credit restraint through 1968 and 1969. In June 1969, the federal government announced a new measure to ease the strain on the nation's economy – capital cost allowances (i.e. depreciation allowances) were to be deferred for tax purposes on buildings constructed between 4 June 1969 and 3 December 1970 in metropolitan and major urban areas in Ontario, Alberta, and British Columbia, where economic pressures were considered to be most intense. This development seemed to call for fresh instructions within the Bank, and, in addition, it had become clear that the instructions of 1966 were not precise enough. These had instructed the Bank's officers to avoid making loans that conventional lenders would normally make, but if a company approached the IDB for a loan for working capital, was this not something that a 'conventional lender' (a chartered bank) would normally do? The management of the Bank had been encouraging its staff to make working capital loans for many years, but how could one distinguish between those cases meriting consideration and those excluded by the directive of 1966? Was not a working capital loan under these conditions a kind of 'refinancing' of accommodation from a chartered bank and therefore contrary to policy? The situation was further complicated by the fact that in 1967 chartered banks had been given the power to lend to businesses against mortgages so that they now had greater freedom to function as term lenders. Policies on working capital loans, on the refinancing of debts owed to other lenders, on the availability of financing from alternative sources, and on the current tight liquid position of the chartered banks and others were now all mixed up.[19]

In October 1969, fresh instructions were issued. First, loans to refinance debts and provide working capital were identified as requiring special care because of the tight liquidity situation. The Bank's staff was reminded of the standing instructions that the Bank should be reluctant to refinance term obligations recently incurred and that the purpose of an IDB loan should be to benefit the borrower and not the other creditor. These considerations were now to be applied to applications for loans to reduce or replace current chartered bank loans. Second, the limit above which particular care was to be exercised was reduced to $150,000; above this level, proposals should be accompanied, if possible, by a greater investment by others than might normally be considered satisfactory, particularly if the business were owned by a wealthy individual or a larger company. Regarding the new tax deferrals, the Bank's staff was instructed, also in October 1969, that loans to finance buildings to which this policy applied were not to be authorized – except (in accordance with IDB traditions) 'in special circumstances.'

In November 1970, all these directives were withdrawn. Economic conditions had changed, and the Bank of Canada had relaxed the policy of restraint that had been introduced in response to the pause in growth that occurred that year. By 1973, the resumed accelerated business expansion had aroused fresh concerns that the Canadian economy was beginning 'to press against the limits of its capacity,' and 'the Bank of Canada took steps to moderate the pace of domestic monetary and credit expansion.' As on similar occasions, the central bank encouraged the chartered banks to 'minimize the impact on small business borrowers' and to ensure 'a reasonable flow of funds' to them.[20] In May 1974, when the liquidity of the chartered banks was again tight, the IDB reintroduced its policy directives almost verbatim, and, at the urging of the board of directors, particularly of the deputy minister of finance, additional cautions were added against entertaining proposals to finance a change in ownership apparently designed largely to benefit the vendor with a substantial short-term capital gain.

While these various instructions in 1969 and 1974 affected individual cases, they did not seriously check the Bank's growth in loan volume. As Table 22 showed, the number of loans approved in 1970, when the 1969 instructions were in effect, showed a slightly greater increase over the preceding year than had been recorded in 1968 or 1969. The proportion of loans approved for more than $200,000, which was the category to which the instructions applied particularly, did decline slightly, however, from 2.9 per cent of the total number of loans approved in 1969 to 2.1 per cent in 1970. This category remained around that position until 1975 when, because of new limitations on the Bank's power to make larger loans, the proportion fell to 1.2 per cent, but it did not represent a large number of loans in any event. In 1975, there were only 117 approved for over $200,000 out of a total of 9,461.

New branches

A most important factor in the volume of business done in the years 1968–75 was the opening of new branches. Once the initial 4 offices were set up 1945–7, only 2 more were opened (in 1956) before 1959. In

1959–62, 16 more were established in the first major program of branch openings. There then followed another quiet period when, for eight years, only 1 branch was opened each year. In 1971, by which time the Bank had 30 branches, it was decided that future development of new branches should be based on a study across the country of the needs for the improved service that more branch offices would provide. The study was made by one of the administrative assistants at GMO, P.M. Bourassa. It took into consideration the population and number of businesses in the area to be served by a new branch, the growth in the area in recent years, the volume of IDB loans already made there, the relation of this to the population of the area, the distance from existing branches, the present and expected lending activity in the area, and the administrative burden that existing branches carried in serving it. These became the general bases on which branch sites were considered.

This study launched the second major program of openings. A planning committee made up of Mr Bourassa; J.B.S. Oldaker, assistant superintendent, personnel; and M. Pellegrino, assistant controller, was set up to review proposals for new branches, and early in 1972 a conference with regional assistant general managers laid the groundwork for permanant procedures to provide for ongoing consideration of branch expansion. Prospective locations for new offices were proposed each year by the regional offices, studied by the planning committee, and then recommended to the board of directors for approval. A feature of such a recommendation to the board was an estimate of income and expenses to show whether the proposed branch was going to carry itself. This was invariably the expectation, and almost invariably it proved to be the case.

The record of branch openings throughout the Bank's history is set out in Chart 3. The second major program of branch openings, which started in 1971, is clearly shown. By 1975, it had added 45 to the 30 existing in 1970, making a total of 75. With the opening of a branch at Charlottetown in 1971, the Bank had at least 1 office in every province. Sub-branches were opened from time to time; some subsequently became full-time branches. At the end of 1975, there were 5 sub-branches in operation, so that the Bank then had a total of 80 branch offices functioning.

In the 1960s, the lack of sufficient loans on the books to provide adequate portfolios for a large number of new branches, and a shortage of experienced staff following the splurge of branch openings 1959–62, slowed down the process of opening offices, as shown in Chart 3. By 1971, the overall volume of loans was larger, so that new branches could be launched with a good foundation of loan accounts to administer. The

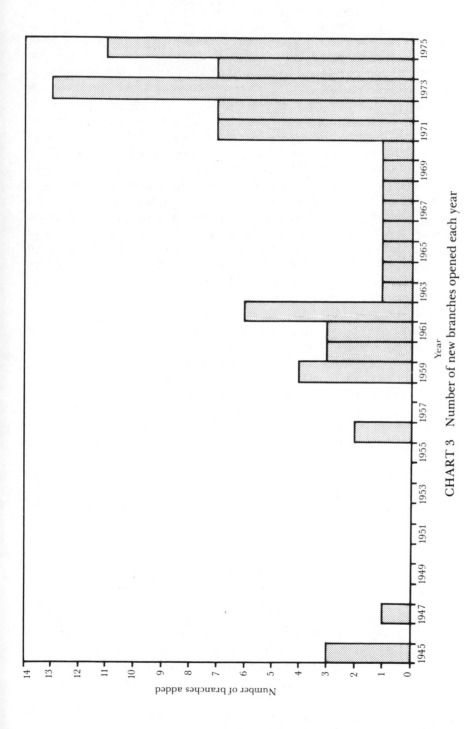

CHART 3   Number of new branches opened each year

branches opened between 1959 and 1967 (apart from the splitting up of Toronto and Montreal branches) started with only 70 accounts on average. In the period 1968–75, however, it was no longer necessary to operate on such a small base, and new branches started with the much more acceptable average of 180 accounts.

The shortage of experienced personnel to provide managers and credit officers for a large number of new branches did not go away quite so easily. To facilitate the appointment of managers for new branches, the regional assistant general managers made up lists of 'promotable' credit officers, with estimates of how much further experience they might need to qualify for a branch appointment. These lists were kept up to date, but by 1973, with fourteen branches opened in the two preceding years, it was becoming difficult not only to find managerial appointees with sufficient experience but also to find candidates who had not already been moved from one town to another quite recently and therefore could not be moved again for a while. As 1973 opened, it was thought that the number of openings for that year might have to be cut back.

In 1974, the problems facing a program of branch openings were listed in an internal memorandum: '(a) The problem of coping with the growing loan volume, and maintaining credit standards. (b) Strain on staff due to expansion of credit plus new responsibilities [assumed by the Bank], (c) Strain on staff from new positions and appointments needed.'

In addition, there was the problem of the cost involved in opening a new branch. The expense of transferring personnel from one town to another had become quite high and now included the cost of a 'housing assistance' plan intended to protect a transferree against inability to sell his old residence. As a result of all these factors, openings in 1974 were reduced to the relatively modest level of 7. For 1975, however, the total was up to 11.

Branch openings naturally lent themselves to publicity for the Bank and to enhancing its image as an institution anxious to be accessible to all. Announcements of a branch's establishment, opening ceremonies attended by local business and government leaders, electric name-signs outside new branches, and attractive, carefully designed premises and street-level locations, such as those at Chilliwack, Campbell River, Terrace, Truro, Scarborough, St Boniface, and Whitehorse, increased public awareness of the Bank. A street-level location in a shopping centre for the new Kelowna branch in 1962 had been regarded as a radical step. Because 'premises on the second floor of some office building' were not available, it was considered, as the supervisor put it, 'that it would not be inappropriate for us to take a ground floor office' in a local shopping centre. To the argument traditionally used against such a location, he responded that the branch would not 'be bothered at this point with people coming in wishing to open deposit accounts'! Such a location was not chosen again for many years, but in the 1970s street-level premises were deliberately sought and became quite common.

Perhaps the Terrace branch might be singled out as taking the most extreme measures to give itself a strong image. Not only was it on street level, with a prominent electric sign, but the staff there (or at least the male staff) cultivated a splendid collection of bushy beards and moustaches and diligently fostered the impression that their spare time was spent hunting grizzly bears.

One would expect a close relationship between the number of branches and the volume of business. This is illustrated in Chart 4. The opening of a new branch usually had a double effect on the Bank's growth. First, the new branch would often, for a few years at least, grow faster than the rest of the Bank. Between 1971, when the second major program of new branches started, and 1974, the number of loan approvals in a year for the Bank as a whole grew at rates of between 24 per cent and 33 per cent, but many new branches were growing at an annual rate of over 40 per cent. Second, a 'parent' branch, relieved of responsibility for the area taken over by the new branch, often grew faster too. Some parent branches, from the portfolio of which accounts of a new branch were taken, grew back to their original size within a year; most would do so in 2½ years at most.

We saw earlier how the character of the Bank changed in the types of business served, in the programs it financed, and in its response to applications for assistance. The Bank also changed in the character of its branches. More and more they were positioned to serve smaller areas and smaller populations. For the first fourteen years of the Bank's existence, each branch served vast areas – whole provinces and groups of provinces – some of them containing millions of people. Even in 1962, following the first major program of branch openings, most branches served fairly large population groups. By 1975, the situation was greatly altered, as Table 28 shows. In 1975, nearly half the branches served smaller population groups than the smallest group served by a branch in 1962.

Publicity

Another important influence on growth was the program of 'advertised visits' by which a branch would advertise in a local newspaper that a credit officer (sometimes two) would be in a town on a certain day to receive

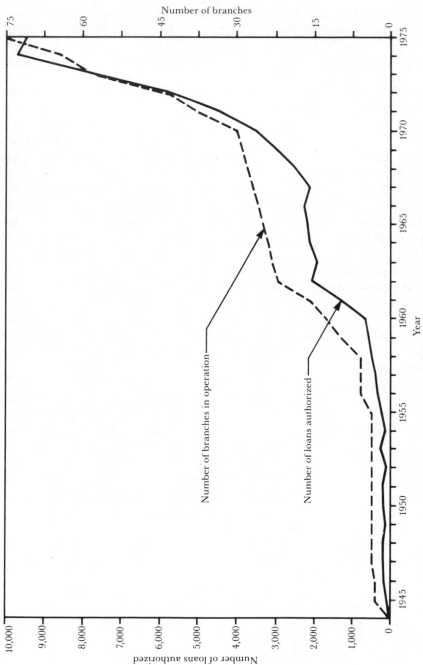

CHART 4 Number of loan authorizations and number of branches in operation

TABLE 28

Approximate population served by branches 1962
and 1975

| | Number of branches | |
Population	1962	1975
Over 1,000,000	6	1
500,000–1,000,000	6	12
200,000–500,000	10	31
100,000–200,000	–	28
Under 100,000	–	3
Total	22	75

TABLE 29

Percentage distribution of sources of reference for loan authorizations to new customers
1968–75

	1968	1969	1970	1971	1972	1973	1974	1975
General knowledge	26	27	30	29	30	30	31	31
Auditors	15	13	12	11	11	10	8	6
Chartered banks	12	12	13	15	14	14	14	14
Another borrower	7	8	6	8	8	8	7	8
Previous borrower	8	7	8	6	4	5	7	7
Advertised visits	12	13	17	19	19	20	18	17
Other	20	20	14	12	14	13	15	17
Total	100	100	100	100	100	100	100	100

inquiries from businessmen about possible financial assistance. In 1967, the Bank's branches had made 696 such visits. Between then and 1975 the number made in a year increased steadily each year until, in 1975, 6,240 visits were made. This increase partly reflected the greater number of branches – 75 in 1975, compared with 27 in 1967 – but each branch was also, by 1975, making many more such visits than previously. In 1967, the number of visits averaged 26 per branch for the year, while in 1975 the average was 83. Advertised visits on this scale represented a considerable burden for the Bank's branches. Some made 100 or more visits in a year, which meant that at least two credit officers were absent from the office for these visits one day of each week, apart from the time required to travel to and from the site of a visit.

Table 29, giving the distribution of the sources by which those who obtained loans each year were referred to the Bank, illustrates the importance of advertised visits. From 1970 on, these visits were the most important identifiable source of reference, displacing auditors from this position. The positions of other sources did not change much, which is quite remarkable, given the number of new branches and the increases in inquiries and loans and also that the Bank was becoming active in parts of the country and in some types of businesses in which it had done much less previously. It is particularly noteworthy that the proportion of borrowers referred to the IDB by the chartered banks was fairly high and scarcely changed from year to year.

The Bank continued with the more usual forms of publicity such as advertisements in newspapers and trade journals, speeches to service clubs and business groups, and showings of the Bank's film, and it also added some new trimmings. The use of display booths at trade fairs was expanded. It was never clear whether they produced many direct benefits, but they were not expensive − several hundred dollars each, as a rule − and they communicated a mood of energy, initiative, and imagination to the Bank's own staff. Inexpensive information leaflets were produced to be given away at these booths; the Bank's regular information booklet was considered to be too costly, at twenty-five cents each, for this purpose. By 1968, the branches were starting to use in these booths slide pictures of the plants and operations of IDB borrowers, and in 1971 this prompted J.W. Sivers, the Bank's information officer, to develop a show of eighty slides, with recorded commentary and music, to be used for automatic display at booths. The slide show proved useful for appearances at luncheon meetings for which the film was too long and where something more colourful than a speech was wanted. The development of the slide show led to the designing of a collapsible, transportable booth that the Bank rented from its manufacturer. A series of coloured posters and charts was also developed for use in booths or where a speech was to be given. Bright electric signs were mounted outside branch offices. In London, a display was placed in sidewalk-level kiosks.

In 1968, it was decided to produce a new film. The old film was now far out of date; the clothes worn in it were out of fashion, the scope of the Bank had been changed by the 1961 amendments, and even the Bank's procedures had changed from those portrayed in the film. Also, field officers felt they needed a new film to get fresh exposure at those clubs or groups where the old film had already been shown. It was intended that the new film should show the broad scope of the Bank in the types of businesses helped, in the regions it served, and in the kind of programs it financed; it was to be lighter in mood than the previous one and with a touch of humour. It was to present the Bank as the responsive, flexible, and helpful organization that those working in it firmly believed it to be.

The film comprised a series of short episodes showing various kinds of businesses, located in different parts of the country, approaching the Bank for help with a variety of problems. The scripts submitted to the Bank caught these ideas very well. One of the first proposed that the film open with a bevy of go-go dancers tossing dollar bills out of their brassières. Somewhere along the way this idea disappeared, and the dancers and their dollars were replaced in the opening, somewhat inadequately, by a construction worker pouring himself a cup of coffee. The film was finished by the end of 1971.[21]

One of the interesting features of the film for the Bank's personnel was that in the English-language version the role of the IDB officer was taken by the same actor, Ed McGibbon, who had played the part superbly in the first film. His earlier performance was considered within the Bank to be a model of what a good IDB credit officer should be like. In the second film, he took the part of a branch manager. This provoked wry comments within the Bank as to the lengths to which the Bank's management seemed to have gone to make the second film realistic in that it had apparently taken Mr McGibbon 11 or 12 years to rise to the exalted position of manager!

In the mid-1960s, branches began to use radio spot announcements to publicize advertised visits, particularly in areas such as northern British Columbia, the interior of Newfoundland, and the Gaspé, where a scattered population was more easily reached in this way than by newspaper advertisements. In addition, by 1972, radio spot announcements were being used regularly in towns where the Bank had branches.

Television also was used quite often, whenever the Bank's branches were able to arrange with a local station for the broadcasting of the Bank's film, usually with a branch officer appearing to introduce it. In 1966, direct television advertising had been considered but rejected. It was felt that the Bank's scale of advertising expenditures, then just under $100,000 per annum, would not accommodate an effort of the magnitude required to be effective. In 1972, however, it was decided to try it, and sixty-second commercials were broadcast after the late national news over a period of eight weeks during the autumn. This resulted in over 1,000 requests for the Bank's booklet, and to this extent the experiment was rated a success. Accordingly, it was repeated the following year, but only in those areas where there was thought to be a particular need for the Bank's services – the Atlantic provinces, the remote parts of Quebec, northern Ontario, Manitoba, Saskatchewan, and northern British Columbia. This reduced the cost somewhat, but advertising expenditures in 1972 and 1973 were greatly increased by these broadcasts. They were not repeated again, and in 1974 advertising costs returned to the normal level of just under $100,000. Perhaps the most obvious effect of the experiment in TV advertising was that it aroused the finance companies to complain about what they interpreted as clear evidence of an intention on the part of the Bank to search aggressively for loans, regardless of the activities of other lenders.

Of the various new ventures in publicity and advertising, one of the most intriguing was the use of a rented van as a mobile office for visits to small communities. The idea was devised in the Atlantic Region by K.A. Powers. It was used first in the autumn of 1973 by the Saint John branch for a week-long trip down the Saint John River valley. The van was rented already fitted up as an office and was driven by a credit officer accompanied by another. In each town or village visited, it was parked for about half a day in a prominent place to receive inquiries. The trip required a great deal of preparation. A month before it was to take place a credit officer went to each town to be visited and called on town officials and bankers to inform them of the plans and to leave literature and posters.

Apart from generating inquiries about possible loans, the van's trips had a great deal of publicity value. The Bank's name was prominently displayed, and the trips effectively conveyed the Bank's interest in the small communities visited and its desire to serve them. That it represented just about the limit in that direction was indicated when those in charge of the van received a visit, during a tour by the van, from a gentleman who asked what the Bank's rate of interest was. When he was told, he was astonished and declared, 'Say, that's the best rate in town. I'll deposit $10,000.' He was naturally disappointed when he learned that the IDB did not take deposits. Other van trips were made in the Atlantic Region, and a van was also used in northern Ontario, southwestern Ontario, northern Alberta, and the interior of British Columbia.

Undoubtedly all this publicity contributed directly to the Bank's growth between 1968 and 1975 by informing businessmen of the services it provided. It also contributed indirectly through its influence on the Bank's own personnel. Branch and regional staffs were directly involved in most of the publicity efforts, with plenty of scope for the exercise of initiative and imagination, and this was probably more effective in increasing the Bank's responsiveness to credit proposals than any number of directives and regulations might have been.

Energetic publicity efforts by the Bank always ran the risk of arousing the criticism that it was breaking away from its statutory role of complementing, not displacing or competing with, commercial sources of financing.

An article in the *Financial Post* on 18 November 1972 suggested that the IDB had 'become a more aggressive competitor to other lenders in recent years'; it was described as employing 'hard-nosed advertising for new business,' illustrated by an increasing frequency of newspaper advertising and the use of television commercials. It was said to be actively competing for business against private sources of capital with ad campaigns, seminars, and solicitations. The IDB, however, saw its publicity efforts as designed simply to inform small businesses about its existence and the services it offered. If a business was unable to get the financial assistance it needed from a conventional source, it would not be able to get help from the IDB if it did not know about the Bank or what it did.

CHAPTER TWENTY

Some consequences of growth

Increasing importance of regional offices

The growth of the IDB 1968–75 affected its organization and the ways in which it did its work. The shifting of more responsibility for authorizing loans to regional offices and branches was accelerated by the enormous flow of credit applications, and the regions became almost small industrial development banks themselves. By 1975, in number of customers, amount of loan balances outstanding, and number of loans authorized in a year, Ontario Region was about the same size as the whole Bank had been in 1966, British Columbia Region was about the size of the Bank in 1967, and Quebec and Prairie regions were each comparable to the Bank in 1962–3. Atlantic Region was smaller – comparable, perhaps, to the whole Bank in 1960.

Before continuing, it might be as well to review briefly the steps by which the Bank had moved from highly centralized control of lending operations to almost complete regional autonomy.

For the first three years of the Bank, all credits had to be approved by the board of directors or the executive committee at head office. In 1947, the general manager, Mr Noble, was permitted to approve loans of up to $25,000; large credits were passed on to the board of directors or the executive committee with the recommendation of the general manager or his assistant, Mr James, first as executive assistant and later as assistant general manager. This meant that all lending was effectively controlled under the supervision of the General Manager's Office.

Alteration of this situation was made possible by the amendments to the

IDB Act in 1956.[1] Within six years, i.e. in 1962, the number of loans approved in one year by the field offices of the Bank was 86 per cent of the total, so that in this fairly short period the direct involvement of the General Manager's Office in the approving of loans had dropped from 100 per cent to 14 per cent. Adjustments in authorizing limits at various levels within the Bank continued to be made, and in 1967, following the setting up of a formal regional structure, the proportion of the number of loans approved by field offices was 90 per cent. By this time, there had also been a substantial delegation of authorizing powers to branch managers and assistant managers; in 1967 they approved on their own authority half of the loans approved at field offices, the other half being approved at the regional level. Decentralization continued, and from 1971 to 1975 the number of loans approved in the field was never below 97 per cent of the total. One might say that, at least with respect to the number of applications, the regions of the Bank were virtually autonomous. In 1975, the proportion approved in the field reached a peak of 99 per cent; the branches authorized 61 per cent, and the regional offices 38 per cent. Some branches of the Bank were strongly autonomous. Even as early as 1971, there were some branches where the managers and assistant managers approved, on their own authority, 75 per cent or more of the total number of loans their branches made.

The steady shift of responsibility to the field offices had been recognized in 1973 by a change in the title of the senior officers in the regions to regional general manager; at the same time the title of the general manager was changed to chief general manager, and the title of the assistant general managers at what was now known as CGMO was changed to general manager.

The distribution of loan authorizations between the field offices, on the one hand, and CGMO and head office, on the other, in terms of dollar amounts was less striking than the distribution by numbers, but even it reflected substantial decentralization. From 1969 to 1973, prior to the revision of authorizing limits in 1974, the field offices approved close to 80 per cent of the dollar total of loans authorized in a year. In 1974 and 1975, the proportion was approximately 82 per cent and 89 per cent respectively.

The strongly decentralized character of the Bank was not always recognized by those outside it. Although the proportion of loans approved in the field was published in the Bank's brief to the Porter Commission, and in the Bank's annual reports as early as 1966 and almost annually thereafter, a favourite comment about the Bank was that it did not give enough freedom of action to its regional offices. In June 1973, the Hon. Duff Roblin, former premier of Manitoba, was reported in the *Financial Times* (25 June) as having said in a speech given in several cities for the Canadian Institute of Public Administration that: 'Government institutions like the Industrial Development Bank are far less effective regionally than they should be. Regional imbalance would be improved if that bank permitted the operation of substantially independent autonomous regional divisions.' The proportion of loans approved by regional offices and branches at the time was 97 per cent, had been at the same level for the two preceding years, and had never been below 90 per cent since 1966!

A few weeks later, the premier of Manitoba, the Hon. Ed Schreyer, was reported in the *Globe and Mail* (18 July) as saying about the IDB and the Export Development Corporation: 'They are operating on a significant scale in Central Canada and the Maritimes and [are] practically non-existent in Alberta and Manitoba, and, in fact, non-existent in Saskatchewan.' As a matter of fact, by 30 September 1973, a couple of months later that year, the Bank had, since it started, approved loans for 1,500 businesses in Manitoba for a total of $94 million, 1,300 businesses in Saskatchewan for $69 million, and 3,600 businesses in Alberta for $200 million.

In fairness, however, to former premiers of Manitoba, it should be said that an inability to realize the extent to which the Bank was decentralized was not limited to observers outside the Bank. From time to time, one regional general manager or another would suggest that regional authorizing limits be raised. The suggestion was partly based on the grounds that inflation had diminished the real value of the proposals being financed, so that the true responsibility represented by a particular limit had decreased considerably. By 1975, in terms of commodity price indices, it would have taken a loan of $200,000 to finance a project for which $100,000 or so would have been sufficient fifteen years earlier. Also, it was felt that an increase in authorizing limits would be a proper reflection of the growing responsibility that management of the regions represented and would reduce the time required to process the larger loans that now required reference to GMO.

Apart, however, from making a small increase in regional authorizing limits in 1974 to mark the raising of the title of the senior regional officers to general manager, the chief general manager rejected the suggestions. He believed strongly that a crown corporation operating in such a sensitive field as that of assisting small businesses had to deal with clients and applicants with a high degree of consistency in the application of policies and credit standards and that this could be done if there were substantial input from a central operational authority on actual credit cases. This could not be done only by issuing instructions and regulations. The most effective way of communicating attitudes and standards was by correspondence and discussions between the regions and the Chief General Manager's Office regarding actual accounts and credit proposals requiring submission to CGMO for authorization or for recommendation to the board of directors. The chief general manager doubted that an input based on 2 per cent or 3 per cent by number, and 12 per cent to 18 per cent by amount, of loans approved was enough, but he did not doubt that anything less would be far too small.

Changing procedures to reduce processing time

The move toward decentralization had been reflected for many years in changes in the procedures by which the Bank dealt with applications for financial assistance. These procedures were most important since they formed the framework within which a decision to make a loan or decline an application was made. Procedures for handling applications had been evolving in three directions. As we saw in the previous section, more and more loans were being approved in the branches or regional offices without being submitted to CGMO. As we shall now see, the proportion of applications processed without a full investigation by one of the Bank's engineers or investigation officers steadily increased, and the amount of documentation required as a basis for approving or recommending a credit proposal decreased.

In all these changes, a principal goal was to cut down the amount of paper and reduce the time needed to process an application. All levels within the Bank were conscious of these needs. One enterprising credit officer suspected that the heavy flow of paper might prevent anyone from reading and appreciating his carefully written interview memoranda. He decided to test the matter by inserting the phrase 'How now brown cow!' in the middle of one of his memoranda. He felt his suspicions confirmed when the insertion was not discovered until it caught the eye of the filing clerk as the memorandum was being placed in its final resting place.

When in 1974 a party was given by the Ontario Region for its retiring assistant general manager, W.C. Stuart, no better way of suitably enriching the occasion occurred to the staff than to honour in song the amount of paper used in the Bank's work. The chorus, written by J.T. Horne, went as follows:

Up then staff and onward
Let not your efforts stop
Keep the paper flying
We may yet reach the top.

The basic approach to the consideration of a credit proposal taken by the Bank was that it should be studied and reported on from two perspectives. One involved a visit to the applicant's place of business and dwelt on the practical aspects of the proposal that could be most easily appraised in this way. This was done by an engineer or, as he was often called, an investigation officer. The other perspective involved a more remote and basically financial analysis carried out by the credit officer who had originally interviewed the applicant and who would administer any loan made.

This dual approach was reflected in the principal documents required in the early days to support a loan recommendation. These were an investigation report prepared by the engineer or investigation officer and a submission letter prepared by the credit officer or by the supervisor, which reviewed the proposal as a whole and analysed its financial aspects. The formal recital of the terms of a proposed loan and the recommendation of its approval were set out on a one-page document (known in the Bank as Form 73). In addition to these documents, which were prepared at the originating branch, there was prepared a one-page summary of the proposal for the information of the board of directors. This gave the terms of the loan, the balance sheet of the applicant, and a brief narrative about the borrower and the merits of the loan.

All the procedures and documents used by the Bank in later years were descendants of this early pattern. Some steps were modified from time to time, others were curtailed or telescoped into each other, and sometimes one person filled more than one role in the processing. These modifications were designed to save time, partly of those who had to read the material, but more generally to obtain a decision faster. Despite these modifications, by 1966–7 little progress had been made in shortening processing time; to deal with an application took just as long in 1967 as it had in 1961. Some idea of the problems faced in this regard can be formed from instructions issued in 1960 requiring that an explanation be put on the summary for any proposal that had taken an 'undue length of time' to be processed; the period beyond which such a comment was required was sixty days!

It became obvious that if the Bank were going to make any progress in speeding up its work it was going to have to know the areas in the processing of an application where most time was consumed. In 1967 and 1968, this was studied by A. Mackay, controller, and by C.B. Ready, assistant controller. The stages through which an application passed were divided into eight steps, and the time taken for each was recorded for a large sample of applications. Three steps seemed to offer scope for saving time, viz. the scheduling of investigations by investigation officers, the writing of investigation reports, and the preparation of submission documents of one kind or another. Thenceforth, a time record of this sort was maintained for every application processed.

The need to amend the Bank's procedures on other, perhaps more fundamental, grounds was dramatically demonstrated when the results of operations for 1969 were established. Shortly before the end of the fiscal year, the controller startled the general manager by expressing the opinion that the net profit for the year would be around $150,000. This was far too close to an operating loss for comfort. In the end, it transpired that the net profit for the year, i.e. the amount to be transferred to the reserve fund, turned out to be $373,000,[2] but even this was the smallest net profit since 1948, and it was clear that major procedural reforms would have to be made.

In 1970, a conference of assistant general managers considered the whole matter, and at intervals up to 1975 further modifications were made to simplify investigations and the amount of reporting required and to reduce enormously the length of credit presentations or submissions. Previous moves toward using credit officers to do investigations were greatly extended. Credit officers were encouraged to do their own investigations for smaller and simpler proposals. Most applications now came from tourist and service businesses, and many did not present the technical aspects that characterized the manufacturing businesses that had made up most of the Bank's borrowers in its early years. For the latter the technical knowledge of engineers and investigation officers had been very valuable, but they were now to concentrate on the larger and more complex proposals. In addition, the amount of work required to prepare credit proposals for a final decision was reduced by raising the authorizing limits of branch and regional officers by amounts ranging from 20 per cent to 65 per cent between 1968 and 1975.

The intention to have investigation officers (mostly engineers) on the Bank's staff deal mainly with larger proposals was related to a plan instituted in 1969 to move these officers into the regional offices. Because of geographical or other factors, some investigation officers continued to be stationed in branch offices, particularly in the Prairie Region, but they all now were to be supervised by regional engineers at the regional offices who would be responsible for training them, for maintaining a proper standard of reporting, and for assigning them to their investigative tasks. Overall, these responsibilities were supervised by a chief engineer, B.K. Heron, at CGMO.

The contribution of this arrangement to improvements in processing loan applications was not considered to be its only advantage. By grouping the investigation officers at one or a few central points in each region, the knowledge of each could be used to greater advantage, they would receive better guidance and training, and they would be provided with a professional line of advancement that had been lacking in the Bank.

There were also disadvantages to the scheme. Most applications would now be processed without the benefit of the second opinion that had been a main contribution of the investigation officers and engineers. Also, the credit officers, who now were responsible for investigating many of the applications they received, had many other preoccupations – interviews with new applicants, administration of existing accounts, advertised visits, and so on – that might interfere with the concentration needed for a good investigation report. Finally, there was now less liaison between credit and investigation officers, when the latter were used, than there had traditionally been. The usual discussions between them before and after an investigation were now difficult to arrange and sometimes non-existent, because the branch credit officer might be hundreds of miles away from the regional office where the investigation officer was located. Relations between branch credit officers and investigation officers lost a great deal of the intimacy that had prevailed when they had worked together on an application in the same office. When an investigation officer had to come from the regional office to investigate a large or complex proposal (which in some branches occurred only two or three times a year), this often seemed to a branch to be an intrusive impediment to rapid processing and something to be avoided if possible. Indeed, some branch managers seemed to feel that investigation officers were unnecessary even for large proposals. This view was not held by the chief general manager in Montreal. After all, the financial penalty for an error in judgment in even just one large loan that might have to be written off was substantial. To ensure that large proposals continued to have the benefit of the 'double view' and technical expertise, instructions were issued in 1975 that for all applications over $150,000 the investigation must be made by an investigation officer. This was not a popular move in the field, although it affected only about 4 per cent of applications handled in a year.

The long process of seeking a more efficient and faster way of handling loan applications had, by 1975, changed the Bank's methods greatly. Submission letters had virtually disappeared, and the summary had become the principal document for the presentation of a credit. For all credits within branch limits and the authorizing limits of assistant supervisors, the summary usually recorded only the terms of the loan and the balance sheet and operating record of the borrowing business. Over these limits, the summary would include a narrative analysis of the proposal that might run to several pages. All credit proposals were still supported by an investigation report of some kind, but most of these were now prepared by a credit officer. Of the 11,800 applications processed in 1975, only 1,300 were investigated by an investigation officer. The remainder were investigated by credit officers; 1,000 reports were written in the full format used by investigation officers, but the remaining 9,500 applications were covered by brief memoranda that were called credit reports to distinguish them from those resulting from a full formal investigation.

By these measures and constant attention to the matter, the Bank reduced the time taken to process credit applications remarkably: an average of 46 days in 1967, 40 in 1968, 33 in 1969, 27 in 1970, 19 in 1971, 17 in 1972, 16 in 1973 and 1974, and 14 in 1975. In 1975, half the applications processed took 8 days or less; in 1967, the corresponding figure was 40 days. In 1975, the 25 per cent of the applications processed most quickly were dealt with in 4 days – or less! In 1967, the comparable figure had been 24 days. Part of the change came from using more frequently the date of receipt of the information required for the consideration of an application as the start of the processing time, but there is no doubt there was a big improvement.

The regionalization of investigation officers was followed, in 1971, by a similar move with respect to lawyers on the Bank's staff. In each region, their work was supervised by a regional solicitor who was, in turn, answerable to the general solicitor, H.M. Scott (succeeded the following year by D.R. Urquhart), and to G. Bousquet, QC, associate general solicitor, both at GMO. As with the investigation officers, in the Prairie Region some legal officers remained at the branches because of the physical size of the region and because a substantial number of the region's loans were in the province furthest from the regional office in Winnipeg, namely Alberta.

Devices were introduced to expedite security preparation and disbursement of loans. Credit officers in branches took on some of the work of instructing outside solicitors in preparing loan security. Legal assistants or legal clerks were stationed at some branches. The Bank's legal officers began cutting down on what they would ask outside lawyers to supply to the Bank in the course of preparing security. They were not expected to spend as much time as previously on corporate niceties such as checking entries in a company's minute book. For loans under $50,000, only a limited search of land titles was required. For small loans, the Bank accepted the outside lawyer's certificate as to security without checking the documentation.

A step that had long been considered was finally taken in using a borrower's solicitor to prepare the Bank's security. The Bank had traditionally resisted such a suggestion because of a fear of a conflict of interest. It was finally adopted, however, because of several advantages. It reduced legal costs for the borrower, placed the onus for expediting security on him and his lawyer, and was a further protection for the Bank against political involvement in its use of lawyers.

The time taken to get the security for a loan completed was reduced to the point that by 1974 half of the loans that had been authorized had had their initial disbursement within about 2 months from the date of authorization, compared with about 3 months in 1967. However, sometimes a borrower needed the proceeds of his loan before the security was ready, especially if the loan was to be used for working capital. In such cases, some field offices would make partial disbursement against a promissory note pending completion of security. In 1974, this practice was recognized as official policy so long as there were no grounds for doubt that the tangible security to be pledged would actually be provided. Alternatively, a partial disbursement could be made on completion of part of the security for a loan 'in exceptional cases where it may be desirable and urgently necessary for a customer who has a pressing need for the proceeds of a loan.'

Changes in structures of regional offices and GMO

Growth in the size of regional offices as a result of regionalization of investigation and legal officers was a visible reflection of the growing importance of these offices. The staff under a regional general manager already included one or more supervisors and assistant supervisors who assisted in both credit and administrative matters. Administration officers were now appointed to look after preparation of reports, planning for new branches, and general administration. Whereas all personnel work had previously been done at GMO, personnel assistants were now attached to the regional offices to handle staff matters for clerical staff. Regional 'directors' for various new activities (which will be described later), such as training for staff and advisory services for businessmen, were also appointed. Ontario and Quebec regions grew to such a size that they were each divided into two districts under supervisors. Both Quebec supervisors operated out of the regional office in Montreal, but in Ontario a district office was opened in Sault Ste Marie to supervise the second district, Northern Ontario. A typical organization chart for a regional office is shown in Appendix II.

Regions also developed their own books of 'circular' directives outlining routines and procedures to be followed within a particular region. The large branches did the same. The instructions for the Ontario Region were famous all over the Bank, not only because they reflected the inimitable personality of the regional general manager, W.C. Stuart, but also because of their attractive acronym, CROONS (Central Region Office Organization Notes). Equally famous were those of Toronto branch, TOONS.

The rapid growth of the Bank also required great changes in the structure of the General Manager's Office in Montreal which from 1968 to 1975 was in an almost constant state of change and adaptation. The Legal, Insurance, and Credit departments had been long established, although the duties of the last-named changed from time to time as the responsibilities of the regional offices increased. The Personnel and Information departments were newer, but their responsibilities also were well recognized, as were those of the controller. Up to 1972, however, a variety of administrative and some credit duties were performed by officers with the general titles of administrative assistant and special assistant, or by one of the assistant controllers. These duties were sorted out in 1973; those of a credit character were taken over by the Credit Department, and the others were assigned to special departments under officers with titles reflecting their areas of responsibilities.

The administrative assistants illustrate the evolution that occurred. This title was introduced first in 1956 and represented a senior position at GMO. The occupant did just what his title implied – he assisted in the administration of the Bank in any way asked of him by the general manager. He might process credits, draft policy instructions, or study some aspect of procedures. However, by 1970, when there were two administrative assistants, their duties had become narrower, and they were each, in effect, heads of small specialized departments. This was recognized in 1973 when one, C.R.T. Bingley, was appointed superintendent, methods and procedures, to prepare circular instructions and directives for the guidance of the Bank's staff, and the other, P.M. Bourassa, was appointed superintendent, planning and supply, responsible for premises, furniture, and equipment and for studies for the creation of new branches.

The same evolution toward specific responsibilities occurred with respect to the assistant general managers at GMO. Following the regionalization of field operations 1966–8, there were two, C.E. DeAthe and H.J. Russell. Mr DeAthe spent the greater part of his time, as he had done for some years, on administrative matters referred to him by the general manager, but both dealt with such credit proposals, submitted by the regions, as might be referred to them by the Credit Department. In 1970, this last part of their work was put on a more precise basis with the assignment of specific regions to each assistant general manager for the processing of incoming credit proposals. In 1973, the next step was taken in the defining of their administrative responsibilities. This was accompanied by the general upgrading of the titles of the senior officers: all assistant general managers became general managers, and the general manager was appointed chief general manager.

At this point, the Bank suffered a great loss in the sudden death of Mr. DeAthe. He had been with the Bank for 24 years; for the last 15 years he had been at GMO, close to the central direction of the Bank's operations as administrative assistant, executive assistant, and assistant general manager. He was a dedicated and very competent senior officer who contributed greatly to the Bank's success.

For the purpose of defining the responsibilities of the general managers at what was now known as the Chief General Manager's Office, their duties were at first divided into three areas – loans, administration, and branch operations – with a general manager in charge of each area. Mr Russell became general manager, loans; G. Bourbonnière, who had been superintendent, credits, became general manager, administration; and E.A. Bell, who had been supervisor, Ontario Region, was appointed general manager, branch operations. In January 1975, the final senior appointment was made, with the transfer of J.E. Nordin, general manager, Quebec Region, to CGMO as general manager, corporate development. He was succeeded in the Quebec Region by J.Y. Milette. Mr Nordin's principal responsibilities were to oversee preparations for the conversion of the IDB into the Federal Business Development Bank and to develop fresh initiatives in the providing of financial assistance through the purchase by the Bank of shares in businesses. Both subjects will be discussed in later chapters.

By 1975, most departments at CGMO were grouped for reporting purposes under one of the four general managers. The only officers at CGMO reporting directly to the chief general manager were those with broad overall responsibility affecting the whole operation of the Bank. These were the director of advisory services (a new department described in chapter 22); the general solicitor; the controller; the superintendent, personnel; the information officer; and the economist. The final organization chart for CGMO is shown in Appendix II.

Although the general management of the Bank was now set up on a more departmentalized basis than ever before, it still retained some marks of its early, loosely structured days when any senior officer at GMO might have had a hand in almost any aspect of management. All the general managers at CGMO continued to the end to deal with credits recommended by the field, just as the assistant general managers had done, irrespective of their responsibility. While the general manager, loans, had certain special concerns in the field of credits, each of the other general managers had credit submissions referred to him also for disposal. The largest credits would be referred to the chief general manager, although he would often refer them back to one of the general managers for consideration. These things were done partly to spread the credit work around, partly because it was considered undesirable that any of the senior officers lose touch with the real purpose of the Bank's existence, namely the making of loans, and partly because it was thought best that the kinds of difficult questions that might typically arise in the consideration of large credit proposals be exposed constantly to a number of persons' judgments.

In addition to this clarification of responsibilities, a number of committees were set up covering staff, job evaluation, branch planning, data processing, and so on. Apart from a staff committee chaired by the chief general manager, each was presided over by one of the general managers at CGMO. This elaboration of CGMO structures meant that senior officers were less likely than before to know what was going on in areas not under their surveillance. A steering committee of the general managers at CGMO, chaired by the chief general manager, was set up so that each could tell his colleagues about developments in his area of responsibility. It did not function as an instrument of management, and the chief general manager remained the ultimate reference point for credit management or any other operational responsibilities.

One committee was known as the staff advisory group. The membership was intended to represent the various characteristics of the Bank's staff – geographical location, length of service, occupation within the Bank, levels of responsibility, men and women, French and English languages, and so on. It had 15 or 16 members. The membership changed from time to time, but the permanent chairman was K.A.

Powers, general manager, Ontario Region. It was intended to provide the management of the Bank with an input from personnel at all locations and at all levels toward personnel policies and practices when such information would be helpful.

That the staff at CGMO had some trouble making the transition from a relatively informal structure to a more rigid one is suggested by the following rather sad extract from a memo written in 1974 by the chief general manager: 'They [departments] should also not be over-sensitive to apparent trespassing by one department on what they believe to be the responsibility of another. They must not be over-agitated if they learn less directly than they think they should of something which they believe will involve their individual department.'

Inspection of branches

Probably the most important reflection of the growth in the departmental structure of the Bank was the development of a new system for inspecting the operations of the branches. The large number of these and the increasing decentralization of the Bank's lending activities made the methods of inspection that had developed in the 1960s quite inadequate. These had originated in 1963 and had been based on inspection reports by each regional assistant general manager on the branches of his own region. They dealt not with the loans made at a branch but with the branch's efficiency and effectiveness. These characteristics were measured by various yardsticks, such as the number of loans made per 100 inquiries, the proportion of loans in arrears, the advertised visits made, and the workload borne by the staff of the branch. Statistics on these things were compiled by GMO and supplied to each regional assistant general manager to assist him in his inspections.

This system was handled at GMO for many years by an administrative assistant, but in 1972 it was turned over to the superintendent, credits, G. Bourbonnière, who had the staff of his department to call on for assistance in preparing the data and analysing the reports. The reports by the regional assistant general managers were then replaced by reports by Mr Bourbonnière following visits by himself, accompanied by one of his credit officers, to each regional office. During these visits, the work of each branch was discussed on the basis of statistics prepared at GMO as outlined above.

It was becoming obvious, however, that with operations highly decentralized there would have to be some more intensive system by which central management could be satisfied that directives on policy and procedures were being followed and that uniformly high standards of performance and service were being maintained. The successful efforts made by the Bank to relax its response to credit proposals, to streamline its procedures, and to shorten the time taken to process applications, while most successful in their immediate objectives, were themselves producing problems. The flood of statistics on the number of loans made, on the number of inquiries received, on the proportion of these that produced loans, and so on created a state of mind in some parts of the Bank that earned the name 'the numbers game' – all that mattered was the number of loans racked up.

This was not regarded as wholly bad, since at least it ensured enthusiasm for giving good service to small businesses. There was a danger, however, that the importance of quality in lending might be overlooked. One major branch manager reported one year on his credit officers, in the annual staff review, merely by giving the number of loans each had made. All his reports were returned to him by GMO for rewriting to make clear to him that this was not regarded as the critical measure of performance. Even the more extensive budgeting procedures, which naturally developed as the Bank grew, contributed to these problems. A budget for a branch, a region, or the Bank as a whole depended first on a forecast of the number and amount of loans expected to be made in the coming year. Once a branch or region had made such a forecast, it was only a short step to regarding it as a target to be aimed at and striven for.

The chief general manager, when attending once a regional conference of branch managers in British Columbia, stressed that 'numbers' were not used by CGMO in assessing a credit officer's work. He was startled to receive the response from a branch manager: 'That is all very well, but you are only out here for one day!'

To some extent, the long-maintained efforts to shorten the time taken to process an application were contributing to these problems. Even though by 1972 and 1973, quite satisfactory results had been obtained, the matter became almost an obsession. In January 1974, when processing time had been reduced to an average of 16 days, when 68 per cent of loans were approved in that time, and when 50 per cent of loans were approved in 10 days, the issue was still being hammered at, even more strongly than when the average time had been 45 days. An internal memorandum that took this line at that time said that 'processing time continues to be most important for the Bank' and urged various drastic measures including 'the elimination of all investigation reports under, say, $50,000,' i.e. for 75 per cent of all loans being made!

However, the important problem was no longer simply that of reducing processing time. As expressed in another internal memorandum written in 1974, it was to 'work as quickly as possible while maintaining necessary standards of investigation and consideration' and following procedures that would 'instil into our officers work habits and methods that would ensure the operation of the Bank in a sound way in future years.' That this was a difficult task is indicated by the pace at which the number of credit officers on the Bank's staff was growing. In the years 1962−7, when the volume of loan authorizations was relatively stable, the number of credit officers was increased each year by, on average, 6 per cent; from 1968 to 1970, an average of 8 per cent was added each year. From 1971 to 1975, however, the average annual increase was 19 per cent, and in 1973 and 1974, when there was a large increase in loan activity, the yearly increase averaged 25 per cent. In 1974, about 40 per cent of the Bank's credit officers had less than one year's service with the Bank.

The next step toward a full-fledged inspection system, as recommended in 1962 by the management consultants, was taken with the appointment of E.A. Bell to be general manager, branch operations, to further develop the inspection program. Visits to the regional offices to discuss the work of the branches were continued, but starting in 1974 visits were also made to the branches themselves by 'inspectors' working under Mr Bell. These branch inspections went beyond the checking of efficiency and effectiveness that had been the sole concern of previous inspection systems and now included a review of recent credit authorizations, loans in arrears, and other credit matters, 'to arrive at an opinion regarding adherence to the Bank's current lending policy and to the relevant principles of sound credit judgment.' This was the first time that such a broad review of operations had been conducted in the field on behalf of the general management. Some regional general managers saw this review of branch credit work directly by officers from CGMO, which by-passed, as it were, the regional offices, as an infringement on their responsibilities. To a complaint of this sort, the chief general manager replied: 'I have no doubt whatever that very quickly the regional offices will appreciate the value of having an outside objective view taken of the operations of their branch offices by someone from outside the region who has knowledge of what is going on in other parts of the Bank and, while respecting the authority of the regional offices, is just as interested as they are to see the efficiency and effectiveness of field operations brought to the highest possible level.'

In the first inspections under the new system, few departures from the Bank's lending policies were found, but some important deviations from prescribed procedures were reported. One branch had, in the interests of saving time, given up writing to an applicant's chartered bank for a report, one of the oldest procedures in the Bank and a most important one. In other cases, there was not a proper liaison between credit officer and investigation officer; a growing number of branches were not taking time to set down an applicant's financial statements on paper for study and analysis; the reviewing of financial statements of existing accounts was not following prescribed lines; and some branch managers were authorizing credits on the basis merely of a verbal discussion with the credit officer and without a written credit report from the latter.

All this was not surprising. There had never been a strict policing of such matters, and many improvements in the Bank's procedures had come from experimental departures by branches and regional offices from those prescribed. Nevertheless, the volume of work handled by the Bank and the extent to which procedures had been modified through the years seemed to make it desirable that there be a closer surveillance of the Bank's work through a broad inspection system.

Staff training

To cope with the growing intake of new credit officers, a formal training program was instituted on a bank-wide basis for the first time. In the early years of the Bank, a new credit officer was given on-the-job training simply by being attached for several weeks or months to an experienced credit officer. As the Bank grew, the larger offices such as Toronto and Montreal set up fairly formal training programs of their own, but there was no plan for the Bank as a whole. Early in 1969, E.C. Scott, in charge of the Bank's Personnel Department as personnel officer, was asked to form a task team 'to design a training program or manual that could be used throughout the Bank in preparing newly engaged credit officers to meet their responsibilities in a more efficient manner and in the shortest possible time.' The team comprised J.A. McKee, assistant personnel officer, as chairman; J.M. Dunbar, assistant supervisor, Quebec Region; J.T.D. Mulqueen, a credit officer at the Metro-Toronto branch and later training director for the Bank; and D.C. Sedgwick, a credit officer at GMO and later manager of the Kitchener-Waterloo branch. The team thus represented experience at GMO, regional, and branch levels.

At the end of 1969, the team produced a manual and syllabus for a bank-wide training system, and the program was introduced early in 1970 under a training director at GMO and regional training directors at the regional offices. The actual training was carried out at the branches under branch training officers.

In spite of the generally uniform introductory training received by new credit officers from 1970 on, their real training still came on the job, when they started to handle loan applications on their own. There were sufficient differences among the styles and attitudes of the various regional general managers so that what was expected from a credit officer once his formal training was completed could vary from one region to another. In fact, occasionally a regional general manager might express reluctance to accept the transfer of a credit officer from another region on suspicion that he would not be properly trained.

Between 1970 and 1975, the training program grew to include week-long seminars on personnel management for branch managers, training periods with classroom instruction in regional offices, film strips, and other aids to training.

Computer

An inevitable result of the Bank's growth was the switching of its loan accounting to a computer. Studies started in 1969 to take advantage of the installation of a large computer by the Bank of Canada in Ottawa. By the summer of 1970, the switch-over was complete. A peculiarity of the arrangements was that, since the data cards for the computer were punched in the loan accounting department in Montreal, they had to be sent to Ottawa by inter-urban bus or by courier. This paradoxical combination of the fastest form of account processing with automotive transport introduced a trying delay into the procedure, and at least once the cards went astray. In 1973, the IDB set up its own computer department at CGMO using rented time on local computers for the actual processing.

The principal task of the computer was to take over the growing burden of keeping track of the loan accounts and payments on them and of calculating interest, but it was also hoped that it would reduce arrears on loan payments. Very early the Bank had sought to do this by asking its borrowers to lodge with it each year post-dated cheques for the payments due in the ensuing twelve months. About 85 per cent would normally agree to this arrangement. Thus, the Bank had custody of a growing number of cheques; by 1973, the number was close to 250,000, and in 1975 it was close to 400,000. The physical task of storing the cheques, extracting the right ones each month, sorting them, and making up the Bank's monthly deposit from them was enormous. It was hoped that the computer would clear away all this by preparing each month debits to the various chartered bank accounts of the IDB's customers, together with the monthly deposit slip for the IDB. By 1975, when the IDB was absorbed into the FBDB, the many arrangements required for this had not been completed.

Staff journal

Another consequence of growth was the establishment in 1973 of a staff paper called *Rapport*. This was to reflect the interests and activities of the staff and to help preserve the intimacy and the family feeling that had always characterized life in the IDB and that were endangered to some extent by its growth.

Language training

One development that was partly a 'consequence of growth', as represented by the opening of new branches in the province of Quebec, was an expansion of the use of the French language in the Bank's work. In 1963 the federal government, responding to desires of French-speaking Canadians that their language have a bigger role in the life of the country, and particularly in business and government, appointed the Royal Commission on Bilingualism and Biculturalism[3] to examine the relative positions of the French and English languages and cultures in Canada. In 1969 Parliament passed the Official Languages Act to enhance the position of French in federal institutions and in the federal civil service.[4] There was a great flurry among large business corporations to teach French to unilingual English-speaking executive officers, and in the civil service numerous and costly programs were introduced to give language courses, principally in French.

The IDB had, from its very beginning, used both French and English in dealing with applicants and customers as they might wish. Internal correspondence, memoranda, and reports, however, were for many years almost invariably written in English. As additional branches were opened in the province of Quebec, dealing almost entirely with French-speaking business people and staffed with French-speaking employees, this practice became, for these offices, an awkward anomaly. When offices were opened in Quebec City (1959) and Trois-Rivières (1962), their staffs gradually slipped naturally into the use of French for many of their memoranda and reports. At the end of 1964, by which time another branch staffed entirely by French-speaking personnel had been opened at Rimouski, the general manager, A.N.H. James, decided to encourage this trend toward increased use of French internally by providing officially for its optional use in the processing of credits up to branch managers' limits. In November 1965, it was observed that this practice had been established 'without a ripple of difficulty,' and the option of using French or English was extended to include credit proposals up to an assistant supervisor's limit. This covered about 70 per cent of a branch's loans. By 1968, this option was enlarged to include the processing of credits of any size.

Since it was then the practice to send to all regional offices copies of the summaries of all credits authorized anywhere in the Bank, this had the useful result of demonstrating to all parts of the Bank the status of French as an optional working language and of doing so in a natural way, reflected from the ordinary operations of the Bank. At GMO, in effect the meeting point for the two languages, the increased use of French internally had the gratifying result that a French-speaking credit officer in the Credit Department dealing with a credit proposal submitted in English by, say, the Prairie Region or the British Columbia Region, would write his analytical memoranda in French for the guidance of the English-speaking officer who was to make the final decision on the proposal.

The Bank also set up programs of instruction in French for English-speaking personnel and in English for those whose first language was French. Participation in these programs was voluntary.

As a result of these actions, the Bank's operational management was able, when visited in 1965 by representatives of the Royal Commission on Bilingualism and Biculturalism, to surprise them when they asked about the Bank's translation facilities by saying that the Bank did not have any because it did not need them; documents were handled in the language in which they were written, whether French or English. This boast was not long maintained, however, since, in 1968, the Bank had begun translating its operational instructions, by then quite a bulky book, into French. The use of outside or government translators for this did not work out satisfactorily, and in 1973 the Bank set up its own translation bureau.[5]

By 1971, approximately 200 of the Bank's staff had taken part in language instruction programs, and two senior officers had taken immersion courses at Laval University. The total number participating represented about 25 per cent of the total number of employees at the end of 1971. The courses had been conducted for the Bank by various language schools or taken by individuals at local colleges or schools. Although the number of employees volunteering for instruction had been very satisfactory, it was pretty clear that few of those who started with little or no knowledge of the language studied were becoming bilingual to any practical degree. Accordingly, it was decided to set up the Bank's own program under a full-time language co-ordinator. Classrooms and a language laboratory were established at GMO for local staff. For employees elsewhere, the co-ordinator provided individual instruction by lessons recorded on tape cassettes that were passed back and forth between student and co-ordinator as the course progressed.

Even with this change, the management of the Bank took, on the basis of experience, a modest view of what could be accomplished through language instruction for adults, particularly for any who had no knowledge whatever of the language being studied and no opportunity of using it. The achievement of a high degree of competence in the language was placed second among the aims of the program. The first aim was as broad a participation as possible. The general manager believed that the Bank could give a good response to the language problems that had come to the fore in Canadian society by basing it on voluntary goodwill on the part of its staff and on the practical needs of an efficient and effective operation. Even if those studying a second language did not become truly bilingual, the Bank would benefit if, out of an employee's willingness to study another language, he or she developed an interest in and sympathy for the milieu and culture it represented, so that the employee established a better rapport with his or her colleagues of the other language group. The general manager wanted the optional status of French and English in the Bank to be seen by its employees not as the result of regulations and requirements established outside but as necessary for doing the Bank's work, as a proper courtesy extended by members of the Bank's staff to each other, and as an interesting and attractive circumstance of employment by the Bank.

These thoughts were reflected in a memorandum written by the general manager in 1972: 'I think we should avoid references to "official" languages. To do so [i.e. make such references] leaves an impression linking us with the bilingualisation program of the Civil Service. I think we should strenuously avoid such a linking. That program has problems and implications with which we have no need to involve ourselves. We are simply teaching English and French to those who wish to improve their knowledge of them, and we want to do it in as attractive and stimulating a way as possible, so as to appeal in interest and motivation to as many employees as we can.'

The cassette program of instruction proved difficult to administer, and the number of personnel who became even partially bilingual through it was not large. Nevertheless, the first aim of the program at least was achieved. Up to the conversion of the IDB into the Federal Business Development Bank in September 1975, there were usually each year more than 300 employees, representing between 20 per cent and 25 per cent of the total staff, taking language courses. The greater number were studying French, and they were located in every region from coast to coast.

Operating results

Revenues and profits

The financial results of operations for the eight years 1968–75 are set out in Table 30. For comparative purposes it also gives results for 1967, which terminated the previous period. The table reflects many of the characteristics of the Bank's operations in the years 1968–75 and the problems faced – the tremendous growth in loans on the Bank's books, increasing dependence on debentures for new funds, dwindling profits in 1969 and 1970, the importance of controlling operating expenses, and the improvement in profits that occurred in the final years.

Interest rates on loans and debentures

Income, which came almost entirely from interest on loans, increased as loan balances grew in response to the great upsurge in new authorizations. In 1967, loan balances outstanding were $333,541,000, while at the end of 1975, they were $1,175,234,000. Interest income also reflected frequent and substantial rises in the Bank's lending rates from 1968 on. In the 8 years 1968–75, the IDB changed its rates about the same number of times as it had in the preceding 22 years, and usually in an upward direction.

In Appendix I is given a chart of the IDB's lending rates, of other important interest rate series, and of such rates for term loans as came to the notice of the IDB. Not all interest rates are comparable with those of

TABLE 30

Operating results ($millions) 1967–75

	1967	1968	1969	1970	1971	1972	1973	1974	1975
Interest on loans	22.8	26.4	30.6	38.3	47.5	55.1	64.6	84.4	113.6
Other income	0.6	0.7	0.5	0.6	1.2	1.5	2.5	1.9	1.9
Total income	23.4	27.1	31.1	38.9	48.7	56.6	67.1	86.3	115.5
Operating expenses	7.0	7.8	8.9	10.2	11.9	14.7	18.1	24.2	30.0
Interest on debentures	13.9	16.5	20.1	26.1	30.7	33.9	40.3	54.8	73.4
Total costs	20.9	24.3	29.0	36.3	42.6	48.6	58.4	79.0	103.4
Net income	2.5	2.8	2.1	2.6	6.1	8.0	8.7	7.3	12.1
Provision for losses	1.9	2.0	1.7	2.1	4.1	4.4	4.9	4.6	7.7
Transferred to reserve fund	0.6	0.8	0.4	0.5	2.0	3.6	3.8	2.7	4.4
Percentage rate of return on capital (shares plus reserve fund)	1.0	1.2	0.5	0.7	2.6	4.4	4.3	2.7	4.0

SOURCE: *Annual Reports.*

the IDB in a meaningful way, but this chart at least shows where the Bank's lending rates lay in relation to the market as a whole.

As the period opened, it was obvious that the Bank's lending rates would have to be increased. The general level of interest rates on the market was rising, the IDB's rates seemed low compared to those of other lenders, and the rate of interest paid on the Bank's new debentures was increasing and steadily pressing more closely on its lending rates.

Table 31 gives the annual 'weighted' average rates of interest on new loans and on new debentures combined with new issues of share capital, for the years 1968–75. It shows clearly the difficult position the Bank was in by 1968 and 1969, being squeezed between lending rates and rising debenture rates. Although the Bank was doing more business, it was deriving less and less benefit from it. This is shown in Table 32, which compares various aspects of the Bank's operations for the years that ended each of the three previous periods with the situation at the end of fiscal 1969. To respond to the situation, lending rates were raised by ½ of 1 per cent in the early months of 1968, and by 1 per cent twice in 1969. These three increases in less than two years were just about equal to the total amount by which the Bank's lending rate rose from 1944 to 1966.

Nevertheless, the changes corrected the situation only gradually. First, changes in lending rates for new loans affected total earnings slowly

TABLE 31

Weighted average rates of interest on new loans made and on new capital funds 1968–75

	Weighted average rate (percentage) on new loans made	Weighted average rate (percentage) on new debentures issued plus new share capital	Difference or spread (percentage)
1968	8.37	6.62	1.75
1969	9.45	7.29	2.16
1970	10.56	7.79	2.77
1971	10.40	5.83	4.57
1972	9.63	6.16	3.47
1973	9.71	6.95	2.76
1974	11.52	8.02	3.50
1975	12.59	7.28	5.31

TABLE 32

Results of operations 1955, 1961, 1967, and 1969

	Loan balances outstanding at end of fiscal year ($millions)	Net income transferred to reserve fund ($millions)	Percentage return on average loans and investments
1955	44	1.2	2.78
1961	123	1.2	1.06
1967	334	0.6	0.20
1969	419	0.4	0.09

SOURCES: *Annual Reports* and Brief, Tables 1, 3, and 4.

because of the time taken to effect disbursement of loan proceeds as the programs being financed were executed and because the great majority of loan balances outstanding represented loans made earlier and at lower rates. Second, the rates applicable to new debentures changed constantly and automatically as the rates for government securities on which they were based fluctuated, whereas lending rates were adjusted much less frequently and only after long consideration. If, as sometimes happened, the president felt that the minister of finance should be apprised of an intention to raise lending rates, this added to the delay. It might take two to six weeks after a change was recommended before it was effected. At a time when interest rates on the market, and therefore the IDB's debenture rates, were rising quite rapidly, the slower response of lending rates was a great disadvantage to the Bank's operating results. Third, debentures were sold in series of up to six-year maturities. In 1967, the average term for loans was just over seven years and in the 1970s it ranged between eight and nine years. This meant that the debentures that had financed a loan in the first instance would probably have to be replaced by renewal debentures before the loan was paid off. If the trend of debenture rates was upward, these renewal debentures would bear higher rates than those in effect when the loan was made and its rate of interest was established.

The effect of all these circumstances was magnified by the continuing move toward increased dependence on debentures for new funds. Debentures outstanding at fiscal year-end amounted to 22.7 per cent of total capital funds employed in 1955, 65.5 per cent in 1961, 80.5 per cent in 1967, and 89.7 per cent in 1975.

The original IDB Act had given the Bank power to sell debentures up to three times the total of issued shares plus the reserve fund. In 1961, this ratio of 3 to 1 was raised to 5 to 1. At that time, outstanding debentures were slightly more than twice the total of shares plus reserve; in order gradually to bring their relationship up to the new ratio, the board of directors decided that any new issues of debentures and shares would be made in the ratio of 10 to 1. By the end of 1967, this practice had brought outstanding debentures up to 4.1 times shares plus reserve, slightly below the statutory limit of 5 to 1. In December of that year, the IDB Act was amended again to increase the amount of share capital that could be issued to $75 million and to raise the Bank's borrowing power once more. This time the limit on debentures was set at 10 times issued shares plus the reserve fund.

This drastic increase in the extent to which the IDB would have to depend on borrowing for such new funds as it might require reflected a desire on the part of officials at the IDB's head office (i.e. at the Bank of Canada) that the Bank's financial base, while shaped by the IDB's special role, should be as free as possible from any suggestion of subsidization. The IDB would now pay, through interest charges, for nearly all the money it would lend.

The new ratio of 10 to 1 was very similar to the ratio of 12½ to 1 under which federally incorporated mortgage loan companies operated. Their financial structure was influenced by profit and tax considerations that favoured a high debt-to-equity ratio. These did not affect the IDB, but at least the Bank's new debenture-equity relationship had the appearance of approximately matching that applied to commercial lenders in the mortgage field.

Although this increased the IDB's costs, it was believed that the practice followed since 1961-2 of supplying new funds to it on the basis of a 10 to 1 ratio between debentures and equity had shown that the Bank was mature enough and strong enough to depend on borrowed money to this extent.

TABLE 33

Increases in shares and debentures 1967–75

	Increase in shares ($millions)	Increase in debentures ($millions)	Increase in debentures as multiple of increase in shares
1967	3	30	10.0
1968	3	31	10.3
1969	4	38	9.5
1970	2	63	31.5
1971	2	51	25.5
1972	3	56	18.7
1973	4	104	26.0
1974	9	231	25.7
1975	7	170	24.3

In 1969, the IDB's board of directors decided that any new issues, after outstanding shares reached $50 million and debentures reached $325 million (which occurred that year), should be made in the ratio of 25 to 1, in order to hasten the day when the totals of outstanding debentures, issued shares, and reserve fund, as shown on the Bank's balance sheet, would achieve the new statutory ratio of 10 to 1. For every dollar of new capital made available to the Bank through the purchase of shares by the Bank of Canada, and therefore free of an interest charge, the IDB would have to borrow $25 through the sale of debentures before another dollar of shares could be issued. The effect of this is shown in Table 33, starting in 1967, when debentures and shares were being issued in the ratio of 10 to 1.

The IDB was now in a position where 96 per cent of new capital funds were borrowed and required the payment of interest. This was a far cry from its position in its early years when all new capital funds were in the form of equity, on which no interest had to be paid.

As Table 31 shows, the changes in the Bank's lending rates in 1968 and 1969 had improved the interest rate situation very little. The second increase in 1969 had been made near the end of the fiscal year and was reflected in higher average rates in 1970, but, even so, it appeared that year that a further increase was required, and in January the general manager recommended an increase of 1 per cent. By this time, however, the Prices and Income Commission appointed by the federal government to maintain a watching brief on inflationary tendencies was policing rises in price levels, and it discouraged any increase in the IDB's rates of interest for loans.

In 1971, market rates fell, and the IDB lowered its lending rates. However, by reducing them more slowly and to a lesser extent than was happening on the market and by enduring complaints on the part of the public and politicians that its rates were too high, the Bank brought its rates on new loans into better relationship with debenture rates, as Table 31 shows.

By 1973, rates on the market were starting to rise again, and the Bank's lending rates slipped back into their old position vis-à-vis its debenture rates. In the first half of 1973 there was, as we shall see later, a controversy in political circles about the future of the IDB, and this may have interfered with consideration of interest rates. In any event, although the matter was considered in the latter part of May and in June, it was not until early July that an increase was actually approved by the board of directors. From then on, there was a steady increase in the spread between the two rates.

Part of the increased spread in 1975 was due to a change in August 1974 in the way in which the rate of interest on new debentures was determined. The amount added to the yield on government bonds to determine the debenture rate was cut from 0.60 per cent to 0.125 per cent. This last percentage was the basis upon which debenture interest was based for all crown corporations that came under the section of the Finance Administration Act that was to apply in the future to the Federal Business Development Bank into which the IDB was to be converted. The governor of the Bank of Canada felt it reasonable to give the IDB the advantage of these easier terms, since it would shortly be operating under them anyway.

Policies on prepayment of loans and various fees

While interest on loans provided the bulk of the Bank's income, other sources were extremely important in the years 1968–75. From 1967 to 1970, the Bank operated at virtually a break-even point as far as lending operations were concerned. 'Other Income,' mostly from various fees, provided whatever net income was transferred to the reserve fund as profit. This was clearly shown in Table 30. Details of 'Other Income' are given in Table 34.

The collecting of a stand-by fee does not appear to have disturbed borrowers. The payment of a commitment fee was sometimes disputed, but after the Bank was successful in 1969 in a court action to collect a large one for over $13,000, there was little difficulty; in 1973, the Bank put a limit of $5,000 on the amount of commitment fee that could be recovered from a single loan. Regarding the prepayment indemnity, there was a

TABLE 34

Other income ($thousands) 1968–75

	Prepayment indemnity	Stand-by fees	Commitment fees	Discount on Treasury Bills	Other	Total
1968	192	245	27	3	192	659
1969	172	256	63	5	39	535
1970	156	327	39	69	28	619
1971	465	269	153	114	236	1,237
1972	906	313	82	112	101	1,514
1973	1,456	439	124	144	360	2,523
1974	875	708	127	190	15	1,915
1975	816	675	171	325	(107)*	1,880

*Sundry adjustments.

good deal of doubt expressed 1968–75 by officials within the Department of Finance, and sometimes even by the IDB's head office. The department thought it incongruous that the IDB, supposedly making a loan where the borrower could not obtain money elsewhere on reasonable terms and conditions, should impose a special charge on a borrower that had ultimately been able to attract other lenders and retire its IDB loan. Officials at Finance saw this policy as evidence that the Bank clung to its borrowers and sought to prevent their financing elsewhere. They were particularly critical of fees collected by the Bank from IDB loans refinanced from the proceeds of loans by other crown agencies such as the Adjustment Assistance Board.

The general manager of the IDB took a different view. In a letter to the president written in February 1973, he recited the basic arguments for collecting a prepayment indemnity – the generous attitude of the Bank toward accepting prepayments, the need to cover costs, the rapid decrease of the indemnity to zero within six years, and the unsuitability of the Bank's becoming a shopping centre for other lenders – he concluded: 'Quite frankly, I think there is no more justifiable source from which our operations can be sustained than those who, having received assistance from us when they were unable to obtain financing elsewhere, find themselves, through the success of their operation, through the sale of their business, or through their having become attractive to other sources of financing, able to retire our loan ahead of time.'

Figures on prepayments that retired IDB loans in full suggest that the Bank's policy did not seriously interfere with prepayments or with a borrower's wish to switch its loan over to another lender. Table 35 shows the sources of full prepayments for 1968–75 and the number of loans

TABLE 35

Sources of prepayments ($thousands) that retired IDB loans in full 1968–75

	Other lenders	Sale of assets or business	Working capital or earnings	Other sources	Total	Number of prepaid loans as percentage of number of customers at previous year-end
1968	1,255	2,581	116	1,228	5,180	3.3
1969	1,335	2,087	249	1,760	5,431	3.3
1970	1,236	2,652	97	1,084	5,069	2.7
1971	1,984	3,506	338	5,179	11,007	3.3
1972	10,061	6,559	1,830	5,455	23,905	6.2
1973	25,037	11,469	2,750	7,269	46,525	8.3
1974	10,973	12,308	1,047	10,152	34,480	6.4
1975	7,517	9,958	1,957	7,723	27,155	4.8

prepaid in full in each of these years as a percentage of the number of customers on the Bank's books at the previous year-end.

The proportion of prepayments from each source naturally fluctuated from year to year, but the amount prepaid by other lenders increased to a substantial level 1972–5. Also, although the table does not show it, there was a steady tendency toward earlier prepayments. In 1968, 63 per cent of the number of loans prepaid in full were paid off after they had been reduced to 50 per cent or less of their original amount, i.e. the majority of prepayments occurred in the latter years of a loan's life. By 1972 the proportion had swung the other way. In that year, 58 per cent were prepaid while more than 50 per cent of the loan was outstanding; i.e. the majority of prepayments occurred in a loan's early years. This trend toward early prepayment continued, and in 1975 62 per cent of the prepayments in full retired loans with more than 50 per cent of the original amount outstanding.

The table also gives, for each year, the number of prepayments in full expressed as a percentage of the number of customers on the Bank's books at the beginning of the year. From 1968 to 1971 inclusive, this averaged 3.2 per cent. From 1972 to 1975, the average was 6.4 per cent. In other words, of the loans outstanding at the beginning of each year 1972–5, 1 in 20 or less was, on average, prepaid in full in the ensuing year. These figures suggest that prepayments were not seriously discouraged by the Bank's policies.

Among the sources of 'Other Income' shown in Table 34, an important one from 1971 on was 'Discount on Treasury Bills.' It was the practice of the Bank of Canada to buy the IDB's debentures in round amounts to

TABLE 36

Operating results expressed as percentage of average loans and investments outstanding
1967–75

	1967	1968	1969	1970	1971	1972	1973	1974	1975
Income as percentage of average loans and investments	7.40	7.67	7.88	8.58	9.46	9.81	9.97	10.03	10.68
Less:									
Debenture cost	4.38	4.67	5.09	5.76	5.96	5.88	5.99	6.37	6.79
Operating cost	2.22	2.22	2.25	2.25	2.30	2.55	2.69	2.81	2.77
Net profit before provision for losses	0.80	0.78	0.54	0.57	1.20	1.38	1.29	0.85	1.12

SOURCE: *Annual Reports*, 1971 and 1975.

cover anticipated cash needs of the Bank. Unexpected inflows of cash, as, for example, from prepayments, and unexpected delays in disbursements could create surplus balances from the proceeds of debenture sales. In 1970, the general manager proposed that these cash balances be invested in short-term treasury bills. By 1971, the annual income from this source was over $100,000. From 1968 to 1975 inclusive, the total earned in this way was $962,000.

Operating costs

As we have done for other periods, we can bring together on a common basis all the elements of the Bank's operating statements by expressing each of them as a percentage of average loans and investments outstanding, as in Table 36. Figures for 1967 are given for comparative purposes. The table shows the narrow margin of profit on which the Bank operated up to 1970. In that year and in 1969, the margin was the lowest in the Bank's history. In the next four years it increased, although it was still well below what it had been in the 1950s, before debenture financing was predominant.

The table shows the relative steadiness of operating costs during a period when the economy was experiencing a general rise in costs and prices. Including figures from Table 21, it will be seen that from 1964 to 1971 inclusive they remained in the narrow range of 2.19 per cent to 2.33 per cent of average loans and investments outstanding. Even when they then rose, they did not pass what they had been in 1962 (the start of the previous period), 2.83 per cent.

TABLE 37

Staff costs per employee and operating costs per customer 1945−75

	Average annual staff costs ($) per employee	Average operating costs ($) per customer on books of Bank
1945−55	4,785	1,264
1956−61	6,388	1,132
1962−7	7,505	939
1968−75	11,857	982

A rough measure of inflationary influences is presumably given in the rising staff costs per employee. From 1962 (the start of the previous period) to 1975, these increased from an average of $6,900 to an average of $14,700. In the same period, average operating costs (including staff expenses) per customer actually declined from $1,209 to $1,174. Table 37 compares these figures for the four periods of the Bank's history.

In spite of a rising burden of expense as reflected in staff costs per employee, the Bank had some success in reducing costs measured in terms of customers. Presumably, this resulted from greater efficiency following the various procedural reforms carried out after 1963−4, particularly between 1968 and 1975. Nevertheless, 'unit costs' in terms of customers were rising in the Bank's final years, as the table shows. The credit staff in the branches was, year by year, performing new tasks to an ever-growing extent in the form of advertised visits, speeches, and other publicity activities and management seminars for businessmen. Also, from 1973 on, the Bank was carrying a growing expense for the advisory services department, which produced virtually no income. In 1974, the net operating cost of the department was between $400,000 and $450,000. By 1975, this was considerably increased by preparations for the expanded duties to be assumed in the new bank. The total for that year was approximately $550,000. This represented 1.8 per cent of the operating costs of $30 million in 1975, as shown in Table 30.

Loss experience

We now come to the final steps in determining the Bank's operating profit at the end of each fiscal year − the transferring from earnings into the reserve for losses of an amount to protect against future write-offs on loans outstanding. The growth in loan volume was naturally reflected in a build-up of the reserve for losses. At the end of 1967, the balance was $7,500,000; at the end of 1975, it was $26,800,000.[1] Each of these figures

TABLE 38

Various aspects of reserve for losses 1945–75

	Average proportion (percentage) of loan balances outstanding regarded as satisfactory	Average reserve as a percentage of 'loan balances outstanding plus undisbursed commitments'	Average margin (percentage) in reserve for losses, in excess of estimated probable losses
1945–55	n.a.	1.37	46
1956–61	84.6	1.56	26
1962–7	85.8	1.72	52
1968–75	90.0	2.11	104

was close to being the same percentage of loan balances and undisbursed commitments. The 1967 figure was 1.94 per cent, and that for 1975 was 2.06 per cent. In the years between, however, the percentage rose to peaks of 2.37 per cent in 1972 and 2.36 per cent in 1973; at these levels the Bank's auditors felt quite strongly that the balance in the reserve for losses account was as large as could be justified and that to increase it would diminish the final profit unreasonably.

Although the reserve in 1975 was just about the same percentage of loan balances and undisbursed commitments as in 1967, the 1975 balance was considered to provide a much greater margin of safety. This margin was equal to 143 per cent of estimated probable losses, as compared with a margin of 79 per cent in 1967. It must be remembered that the margin is the surplus that would be left in the reserve if all estimated possible losses had been charged against it first. In other words, the reserve held at the end of 1975 was nearly equal to $2\frac{1}{2}$ times the estimated probable losses. In spite of moves made to relax credit criteria, to diminish the emphasis on security, and to expedite the processing of loan applications, the quality of the Bank's loan portfolio was believed to have improved. In 1967, 86.4 per cent of loan balances outstanding had been categorized as 'Satisfactory,' but in 1975 91.2 per cent were so classified.[2]

Table 38 gives figures for these various aspects of the Bank's loan portfolio and reserve for losses for each period of the Bank's history.

In 1974, the method for determining the amount to be held in the reserve was changed slightly. The traditional method had been to set a reserve at whatever seemed an adequate percentage of the sum of loan balances outstanding and undisbursed commitments, on the basis of experience and business conditions and in light of the estimate of probable loan losses, but without using the latter in any more precise way.

It was recognized in 1974, however, that the adequacy of the reserve could be affected drastically from one year to another if a large loan of several hundred thousand dollars or more suddenly presented the prospect of a substantial write-off or, conversely, as actually happened then, if some among such large accounts previously expected to produce large write-offs improved to the point that this was no longer the case. Accordingly, a new procedure was approved with the concurrence of the auditors, as described in the following extract from a letter from the chief general manager to the president: 'We wrote to the external auditors some time ago ... suggesting to them that this year we should seek to arrive at our reserve by a different method. This would involve ensuring that the reserve had in it, first, a reasonable percentage of outstanding loans and commitments to cover probable losses on all loans, and secondly, a specific amount to cover probable losses on large loans ... They were in complete agreement with this change of approach.' The 'reasonable percentage' was still set arbitrarily at whatever seemed appropriate on the basis of experience and in light of estimated probable loan losses. This procedure was followed in 1974 and 1975 and resulted in a somewhat smaller reserve.

Few aspects of the Bank's operations were more frequently spoken of in public discussions or were more misunderstood than its loan-loss experience. In 1973, a large trust company announced its intention to make term loans to small and medium-sized businesses, partly on the grounds that the IDB's low loss rate, described in the announcement as 'around 0.5% of annual disbursements over recent years,' indicated that the risk of financing such businesses was extremely small.[3] An understanding of the Bank's policies on the management of bad loans and loan write-offs would have shown that the Bank's true loss rate was much higher than 0.5 per cent.

We have, in this book, been viewing the Bank's loss experience by relating actual write-offs to net authorizations made in the years in which the loans written off originated.[4] As we approach the end of the Bank and its absorption into a new bank, this exercise becomes less satisfactory; for some loans insufficient time may have passed yet to determine their final fate, and the practices and policies of the new bank for dealing with such cases may differ from those of the IDB.

The IDB found that 80 per cent or more of its write-offs would occur within the five or six years following the year of authorization. For loans approved up to 1974 or 1975 most write-offs would probably have developed by 1981, the last year for which full figures are available at the

TABLE 39

Percentage of net authorizations written off less any amounts
recovered later 1945–75

Year of authorization	Percentage of net authorizations
1945–55	0.47
1956–61	1.18
1962–7	1.34
1968–75	2.12
1945–75	1.84

time of writing. Of course, a certain portion of loss experience presumably has yet to be established for these loans. While bearing this in mind, however, and recognizing that the record is still incomplete for loans made in the IDB's closing years, we can obtain a picture of loss experience for the IDB's loans up to the end of the new bank's fiscal year ended 31 March 1981. Bringing forward the figures for previous periods, we can make up Table 39.

This table illustrates about as well as a set of figures could the evolution of the Bank's lending policies and practices: the extension of the Bank's operations to embrace all types of business enterprises, the steady movement toward placing less emphasis on security, the conscious desire to be ever more responsive to requests for help and to take greater risks, the extension of the branch network into less well-developed parts of the country, the simplification and shortening of procedures for loan applications to improve service to applicants and the steady decentralization of decision-making authority. All these developments undoubtedly increased the risks of the Bank's loans and were reflected in the increasing proportion of loans written off. In addition, the impact of the economic recession of the late 1970s and the early 1980s on borrowers of the Bank's last years, and particularly of 1974 and 1975, contributed to a sharp increase in write-offs of loans made in the period 1968–75. The end result of all these factors was a rate of loss over the life of the IDB somewhat higher than the estimate of 1.50 per cent made by Mr Towers back in 1944.

The amount written off in 1975 deserves a brief comment. As was explained earlier, it was the IDB's practice not to write off any portion of a loan until the tangible security for it had been realized on. There was then no source from which the balance of the loan could be recovered, except perhaps for personal guarantees, so that the full loss faced by the Bank was known, to all intents and purposes. One reason for this policy was that it was considered sound discipline, and favourable to achieving the greatest recovery on a loan, that the account should remain under administration for the outstanding balance until at least the tangible security was disposed of. Even then the possibility of recovering under guarantees was not lost sight of, though often the circumstances of the guarantor might require some sort of a compromise. In the life of the Bank, nearly $1 million was recovered from guarantees and other items of miscellaneous security after items of tangible security had been disposed of and the remaining loan balances written off.

In the fall of 1974, however, the policy on write-offs was changed to permit writing off whatever portion of a large 'doubtful' loan did not appear to be covered by the expected sale value of the fixed asset security. This new policy was only applied in 1975; in that year four large loans were partially written off before the tangible security was disposed of. These partial write-offs added up to $1,030,000 out of total write-offs of $3,735,000. Normal practice was departed from in this way because the individual potential losses in these accounts were considered fairly large, and it was felt that the Bank's statement as it entered the new bank (the FBDB) should reflect these substantial anticipated losses.

The Bank's loss experience is not the only measure of the quality of its loans. A survey made in 1973 of loans authorized from 1958 to 1970 showed that from 20 per cent to 40 per cent of loans would be regarded as in an unsatisfactory condition at one time or another before they were retired; most of these, however, would ultimately work out of their difficulties and regain a satisfactory position.[5] Also, for the Bank as a whole, payments on approximately 10 per cent of loan accounts would usually be in arrears following the monthly date for instalment payments. In fact, at some branches the proportion of accounts in arrears was sometimes 25 per cent or more. The arrears situation at a branch, however, was often regarded as a reflection of a branch's administration of its loan accounts rather than as an indication of potential loss for the Bank.

The best continuing insight into the state of the Bank's loans was provided by the annual loan review at the end of August each year, when all loans were carefully analysed and classified. At the review in 1967, 86 per cent of outstanding balances had been considered fully satisfactory. At the review in 1975, the proportion was 91 per cent; of the remainder it was believed that a further 5 per cent, although not wholly satisfactory, would be repaid without the Bank's having to resort to its security.

TABLE 40

Annual average net profit yield on equity and additional interest as percentage of equity (shares plus reserve fund) 1945–75

	Average annual yield of net profit	Average annual yield of additional interest	Combined 'yield'
1945–55	2.6	–	2.6
1956–61	3.7	–	3.7
1962–7	1.3	1.4	2.7
1968–75	2.6	3.5	6.1

SOURCE: See Appendix v.

Yield on the IDB's equity

Perhaps we should end our review of the Bank's operating results by looking at them from the standpoint of its shareholder, the Bank of Canada. The first president of the IDB, Graham Towers, had been hopeful that the profits earned by the Bank would represent a reasonable return on the Bank of Canada's investment in it. These hopes faded as the years went by, but the addition to the rate of interest paid on debentures of an extra fraction of 1 per cent did provide further revenues for the Bank of Canada from the IDB's operations and perhaps compensated for Mr Towers's hopes not being fully realized. In Table 40, there are given, for the four periods of the Bank's history, figures for the average annual yield on equity represented by profits transferred to the reserve fund, estimates of the additional yield from payments of debenture interest (amounting to o.60 per cent from 1962 to 1974 and o.125 per cent thereafter), and a combined 'yield' resulting from these two figures taken together.[6]

When ownership of the IDB was transferred from the Bank of Canada to the federal government at the end of 1975, the Bank of Canada received payment only for the face value of its IDB shares and no payment for the reserve fund. This means that, whether or not the extra payments on debenture interest to the Bank of Canada formed part of the return to it on its investment in the IDB, this additional interest payment proved in the end to be the only sort of extra revenue or 'yield' received and retained by the Bank of Canada for its having invested in the IDB.

Review of the Bank's record

This completes our last survey of the results of the operations of the IDB. In its thirty-one years, it approved 65,000 loans totalling over $3 billion for slightly more than 48,000 businesses in all parts of Canada. In some fields of business, the Bank's assistance was undoubtedly very important.[7] Over 18,000 loans were approved for more than 12,000 manufacturers, nearly 5,000 loans were authorized for 4,000 restaurants, and 4,500 loans were approved for 3,300 motels and hotels. Even in agriculture, the Bank made a significant contribution through 4,500 loans approved for 3,600 enterprises.

Although some opposed to the Bank's establishment in 1944 had said that it would finance only bankrupts, nearly all its borrowers succeeded. More than 90 per cent of them were able to retire their IDB loans in a normal manner from their operations.[8]

This large amount of financial assistance to business was achieved on the basis of a share investment in the Bank that never exceeded $78 million and averaged only $35 million or so during the life of the Bank. The Bank earned a profit each year, although sometimes it was small, and in no year was it large. From its revenues, it paid interest on its debentures, met all its expenses, covered any loan losses, and built up a reserve against future losses which, when the Bank reached the end of its last fiscal year, was equal to $2\frac{1}{2}$ times estimated possible write-offs of loans then outstanding. After all this, the Bank was able to build up an accumulated surplus of nearly $38 million from its earnings.

The following quotation from the Winnipeg *Free Press* for 7 February 1975 provides a fitting close to this review of the IDB's operational results: 'It isn't often one hears the competition dispense words of admiration – particularly when the rival happens to be the government. John D. Thompson, president of RoyNat, the largest supplier of funds to small and medium sized business in the private sector, makes no bones about it. RoyNat's major single rival, the Industrial Development Bank of Canada, is the "best-run" of all federal government agencies, he said this week when visiting Winnipeg. "The IDB has done a good job" in backing the smaller business enterprises of Canada, said Mr. Thompson, speaking of an organization that has done much in making RoyNat's market more competitive during the last decade.'

New initiatives

Advisory services

The regional structure was completely in place by 1967–8, and the Bank was able, on the basis of the growth that started then and the momentum it generated, to undertake some new initiatives. The most important was probably the establishment of a new department to provide a variety of advisory services to the owners and managers of small businesses, intended to improve their managerial skills.

At a regular meeting of the board of directors on 1 September 1970, D.F. Matheson, the director from Saskatchewan, referred, during a discussion of the Bank's loan experience, to the special skills represented on the IDB staff in engineering, financial analysis, and accountancy and suggested that these might be made more available to assist small businesses in organizing themselves and handling their problems. He had heard some complain that the Bank became very active in a borrower's affairs when the latter became bankrupt, but was not nearly so active or helpful before the event. He suggested that a change in this practice could help small businesses significantly.

The operational staff of the Bank had always believed that it did give 'counsel' when it investigated a loan application or in the course of administering a loan. The Bank's engineers would discuss with an applicant or borrower the costing methods used, the suitability of a machine to be purchased, the best layout for a plant, and whether building plans were sound, and a credit officer would analyse working capital needs and the adequacy of investment. The Bank's annual reports regularly included references to this sort of advisory help. In a directive to the staff in 1967, Mr James, the general manager, quoted from a memorandum he had prepared for the Porter Commission on the subject: 'We have always taken the view that we are not in the management consulting business, and we have usually avoided giving direct advice, as such, to borrowers ... The approach normally taken by the Bank is to avoid involvement or interference in the operations of the business, but to discuss the problems with the customer.'

The day following the board meeting at which Mr Matheson had spoken, the matter was discussed by the general manager and E.C. Scott, the chief engineer. A couple of weeks later, Mr Scott made a preliminary report recommending that the Bank set up specialist teams in each region to take over the administration of any loan account where the borrower was in trouble and to help the business find a solution to its problems. Insofar as this might represent 'counselling,' there was no specific statutory authority for it, but it was felt that subsection 24(e) of the IDB Act, which empowered the Bank to 'do all such things as may be necessary for carrying out the intention and purposes of this Act and not specifically prohibited by this Act,' covered any plan to counsel a borrower or carry on related activities.

Mr Scott saw the potential for management assistance as extending far beyond the mere administration of loans in trouble and as including the development of management expertise among small businesses through research, seminars and discussion groups, industry studies, and information booklets. In May 1971, a committee was set up to study the matter further, comprising Mr Scott as chairman; J.E. Nordin, supervisor, Quebec Region; K. Elliott, a credit officer in the Ontario Region; and D.M. Carter, a credit officer at GMO. Mr Scott visited organizations carrying on the kind of activities contemplated, in England, Ireland, the Netherlands, and the United States, as well as various agencies in Canada, such as the National Research Council and provincial bodies providing some kind of business advisory service. In September, fresh instructions were issued to the Bank's staff stressing the opportunities for offering helpful guidance that would occur during interviews with loan applicants and in the administration of accounts.

In November, the committee made its report. Its principal recommendations were that the Bank publish a series of pamphlets on management problems; that it organize local training seminars for operators of small businesses, particularly in localities where such seminars were not regularly available; that libraries of relevant material be established at regional and branch offices; that the Bank publish industry and economic studies for internal and external use; and that it at least experiment with 'diagnostic / realization teams' to administer loan accounts in trouble, 'to provide early advice and initiate corrective action,' and to handle any realization of security that became necessary.

The recommendations were adopted, except for the last one. The idea of special teams to administer accounts in trouble had arisen before in the Bank, and there were two views on it. Those in favour saw it as effective in the concentrated and experienced attention given these accounts and efficient in the freeing of credit officers to concentrate on the processing of new applications. Others saw it as limiting the experience of credit officers; they felt that it was healthy for every credit officer to wrestle with the problems that could arise once a loan was made and, where liquidation of security was ultimately necessary, to gain first-hand experience of it. Accordingly, although at least one region, Quebec, did introduce the practice, it was not adopted as Bank policy.

In December 1971, the program was announced to the Bank, and shortly afterwards Mr Scott was appointed director of advisory services to be in charge of it. He was succeeded as chief engineer by A. Mackie.

Special efforts were made to give the program an attractive and lively public image. A special logo, in two colours, was designed for it, it had its own stationery letterhead, and its publications had colourful and well-designed covers. These were also ingeniously economical. The pamphlets on management problems were designed so that, once printed, they could be assembled by the staff in the Bank's own mailing room, and the cover of each pamphlet had a circular hole in it through which could be read the title of the pamphlet on the page underneath. In this way, one stock of covers could be used for all pamphlets. A special bookcase and display rack with an electric name panel was supplied to branches for the display of booklets on management problems published by others as well as those published by the Bank.

The program was an extraordinary success. In the first full fiscal year following its adoption, 1973, over 100 seminars were held attended by about 2,000 owners and managers of small businesses and by 1974 200 seminars were being held annually. These were usually conducted in small communities – some with a population of less than 5,000 people – where services of this sort were not usually available. Each seminar dealt with some aspect of management. For example, the first series taught the basics of the financial statement of a small business, its effect on expansion, and the use of an operating forecast in choosing a plan for growth. A seminar usually lasted one day, and case studies, group discussions, and brief lectures were used. Members of the staff from one of the Bank's branches presented the seminars, but they were usually associated with a teacher of business or an accountant or some other professional person from the local community. A great deal of advance preparation, publicity, and careful selection of equipment and premises was required, although in a report in 1973 Mr Scott said: 'Improvisation has been the key in many locations where facilities for meeting are often far from ideal. Seminars have been held in basements, restaurants, motels, golf clubs, Legion halls, schools, and, in one case, in the basement below a strip-tease establishment.'

The pamphlets issued by the Bank were just as big a success. The English series was entitled Minding Your Own Business and the French, Votre affaire, c'est notre affaire. Examples of early titles were: *Giving Credit to Your Customers*, *Forecasting for an Existing Business*, *Managing Your Current Assets*, and *Managing Your Cash*. These pamphlets were issued free, and within a year the Bank had a regular mailing list of 5,000 names, including all the chartered banks, most of the national accounting firms, high schools, colleges, universities, libraries, consulting firms, and large corporations. In addition, it was responding to requests for individual pamphlets at the rate of 200 or so per day. By 1974, the mailing list had grown to 15,000, and a total of 500,000 pamphlets had been distributed.

The Bank's view of its work in the seminars and the pamphlets is illustrated by the following quotation from an internal report on the seminars: 'It is quite apparent, as we had expected, that much of the management training material on the market is completely unsuitable for the operator of a small business. The programs (and pamphlets) we are presenting have been specially written for small operators in simple language without management training jargon.'

A serious attempt was made to generate industry studies out of the Bank's lending experience, but it was concluded that not enough useful material would emerge to make the effort worthwhile. Successful (and unsuccessful) enterprises in the same line of business displayed few common elements in working capital, debt-equity relationships, or cost and profit patterns; each business was a story unto itself, so that the idea of publishing studies of this sort was dropped. However, in November 1973, the Bank started publishing a *Small Business Bulletin* for free distribution to inform the public, particularly the small business community, of sources of business assistance and to report developments of interest to business. This had a mailing list of about 25,000. The Bank also designed courses on management suitable for business or community colleges, but the use of these involved financing that the Bank could not supply. As a result, they were adopted only slowly by colleges and educational institutions.

The department also took over responsibility for one of the oldest of the IDB's activities: providing training and guidance to development banks in other countries. Its reputation, as one of the oldest, largest, and most successful development banks, was high in all parts of the world, and other banks, often under the auspices of the World Bank, would send senior employees to the IDB to study its methods. From 1945 to 1975 inclusive, approximately 150 visitors from development financing institutions in forty countries visited the Bank for periods varying from a few days to several weeks.

Sometimes the IDB was asked to lend someone as a consultant to another country. In 1965, the general manager, A.N.H. James, made a study for the World Bank of the possibilities for a development bank in Jamaica. In 1967, he headed up a Mission of the United Nations Development program to investigate the prospects for a regional bank in the Caribbean. As a result, the Caribbean Development Bank was established. In 1969, R.V. Crank, a credit officer with the IDB, was loaned for a year to the Asian Development Bank to give assistance to the Vietnam Development Bank in Saigon.

In 1971, on the strength of Mr James's and Mr Crank's experiences, it was decided that the Bank would be willing to make occasional arrangements of a similar sort as long as the officer's absence was not for more than three months, preferably for a shorter period. It was believed that experiences of this sort would benefit the IDB through broadening the outlook of any of its officers that might participate in such a program. The willingness of the IDB to help other development banks in this way was communicated to them regularly at international conferences. As a result, between 1971 and 1975, officers were loaned for short periods to development financial institutions in St Lucia, Iran, Jamaica, Uganda, Nigeria, Ghana, Antigua, Tanzania, and Zambia. In addition, in 1973 a particularly close association for providing assistance in training and guidance was developed with ALIDE, the association of development banks in Latin America.

Apart from such expertise in their work as the IDB's officers might possess, they were found to command a remarkable range of languages, and this added to their qualifications for offering guidance in the international field. Among the Bank's officers, there was a capability in eighteen languages apart from English and French; these included Afrikaans, Arabic, Hindi, Hindustani, Russian, and Urdu.

Quest for fresh policy on the acquisition of equities

The second major initiative undertaken by the Bank 1968–75 was the search for a fresh orientation of policy on the extension of assistance to a business through the acquisition of its shares. The powers given to the IDB to extend financial assistance were set out in subsection 16(1) of its act (*Revised Statutes*, 1970, cap 1 9) which said in part: 'the Bank may lend or guarantee loans of money to that person, and where that person is a corporation, (d) enter into underwriting agreements in respect of the whole of any issue of stock, bonds or debentures of the corporation, and (e) purchase or otherwise acquire (i) with a view to resale thereof, the whole or any part of any issue of stock, bonds or debentures of the corporation.'

As a rule, references in this book to financial assistance extended by the IDB have been in terms of loans. This has been done for brevity and convenience and is only very slightly inaccurate. The Bank participated in an underwriting only once, and it approved approximately 60 guarantees and 81 investments. By comparison, it authorized a total of 65,000 loans.

For many years, the acquisition of shares was seen as a means by which the Bank could, through sharing in the growing worth of a company to which it had made a particularly risky or seriously under-secured loan, derive a greater compensation for the risk it took than the payment of interest on the loan would provide. Most examples involved fairly large loans. To the extent that a loan was seen as under-secured, the Bank might consider itself as sharing the financial risks and hazards faced by the owner himself and entitled, therefore, to share with him in whatever profits or growth in equity value the business might develop. The Bank's participation in equity might take various forms, including shares by way of a bonus, the convertibility into shares of some part of a loan, the actual purchase of common shares, or the right to purchase shares at a future date. Each investment was tailored to fit the circumstances of individual cases.

Mr. Towers stated the earliest version of policy in a memorandum in January 1947: 'Loans which justify our asking for a share in the profits are ones in which (a) the amount of capital invested by the proprietors is on the "thin" side compared with our advances and / or (b) heavy dependence is placed on the success of operations rather than on the realizable value of our security. Without rigidly ruling out acquisition of common stock either by purchase or as a bonus, our normal policy should be ... to lend part on mortgage security and part in the form of preferred, with some percentage of participation in profits.'

This seemed to imply that shares would usually be acquired only as part of a loan arrangement, that they would usually be preferred shares, and that they would normally be paid for. Within a year, however, they were being obtained as a bonus in connection with a loan, and common shares were more often acquired than preferred.

In 1954, the appearance in the Bank's profit and loss statement of a large profit from the sale of some shares held by the Bank led to the inclusion in the annual report of the first public statement of policy: 'In a relatively small number of cases the Bank has taken minority equity positions in companies financed by the Bank. These have been cases in which the Bank's loan was fairly substantial both in absolute amount and in relation to the capital invested by the proprietors, and in which heavy dependence was placed on the success of the business rather than on the realizable value of the security ... During the past year the majority shareholders of several such companies whose affairs had prospered arranged to sell out to other interests, and the Bank took advantage of this opportunity to sell its shares also.'[1] The first two sentences state the Bank's established policy; the last sentence illustrates the principal way in which the Bank hoped to realize from the shares that potential additional return that had induced it to make a loan.

In the next few years, the matter was a lively topic within the Bank, at least for discussion at supervisors' conferences. At the 1956 conference, the president, J.F. Coyne, is reported to have 'led the meeting to a discussion of whether we are liberal enough, and whether we should take equity positions.' At the 1957 and 1958 conferences, enthusiasm was carried to the point of contemplating the Bank's acquiring as much as 30 per cent to 50 per cent of the capital stock of a business. At the same time, the taking of shares as a bonus for making a loan was dropped from the Bank's policy; any shares acquired were to be paid for. At the 1964 conference, the subject aroused the usual excitement, and one supervisor was moved to exclaim: 'IDB has pioneered the mortgage lending field. Let us now do the same in equities!'

This was followed in 1965 by the issuance of a new circular on policy. It changed things little, but a few features are worth recording. It was not expected that the Bank would hold more than 30 per cent of the common stock of a company, although it might acquire 100 per cent of an issue of preferred. The Bank's investment in one company should not normally exceed 1 per cent of the Bank's total assets, and total stockholdings in all companies should not be greater than 10 per cent of the Bank's total assets. These were pretty generous limits and suggest that those drawing them up had great expectations. The first guideline would have permitted an investment at that time of $2 million in the stock of one company; even as a loan, this amount would have been one of the largest the Bank ever made. The second limit would have permitted total investments of $23 million at the time (1965), as compared with a total of $800,000 actually held five years later. It was not expected that the Bank would normally exercise its voting rights as a shareholder or nominate a person to a board of directors. In spite of all this, little happened. In some years, one, two, or three equity transactions would be approved at a time when, by contrast, the Bank was making 2,000 or more loans per year.

There were many reasons for this inactivity. Despite their oft-stated desire to get involved in the equity field, for most of the Bank's officers it was strange country. They were more comfortable making loans. Holding shares involved difficult problems. If the Bank held a minority interest in a small or private company, how could it be sold so that the Bank's investment could be recovered? Might it not be 'locked in' in such a case? If it purchased shares, how could a price acceptable to the Bank and the other shareholders be arrived at? What if the shares held by the Bank represented the 'balance of power' between two other contending groups of shareholders? What if the other shareholders sold their shares and left the Bank associated with an entirely new group unknown to it but exercising majority control? How could the Bank extend financial assistance through the purchase of shares if most other shareholders had put their money into the business through loans, so that the dollar figure for share capital on the balance sheet of the business was very small? In the event that the Bank wanted to sell its shareholdings, should it give other shareholders the right of first refusal? If so, at what price?

A peculiar problem that had received attention since the early days of the Bank was that the IDB Act required that any share acquisitions must be made 'with a view to resale.'[2] This was interpreted in various ways. One view was that these words were put in the act merely to reassure people that it was not the intention that the Bank become the permanent holder of stock in corporations. Another was that the phrase required that, when shares were acquired by the Bank, there should be a specific plan for their resale to be carried out quite soon. Uncertainty about the legal import of these words may have inhibited the Bank's staff regarding the whole matter of share acquisitions.

The development of much activity in equities was also discouraged by the violent criticism the Bank sometimes encountered as a result of share acquisitions. During the 1960s small businesses were sometimes pictured in the press as eager to find equity money to be invested in them, but this was not the Bank's experience. The IDB found a marked unwillingness on the part of the principals of many small businesses to dilute their equity. The principals were usually optimistic about the prospects of their business and did not want to share the fruits of success with others. If they needed financing, they did not want to give up equity in order to obtain it. In fact, if even the possibility of the Bank's acquiring some equity were raised, the principals would often regard the Bank's desire to share in the future growth of the business as almost scandalous, and not at all appropriate to a public agency such as the IDB. In the early evolution of the Bank's policy, special circumstances had sometimes seemed to justify some degree of equity participation by the Bank. However, these circumstances, such as a small capital base in an applicant business or a small security position relative to the size of a loan, had more and more become acceptable to the Bank as a satisfactory basis for a loan without bothering about shares or any extra compensation. In fact, lending policy in the late 1960s deliberately encouraged the making of loans in these very circumstances, and so the idea of asking a borrower for stock seemed to fade. The years 1969–71 saw no equity acquisitions.

Following the full regionalization of the Bank's operations 1967–8, when it began to re-examine various aspects of its operations, one that attracted thought was the extension of financial assistance through the acquisition of shares. Accordingly, in the autumn of 1970, when E.C. Scott was giving preliminary consideration to prospects for an advisory service program, the general manager asked Mabel Sprott, assistant superintendent, credits, to study the Bank's past experience with equities. Up to 31 December 1970, shareholdings that had cost the Bank some $900,000 had been disposed of at a profit of $1,500,000, so that, even though allowances were made for their having been held as a rule for five or six years without the interest income a loan would have produced, they had been quite profitable. Shortly afterwards, a committee was set up to make a broader study 'to include consideration of what guidelines of a simple and clear character might be laid down towards indicating where and when the taking of equity should be considered.' The committee comprised Miss Sprott, as chairman, and D.M. Carter and M.D. Légaré, credit officers at GMO. The regional assistant general managers were also canvassed for their ideas.

The committee recommended, in effect, that the Bank's policy should not be changed materially. In May 1972, fresh instructions were issued, but these did not change in any substantial way those previously in force. They were still based on the expectation that the acquisition of shares in a company would 'normally be only part of the financing provided by the Bank, with other financing taking the form of the normal term loan secured by a mortgage on fixed assets.'

This left still unanswered the question that had prompted the study and had arisen regularly within the Bank at conferences: 'Do we really know whether there is not something more that we can do for businesses through share capital purchases rather than with loans?' In June, the president, Louis Rasminsky, inquired of the general manager what initiatives seemed to present themselves for the Bank's further growth. The reply gave, as the most promising, the field of equities, if a policy could be established 'geared towards the needs, not of ourselves from the standpoint of profit realization, but from the standpoint of the requirements of the small businesses.' In September 1972, a conference with the regional assistant general managers was held, with the formulation of a new approach to equity transactions virtually the only item on the agenda.

Based on this conference, GMO set out the general terms of a new policy. 1 / The Bank should consider providing equity when it would best meet the needs of a business as opposed to debt financing and when the principals of the applicant company recognized that their real need was for equity and not a loan. 2 / Such a decision should be based principally on the needs of the business, not on the prospects of gain for the Bank itself. 3 / The Bank should be prepared to sell its interest in a private company to the other shareholders at any time at a reasonable price. 4 / In order to get the initiative and drive of the regional offices behind the program, they, as well as GMO, should have limits within which they could authorize investments. (Up to that time, all investment proposals had to be submitted to the board of directors for approval.) The results of the conference were reported to head office with the recommendation that the regional offices, as well as GMO, be given authority to approve share acquisitions up to some amount. At this point, however, other circumstances intervened, and we shall have to consider these now.

Government study of the IDB

While the IDB was re-examining its operations in these various ways and branching out into new activities, the government was perhaps casting around for programs and policies to extricate it from the toils in which 'the modern riddle of high unemployment combined with continuing inflation'[3] had entangled it and was showing more than usual interest in the Bank. In October 1970, the secretary of the Bank, Gray Hamilton, learned that the Department of Industry, Trade and Commerce had been asked by the government to make a study of all forms of government assistance to industrial development in Canada, including the Industrial Development Bank, and to analyse their strengths and weaknesses. A few months later, in April 1971, it was learned that the Department of Finance was also looking at the IDB as part of a study on the impact of foreign investment in Canada. In July, a further study of the Bank was made by the Department of Finance, this time in connection with IDB activity in the economically depressed parts of Canada. In December 1971, all this interest in the Bank seemed to come to a focus in a request by the cabinet for a review of IDB operations in general. Head office and GMO began preparing a large amount of reference material for what was expected to be a presentation to the cabinet by the president. This presentation was repeatedly deferred by the minister of finance, and in August 1972 the secretary learned that more than two months earlier the government had directed the minister of finance to bring forward himself a review of the IDB indicating possible changes in its operations. A deadline of 15 November was set for this review, and the on-again–off-again presentation by the Bank's president was now deferred to the same date.

In addition to these signs of special interest in the IDB, several references to the Bank appeared in the report on foreign direct investment in Canada prepared by a federal government working group under the Hon. Herb Gray and issued, after two years' preparation, in May 1972. The references included suggestions that implied a much closer connection between the government and the IDB than had existed in the past. One proposed a directive to the management of the Bank on its role in providing venture capital. Another envisaged removing the financing of manufacturers from the activities of the IDB entirely! This field was then to be combined with a General Adjustment Assistance Programme 'to provide a single instrument for assisting small and medium-sized Canadian-controlled firms to start up, rationalize and expand.'[4]

The accumulated effect of these incidents was to suggest that the government was considering drastic proposals affecting the future of the IDB. This aroused concern at head office and on the part of senior management personnel at GMO as to the amount of influence they might have on any decisions. The general interest in the Bank in government circles had resulted in a number of studies that seemed, to the Bank's officers, to have been prepared by departmental officials whose responsibilities had not previously involved a close acquaintance with the Bank. These studies were usually drafted, in their first versions at least, without reference to Bank personnel. Corrections of what were regarded as erroneous views were supplied by the Bank whenever the opportunity was presented, but there seemed no means by which such corrections could be communicated to the higher levels in government for whom the departmental studies were prepared, if the authors of these did not accept the Bank's comments, which was sometimes the case.

It was surprising for senior operational management personnel at GMO that such studies did not necessarily involve discussions with them on the part of the departmental officials making the studies. Operational management, knowing as it did how complex the Bank's operations were, how subtle were the concepts by which policies were defined and applied, and the extent to which the Bank's operations depended on the dedication of its employees to the Bank's difficult role, were disappointed that, within some departments, recommendations about the Bank might be made that had not been discussed with them first.

It was clear by the summer of 1972 that major decisions about the IDB were impending. It was important that the Bank find means of getting its story through to the members of the government who might be going to make these decisions. Those within the Bank believed that the IDB had been an enormous success, but there was not a great deal of evidence that this view was shared in the political world. The deputy minister of finance once confided to a meeting of the Bank's executive committee that anyone who mentioned the IDB at a cabinet meeting had to duck very quickly. Although the president of the Bank met with the minister of finance from time to time, he did so in his capacity as governor of the Bank of Canada. Their discussions usually dealt with matters of monetary and financial policy. Rarely would they discuss the IDB. The staff of the Bank believed that its achievements were fully documented in its annual reports, which were presented to Parliament each December and a copy of which went to each member of Parliament, but obviously this was not enough.

To communicate to the government, then, its thoughts on the various proposals that were appearing, the Bank was depending, first, on the presentation by the president for which the Bank had been waiting since December 1971. Second, the request of the government to the minister of finance in the summer of 1972 to bring forward a review of IDB operations was seen as opening up another avenue, since it was arranged that the Bank would formulate its own response to this request, apart from anything the Department of Finance itself might say.

It was at this point that the conclusions of the assistant general managers' conference held on 26 September 1972 to consider a new approach to equities were forwarded to the president for consideration by the board of directors. The conference results were accordingly weighed at head office in light of discussions obviously going on in governmental circles as to future roles for the Bank, and vigorous and forceful statements about the prospects for activity in equity investments were incorporated in the submission prepared as a response to the cabinet's request for a review of IDB operations. What had started inside the Bank simply as a cautious search for a more satisfactory and productive way of using a power to acquire company shares that the Bank had had from the beginning became now more a bold thrust by the Bank to impress the government with the force and energy of its future plans. Viewed in this way, the proposed new principles for equity acquisitions seemed to be not merely a revision of policy but an aggressive sortie into unknown territory and one that might not, in the eyes of some directors, be a suitable venture for the IDB to undertake. As a result, the directors did not approve the proposed delegation to GMO and the regions of some power to make equity investments, and it continued to be the case that any proposal for the acquisition of shares still had to be submitted to the directors.

There was little in subsequent events to indicate that all the strenuous efforts that went into preparing a submission for the minister of finance's review of IDB operations, or getting ready for the president's presentation to the cabinet, were particularly fruitful. The presentation took place in mid-December before the cabinet committee on economic policy. Once the president had made an introductory statement, however, the meeting passed off with a couple of hours of questioning of the president and general manager about some of the Bank's policies and practices. Much more significant as an indication of what the government was thinking of was an item in the *Financial Times* on 11 December that reported the Hon. John Turner, the minister of finance, as having given a strong hint that the next budget would contain new assistance programs for small businessmen. The reporter went on to comment: 'This might include extended lending, equity investing and management services from the IDB ... There could be extra help to train management. It is virtually an article of faith in Ottawa that money for new and small businesses is plentiful and that management skills are in short supply.'

Government proposal regarding the IDB

Support was given to Mr Turner's forecast about the government's intentions when the speech from the throne on 4 January 1973 referred to plans for aid to small business and for the extension and improvement of the IDB.[5] There ensued several months of hectic activity, with the departments of Finance and of Industry, Trade and Commerce producing numerous reports and memoranda about what to do about the IDB. Also, a new element entered the scene with the establishment by the government on 22 December 1972 of an interdepartmental committee on small business programmes, including the IDB, to review programs assisting small businesses with a view to the programs' co-ordination and integration. Nine departments were represented on the committee, plus the secretary of the IDB and of the Bank of Canada, Gray Hamilton.

The inclusion of the IDB in a list of 'programmes' to be studied by the committee illustrates the difference between how government departments viewed the Bank and how the Bank's employees saw it. To the latter it was not a program but a bank, or at least a development bank and an independent crown corporation.

The IDB now passed again through the experience with which it had become familiar in the previous year – trying to correct what it regarded as erroneous or unjust comments on its operations by anonymous memorandum writers – and, to all appearances, with no more success than before. The ideas about the Bank's future surfacing in the two departments as well as in the interdepartmental committee were now becoming clear. The two fields in which the Bank had seen scope for new initiatives – advisory services and equities – figured prominently in one degree or another. Regarding the former, it was suggested that, in addition to what the Bank already was doing or planning, such as seminars, pamphlets, libraries, and a business bulletin, it should offer a consultancy service to small businesses, act as a centre of information for all government assistance programs, and provide training in management. One possibility raised was that this whole group of advisory activities should be handled by a new crown corporation set up for the purpose, but the general view favoured leaving them with the IDB. Regarding equities, there was a variation in emphasis, depending on the view taken of the adequacy of existing sources of this kind of financing, but all proposals included some degree of equity activity by the Bank. To convey the full flavour of the whole bag of services that the Bank would offer, the favourite phrase among departmental personnel was a 'one-stop shopping service' for small businesses.

For this expanded role, it was suggested that the Bank should be separated from the Bank of Canada and set up as a separate crown corporation. This meant, of course, that the Bank would no longer obtain its financing from the Bank of Canada, but would probably be financed, like many other crown corporations, through the government. Some who made this proposal saw this last feature as an argument in favour of the change because it would subject the Bank to what was called 'normal budgetary control.' The deputy minister of finance phrased it differently one time when he said to the general manager with a cheerful grin: 'You won't be able to get your money from Big Daddy any more!'

In departmental circles, within the government, it was considered desirable that programs to help small business, which were threatening to proliferate, be concentrated under one co-ordinating head, viz. the Department of Industry, Trade and Commerce. Also, it was felt desirable to bring together the Bank's lending activities and the government's various counselling and advisory programs aimed at small business, since the guidance resulting from these latter had often a financial dimension. Finally, the view was held that a basic need of small businesses was for equity financing and that a change in the structure of the IDB might produce more activity in this field.[6] All three considerations were believed to support the idea of separating the IDB from the Bank of Canada.

The Bank, and particularly the operational management at Montreal, did not think that advice from outside as to what the IDB should or could do was needed. It attached great importance to the energy and spirit generated in the Bank's staff and felt that these were based partly on the freedom of decision that resulted from the Bank's independent corporate character. It believed that the success and integrity displayed by the Bank in its operating record warranted its being permitted to evolve on the basis of its statute and according to its best judgment. As far as equities were concerned, the Bank was in the process of developing a new approach which it expected to result in more activity. In advisory services, it was already doing some of the things proposed and was considering others. Regarding a management consultancy service, there was a feeling in the Bank that there was potentially a conflict of interest with the providing of financing. The original plans considered by the Bank for its advisory services had included a degree of counselling for any of its own borrowers in trouble. It had not yet been decided to implement this idea, although there were prospects that something might be done along this line in due course.

The position taken by the Bank was that it should continue to evolve and specialize as a source of capital assistance, instead of becoming a multi-purpose organization. It could extend and improve its own modest program of advisory services and perhaps add to it the providing of information on other assistance programs. However, to assign it a major mission in the provision of management counselling and training services would to a considerable degree alter its character and identity, with attendant risks of confusion of personality and conflicts in role as management consultant and lender. Any major efforts in these directions would also raise questions as to how they would be financed.

The proposed separation of the IDB from the Bank of Canada was opposed by the IDB's board, president, and chief general manager. The Bank of Canada was considered to be a valuable buffer between the IDB and the government and its various departments. It meant that it was not only free, but also seen to be free, of political involvement. It created a climate in which the officers of the Bank were able to do their work and exercise their judgment in a business-like manner and free of outside interference.

Governmental plans to convert the IDB into a new bank owned by government, with extended responsibility for advisory services

Through April, May, and June 1973, the views of the Bank were conveyed by the president to the minister of finance and the prime minister, in the latter case with the support of a committee of the directors and the chief general manager. However, on 6 July, the president was informed by the Hon. Alastair Gillespie, minister of industry, trade and commerce, that the government had decided to proceed with plans to set up a new corporation to absorb the IDB, and on 10 July the president and the chief general manager, along with Gray Hamilton, secretary; H.J. Russell, general manager, loans; W.C. Stuart, general manager, Ontario Region; and K.A. Powers, general manager, Atlantic Region, met with Mr Gillespie to review the statement by which he planned to announce this decision on 11 July.[7] The government's intention was to establish an independent crown corporation, to be called the Industrial Bank and Development Agency, to aid small business. The new agency was to incorporate the operations of the IDB, to the financing activities of which were to be added some new management services. The link with the Bank of Canada was to be severed. The agency would be owned directly by the federal government. It was to have its own board of directors and a full-time president as its chief executive officer, and it was to report to Parliament through the minister of industry, trade and commerce instead of through the minister of finance.

As part of the management services of the new agency, it was to take over the CASE program (Counselling Assistance to Small Enterprises) which had been set up in 1972 by the government to use retired business executives to counsel small businesses at low cost. Owner-manager training programs and technical advice programs were to be taken over from the Department of Manpower and Immigration and the National Research Council, respectively. The agency was also to act as a focal point for information on the whole range of federal programs and services available to small businesses. The transfer of some responsibilities from the National Research Council was subsequently dropped.

According to Mr Gillespie, the 'backbone and heart' of the new agency were to be the IDB, on the 'established and recognized strengths' of which the new organization would build. On the basis of this statement, the chief general manager communicated Mr Gillespie's announcement to the Bank's staff with the following message: 'The IDB is to play an integral part in these plans which will open up to the Bank and its personnel new and interesting avenues of service and of assistance to business. The Minister acknowledges in his statements the great achievements of the Bank, and makes clear that it is on these that it is to be built ... With a continuation of the dedication and enthusiasm on the part of the Bank's staff which have distinguished its operations in the past, I have no doubt that the enlarged scope now to be opened up will bring the Bank to even greater levels of achievement.'

References to the IDB at the
Western Economic Opportunities Conference

Mr Gillespie's announcement preceded by a couple of weeks a special conference of the federal government with western provincial premiers bearing the title 'Western Economic Opportunities Conference.'[8] The remarks attributed in an earlier chapter to Premier Schreyer and former premier Duff Roblin of Manitoba were made just prior to that conference, and the position paper of the premiers dwelt at considerable length on the alleged failure of the IDB adequately to assist businesses in the prairie provinces.

The conference took place at Calgary 24–26 July 1973. Regarding the IDB, the comments made in the position paper of the western premiers began, as criticisms often did, with an acknowledgment that the Bank had done useful work: 'While the Bank has assisted the development of many small-scale enterprises ...'[9] Considering that by the end of 1973 the IDB had approved loans for 14,625 businesses in the four western provinces (of a total of 34,159 businesses[10] in all parts of Canada for which loans had been approved), this would seem a very modest comment on the Bank's work in that part of the country.

The position paper added that the IDB's 'contribution to development has been limited for a number or reasons.'[11] First, it was too conservative. This view was subsequently put forward in the House of Commons on the grounds that the provincial agencies had had to make the risky loans the IDB had declined and in so doing had acquired a bad record![12] Second, the Bank was said to have 'an inordinate appetite for tangible security.' Third, assistance to small business had been limited because of reluctance to enter into joint ventures with privately owned firms. Fourth, beneficiaries of the Bank's assistance had been the central provinces, with the exception of British Columbia. The prairie provinces were said to have received a relatively small amount of loan capital.[13]

A glance at Table 23 and Table 24 in chapter 19 would suggest that the central provinces might have been more justified to complain of a bad distribution of IDB loans. Both by number and amount, those made in the prairies were in about the same proportion of total loans as was population in those provinces of the population of Canada. British Columbia's share of loans was, of course, greatly in excess of its share of population. The only provinces where the share of IDB loans was far below the proportion of total population were Ontario and Quebec.

The western premiers proposed that the Bank make riskier loans, that it do more in the way of acquiring shares in applicant businesses, and that it provide additional services such as guidance in business management.[14] In all respects, the federal government's plans for the IDB seemed to anticipate these ideas, so the conference spent little time on the IDB.

Preparing for a new role

Preparation of legislation
to absorb the IDB in a new institution

Preparations for the legislation to be presented to Parliament began under the oversight of a steering committee comprising the president and chief general manager of the IDB, the deputy ministers of finance and of industry, trade and commerce, and two further representatives of the last department. One of these, Fred Raubach, acted as secretary, and the other, Frank Hooten, acted also as chairman of a task force formed to assist the steering committee in preparing a memorandum to cabinet outlining how the government's intention could be carried out in legislation. The Bank's representatives on the task force were H.P. Carmichael, assistant superintendent, credits; H.J. Russell, general manager, loans; and E.C. Scott, director of advisory services. Later Mr Russell's place was taken by J.E. Nordin, general manager, Quebec Region.

This was a useful experience for the Bank because it introduced it to the world of government in which it was going to have to move in the future. The novelty of the experience and the practical attitude of the Bank's personnel toward it are illustrated in the following extract from a memorandum written by one of the Bank's representatives on the task force to review its work:

It should be noted that a Task Force is a very fluid body which expands and contracts in relation to the interests of whoever may become involved. For example, it was not unusual for someone to forcefully support a particular position at the morning meeting and then not show up after lunch.

It became important to appreciate who represented what interests as early as possible in order to know where you might look for support or otherwise.

The Task Force was essentially the lowest rung in the power structure. Its objective was to arrive at a consensus. However, individuals who failed to agree on a given issue had open to them the option of promoting their respective departments, possibly right on up to their Minister who in turn was free to present his department's position to the Cabinet.

In November 1973, another committee was set up by the Department of Industry, Trade and Commerce. This was another interdepartmental committee on small business to co-ordinate relevant government programs until the new bank was established and to oversee the transfer to the new bank of such already established programs as the new legislation might assign to it. The Bank was represented on this by H.P. Carmichael.

In addition to serving on these committees, the Bank formed its own internal implementation committee in October 1973 'to identify all the steps required in the organization, administration and operation of the Bank to effect the establishment of the new organization which is to carry on the work of the Bank.' The chairman was G. Bourbonnière, assistant general manager at CGMO; H.P. Carmichael was vice-chairman; and R.L. McLean, controller, and E.C. Scott, director of advisory services, were the other members. Interaction with the task force was achieved through Messrs Carmichael and Scott.

The steering committee and the task force completed their memorandum to cabinet by mid-November, and the Department of Justice took over the task of drafting the bill. The Bank contributed materially to this work. D.R. Urquhart, who had become general solicitor on the retirement of H.M. Scott, consulted constantly with the department. The Bank's implementation committee held regular meetings with department heads and general managers at CGMO to review in detail each draft of the bill as it was produced.

As the work of the committees proceeded, the Bank's representatives found that much of their time was taken up in explaining the Bank's policies and practices to the other members representing government departments. Although the two departments principally interested in the IDB each had a deputy minister on the Bank's Board – helping to set its policies and oversee the work of operational management – those departmental representatives who sat on the task force and related committees did not always appear familiar with the Bank's character as it had evolved or to fully accept the integrity of its policies and practices. Also, the Bank's representatives and those representing the various departments seemed sometimes to take different views of what the new Bank was. The IDB saw it as a continuation of the old bank with additional responsibilities. Departmental representatives on the committees appeared to view it as a new creation which they were helping to shape. This led to comments on their part about internal procedures and organization that those representing the IDB regarded as matters for management to deal with. It sometimes seemed as if in departmental circles it was open season for telling the IDB how its affairs or those of its successor should be conducted. Senior officers with long experience in the Bank were surprised to hear proposals about the smallest and most delicate aspect of policy or practice put forward by someone who had had no previous direct contact with the Bank. As a result, the Bank's representatives had to discuss patiently and at length matters that they believed the Bank's experience had settled long ago. Unfortunately, the situation occasionally got the better of patience, and one of the Bank's representatives once gave vent to this exasperation by demanding of a startled departmental official: 'When did you last loan five bucks?'

The chief general manager of the Bank was desirous that relations with departmental officials be established on a basis that did not weaken the tradition of independence that Mr Gillespie had said was to be carried into the new bank. Within the IDB, this was regarded as meaning that the new bank's personnel should be answerable only to its board of directors and not open to comments or suggestions about the bank's work from departmental officials other than those who sat on its board. In a memorandum written by the chief general manager in 1975, the view was expressed: 'I do not see how we can maintain any degree of independence ... if we lay our concept of our role open to alteration or interpretation by someone other than ourselves or our Board.' As the staff waited for the structure of the new bank to be put together, the same view was expressed somewhat more picturesquely: 'If every Tom, Dick and Harry is going to have to be persuaded about every detail of how it [i.e. the IDB or the new bank] sets about its work, then there will be no way in which it can be spoken of as an independent Crown Corporation.'

In the spring of 1975, several proposals for the involvement of the Bank in departmental projects provided an opportunity to clarify the situation. One was a suggestion by the Department of Industry, Trade and Commerce that senior officers of the Bank should sit on regional advisory committees of the Program for Advancement of Industrial Technology (PAIT). This program provided assistance to Canadian industry for the development of new products or processes that incorporated new technology and that appeared to offer good prospects for commercial exploitation. The assistance was in the form of a grant that normally represented 50 per cent of the allowable research and development cost of the project.[1] The chief general manager declined because he felt that there would be a potential conflict of interest if a Bank customer or applicant were involved and because he believed that the delicate judgments required of one of the Bank's officers in making IDB-type loans and weighing the chances of the Bank's recovering its money might be disoriented if the same IDB officer sat on a PAIT committee and took part in decisions involving an entirely different principle of assistance. Another proposal, most energetically pressed by some departmental officials, was that the Bank make special loans on soft terms to assist small businesses to convert to metric measurement. After many discussions, the Bank was able to show that neither its act nor the proposed bill of the FBDB gave authority for such a thing. Still another proposal was that the new bank be used as the government's instrument for balancing growth in metropolitan and non-metropolitan areas. To the memorandum recording this suggestion, there is attached a handwritten note: 'If we don't get a Board [for the new bank] soon, we are going to drown in a sea of "new initiatives".'

All these experiences were a natural and useful part of a getting-acquainted process for officers of the IDB and departmental officials who were going to have to co-operate with each other in the future. They also suggested to the operational management of the IDB the desirability of moving quickly, even if only partially, into the new activities assigned to the new bank. It was also believed that this would stir interest in the new bank among the IDB's personnel and encourage them to carry over to it the loyalty and dedication they had shown toward the work of the IDB. It would enable the new bank to start with some understanding on the part of its staff of the work that was now to be done. Normal staff movements and appointments could be co-ordinated with the prospective staff needs for carrying out the new responsibilities. These views are reflected in the following extract from a memorandum written by the chief general manager in February 1974:

Although a new corporation is to be established by legislation, with a new name and additional responsibilities, from a practical standpoint all this will really amount to will be an enlargement of an existing dynamic corporation which is itself growing very rapidly in all its parts and activities ... A simple approach for the Bank to take would be to do nothing until the legislation was passed. In our view, this would be impractical and irresponsible. It would appear to imply a disinterested attitude on the part of the Bank which would be completely incorrect. It would certainly delay very considerably the exercise of the new responsibilities, and it would make it difficult to build the expanded responsibilities truly upon the Bank's successful record of operations, as the Minister announced was to be done.

Move by the IDB towards gaining experience in new responsibilities

The two activities most involved in the plans for the new bank and therefore requiring preliminary preparation were advisory services and the acquisition of equities. For both of these, the IDB had been developing policies, but these now had to be given a fresh orientation. In advisory services, studies were made of the best structure for the numerous tasks to be performed and position descriptions, forms, preliminary operating instructions, and training material were prepared. In May 1974, regional directors of advisory services were appointed to supervise all these activities in the field.

The next step was to set up a limited exercise in providing information on other federal assistance programs. This proved to be a bigger undertaking than had been expected. The IDB's staff had identified over 100 federal government programs of interest to small businesses. Some of the programs were so little known that there was not even printed literature describing them. Some departmental officials believed that an information service would consist of handing out pamphlets. The Bank found, however, that it was necessary to discuss a company's problems in just about the same way as if it were asking for a loan before one could tell to which program of assistance the company should be referred. This, of course, took time and added to the cost.

The first information services were provided in Halifax and Saint John, and it was intended to extend them initially to 25 branches. The response was great, however. In a month, Saint John received as many requests for information as it did inquiries about financing. The cost of an exercise on this scale was considered much too large for the IDB to assume on its own. It was estimated that to provide information services at 25 branches would require an expenditure of about the same amount as the Bank was spending on the whole range of its advisory services. Accordingly, the pilot information program was held down to 11 branches.

The next step considered was the setting up of a program to gain experience in counselling. The internal committee of the Bank, which in 1971 recommended the establishment of advisory services, had proposed that a form of counselling be provided to Bank customers in trouble, but the proposal had not been adopted. The government's plans for the new bank now made the provision of counselling on a broad scale inevitable, and a service of some sort for the Bank's customers seemed to operational management a legitimate and effective way to gain insights into this activity before the new bank took over. E.C. Scott expressed the intent in a memorandum in May 1974: 'One purpose of a counselling service for IDB customers would be to try and provide better service in the form of advice to accounts when they first show signs of difficulty and to try to direct such accounts to corrective action faster than is sometimes possible under our present organizational framework.'

The possibility of setting up a counselling service for customers had been discussed at a meeting of Mr Scott, the president, the secretary, and the chief general manager in March 1973, before the government had reached a decision to set up a new bank, but no action had been taken. Nevertheless, the operational management of the Bank believed strongly that it would be desirable for the IDB's staff members to be equipped with some experience in all the duties they were to perform in the new bank before being taken over by it. Accordingly, the chief general manager recommended to the board of directors in September 1974 that a counselling service for the Bank's own customers be set up. The normal lending operations of the IDB had, from the very beginning of the Bank, involved a kind of counselling for loan applicants as credit officers analysed and discussed the financial needs of the applicant business and engineers and investigation officers reviewed the physical and technical aspects of its plans.

Many thousands of the applications processed by the Bank had involved this sort of work. B.K. Heron, the Bank's first chief engineer, has supplied some examples. A furniture manufacturer was suffering from labour strife and a sales portfolio dominated by one buyer; in addition to financing modernization of the plant, the IDB helped the company find a new manager. A ceramic business, under foreign management, was suffering from contamination of inventory from glaze dust; the Bank suggested the installation of dust-collecting equipment and rigid control of work in process. A sawmill, rebuilt with IDB assistance following a fire, showed weakness in log management, poor equipment maintenance, and excessive labour costs; the Bank suggested the forestry manager be replaced.

The chief general manager's proposal of a counselling service for the Bank's customers was merely an extension and formalization of what was being done all the time anyway. To his surprise, the recommendation was not approved. Some directors, particularly the two deputy ministers, felt doubtful that the IDB should be involved in counselling or setting up even modest programs anticipating the responsibilities of the new bank. The idea of moving into counselling on a limited scale also seemed to raise special difficulties because the Department of Industry, Trade and Commerce intended to transfer its CASE program (Counselling Assistance for Small Enterprises) to the new bank as the means by which it would carry out its counselling assignment. This program used only retired business executives as its counsellors. The scheme proposed by the chief general manager was to involve the use of the Bank's own full-time employees, and the Department of Industry, Trade and Commerce saw this as increasing the cost of counselling and as conflicting with CASE. The IDB's management expected that the new bank would use both full-time and part-time counsellors, but the board's decision postponed further steps toward a system of counselling until the new bank should take over.

The effort to move toward counselling had, however, some practical benefits: the director of advisory services and his staff thoroughly clarified their thoughts as to the advantages and disadvantages of different ways of proceeding. Also, it brought Mr Scott into direct contact with those working in CASE. There had been some apprehension on their part about coming under the supervision of a bank, and Mr Scott was able to do a great deal to allay these concerns.

Exploration of equity field

Regarding equities, there was no question that the government expected much more activity in this area in the new bank than there had been in the IDB. In his statement announcing the government's plans in July 1973, Mr Gillespie had said: 'The new Agency would make greater use of its authority to provide equity financing.'[2] The idea that small businesses badly needed a source of equity funds was a modish one at the time; in its issue of 21 July 1973, the *Financial Post* expressed the view that 'the real test [of the new bank] will come over the agency's role in arranging equity financing for growing Canadian companies.'

Work that the IDB had been doing on new policies in the equity field had been set aside while the decision about the Bank's future was still pending. With that decision taken, this work was resumed. In July 1973, following the government's announcement, the chief general manager obtained clearance from the president to circulate to all offices of the Bank a policy memorandum continuing the efforts made for many years to improve responsiveness to applications and setting out lines along which the conditions for extending financial assistance might be relaxed. In addition to such usual things as longer terms of repayment, seasonal repayment schedules, simplified security, working capital assistance, and inventory financing, the memorandum included a new approach to equities. This memorandum made the new principles outlined in chapter 22 official policies.

Regional offices were asked to contact local sources of equity financing for small and medium-sized businesses to build up the knowledge necessary to apply to requests for equity funds the usual tests as to 'the availability of financing elsewhere.' An outside study claimed to have identified 151 sources of 'venture capital' in Canada; nevertheless, in some parts of the country inquiries by regional and branch offices turned up virtually no sources of the sort of equity financing the Bank had in mind. Even where there was a good local investment market, interest in small stock issues was itself small, and those in the investment business generally extended a warm welcome to the Bank's prospective involvement. There seemed to be room for a special role for the IDB in the equity field. A memo written in September 1975 observed: 'We do not really know whether there will be any similarity between our activities in this area and the operations of private entrepreneurs who are now active. The money these people invest is called venture capital. Perhaps we should think of what we do as warranting the name of "equity assistance". Even this difference in phraseology implies a somewhat different approach.'

By the spring of 1974, new instructions on equity had been issued to the Bank's staff, and following a resubmission to the board of directors of the recommendation for authorizing limits at the regional offices and at CGMO these were finally approved.

It was still the intention of operational management to move into the equity field carefully, even though this might mean slowly. It had been the Bank's practice to build solidly on a foundation of experience; perhaps it was able to approve 10,000 loans a year in the 1970s because for the first ten years it had approved only 200 loans a year. Management had also to bear in mind that the corporation would soon have a new president and a new board of directors, and a desire on the part of the Bank's staff to develop quickly a knowledge of the various facets of equity financing could not be carried to the point of pre-empting the authority of the new bank's board. One advertisement of the interest of the Bank in equity financing was published in the spring of 1974, but, as the chief general manager reported to the president in April, 'We do not have in mind any large or dramatic publicity campaign ... In the first place, I think it would be inappropriate for us to do so just before the new Corporation was set up. In the second place, I should prefer to see us move into this field at a somewhat more moderate speed than a dramatic advertising campaign might produce.'

Investigations into the field of equity financing were conducted most intensively through 1974 and 1975. H.P. Carmichael, assistant superintendent, credits, who was in charge of formulating procedures, was sent on a short course at the Harvard School of Business Administration. He, along with an officer from each region, attended a seminar at the University of Toronto in 1974; perhaps significant of the Bank's growing knowledge of the subject was the fact that J.E. Nordin, general manager, Quebec Region, was invited to be one of the speakers. Training courses and seminars were arranged within the Bank, and at the end of 1974 Mr Nordin was appointed general manager, corporate development, at CGMO, with the further development of an equity initiative as one of his responsibilities. Mr Carmichael was named a special assistant to work with him. Two conferences of general managers were held in 1975, in April and in May, to review the new equity instructions in detail. Mr Nordin visited more than a score of venture capitalists in Canada and the United States to determine what procedures and organization would be best, and numerous seminars and conferences were attended to meet those active in the field.

In addition to this sort of background exposure to the equity field, there was an attempt to acquaint the Bank's staff quickly with the kind of arrangement that might be made by sending to all branches copies of the Forms 73 (the internal document for authorizing a loan) of such equity deals as were made. The first batch was sent out in December 1974, illustrating equity transactions recently entered into. The accompanying letter from P.F. Limoges, superintendent, credits, ended with the rather chilling note: 'As a further caution, we might add that one of the attached examples is now bankrupt!' Finally, to allow for the development of a different chain of consideration of equity proposals from that established for loans, specialized officers were attached to regional offices to handle equity applications apart from the normal procedures for loan applications.

With the new bank in the offing, these various moves were basically taken in preparation for it. They did, however, generate much more equity activity than there had previously been. In the 28 years 1945–72, the Bank authorized 48 transactions involving equity; in the 3 years 1973–5, it authorized 33 such transactions.

Legislation to establish the FBDB

The drafting of the legislation to create the new bank was completed by the end of 1973, and the bill was introduced into Parliament on 9 April 1974. It was expected that the legislative process would be finished by July, but on 9 May Parliament was dissolved and the bill died on the order paper. This presented the IDB with two new problems: it was approaching the limits set by the IDB Act on the Bank's power to raise money, and it was now in imminent danger of exceeding the limits established by the act for loans over $200,000.

The IDB Act authorized the sale of common stock to a level of $75 million and the sale of debentures up to ten times the sum of the issued stock and the reserve fund.[3] Even before the bill was introduced, there were apprehensions on the part of the IDB's operational management that the Bank might come close to or reach the limits of its ability to finance itself before the new legislation was passed to relieve the situation. In both 1973 and 1974, there had been an extremely rapid growth in new business. In 1973, the number of loans approved surpassed by 2,000 the number approved in 1972, itself a very active year. This increase was just about equal to the total loans approved in a single year as recently as 1967. The value of loans approved in 1973 was $345 million, and this was nearly equal to the total amount of all loan balances outstanding on the books of the Bank in 1968.

Fiscal 1974 showed just as much growth. The number of new loans approved exceeded the number in 1973 by 1,900, and the total amount of new authorizations, $470 million, was almost equal to total balances outstanding on the Bank's books at the end of 1970.

Growth on this scale was requiring unusually large amounts of fresh capital. The repayment of loans provided a substantial inflow of cash that could be used for new loans, but this had to be supplemented by the sale of shares and debentures. From 1961, when the IDB Act had last been materially amended, to 1972, the annual sale of shares to the Bank of Canada was between $2 million and $4 million; net sales of debentures varied between $25 million and $60 million per annum. The tremendous surge of new loans in 1973 and 1974, however, coming on top of pretty substantial growth in 1972, changed the Bank's needs drastically. In 1973, debentures increased by $104 million and in 1974 by $231 million. In two years debentures had increased by an amount almost equal to the total balance of debentures outstanding at the end of 1969. Shares had been issued in the fairly normal amount of $4 million in 1973, but $9 million of shares were issued in 1974, bringing shares outstanding to a level of just

$4 million below the limit set by the IDB Act. The Bank's power to raise capital was being used up at an unprecedented rate.

At the end of 1974, debentures outstanding were $837 million. This was very close to the total amount of debentures that the act would permit – ten times the issued shares plus the reserve fund. On the balance sheet, shares issued were $71 million and the reserve fund was $33 million. Since shares were limited by the IDB Act to $75 million, this meant a ceiling of approximately $1,100 million for debentures, apart from such leeway as an increase in the reserve fund might provide. At the end of 1974, the Bank was less than $300 million away from this ceiling. In the summer of 1974, it was expected that the Bank's power to raise money might be used up by January 1975.

The problem regarding loans over $200,000 was even more critical. By the IDB Act, the total loans outstanding in individual balances of more than $200,000 was limited to $200 million.[4] By July 1974, the total of such outstanding loan balances was approximately $177 million. Undisbursed commitments were capable of raising this by $65 million, so that potentially the total of these balances could exceed the legal limit by $42 million.

Normally problems of these kinds had been taken care of by amendments to the IDB Act. With new legislation dealing with the Bank pending, this was not considered practical, and provisions in the bill to incorporate the FBDB were looked to for relief on both of the limitations described above. Since the management of the Bank had no way of knowing when the FBDB bill might be reintroduced and passed (if at all), it set up a careful watch on the growth in capital funds and introduced immediate measures to control any increase in loan balances of over $200,000. No further consideration was to be given to any application for a loan of more than $200,000 no matter how far advanced the processing, and no more applications were to be accepted. Also, the disbursement of any loan of over $200,000 already approved was to be rigidly controlled; where possible, borrowers were asked to find ways of delaying their programs or requests for loan proceeds. An elaborate reporting system was set up, monitored by P.F. Limoges, superintendent, credits.

These steps, taken in the summer of 1974, were described by one regional general manager as 'Draconian measures with a vengeance,' but even more drastic steps had to be taken in October. Early in the month CGMO was told that the bill was to be reintroduced in Parliament immediately, but its recent experiences had diminished its faith in legislative processes. Regional general managers were asked to identify loans over $200,000 that might be disposed of to other lenders, borrowers with loan balances just over $200,000 were asked to see if they could get their loans below the critical level by accelerating principal payments, and rationed limits for disbursements on loans of over $200,000 were set up for each region.

With the limits of power to raise new capital funds expected to be reached by the end of January 1975, tentative consideration was actually given to steps by which the Bank's operations could be wound down if no legislation had been passed by then. As it happened, this was not necessary. The FBDB bill received third reading in the House of Commons on 4 December 1974, passed the Senate on 19 December, and was given royal assent on 20 December.[5] The same day, Parliament adjourned and did not meet again until 22 January. It had been a very near-run thing.

The bill had sections repealing those parts of the IDB Act limiting loans of over $200,000 and increasing the Bank's share capital by $50 million, and these sections came into effect with royal assent.[6]

Although the steps taken by the IDB regarding loans of over $200,000 were only in effect for the last two months of fiscal 1974, and the first three months of fiscal 1975, they had an important and perhaps long-lasting effect on the assistance given by the Bank through larger loans. The programs of many applicants and borrowers were seriously interfered with, and some were abandoned. In 1975, the dollar amount of new authorizations in loans of under $200,000 declined 9 per cent from 1974; authorizations in loans of over $200,000 declined by 45 per cent and reached the lowest total since 1971.

Debate on the bill in the House of Commons had been the usual mixture of compliments and criticisms and showed that there was still a lot of misunderstanding among MPs about the Bank's operations. One complained that the Bank loaned only to manufacturing businesses; in 1974 these had accounted for only 17 per cent of the loans made. Nevertheless, there was also much praise for the Bank and general support for the idea of helping small businesses.[7]

The House of Commons had referred the bill to the Standing Committee on Finance, Trade and Economic Affairs. Its hearings were a historic occasion for the IDB, for it was the first time that the senior operational officer, the chief general manager, appeared on behalf of the IDB by himself. On all other occasions of this sort in previous years, the principal spokesman was naturally the president. It was not inappropriate, however, that just before the Industrial Development Bank should disappear into a new institution, a representative of the Bank's operating personnel, in the person of the chief general manager, should have been able to speak on the Bank's work to members of Parliament in this way.

The hearings were marked by energetic representations against the bill on behalf of the Federated Council of the Sales Finance Companies and by RoyNat Ltd, but among the members of the committee and in the Senate there was little opposition.[8]

A detailed description of the act belongs more to a history of the Federal Business Development Bank than to a history of the IDB. Several features of it are, however, of interest. It added to the responsibilities of advisory services[9] along lines already described, providing for counselling, training, and information services. Powers to extend financial assistance were virtually unchanged, except for the addition of 'leasing,' which was included to make some change in an area where there was little that could be added. The criteria for assistance to businesses were changed. The IDB Act had said that the Bank could lend or guarantee loans if the amount invested in the business by persons other than the Bank and the character of the investment were 'such as to afford the Bank reasonable protection'; the new act merely required that the 'persons other than the Corporation' (the FBDB) have a 'continuing commitment' to the business. This phrase was no more precise than the earlier one, but it was intended to remove from the act what looked like a basis for accusations, regarded by the Bank as unjustified, that it was overly concerned about security protection for the loans it made.[10]

Funds for the new bank were to be derived in two ways. The banking operations were to be self-supporting, with capital funds to be obtained by selling shares and debentures in the ratio of 1 to 10; funds for advisory services were to be supplied by Parliament.[11]

The name to be given to the new bank had provoked a great deal of debate while the bill was being drafted. IDB representatives at meetings with departmental officials objected very strongly to the name used in the government's announcements, Industrial Bank and Development Agency, because they felt that the last word implied that the new bank was to be much more an instrument of government action that they felt it ought to be. The representatives of the Department of Finance on the various committees, however, criticized the name of the IDB because they felt that 'industrial' implied a narrower scope than the Bank really had and that the word 'bank' should be limited to those financial institutions that operated under the Bank Act – chartered banks. They strongly supported the name Enterprise Canada, but this bizarre title the IDB's representatives opposed strenuously. The Bank's operational management attached a lot of importance to the retention of the word 'bank' because it believed it made clear to all concerned that the corporation was to operate on business-like principles. While conceding that the IDB was not similar to the chartered banks, it argued that it was a special type of bank, a 'development bank,' a new kind of institution of which there were scores so-named in all parts of the world. In the end, the name chosen was Federal Business Development Bank.[12] The first word indicated the sponsoring government; the second showed that the bank had a wide scope; and the final words firmly established its character.

The IDB was now entering its final months. Preparations for the Bank's conversion into the Federal Business Development Bank continued to be the principal preoccupations of management. Some of these preparations have already been described. A memorandum written by the chief general manager in February 1975 indicates the policy followed:

My general approach to implementation of the FBDB, insofar as new programmes are concerned, has been to take such action and lay such plans as would be reasonable for the Industrial Development Bank; as would generate and sustain healthy motivation and interest on the part of our staff; as would, by this means, counteract and perhaps eliminate concerns in the Bank over the changes now about to take place; as would present to the departmental authorities in Ottawa a proper reflection of the interest of the IDB in assuming the new responsibilities; as would equip the FBDB to a reasonable degree, in the beginning, for its responsibilities; and as would lay the groundwork and establish plans for the development of the new responsibilities in the FBDB.

Delay in proclaiming the act

Although the bill to create the new bank had been passed by Parliament, and on 20 December 1974 given royal assent, only the sections dealing with the immediate financial problems of the IDB came into effect at that time. The rest of the act was to come into force on a day to be proclaimed. It was expected that this would occur within three to six months, and the Bank set about the tasks required to implement the legislation. For the closer control of these that was now needed, the responsibilities of the implementation committee were taken over by J.E. Nordin, appointed on 20 January 1975 as general manager, corporate development, assisted by H.P. Carmichael.

The first date set for proclaiming the FBDB Act was 1 April. The Bank felt able to meet this date, but around mid-February it was informed that the date would be 1 June. The Bank then worked toward this target, only to learn in mid-April that the proclamation date had been postponed once more, to 1 July. Even this date was only tentative and subject to confirmation by mid-May. Confirmation came on 20 May, and the final step in preparing for the termination of the IDB – the audit that would lead to a closing statement – was started. On 23 June, after the Bank had received a message from the Department of Industry, Trade and Commerce that the Bank must hold firmly to the date of 1 July, the government announced that the proclamation of the FBDB Act was postponed once more, and no new date was set.

These repeated postponements, with, in the end, no date substituted for them, presented the Bank with difficult problems. Dozens of steps under way to effect the change-over to the new bank were 'put on hold.' Work on the audit had to be suspended. Steps taken toward assuming responsibility for CASE were stopped, stranding some CASE people in IDB offices and leaving space rented to house others empty. The five IDB officers selected to be regional counsellors had to be diverted to various temporary assignments without their intended new title owing to the decision of the board of directors of the IDB not to approve further moves toward the provision of counselling. Since some of these officers were to have moved from one city to another to take up the new post, the postponement put a considerable personal strain on them. In addition, the repeated delays in the long-pending change-over to a new bank inevitably had a dampening effect on the morale of the Bank's staff. It was now over two years since the government had announced its decision to convert the IDB into the FBDB, and it is hardly surprising that these repeated postponements in proclaiming the new act led management to weigh, as one of the options to be ready for, the possibility that the FBDB would ultimately not come into being at all.

The announcement of the latest postponement was contained in the budget presented to Parliament by the minister of finance, John Turner, on 23 June.[13] The *Gazette* (Montreal) on 25 June reported: 'Two major new government programs have been postponed and another two ... have been sharply curtailed as a result of the cost-cutting measures announced by Finance Minister Turner's budget. "If this lead is followed ... then we can turn back inflation", he said in his budget speech ... In dollar terms, the most dramatic casualty was the planned Federal Business Development Bank. The Government had been intending to plough $150 million or so this fiscal year into what would have been an expanded and more aggressive version of the existing Industrial Development Bank.' The article added that the start-up date had been pushed beyond 1 April 1976 at the earliest! Early in July 1975, however, it was learned that the government was aiming at 2 October 1975.

It is not clear how delaying the start-up date for the FBDB from July to October was related to the saving of '$150 million or so' referred to in the

Gazette article. However, the delay did relieve the government of the need to purchase new debentures of approximately this amount to be issued by the IDB during the three-month period. As long as the IDB existed as a subsidiary of the Bank of Canada, it was up to the latter to purchase these new debentures.

The selection of a date separated by a day from the IDB's fiscal year-end, 30 September, meant that, after the year-end statement for that date, which was required by the IDB act, the Bank would continue to operate for one more day and would have to prepare a one-day statement for that day on the basis of which the IDB would on the following day, 2 October, be taken over by the new bank. The choice of 2 October instead of 1 October was related to the intention of the budget that there be a cut in government spending. The IDB had $44 million of debentures falling due on 1 October and $21 million of accrued debenture interest due that was also to be covered by an issue of debentures. If the transfer of the IDB's assets and liabilities to the new bank were delayed until 2 October, the switch in debentures would take place under the IDB's standing arrangements with the Bank of Canada, and the latter would purchase the renewal debentures totalling $65 million. However, if the change-over took place on 1 October, the Bank of Canada would be out of the picture and the federal government would have to buy the debentures which would then be issued by the new bank. By delaying matters a day, the government was able to preserve at least the appearance of keeping its outlay down by $65 million.

The final decision as to which day would mark the end of the IDB was not taken until well into September. By that time, it involved deadlines for cabinet meetings, for IDB board meetings, for inserting announcements in the *Canada Gazette*, and for arranging for an audit. In the end, however, the date of 2 October stood. To avoid awkward problems in establishing final records and to facilitate the issuing of an audited statement for the one-day 'year' of 1 October, certain loan transactions, such as the recording of new authorizations in the Bank's books or the making of disbursements, were prohibited on 1 October. The computer was unable to adjust itself to these extraordinary proceedings and accrue interest for one day, and an estimate was made for the accrual necessary. There was a certain symbolism in this partial suspension of activity as the Bank waited for its end as the IDB and its rebirth as the FBDB.

Last letters from the chief general manager to the president

At the close of business on 1 October, the chief general manager, as his last official act, wrote two letters to the president, G.K. Bouey, to mark what was, for the IDB, an emotional and historic moment. The first was written (with the help of P.F. Limoges) in Latin, the solemnity of the occasion seeming to call for the classical language. The letter said:

> *Carissime Domine:*
> *Morituri te salutant,*
> *Cordialiter.*

The second letter was as follows:

October 1st, 1975

Mr. G.K. Bouey
Governor
Bank of Canada
Ottawa, Ontario

Dear Mr. Bouey,
 This being the last day upon which the IDB will operate under that name and as a subsidiary of the Bank of Canada, I should like, on behalf of all the employees of the IDB, to send you and your colleagues warm greetings of affection and esteem. During the thirty-one years that the IDB has been a subsidiary of the Bank of Canada, it has established a record of achievement of such magnificence as to be unsurpassed, I believe, by any other Crown corporation. In looking back on those years, we in the IDB, like any other offspring reaching maturity, recognize the enormous debt we owe to the careful upbringing bestowed upon us by our parent.
 As the Bank now moves on to new and larger work, with a new name and broader responsibilities, you may be sure that we will remember with gratitude the assistance and support freely and cheerfully given to the IDB and its employees by the Bank of Canada, by yourself and your predecessors, and by all your colleagues.

Yours sincerely,
E.R. Clark

J.E. Millard
Joined Bank 1948;
supervisor, Vancouver, 1963–6;
supervisor, British Columbia
Region, 1966–8; assistant
general manager, British
Columbia Region, 1968–73;
general manager, British
Columbia Region, 1973–5
Photo by Williams Photo
Vancouver

I.D. MacLaren
Joined Bank 1957;
general manager, Atlantic
Region, 1974–5

K.A. Powers
Joined Bank 1950;
supervisor, Atlantic Region,
1966–8; assistant general
manager, Atlantic Region,
1968–73; general manager,
Atlantic Region, 1973–4;
general manager, Ontario
Region, 1974–5
Photo by Jarvis Studios,
Halifax

J.Y. Milette
Joined Bank 1960;
supervisor, Quebec Region,
1972–5; general manager,
Quebec Region, 1975

J.E. Nordin
Joined Bank 1953;
supervisor, Quebec Region,
1966–72; assistant general
manager, Quebec Region,
1972–3; general manager,
Quebec Region, 1973–5;
general manager, Corporate
Development, 1975

G. Bourbonnière
Joined Bank 1961;
superintendent, Credits, 1971–3;
general manager,
Administration, 1973–5
Photo by David Bier, Montreal

A cartoon captioned '... and above all ... , help keep me from being transferred,' *from the staff magazine* Rapport, *March 1975, reflects the rapid growth in the branch network in the 1970s and illustrates the general good humour that usually characterized relations within the Bank. Cartoon by Aldo Dolcetti*

Fourth staff administration training seminar, held in North Hatley, Quebec, 25–9 May 1969. Seated (l to r): J.T. Horne, J. Denholme, H.P. Carmichael, E.C. Scott; middle row: C. L'Espérance, J.A. Clinton, G.W. Madore, J.A. McKee, M.T. Collins, L. Crowley, L. Barclay, J.B.S. Oldaker, C.R.T. Bingley, P.H. Johnson; back row: C.B. Ready, R.P. Dohan, D.A. Kerley, D.S. Brown

This unusual business (top left) fabricated specialized glass laboratory equipment for the British Columbia scientific and medical communities on a custom basis. An IDB loan helped it to buy the special equipment required.

The oysters being washed here (top right) were harvested at an oyster farm which cultivated two hundred acres of sea-floor. With several small loans from the IDB the company built up its sales to a substantial volume.
Photo by Svendsen, Victoria

This bus-manufacturing company in Quebec (centre) received a loan to improve its building and equipment.
Photo by Studio Daniel, Enr

Automobile tail-light reflectors are aligned (top left) for entry into a chemical solution for electroplating. This company, which was started with the help of IDB loans, specialized in metal-coating plastic parts for cars.

This long-established company (top right), an IDB borrower in the Atlantic provinces, carried on a successful business rebuilding organs and pianos.

Specialized agricultural operations such as the IDB financed often required large investment in buildings or equipment. Here (centre) a potato harvester is at work in the fields of an IDB borrower.

*When restaurants became eligible, the IDB made many loans to them.
Some loans went to gourmet restaurants in the metropolitan centres,
but many also upgraded facilities in small towns and cities,
as in the case of this restaurant kitchen
in a small prairie city.*

This Nova Scotia company, engaged in industrial and marine repairs, was assisted by several loans.

Appendices

I. INTEREST RATES

On Chart 5, the IDB's lending rates of interest are plotted along with some other lenders' rates that provide a suitable comparison. There are many series of interest rates available – the mortgage rate for conventional residential mortgages, the Bank of Canada rate, the treasury bill rate, and so on – each of which reflects some aspect of the money market. The chart is concerned only, however, with rates at which businesses could borrow. It is not concerned with what rates of interest the lenders themselves might have to pay in order to obtain funds to loan. The rates selected for the chart are, therefore, those used by various sources of term financing for businesses. They include those of the IDB, the chartered banks' average prime rate for business loans, the prime rate for a commercial lender specializing in small and medium-sized industrial mortgage loans, the maximum rate allowed by the federal government for guaranteed loans by the chartered banks under the Small Business Loans Act, and the yield for ten industrial bonds. In addition, crosses on the chart represent interest rates reported to the IDB from time to time by some applicant or borrower as having been quoted by another lender for an industrial mortgage or term loan proposal.

The prime rate of the chartered banks relates to short-term credits and would usually be lower than the rate for term financing by the banks. It shows, however, the general movement and the basic position of chartered bank rates. The rate shown for a commercial lender is also a prime rate. Many loans would be made at rates 1 per cent or more above this rate; the actual rates for loans would usually average $\frac{1}{2}$ to $\frac{3}{4}$ of 1 per cent over the prime. The maximum rate permitted for SBLA loans can be taken to represent the rates associated with various federal government schemes of financial assistance; these rates would usually be below the rates of the IDB.

The rate for ten industrial bond yield averages represents, in contrast, the general level of interest attached in the market to the long-term debts of the larger corporations in the form of industrial bond issues. Because the amounts of these issues were usually much greater than any loans the IDB would make, the level of industrial bond yields was not given an important place in the setting of the Bank's lending rates. In any event, as the chart shows, the industrial bond yield was consistently lower than the IDB's rates and generally by 1 to $1\frac{1}{2}$ per cent.

One thing the chart shows is that there really was no single 'going' or 'market' rate for small and medium-sized industrial term financing

CHART 5

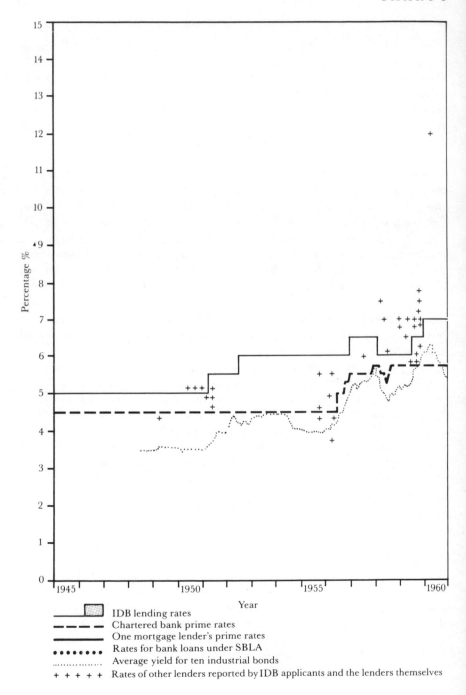

IDB lending rates
Chartered bank prime rates
One mortgage lender's prime rates
Rates for bank loans under SBLA
Average yield for ten industrial bonds
+ + + + + Rates of other lenders reported by IDB applicants and the lenders themselves

INTEREST RATES

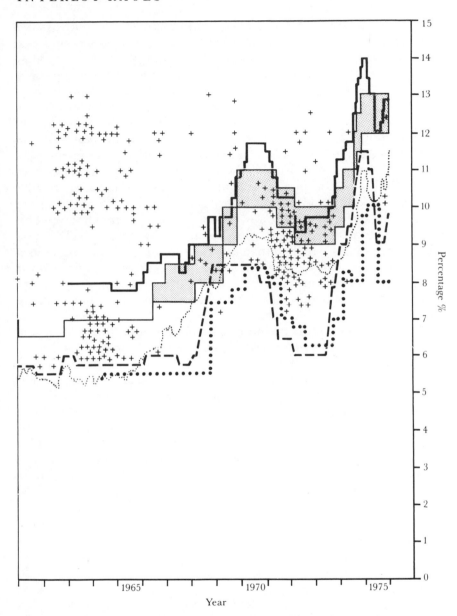

SOURCES: *Chartered bank prime rates: Bank of Canada, 'Selected Canadian and International Interest Rates';* *one mortgage lender's prime rates: supplied by RoyNat Limited; rates under SBLA: as announced from time to* *time in* **Canada Gazette**, *also press release by Department of Finance, 29 June 1973; average yield: supplied by* *McLeod, Young, Weir to Bank of Canada, 'Selected Canadian and International Interest Rates.'*

during the years covered. There was, at times, a spread of as much as 7 per cent between the rate set by one lender for one program and one borrower and the rate that another lender might quote to another borrower for another program. As a rule, the rate offered by a commercial lender would be determined by the circumstances of a particular proposal. This would involve a host of considerations – the financial strength of the borrower, the nature of the program, the security offered and the margin of protection provided by it, the location of the business, the liquidity of the lender and the strength of its desire to make the loan, the extent of the lender's involvement in the industry concerned, a possible desire on the part of the lender to gain a foothold in a particular industry or locality, and the availability of compensation to the lender in other forms such as a stock bonus, conversion or stock purchase options, or a share of the borrower's profits. Then, too, one lender might have a slightly different orientation than others as to the kinds of businesses it dealt with, the kind of security it took, and the way in which it carried on its own operations. All kinds of factors could affect the setting of a rate of interest, and so the crosses representing rates for individual proposals are scattered widely over the chart.

The chart illustrates many aspects of the Bank's story already discussed. It shows how, for the first ten years or so, when the chartered banks were regarded as the most likely alternative source of financing, the IDB held its lending rate $\frac{1}{2}$ of 1 per cent to $1\frac{1}{2}$ per cent above the banks' prime rate. For those years there are few individual rates of other lenders plotted. The increase in the number of such rates reported after 1956 probably reflects the involvement of the Bank with a much wider variety and greater number of businesses after the amendments to the IDB Act in that year and a growing interest on the part of other lenders in industrial mortgage lending. The increase in the number of individual plots after 1961 suggests that the 1961 amendments had similar effects. The IDB was clearly now coming in contact with a much wider variety of lending institutions than ever before. Since many of these were finance companies with rates, as shown on the chart, sometimes several percentage points above the IDB's rate, it is understandable that, as described earlier, there was a period of strain between them and the IDB. Nevertheless, it should be noted that in scarcely any of the examples of individual rates plotted from 1962 on was the rate of interest of the other lender considered an 'unreasonable condition' by the IDB that would justify its displacing the lender, even though in some cases the difference between the rates was quite large.

The chart shows the slow response of the IDB's rates to upward tendencies on the market in 1968. In fact, in that year the chartered bank prime for short-term loans actually rose past the IDB's lowest rate, which was applied to its smaller loans. From 1965 to 1968 the chartered bank prime rate rose by 2.5 percentage points; in the same period, the IDB's rate for smaller loans rose by only 1 percentage point.

The chart shows the efforts of the IDB 1968–70 to bring its rates into a more suitable relationship with other lenders' rates. The whole range of IDB rates was lifted well above the chartered bank prime and above the rate set by the government for guaranteed loans by the banks to small businesses. While some of the rates of other lenders reported still appeared above those of the IDB, many now fell either within the Bank's range of rates or below it. This may be partly because the rates of other lenders reported through the early 1970s were for term loans by chartered banks or by trust and mortgage companies.

The chart shows the slow drop of IDB rates 1971–2, as compared with those of other lenders, as a result of which the Bank was able to move its rates further still into a more appropriate position in the general market interest rate structure as it related to term lending. It should also be remembered that, for the larger loans, which were those of most interest to other lenders, the top of the IDB's range of rates was regarded as a minimum. For these loans, the rate applied to a particular case would usually be $\frac{1}{2}$ of 1 per cent or even 1 per cent above the top of the range shown on the chart.

Finally, the chart reflects the various phases through which the Bank's policy on its interest rate passed, starting with a simple position some distance above the chartered bank prime rate and ending with rates more responsive to market changes and generally seeking a place somewhere in the upper half of the very wide spectrum of rates of other lenders.

Chart 6 shows the organization of the Chief General Manager's Office
(CGMO) as it was when the IDB was converted into the FBDB in 1975. Also
shown is the position of the president and the positions of those officers of
the Bank reporting directly to him.

The Bank's operations were under the overall direction of the chief
general manager. Those sharing this responsibility with him are shown in
three separate groups to reflect the fact that each group had slightly
different relations with him. The first, shown at the left, comprised the
four general managers at CGMO. Each of them was in charge of a large
area of responsibility having to do with the Bank's pursuit of its principal
role of providing financing to small and medium-sized businesses and
with the administration of the structure required for this. Under each of
these general managers were grouped those officers whose functions
appertained to the particular area of responsibility concerned. Most of
the titles shown are self-explanatory, and the reasons for their being
grouped as in the chart are fairly obvious. The position of the general
manager, branch operations, may require explanation. Both he and the
general manager, loans, were concerned in the work of the Bank's
branches. The general manager, loans, had to do with the processing of
credit proposals submitted to CGMO and the general administration of
credits, while the general manager, branch operations, was responsible
for overseeing the effectiveness and efficiency of the branch offices.
Reporting to him were the inspectors, who visited the field offices and
analysed their performance, and the superintendent, methods and
procedures, who studied procedures, especially new ones being introduced, and ensured that all were compatible with other procedures and
instructions.

A second group is shown at the right and includes departmental
officers at CGMO whose responsibilities were of a broad character,
affecting all aspects of the Bank's activities, and to whom the chief general
manager wanted to have direct access. The general solicitor and associate
general solicitor and their department also had a great deal to do with
security documentation for the Bank's loans. In this respect, they
functioned in relation to the general manager, loans, and the various
departments reporting to him.

The director, management services, was included among those reporting directly to the chief general manager because, his department being a

CHART 6

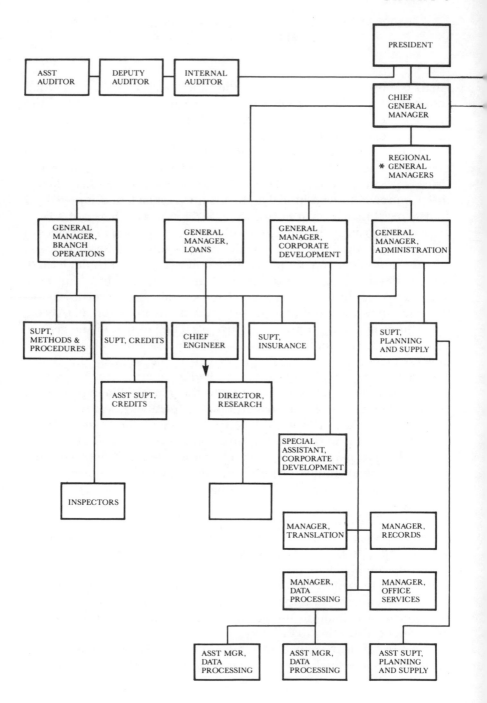

ORGANIZATION OF CGMO

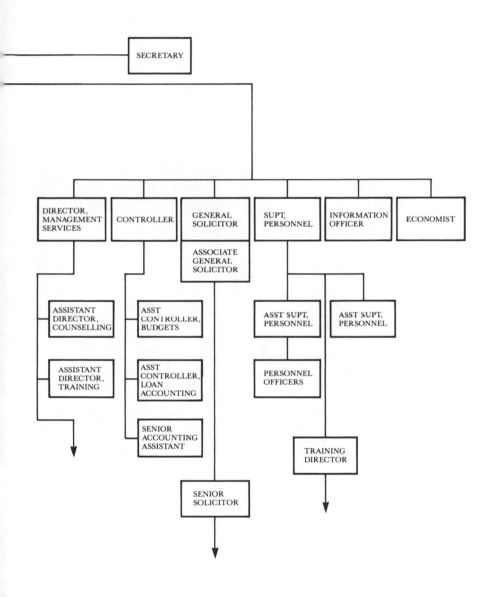

* Regional General Managers were
located at the Regional Offices.

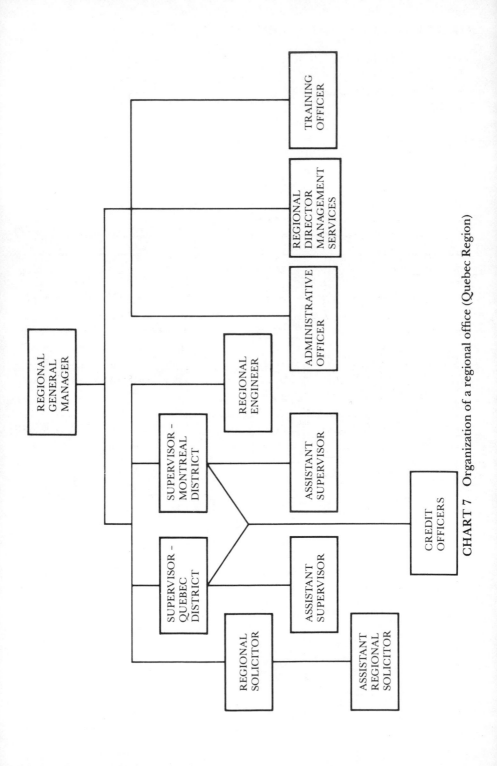

CHART 7   Organization of a regional office (Quebec Region)

REGIONAL GENERAL MANAGER

SUPERVISOR - QUEBEC DISTRICT

SUPERVISOR - MONTREAL DISTRICT

REGIONAL ENGINEER

ADMINISTRATIVE OFFICER

REGIONAL DIRECTOR MANAGEMENT SERVICES

TRAINING OFFICER

REGIONAL SOLICITOR

ASSISTANT SUPERVISOR

ASSISTANT SUPERVISOR

CREDIT OFFICERS

ASSISTANT REGIONAL SOLICITOR

new one, consultations with him occurred frequently. In any event, it was recognized that the activities of management services were destined to become another 'large area of responsibility' and a major function of the Bank.

Four of the blocks in the chart have black arrows attached to them to indicate that the CGMO officers concerned had special relationships with counterparts in the regional offices.

The third group is shown in the centre and comprises the regional general managers. When the Bank was fully regionalized 1967–8, it was intended that the senior regional officers, then called assistant general managers, would act as extensions of the General Manager's Office in Montreal and be frequently called in for consultation. It did not work out this way, apart from attendance at the usual periodical conferences. Nevertheless, the regional assistant general managers (later called regional general managers) had a very close relationship with the general manager at Montreal (later the chief general manager), which the growing departmentalization of the Bank did not diminish. In specific matters, however, they communicated with whatever officer at GMO (later CGMO) was responsible for the matter under correspondence – loans, inspections, administration, personnel, and so on.

Chart 7 shows a typical organization of a regional office, although each region was slightly different from the others in one way or another, reflecting the ideas of the regional general manager, the size and character of the area supervised, and the experience of the personnel available.

III. ASSETS AND LIABILITIES 1945-75

The table presents assets and liabilities (in millions of dollars) as at 30 September of each year.

	1945	1946	1947	1948	1949	1950	1951
Assets							
Government securities	8.9	10.2	14.1	8.2	6.2	5.1	–
Loans and investments	0.9	5.1	11.5	17.5	20.3	21.9	29.2
Other assets	0.3	0.2	2.2	3.5	3.7	4.1	0.7
Total	10.1	15.5	27.8	29.2	30.2	31.1	29.9
Liabilities							
Bonds and debentures	–	–	–	–	–	–	1.3
Other liabilities	–	–	1.9	3.1	3.3	3.5	0.3
Reserve for losses	–	–	0.2	0.3	0.4	0.4	0.4
Capital issued	10.0	15.0	25.0	25.0	25.0	25.0	25.0
Reserve fund	0.1	0.5	0.7	0.8	1.5	2.2	2.9
Total	10.1	15.5	27.8	29.2	30.2	31.1	29.9

	1961	1962	1963	1964	1965	1966	1967
Assets							
Government securities	–	–	–	–	–	–	1.1
Loans and investments	123.5	164.9	201.0	224.4	255.7	299.0	334.8
Other assets	1.5	2.2	3.6	5.0	6.3	6.1	4.9
Total	125.0	167.1	204.6	229.4	262.0	305.1	340.8
Liabilities							
Bonds and debentures	78.9	115.3	147.6	168.1	195.4	232.8	262.5
Other liabilities	1.9	2.8	3.7	4.3	4.9	6.0	7.2
Reserve for losses	2.7	3.1	3.7	4.5	5.3	6.3	7.5
Capital issued	26.0	30.0	33.0	35.0	38.0	41.0	44.0
Reserve fund	15.5	15.9	16.6	17.5	18.4	19.0	19.6
Total	125.0	167.1	204.6	229.4	262.0	305.1	340.8

NOTE: Figures for 1945–61 inclusive are from Brief, Table 1. For subsequent years, they are taken from individual annual reports. The figures are taken to the nearest decimal or the appropriate decimal to make rounded figures balance.

The figures for 'Loans and investments' include 'Property held for sale,' in accordance with the practice adopted in 1974.

Although in 1971 the practice was adopted by the auditors of deducting the 'Reserve for losses' from the 'Loans and investments' in making up the balance sheet, the 'Reserve for losses' is shown here separately on the 'Liabilities' side as a convenient way of showing this figure for each year.

'Interest due and accrued' on loans is included in 'Other assets.'

The figures used for 1975 are those of the balance sheet for 1 October 1975.

1952	1953	1954	1955	1956	1957	1958	1959	1960
–	–	–	–	–	–	–	–	0.5
33.5	39.0	42.3	44.3	52.4	72.1	88.9	97.0	103.4
0.6	0.8	0.8	1.7	0.7	1.7	1.5	1.7	2.9
34.1	39.8	43.1	46.0	53.1	73.8	90.4	98.7	106.8
3.9	9.0	10.7	9.5	17.7	35.5	51.0	57.7	63.6
1.0	0.6	0.5	3.4	0.8	2.2	1.4	1.6	1.4
0.5	0.7	0.7	0.7	0.9	1.1	1.7	1.6	2.5
25.0	25.0	25.0	25.0	25.0	25.0	25.0	25.0	25.0
3.7	4.5	6.2	7.4	8.7	10.0	11.3	12.8	14.3
34.1	39.8	43.1	46.0	53.1	73.8	90.4	98.7	106.8

1968	1969	1970	1971	1972	1973	1974	1975
1.0	–	4.9	7.6	7.0	7.8	8.5	11.9
373.5	420.4	489.7	545.9	614.6	736.2	987.3	1,175.2
4.4	3.0	3.4	4.2	4.6	5.9	7.8	10.5
378.9	423.4	498.0	557.7	626.2	749.9	1,003.6	1,197.6
293.6	331.5	394.1	445.5	501.7	605.9	837.3	1,027.8
9.1	10.9	19.2	20.1	22.7	30.9	39.2	26.3
8.8	9.3	10.5	13.9	17.0	20.5	22.8	26.8
47.0	51.0	53.0	55.0	58.0	62.0	71.0	79.0
20.4	20.7	21.2	23.2	26.8	30.6	33.3	37.7
378.9	423.4	498.0	557.7	626.2	749.9	1,003.6	1,197.6

IV. INCOME AND EXPENSES, PROFIT AND LOSS, 1945–75

The table presents income and expenses and profit and loss (all in millions of dollars) for fiscal years ending 30 September.

	1945	1946	1947	1948	1949	1950
Income						
Interest on loans	–	0.1	0.4	0.7	0.9	1.0
Fees	–	–	–	–	–	–
Interest on government securities	0.2	0.2	0.2	0.2	0.2	0.1
Other	0.1	0.2*	0.2	–	0.2*	0.2*
Total	0.3	0.5	0.8	0.9	1.3	1.3
Expenses						
Staff costs	0.1	0.1	0.2	0.3	0.4	0.4
Other operating costs	0.1*	0.1	0.1	0.4*	0.1	0.1
Debenture cost	–	–	–	–	–	–
Total	0.2	0.2	0.3	0.7	0.5	0.5
Net income	0.1	0.3	0.5	0.2	0.8	0.8
Transfer to reserve for losses†	–	–	0.2	0.2	0.1	0.1
Net transfer to reserve fund†	0.1	0.3	0.3	–	0.7	0.7

	1961	1962	1963	1964	1965	1966
Income						
Interest on loans	7.1	9.4	12.2	14.2	16.6	19.3
Fees	0.2	0.3	0.4	0.4	0.4	0.5
Interest on government securities	–	–	–	–	–	–
Other	0.1	–	–	0.1	0.1	–
Total	7.4	9.7	12.6	14.7	17.1	19.8
Expenses						
Staff costs	2.0	3.0	3.4	3.6	3.9	4.8
Other operating costs	0.8	1.1	1.2	1.3	1.4	1.6
Debenture cost	3.0	4.5	6.6	7.9	9.5	11.5
Total	5.8	8.6	11.2	12.8	14.8	17.9
Net income	1.6	1.1	1.4	1.9	2.3	1.9
Transfer to reserve for losses†	0.4	0.7	0.7	1.0	1.3	1.4
Net transfer to reserve fund†	1.2	0.4	0.7	0.9	1.0	0.5

NOTE: Figures for 1945–61 inclusive are from Brief, Tables 2 and 3. Subsequent years are from individual reports.

The figures marked * include the various adjustments shown in Table 3. Of the items

1951	1952	1953	1954	1955	1956	1957	1958	1959	1960
1.2	1.6	1.8	2.1	2.2	2.6	3.5	4.5	5.5	6.3
–	–	–	–	–	0.1	0.1	0.1	0.1	0.1
–	–	–	–	–	–	–	–	–	–
0.1	–	0.1	0.8	–	–	–	0.1	0.3	0.1
1.3	1.6	1.9	2.9	2.2	2.7	3.6	4.7	5.9	6.5
0.5	0.5	0.5	0.6	0.6	0.7	0.8	1.0	1.2	1.4
0.1	0.1	0.1	0.1	0.1	0.2	0.3	0.3	0.4	0.6
–	0.1	0.2	0.4	0.3	0.3	0.9	1.5	2.0	2.5
0.6	0.7	0.8	1.1	1.0	1.2	2.0	2.8	3.6	4.5
0.7	0.9	1.1	1.8	1.2	1.5	1.6	1.9	2.3	2.0
–	0.1	0.2	0.2	–	0.2	0.3	0.7	0.7	0.5
0.7	0.8	0.9	1.6	1.2	1.3	1.3	1.2	1.6	1.5

1967	1968	1969	1970	1971	1972	1973	1974	1975
22.8	26.4	30.6	38.3	47.5	55.1	64.6	84.4	113.6
0.5	0.5	0.5	0.5	0.9	1.3	2.0	1.7	1.7
–	–	–	0.1	0.1	0.1	0.1	0.2	0.2
0.1	0.2	–	–	0.2	0.1	0.4	–	–
23.4	27.1	31.1	38.9	48.7	56.6	67.1	86.3	115.5
5.3	5.9	6.8	7.6	8.9	10.8	13.2	17.8	21.7
1.7	1.9	2.1	2.6	3.0	3.9	4.9	6.4	8.3
13.9	16.5	20.1	26.1	30.7	33.9	40.3	54.8	73.4
20.9	24.3	29.0	36.3	42.6	48.6	58.4	79.0	103.4
2.5	2.8	2.1	2.6	6.1	8.0	8.7	7.3	12.1
1.9	2.0	1.7	2.1	4.1	4.4	4.9	4.6	7.7
0.6	0.8	0.4	0.5	2.0	3.6	3.8	2.7	4.4

marked †, the 'Reserve for losses' represents amounts set aside from earnings to take care of any loans subsequently written off. The 'Reserve fund' represents accumulated earnings that remained after these amounts had been set aside and all expenses met.

V. AUTHORIZED LOANS, BY INDUSTRY, PROVINCE, AND SIZE 1945–75

	Number of loans	Number of borrowers	Amount ($millions)
By industry			
Manufacturing	18,839	12,197	1,073
Transportation and storage	2,771	1,852	175
Construction	3,670	2,742	141
Wholesale	3,624	2,725	175
Retail	12,086	9,647	394
Agriculture	4,476	3,572	178
Restaurants	4,933	3,924	194
Hotels and motels	4,461	3,264	278
Other	10,522	8,123	467
Total	65,382	48,046	3,075
By province			
Newfoundland	1,482	1,107	49
Prince Edward Island	452	334	19
Nova Scotia	1,991	1,465	68
New Brunswick	1,959	1,397	76
Quebec	11,994	8,526	672
Ontario	18,589	13,748	850
Manitoba	2,509	1,826	119
Saskatchewan	2,155	1,654	88
Alberta	6,569	5,142	286
British Columbia	17,127	12,451	814
Yukon and Northwest Territories	555	396	34
Total	65,382	48,046	3,075
By size			
$5,000 or less	2,642		11
$5,000+–$25,000	28,739		457
$25,000+–$50,000	18,238		696
$50,000+–$100,000	10,676		798
$100,000+–$200,000	3,724		546
$200,000+	1,363		567
Total	65,382		3,075

*Figures for numbers and amounts of loans are from Brief, Tables 10, 11, and 12 for 1945–61; *Annual Report*, 1967, for 1962–7; *Annual Report*, 1969, for 1968–9; and *Annual Report*, 1975, for the remaining years. Figures for number of borrowers are from internal records.

VI. IDB LENDING RATES 1944-75

Date	Interest rate (percentage)	Date	Interest rate (percentage)
15 September 1944	5	12 September 1966	$7\frac{1}{2}$–$8\frac{1}{2}$
5 February 1951	$5\frac{1}{2}$	4 December 1967	8–9
7 April 1952	6	17 February 1969	9–10
16 June 1952	6	18 June 1969	10–11
16 September 1956	$6\frac{1}{2}$	22 March 1971	$9\frac{1}{2}$–$10\frac{1}{2}$
15 November 1957	6	29 November 1971	9–10
13 March 1959	$6\frac{1}{2}$	5 July 1973	$9\frac{1}{2}$–$10\frac{1}{2}$
21 September 1959	7	22 October 1973	10–11
12 September 1960	$6\frac{1}{2}$	19 April 1974	11–12
31 August 1962	7	17 May 1974	$11\frac{1}{2}$–$12\frac{1}{2}$
14 February 1966	$7\frac{1}{2}$–8	26 July 1974	12–13

Notes

In these notes, references are given only for material available to the public. Some short forms of titles are used. *'Debates'* means the record of the House of Commons debates; the year and page number are given. *'Proceedings'* means proceedings of the House of Commons Standing Committee on Banking and Commerce, the year and page number also being given; in 1944, the page references are from the printing of the proceedings in the appendices to the committee reports. When an act of Parliament is referred to for the first time, it is given its official designation. This is usually followed in parentheses by a briefer description such as 'IDB Act, 1956,' which is used thereafter. 'PAC' means Public Archives of Canada, Ottawa.

Royal commissions are referred to by their full title the first time. Thereafter, they are referred to by the colloquial name by which they are commonly known, such as Porter Commission, Glassco Commission, and so on. References to evidence given at hearings held by these commissions are indicated in the same way, e.g. Porter Hearings. Any brief referred to was submitted to the Porter Commission; the single word 'Brief' means the brief submitted to the Porter Commission by the IDB.

References to the *Britannica Book of the Year* are to the annual publication bearing this name issued by Encyclopaedia Britannica Inc, University of Chicago, Chicago, Illinois. References to the *Canadian Annual Review* are to the publication bearing this name issued annually by the University of Toronto Press, Toronto; latterly, it was published as the *Canadian Annual Review of Politics and Public Affairs* and with the support of York University.

For figures and statistics, only publicly available sources are cited. Where no source is given, the figures or statistics have been taken from internal records of the Bank.

Introduction

1 *Bank of Canada Annual Report*, 1947, pp. 13, 15; *Britannica Book of the Year*, 1946, p. 164, 1948, p. 163.
2 *Canada Year Book*, 1976–7, p. 1016. The figures used throughout for the gross national product are those published in terms of constant (1971) dollars.
3 Ibid.
4 *Bank of Canada Statistical Summary Supplement*, 1966, p. 133; *Bank of Canada Review*, December 1976, p. s105.
5 *Bank of Canada Statistical Summary Supplement*, 1960, p. 142; also *Supplement for 1966*, p. 142, and *Bank of Canada Review*, December 1976, p. s105.
6 See Appendix I.
7 For example, *Bank of Canada Annual Reports*, 1948, pp. 7–9, 1956, pp. 35–6, 1957, pp. 20–1, 28, 1958, pp. 9, 42, 1959, pp. 6–7, 37, 1969, p. 13, 1973, p. 6.

Chapter one: The background

1 *Report of the Committee on Finance and Industry*, HM Stationery Office, London, Cmd. 3897, 1931 (generally known as the Macmillan Report). The Committee on Finance and Industry was appointed in 1929 by the Treasury Board 'to inquire into banking, finance and credit ... and to make recommendations calculated to enable these agencies to promote the development of trade and commerce and the employment of labour' (page vi). The chairman was the Rt Hon. H.R. Macmillan, who in 1930 was given a life peerage and appointed to the bench as a lord of appeal. Although the report is usually spoken of as the Macmillan Report, much of it is supposed to have been written by another member of the committee, John Maynard (later Lord) Keynes.
2 Macmillan Report (p. 173), quoted by Graham Towers before House of Commons Committee on Banking and Commerce during hearings on IDB bill (Proceedings, 4 August 1944, p. 1469). The Macmillan Report (p. 172) identified another 'gap' – the lack of specialist advice to industrial companies seeking long-term capital or involved in mergers or in negotiations with international groups. This gap, however, does not concern us here.
3 In the United Kingdom, the Bankers' Industrial Development Company was set up in 1930 by the Bank of England and some of the commercial banks to assist in finding finance for industries seeking amounts of 250,000 pounds or less through public issues (Macmillan Report, p. 173). See also William

Diamond, *Development Banks* (Baltimore and London: World Bank – The Johns Hopkins University Press, 1957), pp. 30–1.

In addition, several commercial financial institutions were established in Britain prior to the Second World War to supply capital and credit to small firms, e.g. Credit for Industry Limited (1934), Charterhouse Industrial Development Company (1934), Leadenhall Securities Corporation (1935), and New Trading Company. See *Report of the Financial Committee to the Council of the League of Nations on the Work of the Sixty-eighth Session of the Committee, June 15th–20th, 1939, Geneva*, pp. 16–17.

In the United States, commercial banks are a normal source of term financing for industry, but from 1932 to 1938 the Federal Reserve Banks and the Reconstruction Finance Corporation (RFC) were given special powers to make industrial loans on liberal terms as to maturity, interest rates, and collateral. Neither the Reserve Banks nor the RFC made any considerable volume of advances under these powers. Ibid, pp. 15–16.

When the IDB bill came before the House of Commons Standing Committee on Banking and Commerce, Dr W.C. Clark, deputy minister of finance, cited both the Bankers' Industrial Development Company and US experience as precedents for the proposed IDB. See *Proceedings*, 1944, p. 12.

4 *Official Journal*, League of Nations, February 1939, Geneva, p. 119.

5 *Report of Financial Committee of League of Nations*. This report has very close links with Canada's Industrial Development Bank. Dr W.C. Clark who, as deputy minister of finance, later was associated with Graham Towers, governor of the Bank of Canada, in establishing the IDB, was a member of the League of Nations Financial Committee. Louis Rasminsky, later governor of the Bank of Canada and president of the IDB for approximately thirteen years, wrote the committee's report as a member of the League of Nations Secretariat.

6 Ibid, p. 14. This particular passage and several of the accompanying paragraphs of the League of Nations report were quoted by Graham Towers in his evidence on the IDB bill before the House of Commons Standing Committee on Banking and Commerce; *Proceedings*, 1944, p. 1468.

7 Ibid, pp. 21–2.

8 Ibid, p. 22.

9 Shirley Boskey, *Problems and Practices of Development Banks* (Baltimore and London: World Bank – The Johns Hopkins Press, 1959), pp. 4–7. The term *development financing institutions* is now sometimes used to refer in a broad sense to development banks. The matter of nomenclature is discussed in a speech by William Diamond delivered to the World Federation of Development Financing Institutions on 22 June 1981, as reported in the *News Letter*

of the Association of Development Financing Institutions in Asia and the Pacific for September 1981.

10 Boskey, *Problems*, pp. 5–6.

11 *Report of the Royal Commission on Banking and Currency in Canada* (Ottawa: King's Printer, 1933).

12 J.L. Granatstein, *Canada's War: Politics of the Mackenzie King Government, 1939–45* (Toronto: Oxford University Press, 1975), pp. 252–9.

13 Ibid, pp. 249–50, also 276–7.

14 *Annual Report of Bank of Canada*, 1943, pp. 11–12.

15 PAC, Record Group (RG) 19, vol. 4660, file 187, E.A.C. – 1.

16 Undated memo, Post-war Financial Needs of Business Agriculture and for Housing, PAC, RG 19, vol. 4660, file 187, E.A.C. – 1.

17 Memorandum from J.E. Mackey to W.A. Mackintosh, 16 August 1943, PAC, RG 19, vol. 3562, file E01.

18 These circumstances were referred to several times by Dr W.C. Clark and Graham Towers in their evidence before the House of Commons Standing Committee on Banking and Commerce when it considered the bill to incorporate the IDB; e.g. *Proceedings*, 1944, pp. 8–11, 14, 1408, 1425–6.

19 This long quotation is an extract from an unpublished monograph on the IDB's history by W.E. Scott. Apart from the specific sources referred to in other notes, the comments on the background and origins of the IDB in this chapter have drawn heavily on this monograph. Mr Scott took a very intimate part in the events described. As a member of the Bank of Canada's staff at the time, he worked with Graham Towers in developing plans for the IDB and made the early drafts of legislation to incorporate the Bank. Later, from 1966 to 1972, he was inspector general of banks.

20 Granatstein, *Canada's War*, pp. 267, 268–9.

21 PAC, RG 2, series 18, vol. 12, file w-50-2.

22 Debates, 1944, p. 2.

23 Ibid, pp. 500 and 6503; Granatstein, *Canada's War*, p. 278.

Chapter two: Legislation

1 *Debates*, 1944, pp. 913–14. The act, when passed, was 8 George VI cap. 44 (IDB Act, 1944).

2 *The Canadian Banker* (Toronto 1945), p. 35.

3 It is difficult to determine when commonplace phrases first emerge into general use. There was an industrial bank in Japan as early as 1902–4, and in Great Britain the Bankers Industrial Development Company was set up in 1930. However, the naming of Canada's Industrial Development Bank seems to have been the first use of the three words together and may, in

effect, have coined a name that was used quite often by others for this new kind of financial institution. Of the 110 or so development financing institutions sponsored by the World Bank referred to in chapter 1, 50 are actually named development banks, and at least 10 have an identical name to that of Canada's bank.

4 *Proceedings*, 1944, pp. 32–3.

5 Ibid, p. 34.

6 Ibid, p. 15: 1457.

7 Ibid, p. 1457; also *Debates*, 1944, p. 1059. D.C. Abbott, parliamentary assistant to the minister of finance, said that it was anticipated that they, i.e. the IDB's bonds and debentures, would be marketable elsewhere as well as with the Bank of Canada.

8 24–25 George V cap. 43 (Bank of Canada Act) sec. 7. In the act of 1944, the assistant deputy governor of the Bank of Canada was included in the board of the IDB. In 1954 this position was discontinued by an amendment to the Bank of Canada Act, and in 1956 it was removed from the IDB board by that year's amendments to the IDB Act.

9 *Debates*, 1944, pp. 1375–6, 1441–2, 1465–6, 1468; *Proceedings*, 1944, p. 12–13.

10 *Proceedings*, 1944, pp. 13, 33, 1459.

11 Ibid, pp. 10–11.

12 *Debates*, 1944, pp. 1441–3, 1465; *Proceedings*, 1944, pp. 15, 11.

13 *Proceedings*, pp. 1402, 1403, 1406.

14 Ibid, p. 29.

15 Ibid, pp. 1432, 1504.

16 Ibid, pp. 25–6, 1398–1402.

17 Ibid, p. 31.

18 *Debates*, 1944, pp. 1387, 1464.

19 Ibid, p. 6250; *Proceedings*, 1944, pp. 1405, 1470.

20 *Debates*, 1944, p. 1281, 1351, 1473; *Proceedings*, 1944, pp. 1515–16.

21 *Proceedings*, 1944, p. 1470.

22 Ibid, p. 1421.

23 Ibid, p. 1469.

24 Ibid, p. 1428.

25 Ibid, pp. 1409–10, 1440, 1470, 1514–16.

26 Ibid, p. 1450.

27 Ibid, pp. 1470, 1515, 1439–41.

28 Ibid, pp. 1409–10.

29 Ibid, pp. 1514–15.

30 Ibid, p. 1470.

31 Ibid, p. 11.

Chapter three: Early organization

1 IDB Act, 1944, sec. 4.
2 24–25 George V cap. 43 (Bank of Canada Act – as amended 1938) sec. 7(1). In 1973, the title of the chief operational officer was changed to chief general manager.
3 The comments in the preceding two paragraphs on the IDB's recruiting problems in its early days are based largely on a letter on the subject written to the author by W.C. Stuart, a long-time employee of the IDB who retired in 1974 as assistant general manager, Ontario Region.

Chapter four: Procedures

1 *Debates of Senate*, 1944–5, p. 443.
2 *Proceedings*, 1944, p. 8. In 1973, the title of the chief operational officer was changed to chief general manager.
3 IDB Act, 1944, sec. 15(1). The wording was changed slightly in subsequent amendments.

Chapter five: Policies

1 IDB Act, 1944, sec. 2(d), sec. 15(1).
2 13 George VI cap. 26 (IDB Act, 1949) sec. 2, amending sec. 15(1).
3 IDB Act, 1944, sec. 2(d).
4 IDB Act, 1944, sec. 15(1)(c).
5 Brief, Table 14.
6 *Proceedings*, pp. 1409–10, 1439–41, 1470, 1514–15.
7 IDB Act, 1944, Preamble, and sec. 15(1).
8 'The Bank will not furnish all or a major portion of the funds required to start a new enterprise'; article by S.R. Noble in the *Canadian Banker* (Toronto 1945), p. 36.
9 Ibid.
10 Later, the annual report, with pictures of borrowing businesses, became a principal means of communicating just what the IDB did. Its 1974 report tied for first prize with that of one of the chartered banks in a competition conducted by the Canadian Public Relations Society, Inc, in 1975.

Chapter six: Finances

1 *The Canadian Banker* (Toronto 1945), p. 43.
2 See Appendix I.

3 Brief, Table 1.
4 Ibid.
5 Brief, Table 3. Regarding the addition of a further fraction of the rate of interest paid by the IDB on its debentures, R.B. McKibbin, who, as securities adviser on the staff of the Bank of Canada at the time, was responsible for arranging the debenture financing of the IDB, has written to the author as follows: 'It was a constant struggle to persuade successive Ministers of Finance that they should reflect the pricing practices in other more mature capital markets and add a surcharge of the Government's own direct borrowing costs when advancing capital funds to crown corporations from the Consolidated Revenue Fund; frequently I failed and 'pet' projects were charged inadequate or no premiums. However, the logic seemed sound to me and hence the surcharge of 0.60 added to G. of C. [Government of Canada] rates in pricing IDB debentures acquired by B/C [the Bank of Canada].'

Chapter seven: Operational developments

1 *Bank of Canada Annual Report*, 1946, pp. 15, 21, 1947, p. 15, 1948, p. 19; *Britannica Book of the Year*, 1947, p. 173, 1948, p. 162.
2 *Britannica Book of the Year*, 1956, p. 138.
3 Statistics for prices and unemployment from *Bank of Canada Statistical Summary Supplements* for 1960, 1966, and 1975; statistics for GNP from *Canada Year Book*, 1976–7, p. 1016.
4 *Bank of Canada Annual Report*, 1948, pp. 7–9, 1956, pp. 35–6, 1957, pp. 20–1, 28, 1958, pp. 9, 42, 1959, pp. 6–7, 37. The figures used throughout for gross national product are those published in terms of constant (1971) dollars.
5 *Bank of Canada Annual Report*, 1947, p. 6, 1948, pp. 7–9.
6 News release by Bank of Canada, 22 February 1951; *Bank of Canada Annual Report*, 1951, pp. 1–2, 9.
7 IDB *Annual Report*, 1951, p. 3.
8 IDB Act, 1949, sec. 2, amending sec. 15(2); 1 Elizabeth II cap. 30 (IDB Act, 1952), sec. 1, amending sec. 15(2).
9 Brief, Table 10; *Annual Reports* 1968, 1969, and 1975; the number of air service companies was obtained from internal records.
10 Recalled by B. Heron.
11 The account of this episode is based on William Kilbourn's book *Pipeline* (Toronto 1970) and on conversations and correspondence with J.E. Coyne, the Hon. Jack Davis, MLA, R.B. McKibbin, and W.C. Stuart, all closely involved in the negotiations, and with K.K. Hay-Roe, then a credit officer in the IDB. IDB records in the files of the Bank of Canada were also consulted.

Chapter eight: Operating results

1 *Proceedings*, 1944, p. 29. The 'opinion' was arrived at, as Mr Towers explained, by simply doubling the 'normal losses' of a commercial bank. These were estimated by Mr Towers to be 'something a little less than ¾ of 1 per cent per annum of total loans.'
2 Brief, Table 9.
3 This includes write-offs made after the FBDB had superseded the IDB.

Chapter nine: Political developments and legislation

1 4–5 Elizabeth II cap. 25 (IDB Act, 1956); *Debates*, 1956, pp. 1921–2, 5884.
2 IDB Act, 1956, sec. 1, amending sec. 2(d).
3 Ibid, sec. 5, amending sec. 15(1) and (2).
4 *Debates*, 1956, pp. 1921–34, 3650–8, 3675–8.
5 *Proceedings*, 1956, pp. 256, 254.
6 *Debates*, 1956, p. 3651.
7 Halifax *Mail-Star*, 21 September 1956.
8 *Debates*, 1957, pp. 2466–7.
9 Ibid, 1957–8, pp. 1029, 1611, 3120.
10 Ibid, 1958, p. 1817.
11 Ibid, 1957, pp. 1–2.
12 Ibid, 1958, p. 6.
13 Ibid, 1958, pp. 1810–13, 1818, 1817.
14 Ibid, 1960, pp. 817–20, 1734.
15 Ibid, 1960–1, pp. 3, 29, 54–6, 1018.
16 *Proceedings of Senate Standing Committee on Banking and Commerce*, 1960–1, 7 December 1960, pp. 8–9.
17 9 Elizabeth II cap. 5 (Small Business Loans Act, 1960–1); *Report of Operations under the Small Business Loans Act* (Ottawa 1961).

Chapter ten: Policy problems

1 *Britannica Book of the Year*, 1957, p. 198, 1958, p. 137, 1960, p. 136; *Canadian Annual Review*, 1960, p. 143; *Britannica Book of the Year*, 1959, p. 138, 1961, p. 135, 1959, p. 138, 1961, p. 135, 1958, p. 137, 1961, p. 135; *Canadian Annual Review*, 1960, p. 144; *Britannica Book of the Year*, 1961, p. 135.
2 *Bank of Canada Annual Report*, 1955, p. 3.
3 *Britannica Book of the Year*, 1956, in a feature article, 'Canada: The Land and the People,' by Pierre Berton.

4 *Bank of Canada Review*, October 1972; *Bank of Canada Statistical Summary Supplement*, 1960, p. 142.
5 *Bank of Canada Annual Report*, 1955, p. 10, 1956, pp. 3–4, 37, 1955, pp. 17, 11.
6 Ibid, 1955, pp. 10–11, 1956, pp. 33, 34, 9.
7 Ibid, 1959, p. 6, 1957, p. 20.
8 Ibid, 1957, pp. 28–9.
9 IDB Act, 1956, sec. 5, amending sec. 15(1)(b).
10 Brief, Table 13.

Chapter eleven: Operational developments

1 Recalled by D.G. McCrae.
2 Recalled by E. Wilk.
3 Mr Ingram, one of the Bank's first supervisors, had left the Bank for outside employment in 1956. He rejoined the Bank in 1962.
4 Figures in this paragraph are from Brief, Table 11.
5 Ibid, Table 8.
6 These various 'chief' titles were later changed to ones more suitable to ordinary business practice: general solicitor; superintendent, credits; and superintendent, insurance. The same three men were appointed to these positions.

Chapter twelve: Operating results

1 Bank of Canada, *Selected Canadian and International Interest Rates*, Table of Government of Canada Securities – Bond Yield Averages 10 Years and Over.
2 See also Appendix I.
3 *Proceedings*, 1944, p. 11.
4 *Debates*, 1960, pp. 817–51.
5 Brief, Table 1.
6 Ibid, Table 8.

Chapter thirteen: Legislation again

1 *Britannica Book of the Year*, 1962, p. 124; *Canadian Annual Review*, 1967, p. 279; *Britannica Book of the Year*, 1968, p. 187; *Bank of Canada Annual Report*, 1967, p. 5; *Britannica Book of the Year*, 1964, p. 218; *Canadian Annual Review*, 1964, p. 249; *Britannica Book of the Year*, 1965, p. 215, 1966, p. 163; *Bank of*

Canada Annual Report, 1966, p. 3; *Canadian Annual Review*, 1966, p. 251; *Canada Year Book*, 1976–7, p. 1016.

2 *Britannica Book of the Year*, 1963, p. 241; *Bank of Canada Annual Report*, 1962, pp. 3–6; *Britannica Book of the Year*, 1963, p. 23; *Bank of Canada Annual Report*, 1962, pp. 3–4; *Britannica Book of the Year*, 1964, p. 213, 1965, p. 209; *Bank of Canada Annual Report*, 1963, p. 3, 1964, p. 3; *Bank of Canada Review*, October 1972, s96; *Bank of Canada Statistical Summary Supplement*, 1966, p. 142; *Bank of Canada Annual Report*, 1965, p. 3, 1966, pp. 3, 8, 1967, pp. 6, 28–31; *Britannica Book of the Year*, 1967, p. 191, 1968, p. 187; *Canadian Annual Review*, 1965, p. 302, 1966, p. 251; *Bank of Canada Annual Report*, 1966, p. 8–11.

3 *Britannica Book of the Year*, 1965, p. 208; *Canadian Annual Review*, 1963, p. 174; 1964, p. 252, 1965, p. 305; *Bank of Canada Annual Report*, 1965, p. 24, 5, 1966, p. 6, 1967, p. 5; *Bank of Canada Annual Report*, 1967, p. 36; *Canadian Annual Review*, 1967, p. 279; *Bank of Canada Annual Report*, 1967, p. 5; *Bank of Canada Annual Report*, 1966, pp. 8–11, 1967, p. 6.

4 *Britannica Book of the Year*, 1963, p. 37; *Bank of Canada Statistical Summary*, 1966 Supplement, p. 135.

5 *Resolutions of the Progressive Conservative Association of Canada, Annual Meeting March 16–18, 1961*, section N-1.

6 *Debates*, 1960–1, pp. 6646, 6934.

7 9–10 Elizabeth II cap. 50 (IDB Act, 1961).

8 *Debates*, 1960–1, pp. 7311–12.

9 Ibid, pp. 7312, 7315, 7442–3.

10 Ibid, 1960, p. 830.

11 Ibid.

12 *Debates*, 1960–1, pp. 7437, 7445.

13 Ibid, p. 7312 (see also other comments on p. 7440 referring to party rally the previous January), p. 7317.

14 Ibid, p. 8050.

Chapter fourteen: The Bank under study – organization and procedures

1 The members of the commission were J. Grant Glassco, R. Watson Sellar, and F. Eugène Therrien.

2 Brief, Table 16.

3 Ibid, p. 39A.

4 *Report of Royal Commission on Government Organization*, vol. 3 (Ottawa: Queen's Printer, 1962), Report 16, pp. 283, 282. The sort of 'independence' the commission had in mind was illustrated by the belief expressed in the report (p. 283) 'that in the current situation, it would be in the public interest ... to

subject the Industrial Development Bank to such general policy direction as the Minister of Finance may deem to be in the public interest.'
5 Ibid, p. 283.
6 Ibid, pp. 282–3.

Chapter fifteen: The Bank under study – policy

1 The members of the commission were the Honourable Chief Justice D.H. Porter, W.T. Brown, J.D. Gibson, G.L. Harrold, P.H. Leman, J.C. MacKeen, and Dr W.A. Mackintosh.
2 Brief of Canadian Bankers' Association, Porter Hearings, p. A-283; see also pp. 7964–78. The chartered banks also complained that monetary policy might, at times, restrict their resources while the IDB might not be subject to the same constraints. Nevertheless, several of the banks' representatives expressed the opinion that there was a role for the IDB in the lending field.
3 Porter Hearings, p. 7965. After the chartered banks' powers were changed in these ways, the IDB's volume of loans grew faster than ever!
4 Brief of Retail Merchants Association of Canada Inc, Porter Hearings, p. A-27–8.
5 Porter Hearings, pp. 5212–13; Brief of Canadian Federation of Agriculture, p. A-51.
6 Porter Hearings, pp. 5280–2.
7 Brief of Canadian Manufacturers' Association, ibid, pp. A-28–30.
8 Brief of Investment Dealers' Association of Canada, ibid, p. A-77.
9 Ibid, pp. 2225–6, 2048, 2097.
10 Brief of the Government of Ontario, Porter Hearings, A-51–2; p. 7043, A-52.
11 Porter Hearings, p. 7130.
12 Ibid, pp. 792, 794, A-440, 861.
13 Ibid, pp. 792, A-440.
14 Ibid, p. 858.
15 Ibid, p. 665.
16 See pp. 179–80 above.
17 *Montreal Star*, 9 March 1962.
18 Brief of Federated Council of Sales Finance Companies, Porter Hearings, pp. A-96–9.
19 Brief of Federated Council, Porter Hearings, pp. 186–7.
20 F. Wildgen, 'Financing Small Business,' Ottawa, 1963, prepared for the Porter Commission (available in the National Library of Canada, Ottawa).
21 *Report of Royal Commission on Banking and Finance* (Ottawa: Queen's Printer, 1964).

22 Porter Report, p. 230.
23 Porter Hearings, pp. 8663–4.
24 Brief, pp. 13A–14A; Porter Report, p. 229.
25 Porter Report, p. 229; Porter Hearings, pp. 8691–3; Wildgen, 'Financing Small Business.'
26 Porter Hearings, p. 8694.
27 Porter Report, pp. 229, 228.
28 Ibid, p. 229.
29 Ibid, p. 228.
30 Ibid, p. 230.
31 Ibid, p. 230. See also Glassco Report, vol. 3, Report 16, p. 283: 'A hazardous and competitive business such as the Industrial Development Bank needs directors whose qualities and experience are distinguishable from those appropriate to a director of a central bank.'
32 Porter Report, p. 230; *Debates*, 1962–3, pp. 3027, 3463.
33 Porter Report, p. 229.

Chapter sixteen: Operational developments

1 *Statistical Summary*, Bank of Canada, 1966, p 31, IDB *Annual Reports*.
2 IDB *Annual Report*, 1971.
3 *Winnipeg Free Press*, 28 October 1958; Winnipeg *Tribune*, 30 October 1958.
4 There is a comment on this in E.P. Neufeld *The Financial System of Canada: Its Growth and Development* (Toronto: Macmillan, 1972), p. 433: 'Since their customers [i.e. those of the provincial agencies] for the most part are also ones that are eligible in principle for Industrial Development Bank loans, it means either that there is duplication of facilities or that loans are made to borrowers that the IDB would not regard as being credit-worthy. The expanded activities of the IDB in recent years probably restrained the growth of these provincial agencies.' Although the operations of the IDB and those of the provincial agencies probably affected each other, as suggested in the last sentence of the quotation, the conclusions in the preceding sentence would be difficult to prove. They seem to rest on an assumption that any business that needed the IDB's kind of financial assistance would know about the Bank. This was never true. Even chartered bank branch managers were often quite ignorant about what the IDB did. Further, the comments make no allowance for honest differences in credit judgment. It is quite possible for a lender to reject as too risky a proposal that would be accepted by another lender.
5 SBLA *Report*, 1975.

6 16 Elizabeth II cap. 83.
7 *Debates*, 1965, pp. 2, 2907–8, 2910.
8 Press release by minister of industry, trade and commerce.
9 *Debates*, 1965, p. 2908.
10 In 1969, when the two departments were combined, as the Department of Industry, Trade and Commerce, with only one deputy minister, he was appointed to the board and the executive committee of the IDB.

Chapter seventeen: Some policy issues

1 *Report of Farm Credit Corporation*, 31 March 1962, pp. 5–6; also FCC, *The Development of Farm Credit in Canada. A History of the Farm Credit Corporation* (Ottawa: FCC, 1979), pp. 94, 177.
2 *Report of Farm Credit Corporation*, 31 March 1961, p. 10.
3 Regina *Leader-Post*, 13 June 1964.
4 *Annual Report*, 1967.
5 *Debates*, 1960–1, p. 7437.
6 Brief, Table 2.
7 *Debates*, 1962–3, p. 2295; 1967, pp. 3201–2, 1964, p. 5806, also 1962–3, p. 2295; 1966, p. 5883; 1962–3, p. 2951; 1962–3, p. 2949; 1962–3, p. 3174; 1963, p. 292; 1966, p. 5230; 1967, p. 13146. It was often suggested that the IDB was not making enough loans. To one such complaint in 1967, Mitchell Sharp, the minister of finance, pointed out that a few days previously he had received complaints from an association of financial companies that the IDB was much too active; *Debates*, 1967, p. 13467.
8 Porter Report, 229.

Chapter eighteen: Operating results

1 For 1956, see Table 5; for 1967, see Table 14.
2 Brief, Table 1.
3 *Annual Report*, 1967.
4 See Table 11.
5 See Appendix I.
6 Although the phraseology used in the Bank's instructions to describe 'satisfactory' loans varied slightly from time to time, basically they were those that were 'wholly satisfactory as to credit risk and performance' and operated in accordance with their terms and conditions. See note 2 to chapter 21, below.

Chapter nineteen: Growth and expansion

1 Those who retired included H.M. Scott, general solicitor, who might be considered one of the IDB's founders. He joined the Bank within a few weeks of its formation and was in charge of its legal work until his retirement. Others who retired were four assistant general managers – H.R. Stoker, Atlantic Region, a long-time employee, L. Viau, Quebec, one of the Bank's earliest employees, W.C. Stuart, Ontario, also a very early employee, and J.C. Ingram, Prairies, one of the first three supervisors; W.L. Mundy, chief of the Insurance Department and a long-time employee; G.R. Elliott, superintendent, credits, a long-service employee; C.I. Stuart, a deputy secretary, also with long service; and P.D. Smith, also a deputy secretary, who, although his principal work was in a similar capacity in the Bank of Canada, was a tower of strength to the IDB in an advisory capacity on staff matters.

2 *Canada Year Book*, 1976–7, p. 1016; *Canadian Annual Review*, 1974, p. 348.

3 *Bank of Canada Review*, December 1976, p. s110; *Bank of Canada Annual Report*, 1968, pp. 6, 7; *Canadian Annual Review*, 1969, p. 308.

4 *Bank of Canada Review*, December 1976, p. s110; *Canadian Annual Review*, 1975, p. 338.

5 *Bank of Canada Review*, December 1975, p. s104.

6 *Bank of Canada Annual Report*, 1966, pp. 8–11; *Canadian Annual Review*, 1967, p. 41, 1968, pp. 29, 62.

7 *Canadian Annual Review*, 1968, p. 285, 1969, p. 305, 1970, pp. 3, 374, 1972, pp. 18, 45, 69, 76.

8 Ibid, 1974, p. 3.

9 SBLA Report, 1975.

10 Information obtained from Department of Industry, Trade and Commerce through Henry R. Juelich; see Preface.

11 The agencies referred to in these comments were the Newfoundland Rural Development Authority, the Newfoundland and Labrador Development Corporation, Industrial Estates Ltd (Nova Scotia), the Nova Scotia Resources Development Board, the New Brunswick Development Corporation, the New Brunswick Industrial Finance Board, the Prince Edward Island Lending Agency, Industrial Enterprises Ltd (Prince Edward Island), the Société de développement industriel du Québec, the Ontario Development Corporation, the Manitoba Development Fund, the Saskatchewan Economic Development Corporation, and the Alberta Opportunity Company. Some provinces may have had other lending bodies, but those listed were those operating in the same general area of financial assistance as the IDB.

12 *Annual Reports*, 1969 and 1975.

13 *Annual Reports*, 1969 and 1975.

14 Estimate based on information from G. Phillips of the Air Transport Committee of the Canadian Transport Commission; see Preface.
15 Recalled by E.T. Bringnall.
16 Funeral home: recalled by M.D. Rudkin; mobile home: recalled by R.B. Thomas; motel on skids: recalled by M.D. Rudkin.
17 Recalled by R.T. MacTavish and J.P. Roberts.
18 Figures for chartered bank loans from *Bank of Canada Monthly Statistical Review*.
19 Bank of Canada Annual Report, 1968, p. 7, 1969, p. 7; *Debates*, 1969, p. 9419. E.P. Neufeld, in *The Financial System of Canada: Its Growth and Development* (Toronto: Macmillan, 1972), p. 111, observes: 'But the major change in mortgage lending provisions of the Bank Act did not occur until 1967 when the new Bank Act enabled the banks for the first time to make conventional unguaranteed mortgage loans. There is no doubt that this is the most significant change in bank lending power that has occurred for decades.'
20 *Bank of Canada Annual Report*, 1970, p. 45, 1973, pp. 5, 6, 27.
21 Both films were made by Crawley Films Ltd, Ottawa.

Chapter twenty: Some consequences of growth

1 By the IDB Act, 1956, section 15 was amended to permit the delegation of authority.
2 *Annual Report*, 1969.
3 *Debates*, 1963, pp. 2440–4. The co-chairmen were André Laurendeau and Davidson Dunton. The commission issued a series of reports up to 1969–70, but did not issue a final report; *Debates*, 1971, pp. 4080–1.
4 17–18 Elizabeth II cap. 54.
5 To make clear to the staff the central place of the French language in the life of the Bank, the chief general manager, following two short courses in French at Laval University, established the practice of having a luncheon each week for six or seven staff members, mostly French-speaking, during which only French was permitted. These luncheons were given the name 'La Bonne Fourchette' after a restaurant in France visited by G. Bousquet, QC, associate general solicitor.

Chapter twenty-one: Operating results

1 *Annual Reports*, 1967 and 1975.
2 See note 6 to chapter 18, above. The basis on which loans were classified as 'satisfactory' remained much the same from 1949, when the system of reviews was introduced, to 1975. The definition of the second category of

loans, however, changed. In 1949, these were loans that had developed 'unsatisfactory trends' and might offer 'some problem in liquidation,' but for which it was believed there was no prospect of loss. By 1975, this definition had become narrower. While the second category still included loans with what were now called 'undesirable developments,' the category was limited to such of these accounts as were expected to overcome these developments and retire their loans in full without the Bank's having to proceed to liquidation and realize on its security. Those that might require realizing on the Bank's security were now put in category III. Internally, category II loans were now regarded as a lower category of 'satisfactory' loans than category I. If they were included with the 91 per cent of loans referred to in the text as 'satisfactory,' it would bring the percentage of 'satisfactory' loans in 1975 to 96 per cent.

3 *Financial Post*, 19 May 1973.

4 See pp. 109, 170, 270 above.

5 The same survey showed that 63 per cent of the amounts written off from 1945 to 1973 inclusive occurred in loans authorized in amounts of $100,000 or less and that 32 per cent occurred in loans for more than $200,000. Only 5 per cent occurred in loans of between $100,000 and $200,000. Twenty-two per cent of the total amounts written off in those years occurred in loans authorized for $25,000 or less.

6 The figures for 'Average Annual Yield of Additional Interest' in Table 40 are estimates. An accurate calculation of the extra revenue would be practically impossible. Debentures generally revolved in serial maturities over a six-year period, and it was assumed that the debentures outstanding at the end of fiscal 1961 would be renewed in equal portions over the next six years. The extra 0.60 per cent was then applied to this growing balance of renewed debentures until by 1967 the full amount of debentures outstanding at the end of 1961 was assumed to be bearing the extra interest charge. For the purposes of the table, the amounts of new debenture balances 1962–7 over and above the 1961 balance were given the additional 0.60 per cent interest. These two revenues were then added together for each year and the yield calculated on the shares plus the reserve fund. For 1968–74, the additional 0.60 per cent was applied to all debenture balances. For 1975, 0.125 per cent was applied to the increase in debentures in 1975, and 0.60 per cent to the rest. (See pp. 86–7 above for origin of the 'additional interest charge.') 'Average' balances of debentures and capital were calculated on the basis of opening and closing balances of each year; Brief, Tables 1 and 2; *Annual Reports* 1967, 1969, and 1975.

7 See Appendix V.

8 Only for the last nine years of the IDB's operations (1967–75) does the Bank

have a record of the disposition of those loan accounts that were reported each year as being 'unsatisfactory.' Some of these would later be returned to the 'satisfactory' category due to improvements in a borrower's circumstances, some would be written off, and some would be retired in full from some special source other than earnings. Among these last were some of which repayment came from the sale of the Bank's security, from guarantors, or from some kind of refinancing of the IDB's loan. These could be regarded as making up, together with those written off, those loans for which the Bank had to take some sort of recovery action. From the record for 1967–75, an estimate has been made of the proportion of the total number of loans that would be in this category. This proportion was estimated to be between 6.6 per cent and 7.2 per cent. This would suggest that between 93.4 per cent and 92.8 per cent of the IDB's loans, by number, were repaid out of borrower's operations. Since this estimate is based on a very approximate exercise, however, the statement in the text has been modified to 'more than 90 per cent.' Incidentally, this percentage would include the relatively small number of cases in which a borrower was successful in selling his or her business and the buyer, not wanting to continue with the IDB loan, paid it off.

Chapter twenty-two: New initiatives

1 *Annual Report*, 1954, p. 12.
2 IDB Act, 1944, sec. 15(1)(c).
3 *Canadian Annual Review*, 1973, p. 3.
4 *Foreign Direct Investment in Canada* (Ottawa: Minister of Supply and Services Canada, 1972), pp. 359, 359–60.
5 *Debates*, 1973, p. 5. The *Canadian Annual Review*, 1973, p. 6, commented as follows: 'It [i.e. the program announced by the new Liberal government] incorporated the Conservative Party's campaign proposal to aid small business through new initiatives to strengthen management and consulting resources and to increase access to financing resources.'
6 Any documentary information on the government's views would be in unavailable cabinet documents. The outline given here is based on IDB records and conversations with others, in particular with W.A. Kennett.
7 *Debates*, 1973, pp. 5491–2; also Background to Statement by Minister of Industry, Trade and Commerce, 11 July 1975.
8 *Western Economic Opportunities Conference – Verbatim Record and Documents* (Ottawa: Minister of Supply and Services Canada, 1977).
9 Ibid, p. 309.
10 *Annual Report*, 1973.
11 *Western Conference*, p. 309.

12 *Debates*, 1 April–8 May 1974, pp. 1804–5. One might think that loans so bad that they gave the lenders a bad name would be loans that were not merely risky, but imprudent!

13 *Western Conference*, p. 309.

14 Ibid, p. 310.

Chapter twenty-three: Preparing for a new role

1 Although this assistance is referred to in the text as 'grants,' it was not as simple as that. The following extract from a brochure issued in 1965–6 to introduce the program explains it more fully: 'Cost of an approved development project will be shared by the Department [of Industry] and the company concerned ... If the resulting product or process is put into commercial use, the company will be obliged to repay the Department's contribution with interest. If the results are not used commercially, the Department's contribution will not be repayable ... Companies will be required to give an undertaking that, if the project is successful, they will exploit the results in Canada within a reasonable period of time.'

2 *Debates*, 1973, pp. 5491–2; also Background to Statement by Minister of Industry, Trade and Commerce, 11 July 1973.

3 *Revised Statutes*, 1970, caps. 1-9, secs. 13 and 15.

4 Ibid, secs. 16(3) and (4).

5 *Debates*, 1974–5, p. 2455.

6 23 Elizabeth II cap. 14 (FBDB Act), sec. 59.

7 *Debates*, 30 September–9 November 1974, p. 509; *Debates*, 1 April–8 May 1974, pp. 1793–1810, 2060–63.

8 *Senate Debates*, 1974, pp. 368–71, 417–18.

9 On 2 July 1975 the name of the department was changed to Management Services in anticipation of the broader responsibilities established in the FBDB Act.

10 FBDB Act, secs. 21, 22, and 23; ibid, sec. 20(4); ibid, sec. 20(1)(c).

11 Ibid, sec. 33.

12 Ibid, sec. 3.

13 *Debates*, 1975, p. 7026.

Annotated bibliography

One can scarcely provide a bibliography of other books about the IDB since this is the first to have been written. Short articles about the Bank did appear from time to time in newspapers and magazines, some of them written by officers of the Bank. None of these throws light on the Bank or its operations that would materially supplement what is written in this history. Some publications, however, are useful sources of information about the Bank.

Annual Reports of the IDB. These review each year's operations and give a great deal of statistical information about the Bank. In some of these reports, figures are given for several years. The life of the Bank can be covered statistically with the brief if submitted to the Porter Commission, referred to below, and the Bank's *Annual Reports* for 1967, 1969, and 1975.

Debates of the House of Commons, 1944. These contain the official statement by the government announcing and explaining the plan to set up the IDB. Some of the speeches made in the debate favoured the plan, some recorded objections to it, and some reflected the variety of expectations that the establishing of the Bank aroused.

Debates of the House of Commons, 1956. These deal with the first major amendments of the IDB Act. They contain the government's statement giving the background to the amendments. The speeches in the debate give some idea of the public's impressions of the Bank after eleven years of operation, although, of course, in reading them, one has to make allowance for political considerations.

Debates of the House of Commons, 1961. This was the last occasion on which there was a lengthy debate about the Bank in the House of Commons. The discussion was sometimes a bit disoriented because of its being conducted in the shadow of the government's efforts to have the governorship of the Bank of Canada declared vacant. The bill was not referred to the Standing Committee on Banking and Commerce.

Debates of the House of Commons, 1962–74. There were references to the Bank in the House of Commons in these years whenever amendments to the IDB Act were made, as well as in connection with other business of the House. These references can be found through the indexes to the *Debates.* No occasion produced a major discussion about the Bank, but the comments are interesting as reflecting some public attitudes toward the Bank.

Debates of the House of Commons, 1974. These deal with the bill to convert the IDB into the FBDB.

The Development of Farm Credit in Canada. A History of the Farm Credit Corporation, FCC, Ottawa, 1979. This publication gives a clear and fairly short account of the operations of the FCC and can supplement the comments made in this book.

Economic Development and the Atlantic Provinces, A.K. Cairncross, sponsored by Atlantic Provinces Research Board, Fredericton, February 1961. This brief monograph discusses the role of the IDB in the Atlantic provinces and compares its activities with those of provincial agencies.

The Financial System of Canada: Its Growth and Development, E.P. Neufeld, Toronto: Macmillan, 1972. This book has scattered brief references to the IDB.

'Financing Small Business: A Study Prepared for the Royal Commission on Banking and Finance,' by F. Wildgen, Ottawa, n.d., 195-33 C.M. This study was not printed by the commission, but is available in mimeographed form at the National Library of Canada in Ottawa.

Foreign Direct Investment in Canada (Gray Report), Ottawa: Minister of Supply and Services Canada, 1972, pp. 111–12, 349, 357–9.

Hearings of the Royal Commission on Banking and Finance (Porter Hearings), 1962–3. In the following briefs and / or testimony forming part of the record of the hearings, there was reference to the IDB: Canadian Bankers' Association, Retail Merchants Association of Canada, Canadian Federation of Agriculture, Canadian Manufacturers' Association, Investment Dealers' Association of Canada, Canadian Small and Independent Business Federation, Federated Council of Sales Finance Companies, Laurentide Financial Corporation Ltd, Industrial Acceptance Corporation Ltd, Atlantic Provinces Economic Council, and the provinces of Saskatchewan, Manitoba, Ontario, New Brunswick, Prince Edward Island, and Nova Scotia.

Institutional Financing of Small Business in Nova Scotia, John T. Sears, Toronto: University of Toronto Press, 1972, pp. 142–67. Although the part of this book that refers to the IDB is brief and is related particularly to Nova Scotia, it makes interesting reading. It is a careful and intelligent attempt by someone outside the Bank to understand it. Some of its recommendations about the Bank's operations were met, to a degree, in the 1970s when the IDB opened more branches, enlarged its publicity program, and set up advisory services to improve management skills in small businesses. The book's recommendation that the IDB publicly state that all interest rates over 10 per cent were unreasonable would have meant the Bank's arrogating to itself a responsibility for policing interest rates that it did not have and could not have assumed. The book speaks of the funds loaned by the IDB as coming from the federal treasury. This was never the case.

Pipeline, by William Kilbourn, Toronto and Vancouver: Clark, Irwin, 1970. This deals, in part, with the proposal that the IDB assist in financing Trans-Canada Pipe Lines Ltd.

Proceedings of the Standing Committee of the House of Commons on Banking and Commerce, 1944, pp. 1–76, 1393–1525, 1674–84. These proceedings contain the evidence of Graham Towers, Dr W.C. Clark, J.L. Ilsley, and D.C. Abbott, parliamentary assistant to Mr Ilsley, before the House of Commons committee. These proceedings are the best source of information about the concepts on which the IDB was based.

Proceedings of the Standing Committee of the House of Commons on Banking and Commerce, 1956, pp. 243–302. These record evidence by the Bank's president, J.E. Coyne, regarding the amendments to the IDB Act. Of particular interest are the submissions made by the Hotel Association of Canada Inc that tourist businesses should be eligible for IDB financing.

Proceedings of the Standing Committee of the House of Commons on Finance, Trade and Economic Affairs, 1974, issues No. 5, 6, 7, and 8. These deal with the proposal to convert the Bank into the FBDB, but they provide a great deal of information on the operations of the IDB in the testimony of the chief general manager. They also report representations made by RoyNat Ltd and the Federated Council of Sales Companies regarding the proposal.

Report of the Royal Commission on Banking and Finance (Porter Report), Queen's Printer, 1964. Ottawa: The index to the report gives the numerous page references.

Report of the Royal Commission on Government Organization (Glassco Report), vol. 3, Ottawa: Queen's Printer, 1965, pp. 281–3.

Submission by the Industrial Development Bank to the Royal Commission on Banking and Finance, 3 October 1962. This brief gives a good, short account of the Bank's operations and policies up to 1962 and a great deal of statistical information. It was not published by the Bank, but it is available as part of the evidence presented to the commission and printed by it as part of its Hearings.

Western Economic Opportunities Conference – Verbatim Record and Documents, Ottawa: Minister of Supply and Services Canada, 1977. This report includes a record of the discussions that took place and the background papers prepared by the governments of Canada and the western provinces. This conference took place two weeks after the federal government announced its plans to convert the IDB into the FBDB. The government's paper devoted a half-page to these plans. The new bank was described as 'a loan and development corporation for small business'; pp. 245–6, also pp. 325–7. Pp. 87–95 record discussion by the provincial premiers of the record of the IDB and the federal government's plans. Pp. 305 and 309–10 record the comments about the IDB in the background paper of the provincial premiers.

A great many books have been published on the general subject of development banks. A list of them would not be germane to this history. For brief commentaries on the subject, however, one could hardly find better sources than three books published by the World Bank:

Development Banks, by William Diamond, Baltimore: The Johns Hopkins University Press. A World Bank Publication, 1957.

Development Finance Companies: Aspects of Policy and Operation, edited by William Diamond, Baltimore: The Johns Hopkins Press for The World Bank Group, 1968.

Problems and Practices of Development Banks, by Shirley Boskey, Baltimore: The Johns Hopkins Press, 1959.

Index